Adverse Impact and Test Validation: A Practitioner's Handbook

Third Edition

Daniel A. Biddle

Biddle Consulting Group, Inc.

Reference: Biddle, D. A. (2011). Adverse Impact and Test Validation: A Practitioner's Handbook (3rd ed.). Scottsdale, AZ: Infinity Publishing.

Biddle Consulting Group, Inc.
193 Blue Ravine Road, Suite 270
Folsom, CA 95630
1.800.999.0438

ISBN 0-7414-6606-6

Printed in the United States of America

This is a work of fiction. Names, characters, places, and incidents either are the product of the author's imagination or are used fictitiously. Any resemblance to actual events or locales or persons, living or dead, is entirely coincidental.

Published July 2011

INFINITY PUBLISHING
1094 New DeHaven Street, Suite 100
West Conshohocken, PA 19428-2713
Toll-free (877) BUY BOOK
Local Phone (610) 941-9999
Fax (610) 941-9959
Info@buybooksontheweb.com
www.buybooksontheweb.com

Contents

List of Figures

List of Tables

About the Authors

Daniel A. Biddle, Ph.D. Dan is the CEO of Biddle Consulting Group, Inc., (BCG), a consulting firm specializing in the areas of test development and validation, Equal Employment Opportunity compliance, and Human Resource software development. Dan is also CEO of Fire & Police Selection, Inc. (FPSI), a firm dedicated to providing fair and defensible testing solutions to the protective services industry. BCG has consulted with numerous Fortune 500 companies and hundreds of public sector agencies in matters pertaining to these areas, and maintains over 1,000 software or service clients worldwide. BCG also provides expert witness and consulting services in state and federal litigation matters, or in response to government audits. Dan obtained his undergraduate degree in Organizational Behavior from the University of San Francisco and Master's and Doctorate degrees in Organizational Psychology from Alliant University in California. Dan has over 20 years of experience in the EEO analysis and test validation fields. He resides in Folsom, California, with his wife and four children.

Richard E. Biddle, M.B.A. Dick is the founder of Biddle & Associates, Inc., the preceding company to Biddle Consulting Group, Inc. He was involved in the state and federal framing of regulatory practices in the EEO field, and has 40 years of experience in EEO-related cases and projects.

Stacy L. Bell, M.S. Stacy is the Executive Vice President of Fire & Police Selection, Inc. (FPSI), a consulting firm specializing in the development and validation of testing instruments used in the protective services industry. Stacy has a Master's degree in Industrial/Organizational Psychology and 14 years of experience in the field.

Leonard S. Feldt, Ph.D. Dr. Feldt holds the Professor Emeritus status at the University of Iowa College of Education, and is one of the senior authors of the Iowa Tests of Basic Skills and the Iowa Tests of Educational Development.

Jim Higgins, Ed.D. Jim has worked in the field of human resources and applied human services research for over 20 years. Jim is currently a principle in Affirmative Action Services, LLC. He has taught applied behavioral statistics at the college level, and is the author of a textbook geared toward making applied statistical analysis easy to understand for the non-mathematical professional.

Gregory M. Hurtz, Ph.D. Greg is an associate professor at California State University, Sacramento, specializing in industrial psychology, psychometric theory, and statistical methods. For over 15 years, he has researched, presented, published, and consulted primarily in the areas of employee selection, occupational licensure/certification testing, and applied psychometrics.

Daniel C. Kuang, Ph.D. Dan is a Principal Consultant with Biddle Consulting Group, Inc. He is an expert at developing and validating tests and measures for personnel selection and performance assessment and has many years of experience in evaluating, supporting, and challenging employment practices, procedures, and tests within the context of litigation support. His primary responsibility at BCG is to ensure that clients are in compliance with federal guidelines and regulations, and are positioned to respond to external legal threats and challenges.

James E. Kuthy, Ph.D. Jim is a Principal Consultant with Biddle Consulting Group, Inc. With 17 years of experience working in the field of Industrial and Organizational Psychology, he has conducted job analyses and developed employment-selection devices, including work-sample testing, for a wide variety of industries. In addition, he has taught college-level courses in both Psychology and Business.

Scott Morris, Ph.D. Scott is an Associate Professor and the Assistant Dean at the IIT College of Psychology. He received a Ph.D. in Industrial-Organizational Psychology in 1994 from the University of Akron and teaches courses in personnel selection, covering topics such as job analysis, test development and validation, and legal issues. He also teaches courses in basic and multivariate statistics.

Patrick Nooren, Ph.D. Patrick is the Executive Vice President of Biddle Consulting Group, Inc. With 17 years of experience in the EEO/HR field, he has invested thousands of hours in EEO-related cases and projects. His primary focus at BCG is oversight of the EEO/AA division and development of related software products.

Contact information for Biddle Consulting Group, Inc.:

Biddle Consulting Group, Inc.
193 Blue Ravine, Suite 270
Folsom, CA 95630
U.S.A
800.999.0438

www.biddle.com

Dedications

To my supportive wife, Jenny, and our four children, Makaela, Alyssa, Matthew, and Amanda, who invested greatly in this work. They mean the world to me.

To my father, Richard E. Biddle, who gave me opportunities galore and an incredible head start in life.

To my co-workers at Biddle Consulting Group: Patrick Nooren, Leigh Bashor, Jim Kuthy, and Stacy Bell, who contributed greatly to the completion of this project, and are a joy to work with; Mike Callen, Joe Doane, Dan Kuang, Patrick Krage, Lori Lee, Clifford Tam, and Ellie Callen, who helped at crucial stages along the way; and to Kathy Sharpe, who patiently wrestled everyone's contributions into a seamless finished product.

To my friends and colleagues at Seattle City Light who taught me the importance of converting theory into what actually works, and who contributed greatly to the refinement of the tools discussed herein.

To my mentors, Dr. Frances Campbell-Lavoie, who strengthened me; Dr. Shelly Zedeck, who set a professional standard; and to Mr. R. Lawrence Ashe Jr., who taught me that what does not kill me can only make me stronger.

Most of all, I want to acknowledge and thank my Savior and Lord, Jesus Christ, for the many miracles He has performed in my life. This book is truly the result of His grace.

"This is the Lord's doing; it is marvelous in our eyes."

Psalm 118:23

D.A.B.
June 1, 2011

Chapter 1 - Adverse Impact

Overview

Not long after the passage of the 1964 U.S. Civil Rights Act (now commonly known as *Title VII*), the legislative and judicial fields began hammering out the concept of *adverse impact*. Nearly 50 years later, after thousands of cases and arbitrations and well over one billion dollars[1] spent by employers, government enforcement agencies, special interest plaintiff groups, and law firms, the concept has been highly refined. It has also expanded to apply to settings other than that for which it was first designed (*e.g.,* some U.S. circuit courts have recently approved of using adverse impact calculations for age discrimination cases).

     While the courts still struggle for a definitive explanation of what constitutes a "finding of adverse impact," the term as used today essentially means the same as when it was first written: a *substantially different rate of selection* in hiring, promotion or other employment decision which works to the disadvantage of members of a race, sex or ethnic group (Uniform Guidelines Questions & Answers Supplement #10).[2] The three most common methods for determining adverse impact are the 80% Rule, statistical significance tests, and practical significance tests. Each will be discussed in this Chapter.

Why does adverse impact occur?

Virtually every public sector employer has one or more entry-level positions with adverse impact in the testing process. Written tests typically have higher levels of adverse impact against minorities (Sackett, 2001; Neisser, 1996). Physical ability tests typically have adverse impact against women, especially when they measure upper body strength. Robert Guion (1998, p. 445) cites several reasons why adverse impact can occur:

1. Chance;
2. Measurement problems inherent to the test (*e.g.,* poor reliability);
3. The nature of test use (*e.g.,* ranking versus pass/fail);
4. Differences in distribution sizes (*e.g.,* a selection process with 100 men and only 10 women);
5. Reliable subgroup differences in general approaches to test taking; and,
6. True population differences in distributions of the trait being measured.

     Test bias is another possible reason why adverse impact can occur, but this can only be a valid reason if one or more of the first five reasons above exist and the sixth is rejected. Genuine discriminatory intent and actions can be yet another reason why adverse impact can occur in a selection process.

     Adverse impact has become a loaded term, fraught with suggestions of ill intent on the part of the employer. It should be noted, however, that adverse impact simply describes differences between groups on a testing process. It is not a legal term that implies guilt, nor is it a psychometric term that implies unfairness or test bias.

Virtually every employer that tests for relevant job skills will generate adverse impact in a testing process in one way or another, and most studies show that adverse impact is not normally due to forms of bias inherent to the tests (Sackett, 2001; Neisser, 1996).

History and development

The U.S. government treatise that first mentions the concept of adverse impact was the Equal Employment Opportunity Commission (EEOC) Guidelines on Employment Testing Procedures (issued on August 24, 1966). This document, however, offered no indication as to how to determine (by calculation or otherwise) whether adverse impact existed in an employer's selection practices. This left the higher circuit or supreme courts with the burden of using key legal cases to make judicial findings that provided insight into what is really meant by adverse impact.

The first major adverse impact case was Griggs v. Duke Power Company (1971). At the time, Duke Power was using a high-school diploma requirement and an off-the-shelf intelligence test as a screening device, both of which had adverse impact against blacks. Since the jobs being tested did not appear to really require a high school diploma to be performed successfully, the court held that the employer had to show a "business necessity" for these two requirements; otherwise, Duke Power would be in violation of Title VII. Responding to the adverse impact that these two requirements had on blacks, the court only stated a few words: ". . . they operated to disqualify blacks at a *substantially higher rate* than white applicants."

Exactly what is a "substantially higher rate?" Wanting to answer this question (and many others pertaining to personnel testing) as well as build a set of criteria that employers could use for determining exactly *how* "adverse" a testing process needed to be to represent "adverse impact," an advisory committee called the Technical Advisory Committee on Testing (TACT)[3] was assembled by the State of California Fair Employment Practice Commission (FEPC) in 1971. TACT was charged with compiling the State of California Guidelines on Employee Selection Procedures (which were published in final form in October, 1972). These California Guidelines were designed to "supersede and enlarge upon" (Section 3 preamble) the earlier set of Guidelines on Employment Testing Procedures, issued by the U.S. EEOC on August 24, 1966. These California Guidelines were later incorporated into the Federal Uniform Guidelines on Employee Selection Procedures (1978), a document still in force.

TACT included 32 specialists from various labor, employment, and technical fields who deliberated the specific techniques and steps that would be taken to evaluate adverse impact. It was out of these deliberations that the (now infamous) 80% Rule was born (in short, the 80% Rule is calculated by dividing the focal group's (the focal group is typically minorities or women) passing rate on a selection procedure by the reference group's (typically whites or men) passing rate, and any value less than 80% is said to violate a "threshold test" for evaluating adverse impact). One of the committee members[4] describes its origin as follows:

> During the negotiations of the FEPC Guidelines (which went on for months), one session had a significant debate on an appropriate statistical tool for

determining adverse impact. We wanted to put an operational definition to some words defining what constituted adverse impact. There were about 20 of the committee members in the room. The members agreed that a statistical test was appropriate, but not enough. They also agreed that those who would implement these guidelines (the FEPC consultants) would never have the appropriate training to implement statistical tests [prior to the common use of computers, calculating probability statistics was a difficult task only completed by the technically savvy]. Therefore, we needed an administrative guideline as well as a technical one for cases. I recall a heated debate that went on for way too long (as usual) with two camps: a 70% camp and a 90% camp. The 80% Rule was born out of two compromises: (1) a desire expressed by those writing and having input into the Guidelines to include a statistical test as the primary step but knowing from an administrative point of view a statistical test was not possible for the FEPC consultants who had to work the enforcement of the Guidelines, and (2) a way to split the middle between two camps, the 70% camp and the 90% camp. A way was found to use both. In the way the 80% Rule was defined by TACT, if there was no violation of the 80% Rule, then there would be no reason to apply statistical significance tests. This hopefully would eliminate many calculations and many situations where TACT would not be necessary and the decision could be made in the field. So from the practical point of view, the 80% Rule became a first step. If there was no 80% Rule violation, there was no need to go further and use a statistical test. If there was a violation of the 80% Rule, statistical significance was needed and the 80% Rule then became a practical significance test for adverse impact.

These deliberations resulted in the final text used in the 1972 California Guidelines, which constituted an industry-first, concrete definition of "adverse effect":

Adverse effect refers to a total employment process which results in a significantly higher percentage of a protected group in the candidate population being rejected for employment, placement, or promotion. The difference between the rejection rates for a protected group and the remaining group must be statistically significant at the .05 level. In addition, if the acceptance rate of the protected group is greater than or equal to **80%** of the acceptance rate of the remaining group, then adverse effect is said to be not present by definition (Section 7.1).

Prior to the publication of the California Guidelines, there were no government-endorsed *mathematical* guidelines for proving adverse impact. The EEOC Guidelines issued on August 1, 1970 (replacing the earlier August 24, 1966 version), had discrimination broadly defined in section 1607.3 without providing mathematical guidance. The Office of Federal Contract Compliance (OFCC) Guidelines (issued October 2, 1971) had discrimination defined in section 60-3.3, also without specific guidance. The EEOC used the term "adversely affects" while the OFCC used the term

3

"adversely affected." Neither of these two documents defined how adverse impact was to be actually calculated.

The TACT committee agreed that statistical significance testing for "adverse effect" should be paramount, as a matter of policy, even if the FEPC consultants were not likely to implement that part. So the FEPC Guidelines presented the concept of statistical significance first ("The difference between the rejection rates for a protected group and the remaining group must be statistically significant at the .05 level."). They wrote the 80% Rule as a *practical significance* test ("In addition, if the acceptance rate of the protected group is greater than or equal to 80% of the acceptance rate of the remaining group, then adverse effect is said to be not present by definition.").

After the 1972 FEPC Guidelines were published, the Equal Employment Opportunity Coordinating Council (EEOCC) issued some drafts in August 23, 1973, and June 24, 1974. The Ad Hoc Industry Group found them unworkable as reported in the Daily Labor Report on October 24, 1974. The next attempt at developing an acceptable set of Guidelines was the Federal Executive Agency (FEA) Guidelines published on November 19, 1976. These FEA guidelines applied the 80% Rule in section 60-3.4(b) in the same way the current 1978 Uniform Guidelines apply the 80% Rule in Section 4D. The 1978 Uniform Guidelines may have been the first to specifically refer to the 80% Rule as a "rule of thumb" (Section II, paragraph 2 on page 33291, Federal Register, Vol. 43, No. 166).

The FEPC used the 80% Rule as a *practical significance* test in a technical sense, but only as a rule of thumb in a practical sense. The 80% Rule of thumb was given greater power by the FEA and the 1978 Federal Uniform Guidelines because a literal reading could interpret adverse impact under some circumstances resulting in an 80% rule-of-thumb violation, but with no statistical significance.

Types of Adverse Impact Analyses

Generally speaking, there are two primary types of adverse impact analyses: Selection Rate Comparisons and Availability Comparisons. Each is briefly described in this Chapter.

A Selection Rate Comparison evaluates the selection rates *between two groups* on a selection procedure. It can also be used to compare the selection rates of two groups in layoffs, promotions, or placements. This type of analysis always involves two groups: a focal group (typically women or minorities) and a reference group (typically men or whites). Selection Rate Comparisons are most typically used in litigation settings, as they relate specifically to the type of adverse impact analysis called for in the Uniform Guidelines. There are four variables that are entered into an adverse impact analysis of this type: (1) the number of focal group members who were selected, (2) the number who were not selected, (3) the number of reference group members who were selected, and (4) the number who were not selected.

An Availability Comparison evaluates one group's representation in a position (*e.g.,* 13% of the incumbents in the Manager II position are Hispanic) to their availability for that position (*e.g.,* 15% of the qualified applicants available for the Manager II position are Hispanic). It is useful for showing the extent to which one group may be *underutilized* (*e.g.,* 15% Hispanics available compared to 13% currently in the position shows a 2% underutilization). There are three variables that are entered into an adverse impact analysis of this type: (1) the total number of incumbents in a position, (2) the number of focal group members in the position, and (3) the percentage of qualified focal group members who are available for the position.

There are major differences between these two types of analyses regarding the extent to which they constitute a legitimate finding of adverse impact that could potentially bring an employer to court. Generally speaking, the Selection Rate Comparison is the only type that can be used alone to demonstrate adverse impact in the classical sense; whereas the Availability Comparison only shows a prima facie reason to investigate further into an employer's practices to see why a "gap" may exist.

There are *descriptive statistics* and *statistical significance* tests that can be applied to both types of adverse impact analyses. Descriptive statistics merely show the mathematical difference relevant to the comparison being made. For Selection Rate Comparisons, this is the difference in selection rates between two groups (*e.g.,* focal group members had a 70% selection rate; reference group members had a selection rate of 80%, which constitutes a 10% difference between the two groups). For Availability Comparisons, the extent of underutilization is the relevant descriptive statistic (*e.g.,* 2% underutilized). Statistical significance tests are the most relevant for adverse impact analyses because they show whether the descriptive statistic is statistically meaningful and whether they can be regarded as a "beyond chance" occurrence.

For each of these types of statistical tests, adverse impact can be analyzed for a single event (*e.g.,* one selection test given during a single year) or multiple events (*e.g.,* one selection test administered over several years and aggregated into a combined analysis). The techniques for conducting each type of analysis will be discussed later in this Chapter.

The Concept of Statistical Significance

Karl Pearson (one of the founders of modern statistical theory) formulated the basis of statistical significance testing as early as 1901 and, even a century later, researchers are still applying the concept as the acid test for deciding whether the results of their studies are "onto something meaningful." While the concept of statistical significance can be applied to literally hundreds of different types of statistical analyses, the meaning is essentially the same: If the result of a statistical test (*i.e.,* the final product of its calculation) is "statistically significant," it is unlikely to have occurred by chance. Said another way, a "statistically significant finding" is one that raises the eyebrows of the researcher and triggers the thought, "I think I've found something here that is not likely due to chance." Obtaining a finding of statistical significance in a research study signifies a point at which the researcher is capable of stating that a legitimate trend, and not a chance relationship, actually exists (with a reasonable level of certainty).

Statistical significance tests result in a p-value (for probability). *P-values* range from 0 to +1. A p-value of 0.01 means that the odds of the event occurring by chance is only 1%. A p-value of 1.0 means that there is essentially a 100% certainty that the event is "merely a chance occurrence," and cannot be considered as a "meaningful finding." *P-values* of .05 or less are said to be "statistically significant" in the realm of EEO analyses. This .05 level (or 5%) corresponds with the odds ratio of "1 chance in 20."

The use of statistical tests to identify whether statistical significance exists in a data set is highly contingent on two major factors: (1) Whether adverse impact exists in the first place under the 80% Rule, and (2) whether the analysis has sufficiently high levels of statistical power to find it. The important concept of statistical power is reviewed next.

Statistical power

When a statistical test is calculated to evaluate whether the event being analyzed is "statistically significant," there is always a "power" associated with the test which can be used to describe its *ability to reveal a statistically significant finding if there is one to be found*. Thus, a powerful adverse impact analysis is one that has a high likelihood of uncovering adverse impact if it really exists. When applying the statistical power concept specifically to adverse impact analyses, there are three factors that impact the statistical power of the analysis:

1. Effect size. For Selection Rate Comparisons, this pertains to the size of the "gap" between the selection rates of the two groups (*e.g.,* if the male passing rate on a test is 80% and the female passing rate is 60%, there is a 20% "gap" or effect size between the two groups). For Availability Comparisons, effect size means the size of the difference between a group's representation in the workplace versus their availability (*e.g., qualified applicants*).
2. Sample size. The number of focal and reference group members plays a key role in adverse impact analyses.
3. The type of statistical test used. This includes the actual formula of the adverse impact analyses (some tests are more powerful than others) and whether a one-tail or a two-tail test for significance is used (see discussion on one-tail versus two-tail tests later in this Chapter).

Because the effect size is outside of the practitioner's control when analyzing adverse impact, only the latter two factors will be discussed here.

Sample size

Amassing a large sample size is perhaps the single most effective way to increase the power of an adverse impact analysis. There are at least five ways this can be accomplished:

1. Widen the timeframe of the events being analyzed. For example, rather than analyzing a selection process for just one year, several administrations from previous years can be included to make an overall historical analysis. In EEO litigation settings, including several events into a single analysis requires the plaintiff to successfully argue a "continuing violation" of the employer's practices over a longer timeframe than just the single at-issue event (*e.g.,* a written test administered in a certain year) or that the sample size in the case is simply too small to conduct a meaningful analysis.

2. <u>Combine various geographic areas</u> together into a "regional" analysis, when appropriate. For example, a plaintiff group could challenge all of the employer's sites in a particular state and demonstrate that these sites operated under similar policies or hiring/promotion strategies.
3. <u>Combine events from several jobs</u>, job groups, or divisions. Combining jobs or divisions into an overall adverse impact analysis is a complicated issue that requires considering several factors. Some of these factors are: the similarity in work behaviors between jobs, job groups, or divisions; statistical homogeneity (discussed later in the Multiple Events section of this Chapter); and the consistency and similarity of the patterns and practices.
4. <u>Combine various selection procedures</u>. Under some circumstances, the courts will allow combining various selection procedures into a combined "overall selection process" analysis. While this type of analysis may sometimes yield meaningful results, an event-by-event analysis should be the primary comparison in most circumstances (the 1991 Civil Right Act requires that a "particular employment practice" needs to be identified as the source of adverse impact for a plaintiff to establish an adverse impact case, unless the results are not capable for separation for analysis – see Section 2000e-2[k][1][A][i]).
5. <u>Combine different ethnic groups</u> for analysis purposes. Some EEO litigation circumstances allow plaintiff groups to form a class of two or more ethnic groups who share similar allegations (*e.g.*, "total minorities").

It is important to note that the first four of the five aggregation techniques described above require using the appropriate multiple-events type of adverse impact analyses because statistical anomalies can occur when combining data across multiple strata (see multiple event analyses discussed later). In litigation settings, it is almost always more favorable to the employer to *limit* the sample size used in the adverse impact analysis (because this limits statistical power and makes it more difficult to identify significant findings) and almost always more beneficial for the plaintiffs to *increase* the sample size (for the reverse reason). The courts will typically have the final say on the nature of the sample used.

When is a sample "too small" for adverse impact analysis?
Despite years of debate among statistical practitioners, there is no absolute, bottom-line threshold regarding the minimum sample size necessary for conducting statistical investigations. Courts also frequently take the stance that there is no clear minimum sample size. For example, in <u>Bradley v. Pizzaco of Nebraska, Inc.</u> (1991), the court stated, "There is no minimum sample size prescribed either in federal law or statistical theory."

If one had to pick a minimum number for adverse impact analyses, it would be 30 with at least 5 expected for selection (*i.e.,* hired, promoted, etc.) (OFCCP, 1993). The Uniform Guidelines Questions & Answers Supplement #20 states that a sample of 20 is too small. In some circumstances, however, it can be argued that a sample with fewer than the "30 requirement" from OFCCP or the "20 requirement" from the Uniform Guidelines can still allow a meaningful statistical analysis to be conducted. For example, consider a testing situation where only 5 men and 5 women applied for a position and all 5 of the men passed and none of the women. A statistical significance test of this example reveals a probability value of .008 (or odds of 1 chance in 126, well beyond the 1 chance in 20 required for statistical significance). Below are a few examples of how some U.S. courts have addressed the issue of small samples in adverse impact calculations:

- The courts have provided several rulings in situations where zero (0) focal group members are selected or represented. Such circumstances have been referred to as the "inexorable zero," and almost always result in the court finding adverse impact such as in <u>Association Against Discrimination in Employment, Inc. v. City of Bridgeport</u> (1979) and <u>Franks v. Bowman Transportation Co.</u> (1974, 1976).
- In <u>Watson v. Fort Worth Bank & Trust</u> (1977, 1988), the court stated, "Our formulations, which have never been framed in terms of any rigid mathematical formula, have consistently stressed that statistical disparities must be sufficiently substantial that they raise an inference of causation."
- In <u>Shutt v. Sandoz Corp.</u> (1991), the court stated that it is sometimes necessary to rely on statistics derived from small samples, however, when it is not completely necessary, it is better to base the statistics on a larger sample (the appeals court in this case reversed the district court's ruling which used a sample of 21 employees working in one of two merged companies instead of 106 employees total). This court also referenced two other cases where sample sizes of 30 and 28 were considered too small.
- In <u>Cicero v. Borg Warner Automotive</u> (1999), the court stated that ". . . statistical evaluations ('disparate impact analysis') of an employer's subjective decisions are permissible in a disparate treatment case brought under Michigan law . . . However, the United States Supreme Court has repeatedly warned courts to be wary of simplistic percentage comparisons based on small sample sizes (see Watson, 487 U.S. at 1000, 108 S.Ct. 2777: 'It may be that the relevant data base is too small to permit any meaningful statistical analysis.')."
- A sample size of six was found to be too small in <u>Gault v. Zellerbach</u> (1998).
- A sample size of seven or eleven was insufficient to demonstrate a pretext in <u>Martin v. United States Playing Card Co.</u> (1998).
- A sample size of 13 was too small in <u>Tinker v. Sears, Roebuck & Co.</u> (1997).
- A sample of eight was insufficient in <u>Anderson v. Premier Industrial Corp.</u> (1995).
- An eight-person sample was too small to support a discrimination case in <u>Osborne v. Brandeis Machinery & Supply Corp.</u> (1994).

While the courts will provide only general guidelines on sample size requirements (almost always evaluating this issue on a case-by-case basis), one characteristic is common to all statistical analyses where small numbers are involved: they suffer from having a higher "sampling error" than analyses involving larger data sets. Analyses with "high sampling error" are prone to change in ways that would likely lead to different statistical outcomes if the underlying event hypothetically occurred again.

For example, consider a situation where 10 men and 10 women applied for a job and 8 men were hired (80%) and 4 women were hired (40%) – a substantially different selection rate of 40% between men and women. It is very likely that subsequent selection processes would have different results. A difference of just a few hires could change the 40% selection rate difference to 10%, 20%, or even 30%. In fact, the very next selection process could result in the complete opposite (*e.g.*, 80% selection rate for women and 40% for men). For this reason, adverse impact analyses that are based on small numbers should be viewed as "less stable" than analyses that involve larger sample sizes. The Uniform Guidelines offers some specific guidance regarding this problem with small data sets:

> Where the user's evidence concerning the impact of a selection procedure indicates adverse impact but is based upon numbers which are too small to be reliable, evidence concerning the impact of the procedure over a longer period of time and/or evidence concerning the impact which the selection procedure had when used in the same manner in similar circumstances elsewhere may be considered in determining adverse impact (Section 4D).

Types of statistical tests

"Exact tests" are considered the most powerful statistical tests to use for adverse impact calculations. These are tests that calculate the precise probability value of a circumstance and require mathematical formulas and iterations that typically can only be completed using computer software. The key exact statistical tests are discussed later in this Chapter.

Another methodology to consider when determining the statistical significance levels of a statistical test used for adverse impact analysis is a one-tail versus a two-tail test. A one-tail statistical test investigates the possibility of discrimination occurring in just one direction (*e.g.*, against women when making a men-versus-women comparison). A two-tail test takes the assumption that discrimination *could have* occurred in either direction (*e.g.*, against men or against women) and hence *spends its statistical power* investigating discrimination in both directions. A one-tail test is more powerful than a two-tail test when investigating discrimination cases because it requires only a 5% level of significance level in one direction in the probability distribution, whereas the two-tail test examines 2.5% on each end of the probability distribution (*i.e.*, it assumes that the at-issue group's selection rate could have been either more or less than the comparison group's).

Thus, because a one-tail test is focused on finding discrimination against only one group, it will always find statistical significance before a two-tail test. For this reason, a one-tail test is a more plaintiff-oriented test than a two-tail test. While statisticians sometimes disagree on the validity of the one-tailed test in discrimination cases,[5] the courts have been almost totally consistent in their requirement of using a two-tail test for significance. The cases cited below have discussed the one-tail versus two-tail issue, and some rather extensively, (*e.g.*, Palmer v. Shultz, 1987), and they almost unanimously agree that a two-tail test is the technique they prefer for adverse impact cases:

- Brown v. Delta Air Lines, Inc. (1980).
- Chang v. University of Rhode Island (1985).
- Csicseri v. Bowsher (1994).
- EEOC. v. Federal Reserve Bank of Richmond (1983).
- Hoops v. Elk Run Coal Co., Inc. (2000).
- Moore v. Summers (2000).
- Mozee v. American Commercial Marine Service Co. (1991).
- Palmer v. Shultz (1987).

While these cases and the OFCCP[6] have clearly endorsed the two-tail method,[7] two cases have allowed a one-tail investigation under certain circumstances:

- Ottaviani v. State University of New York at New Paltz (1988). This case did not involve a typical adverse impact analysis, but rather involved using regression analysis for evaluating differences in salary.
- Police Officers for Equal Rights v. City of Columbus (1985).

It would seem allowable to use a one-tail test for adverse impact analyses if the plaintiff can make a showing that the employer's actions were overtly discriminatory. Such actions on the part of the employer would justify a one-tail test because the researcher would have good cause to suspect that the overt discriminatory actions led to some unequal outcome, hence the use of a one-tail test would only look for what was suspected to exist based on credible evidence.

Selection Rate Comparison for a Single Event

This type of analysis can be regarded as the "most typical" type of adverse impact analysis, and is specifically explained in the Uniform Guidelines as a "rates comparison" (Section 4D) of the passing rates between two groups (*e.g.*, men and women) on a selection procedure. This type of analysis can also be used to analyze the outcome of layoffs, demotions, or other similar personnel transactions where there are only two possible outcomes (*e.g.*, promoted/not promoted; hired/not hired, etc.) (see Table 1-1).

This type of analysis should not be used to analyze combined sets of data (*e.g.*, analyzing the passing rates of men and women in several years combined). The Multiple Events Selection Rate Comparison (discussed later in this Chapter) is necessary when multiple years or tests are placed into a combined analysis. This is because statistical anomalies can occur when combining data across multiple strata.

Types of statistical analyses for Selection Rate Comparisons
There are several types of statistical tests that can be used for this type of analysis. The primary types include the 80% Rule test, statistical significance, and practical significance.

Selection Rate Comparisons: The 80% Rule Test
Much of the historical development regarding this test has been discussed previously. This section will limit the discussion of this test to the mechanical aspects, and how this test is sometimes used in litigation settings.

To review, the 80% Rule is an analysis that compares the passing rate of one group to the passing rate of another group (*e.g.,* men vs. women). An 80% Rule "violation" occurs if one group's passing rate is less than 80% of the group with the highest rate. For example, if the male pass rate on a test is 90% and the female pass rate is 70% (77.7% of the male pass rate), an 80% Rule violation has occurred. The 80% Rule is described by the Uniform Guidelines as:

> . . . a 'rule of thumb' as a practical means for determining adverse impact for use in enforcement proceedings . . . It is not a legal definition of discrimination, rather it is a practical device to keep the attention of enforcement agencies on serious discrepancies in hire or promotion rates or other employment decisions (Overview, Section ii).

It is also described by the Uniform Guidelines as having some limitations:

> . . . a selection rate for any race, sex, or ethnic group which is less than four-fifths (4/5) (or eighty percent) of the rate for the group with the highest rate will generally be regarded by the Federal enforcement agencies as evidence of adverse impact, while a greater than four-fifths rate will generally not be regarded by Federal enforcement agencies as evidence of adverse impact. Smaller differences in selection rate may nevertheless constitute adverse impact, where they are significant in both statistical and practical terms . . . (Section 4D)

The 80% Rule has been scrutinized in Title VII litigation because it is greatly impacted by small numbers and does not consider the "statistical significance" of the passing rate disparity between the two groups (see, for example, Bouman v. Block, 1991; and Clady v. County of Los Angeles, 1985). More typically, courts consider the statistical significance of the passing rate disparity between groups:

- "Rather than using the 80 percent rule as a touchstone, we look more generally to whether the statistical disparity is 'substantial' or 'significant' in a given case" (Bouman v. Block, 1991, citing Contreras v. City of Los Angeles, 1981, at 1274-75).
- "There is no consensus on a threshold mathematical showing of variance to constitute substantial disproportionate impact. Some courts have looked to Castaneda v. Partida (1977) , which found adverse impact where the selection rate for the protected group was 'greater than two or three standard deviations' from the selection rate of their counterparts" (Clady v. Los Angeles County 1985).

Notice in the above cases that standard deviations are used to represent the extent of the adverse impact against a group. Because standard deviations sometimes present a more straightforward interpretive tool for the courts to use when discussing statistical significance and probability values, they have widely adopted the common "two or three standard deviations" as a criteria for establishing statistically significant adverse impact. To be exact, however, a standard deviation that equates to the .05 level of statistical significance is *1.96* (see below for further explanation).

Selection Rate Comparisons: Statistical significance tests

There are two categories of statistical significance tests that can be used for analyzing adverse impact for Selection Rate Comparisons: *exact* and *estimated*. Exact tests provide the precise probability value of the analysis. Estimated techniques approximate the exact results without requiring lengthy calculations. See Appendix A for a complete discussion on the recommended *exact* methods for analyzing adverse impact when making Selection Rate Comparisons. Both exact and estimation techniques require using a 2 X 2 contingency table, as displayed in Table 1-1.

2 X 2 Contingency Table		
	Men	**Women**
Pass	50	40
Fail	50	50

Table 1-1 2 X 2 Contingency Table

These 2 X 2 contingency tables will always have *two groups* and *two categories*. Statistical significance tests applied to these tables can determine whether "statistically significant" levels of adverse impact exist.

Any probability value that is less than .05 is statistically significant and indicates a difference in passing rates between two groups that is not likely occurring by chance. A probability value of .05 corresponds with a likelihood of 1 chance in 20, a probability value of .01 to a likelihood of 1 chance in 100, etc. A probability value can also be interpreted as a standard deviation unit, with a probability value of .05 corresponding to a (two-tail) standard deviation value of 1.96. A standard deviation of 2.58 corresponds with a probability value of .01, and a likelihood of 1 chance in 100.

Selection Rate Comparisons: Practical significance tests

A number of alternate rules of thumb have been applied to adverse impact analysis. In some litigation contexts involving adverse impact, these have been referred to as "practical significance" tests. This is described in the Uniform Guidelines, Section 4D, where it states that selection rate differences between groups that do not violate the 80% Rule "may nevertheless constitute adverse impact, where they are significant in both statistical *and practical terms* …" [emphasis added]. The Uniform Guidelines expounds on this definition only slightly in the Questions & Answers Supplement #20 by stating: "If the numbers of persons and the difference in selection rates are so small that it is likely that the difference could have occurred by chance, the Federal agencies will not assume the existence of adverse impact, in the absence of other evidence." The section continues to explain that it is "inappropriate to require validity evidence or to take enforcement action where the number of persons and the difference in selection rates are so small that the selection of one different person for one job would shift the result from adverse impact against one group to a situation in which that group has a higher selection rate than the other group."

This concept has also been applied in different ways in litigation settings. For example, two cases have ruled that the adverse impact finding was not practically significant if the statistical significance findings would become non-significant if just *two more persons* from the focal group would have hypothetically passed selection procedure (Waisome v. Port Authority, 1991; U.S. v. Commonwealth of Virginia, 1978). Some more recent cases have denounced this approach (OFCCP v. TNT Crust, 2004).

The courts have also been known to apply this same principle to see whether the result of the 80% Rule would change (*e.g.,* Contreras v. City of Los Angeles, 1981 Delgado v. Ashcroft, 2003), which is consistent with the intention of the original framers of the 80% Rule (*i.e.,* with the adverse impact result only taking on the "practically significant" label if it was both statistically significant and the 80% Rule was violated). Still other courts have rejected this type of analysis, noting that it is unacceptable to "play hypotheticals" with the actual numbers observed in a discrimination case (*e.g.,* Dixon v. Margolis, 1991; Washington v. Electrical Joint Apprenticeship & Training Committee of Northern Indiana, 1988). Indeed, one could only imagine the reaction from employers defending a test based on criterion-related validity if the plaintiffs hypothetically removed subjects from the validity study until the validity coefficient was no longer significant.

While the Uniform Guidelines are clear that practical significance evaluations are *conceptually relevant* to adverse impact analyses, the indefinite endorsement and inconsistent interpretations in the courts should serve as a caution to practitioners against using hard-and-fast practical significance rules when analyzing adverse impact. Rather, the determination of adverse impact should be governed by a process where the "collective evidence" is weighed. In the typical legal proceeding, this *starts* with a finding of statistical significance which can be supplemented by additional evaluations, such as the 80% Rule (or the "impact ratio") and practical significance analyses. This is because the true definition (per the Guidelines) of adverse impact is essentially a "*substantially different* rate of selection."

Making a final determination of adverse impact for Selection Rate Comparisons

Under most circumstances, a Selection Rate Comparison analysis should result in a firm finding of both statistical and practical significance to constitute a solid finding of adverse impact. However, the myriad of factors involved in litigating adverse impact cases will often lead to differing judicial findings based on the circumstances involved. For this reason, when practices, procedures, or tests show signs of adverse impact (or may show adverse impact if greater sample sizes were evaluated), the employer should consider either conducting validation studies or using alternative employment practices that have less adverse impact (see Section 2000e-2[k][1][A][i]-[ii] of the 1991 Civil Rights Act). For this reason, it is a good idea for employers to keep track of the results of their testing, so that they might consider adjusting the process if adverse impact does occur.

Selection Rate Comparisons for Multiple Events

This section discusses the proper methodology for comparing the passing rates of gender and ethnic groups on several combined "events" or administrations of various practices, procedures, or tests. This technique may also be used to complete an overall adverse impact analysis on several jobs or groups of jobs with similar skill sets, or for comparing group passing rates on an overall selection or promotion process for multiple years, although an event-by-event analysis should be the primary comparison in most circumstances (the 1991 Civil Right Act requires that a "particular employment practice" needs to be identified as the source of adverse impact for a plaintiff to establish an adverse impact case, unless the results are not capable of separation for analysis – see Section 2000e-2[k][1][A][i]).

Simpson's Paradox - The reason for caution when combining data

Statistical anomalies can occur when combining data across multiple strata. While it may be tempting to simply aggregate several years of a particular testing practice into an overall, combined adverse impact analysis, the results will sometimes be misleading unless a special "multiple events" technique is used. A statistical phenomena called "Simpson's Paradox"[8] shows why this can be a problem. Consider the data presented in Table 1-2

Simpson's Paradox Example				
Testing Year	**Group**	**# Applicants**	**# Selected**	**Selection Rate %**
2004 Test	Men	400	200	50.0%
	Women	100	50	50.0%
2005 Test	Men	100	20	20.0%
	Women	100	20	20.0%
2004 + 2005 Tests Combined	Men	500	220	44.0%
	Women	200	70	35.0%

Table 1-2 Simpson's Paradox Example

Notice that the selection rate for men and women in the table is *exactly the same* for each of the two years individually. Thus, a year-by-year analysis of the selection rates between men and women would reveal no differences in passing rates. No 80% Rule violation, statistical significance, or practical significance occurred. However, when the two years are added together for a combined analysis, a significant gap of 9% between men and women becomes apparent. Because the application ratio (the number of men compared to women for each year) has not remained constant for the two years, the combined analysis shows that women have a lower selection rate when the years are combined. When evaluating the data in Table 1-2 statistically, the following results are calculated:

- When calculating the adverse impact for each year individually, no statistical significance exists (the selection rates are exactly equal for each year).

- When calculating the adverse impact for both years aggregated (*i.e.,* simply adding the passing and failing values together for both years into a single analysis), the probability value is statistically significant (p = .031 using the Fisher Exact Test with mid-P adjustment, or odds of about 1 chance in 33).
- However, when calculating adverse impact for both years combined using the proper technique (the Multiple Events technique discussed herein), the probability value is appropriately not significant.

Because of limitations like the Simpson's Paradox, proper aggregation techniques need to be used in place of simple aggregation techniques.

Properly aggregating data for Multiple Event Selection Rate Comparisons

Unlike the Selection Rate Comparison test used for single events, two steps are necessary for evaluating multiple event Selection Rate Comparisons. The first step is to calculate the pattern consistency of the events to evaluate whether the events can be combined into a single analysis; the second is to calculate and interpret the statistical significance test.

Step 1: Evaluate the events for pattern consistency

Before data sets can be combined into an overall analysis, they should first be analyzed to see whether they are similar enough statistically to be combined. This first step involves a test called a *pattern consistency* test or, in technical terms, a *homogeneity of odds ratios* test. While there are several different tools and techniques that can be used to accomplish this, the end goal of these tests is the same: to evaluate whether the "trend" in the passing rate difference between groups is consistent between "events" (*e.g.,* years, tests, etc.).

When one group continually maintains a passing rate that is lower than the other group, the result of this test will be close to 1.0 – indicating there are no significant fluctuations between the events in the combined data set. When there are "flip-flops" between events (*e.g.,* when one group's selection rates are below the other group's for four years in a row, but reverse dramatically in the fifth year), the value will approach 0. When the result of this test is below .05, a statistically significant *reversal* of one or more events has been detected, and conducting separate analyses for these events (or removing them altogether) should be considered.

There are at least two frequently used statistical tests available for analyzing pattern consistency. The first test uses the "Treatment by Strata Interaction" test (Mehrotra & Railkar, 2000); the second is a widely used test called the "Breslow-Day" (1980) with Tarone's (1988) Correction. If the output from these test results is above .05, no significant reversal in the selection rates (between events) has been detected and the results can be safely included in an overall analysis.

Step 2: Calculate statistical test results

If the events can safely be combined into an overall analysis, the next step is to evaluate whether adverse impact occurred in the overall analysis. The Mantel-Haenszel[9] Test is the most commonly used test for multiple 2 X 2 data sets (such as the data required for Selection Rate Comparisons, where there are two outcomes for the two groups being evaluated).

While the Mantel-Haenszel Test is not an exact statistical test (but rather an estimator for the precise probability value), it comes very close. For large data sets, it will match the exact test results almost precisely. The mathematical iterations necessary for calculating the exact test are highly sophisticated and require advanced statistical software.[10]

Two versions of the Mantel-Haenszel estimator formula are included in the Adverse Impact Toolkit Demo Version on the Toolkit Evaluation CD included in the back of this book. Version 1 is likely to be closest to the "exact" probability value, and only uses a modest (.125) continuity correction.[11] Version 2 uses a conventional correction (.5) and will typically overestimate the probability value (especially with small data sets). These tests assess whether the selection rate difference between two groups (*e.g.*, men vs. women) for *all events combined* is extreme enough to be considered "beyond chance." Values less than .05 are statistically significant; values between .05 and .10 should be considered "close to significance." Both versions use the Cochran variation of the Mantel-Haenszel statistic, which weights each event according to its sample size.

Another statistical analysis called the Minimum Risk Weights Test (Mehrotra & Railkar, 2000) can be used for multiple Selection Rate Comparisons. This test does not weight the events by sample size and can sometimes provide a "more powerful" analysis than the Mantel-Haenszel Test (above). The test uses a moderate correction for continuity (.375) and can be interpreted using the same guidelines proposed for the Mantel-Haenszel.

Multiple events Selection Rate Comparisons in litigation

This type of analysis has been successfully applied in numerous EEO litigation settings. A partial list is provided below:

- Arnold v. Postmaster General (1987).
- Covington v. District of Columbia (1995).
- Dees v. Orr, Secretary of the Air Force (1983).
- Dennis L. Harrison v. Drew Lewis (1983) .
- Hogan v. Pierce, Secretary, Housing and Urban Development (1983).
- Johnson v. Garrett, III as Secretary of the Navy (1991).
- Manko v. U.S. (1986).
- McKay v. U.S. (1985).
- Paige v. California Highway Patrol (1999).
- Trout v. Hidalgo (1981).
- Strong v. Blue Cross (2010).
- Delgado-O'Neil v. City of Minneapolis (2010).

Availability Comparison for a Single Event

This type of adverse impact analysis is designed for comparing one group's representation (*i.e.*, the percentage of incumbents in a given position who belong to the gender or ethnic group) to that group's availability in the relevant labor market (using availability data from inside or outside the organization). This type of comparison is useful for determining whether a group is underutilized in a particular position, or group of positions.

This analysis should be differentiated from the Selection Rate Comparison because (under most circumstances) a statistically significant finding (meaning the at-issue group is significantly underutilized) does not automatically constitute a finding of adverse impact.[12] The reason for this is straightforward: a Selection Rate Comparison directly evaluates how two groups fared on a particular selection procedure, so if one group significantly outperforms the other, direct evidence is amassed regarding the impact of a *particular* employment practice on a *specific* group when *compared to another group*. Then the attention can shift toward evaluating that particular selection procedure for job-relatedness (*i.e.,* validity).

By contrast, the Availability Comparison does not (necessarily) consider the impact of a single employment practice. Because the comparison is an overall evaluation that considers one group's makeup in a given position compared to their availability outside of that position, it does not individually consider all of the selection procedures that may have been used to select or promote individuals for that position. Further, it does not take into consideration other factors such as "job interest" or qualification levels of the at-issue group.

For example, if outside availability data shows that men are statistically significantly underutilized for a group of clerical jobs at a given employer, the underutilization could possibly be explained by either lack of interest on the part of men to pursue these positions, or the fact that men performed poorly on the multitude of qualification screens required for entry into the position (or some combination of these two factors and/or others). For these reasons, the Availability Comparison should only be considered as a "threshold" or "initial inquiry test."

Types of statistical analyses for Availability Comparisons

While the 80% Rule is sometimes used by government enforcement agencies for evaluating underutilization of various groups, it will not be discussed here because it has already been discussed in the previous sections relevant to the Selection Rate Comparisons, it is not regularly used in litigation to assess adverse impact on groups,[13] and it is not endorsed by the Uniform Guidelines as a valid adverse impact analysis (it is only referenced as a "rule of thumb" for comparing the selection rates of two groups).

The concept of practical significance, while highly relevant in some cases, is also not discussed here because it has not been referenced or applied in litigation settings of Availability Comparisons. This leaves only statistical significance as the relevant test for Availability Comparisons.

Like the Selection Rate Comparison, calculating adverse impact for Availability Comparisons can be done using exact or estimator techniques. The exact test provides the precise probability value of the analysis. The estimator techniques can approximate the exact results without requiring lengthy calculations. The estimator technique can readily be calculated in Microsoft® Excel® by using the BINOMDIST function and doubling the value to obtain an estimated two-tail probability value. The proper exact test is a (two-tail) Exact Binomial Probability Test, which can also be corrected for discreteness using the mid-P adjustment.[14] This test requires sophisticated iterations that require programming or advanced computer software (this calculation is available on the Evaluation CD). The same conventions used for the Selection Rate Comparison can also be used for this test (*e.g.*, any value below .05 constitutes a statistically significant finding).

Making a final determination of adverse impact for Availability Comparisons

Because this test compares one group's representation to their availability (rather than comparing the selection rates of two groups, such as the test used for the Selection Rate Comparison), statistically significant findings (without other evidence) should not be considered as direct evidence of adverse impact (because both discriminatory and non-discriminatory reasons can possibly account for the group's underutilization). Rather, results that yield probability values of less than .05 should be regarded as "statistically significant under-utilization," but not necessarily as adverse impact.

These findings are sometimes called a "manifest imbalance" or "statistically significant underutilization" in litigation which simply means that there is a "statistically significant gap" between the comparison group's availability for employment or promotion (typically derived from a group's representation in the qualified applicant pool for entry-level positions and the "feeder" positions for promotional positions[15]) and the group's current representation in the at-issue job or group of jobs. When such a statistically significant "imbalance" or "underutilization" exists, any of the five circumstances listed below can possibly lead to a court's finding of adverse impact:

1. The employer failed to keep applicant records (sometimes referred to as an "adverse inference" – see Section 4D of the Uniform Guidelines). If an employer fails to keep applicant data, the government has reserved the right to infer adverse impact on the selection or promotion process if the agency has an imbalance in a job or group of jobs.

2. The employer failed to keep adverse impact data on the selection or promotional processes (Section 4D of the Uniform Guidelines). Similar to #1 above, if employers have an imbalance in a job (or group of jobs) and do not have information regarding the adverse impact of the various practices, procedures, or tests used in the selection or promotion process, an "adverse inference" can be made. Employers should maintain passing rate data for their various selection and promotional processes. Practices, procedures, or tests that have adverse impact should be justified by evidence of job-relatedness and business necessity.

3. The employer's recruiting practice was discriminatory toward the protected group (see Section 4D of the Uniform Guidelines and Hazelwood School District v. United States, 1977). For example, if the employer recruits for certain jobs only by "word of mouth," and the only applicants who are informed about the job opportunities are a certain race and/or gender group, the employer could be held liable in a discrimination lawsuit. Plaintiff groups may also argue that minorities and/or women were "funneled" by the employer's systems and processes into filling only certain position(s) in the organization.

4. The employer maintained a discriminatory reputation that "chilled" or "discouraged" protected group members from applying for the selection process (Section 4D of the Uniform Guidelines). This argument has been successful in several discrimination cases,[16] and is a viable argument for plaintiffs to make in some circumstances.

5. The employer failed to conduct a formal selection process for the position and instead hired or promoted individuals through an "appointment only" process. This "promotion by appointment" practice would certainly lend itself to a viable plaintiff argument because the practice was exclusionary to qualified individuals who were not allowed an equal opportunity to compete for a position. Further, this type of promotional practice could make the use of conventional adverse impact analyses impossible (because there are no clear "promotional processes" or "events" that can be analyzed by comparing the passing rates between two groups), which could limit the adverse impact analysis to a comparison between the disadvantaged group's representation in the promotional position to their availability in the "feeder" positions. While informal selection procedures are not directly prohibited under the various civil rights laws, they are much more difficult to defend against claims of unfairness than are more standardized selection processes.

Unless one of these five situations exists, a plaintiff group will be required to pinpoint the specific selection procedure that caused the adverse impact (using the 80% Rule, statistical significance tests, and/or practical significance tests). The only exception is if the agency's practices cannot be "separated for analysis purposes."[17]

Availability Comparisons for Multiple Events

Availability Comparisons can be made for several different jobs (or groups of jobs) or for the same job across multiple years (the reader is referred back to the "Availability Comparison for Single Events" section of this Chapter for several caveats that apply to these types of analyses). This technique is useful for many personnel assessments, such as:

- Employment trends of specific groups over time
- Utilization rates of groups in various departments at one employer
- Utilization rates of specific groups across different geographic regions of one employer

The Generalized Binomial Test[18] can be used to appropriately analyze multiple Availability Comparison data sets. This type of analysis has been successfully applied in several EEO litigation settings. A partial list is provided below:

- Cooper v. University of Texas at Dallas (1979)
- EEOC v. United Virginia Bank (1980)
- Vuyanich v. Republic National Bank (1980)

Using Logistic Regression to Evaluate Adverse Impact

Logistic Regression (LR) is a statistical method that is useful for evaluating *why* adverse impact may be occurring in a hiring or promotional process. While classic 2 X 2 table analysis can identify whether the observed hiring or promotion rates between two groups are significantly different, LR can determine if job-relevant qualification factors (*e.g.,* experience or education) of the individuals included in the analysis explain the difference in hiring or promotion (as opposed to gender or race being the reason).

From a technical standpoint, LR analyses use multiple predictor variables for the individuals included in the study (such as education, experience, or other relevant qualifications) to predict a single criterion or "outcome" variable that has only two possible values, such as hired/not hired or promoted/not promoted. By including gender or race ("dummy coded," using, for example, 1 = men and 0 = women), the researcher is able to determine whether gender or race played a significant role in the hiring or promotional process, or if the job-related qualification variables statistically accounted for the hire or promotion decisions.

For example, if a promotional process exhibited three standard deviations (3 SD) in adverse impact against women using the classic 2 X 2 table method, an employer could conduct an LR analysis by "controlling" for the factors that were considered in the hiring process, such as education level and tenure. If these two qualification factors were significant in the LR model and gender was not, this would indicate that the management staff responsible for making the promotion decisions was paying attention to each individual's education and tenure, and not their gender.

When using LR in the specific context of adverse impact analyses, it is important to remember that the Uniform Guidelines (and the related Q&As) define adverse impact as a *substantially different rate of selection* in hiring, promotion or other employment decision which works to the disadvantage of members of a race, sex or ethnic group (Uniform Guidelines Questions & Answers Supplement #10; see also Section 4D and 16B). Because adverse impact occurs whenever the observed 2 X 2 table (which includes passed/failed, hired/not hired, or promoted/not promoted counts for two groups) is statistically significant, LR is only useful as a *follow-up analysis* procedure that can evaluate *why* the disparity is occurring, and whether objective, job-related qualifications can justify the differences. In other words, LR should not be used to *back into* a finding of adverse impact where there is initially no showing of adverse impact using a classic 2 X 2 method. There are several reasons for this, expressed below.

First, as a matter of standard practice, the initial EEO investigation is to test for simple differences in selection rates (not controlling for explanatory factors). This "threshold test" is foundational to Title VII and Uniform Guidelines-prescribed analytical methodology. Before a LR (or Probit Regression Analysis)[19] can be used, there must first be a raw, absolute difference in selection *rates* (as per Section 4D of the Uniform Guidelines) that is *substantial* (as per Section 16B of the Uniform Guidelines). Without this, Title VII does not allow employers to be found guilty of discrimination for "theoretical probabilities" (as LR analyses may reveal) based on some (limited) combination of whatever job qualification variables happen to be electronically available (*e.g.,* tenure or education, which may or may not be relevant for each specific position included in the study). This is especially true if the LR analysis is applied to an arbitrary or theoretical assembly of positions (*e.g.,* movement between two broad categories, such as "hourly" to "salary" classifications), as opposed to the actual positions or the lines of progression for positions.

Rather, Title VII clearly outlines that the employer's "specific employment practice" (as per the 1991 Civil Rights Act, Section 703[k][1][A][i]) or the specific "hiring, promotion, or other employment decision" (as per 16B of the Uniform Guidelines) must be identified and called out as having specific adverse impact (using the 2 X 2 table method specifically outlined by the Uniform Guidelines). Otherwise, using an LR analysis, employers could be incriminated for adverse impact on position and qualification configurations that do not even exist in the real world. Further, they could be held liable for a theoretical, probability-based model that did not result in any practical, real-world hiring or promotion disparity between groups.

This is because 2 X 2 table analyses have been used by the courts and regulatory agencies for decades for determining whether the plaintiff has sufficiently carried the first burden in EEO litigation or enforcement settings. Given the sensitivity of LR analyses when large samples are involved, and the fact that a researcher's LR model may or may not include the actual decision factors that were considered in a hiring or promotion process, LR models may trigger possible problems (*e.g.,* a significant race variable) when there are no practically meaningful hiring or promotion differences between the groups. If LR was used as the primary threshold indicator for adverse impact, it could lead to situations where employers (wanting to proactively conduct adverse impact analyses controlling for a variety of variables rather than just using standard 2 X 2 analyses) could find multitudes of additional *potential* problems which, because they may be based on situations where the LR models were inadequate or where no practically meaningful difference was occurring between groups, may not be *actual* problems.

For these reasons, LR should (1) only be used after an initial showing of adverse impact (using the classic 2 X 2 approach), (2) include the relevant job qualification factors for the position (or group of highly-related positions), and (3) consist of an analysis configuration that accurately reflects the progression of employees or applicants (*e.g.,* hiring for a single position, promotion to a position that follows the proper line of progression, etc.). Without such modeling, an LR analysis that crosses job title and line of progression boundaries (where specific positions feed into others) and combines these into an aggregate analysis may not accurately reflect the employer's reality.

In situations where adverse impact is exhibited using a standard 2 X 2 table on a hiring process, an LR analysis based on differences between the two groups on job-related factors (such as experience or education) can be useful for demonstrating two important facts. First, the LR model will reveal the *relative predictive strength* of each job-related qualification factor in the hiring or promotion process. That is, LR models will unveil how much each factor played into the decision process. Second, by including the race or gender variable in the LR model, the researcher can determine how much gender or race played into the decision process. If the gender or race variable starts out significant in the LR model, and then moves to non-significant after including the job-relevant qualification factors, evidence is generated that the hiring or promotional decision process was job-related and free from bias.

Before describing the steps involved in conducting an LR analysis, there are several key outputs generated by LR analyses that will first be explained:

- **B coefficient**: These values reveal the strength of the relationship between the predictor variables (*e.g.,* experience) and the outcome variable (*e.g.,* hires). The values show the amount of increase (or decrease, if the sign is negative) in the outcome variable that would be predicted by a one-unit increase (or decrease) in the predictor, holding all other predictors constant.

- **P-value** (or "Sig" values): This value indicates the significance level of the B coefficient (for the respective predictor) (with values < .05 classified as statistically significant).

- **Exp(B)**: This is one of the more useful outputs from an LR analysis. In technical terms, this value is the exponentiation of the B coefficient, which is an odds ratio that shows the ratio of the probability of an event occurring to the probability of the event not occurring. In practical terms, it is an "odds multiplier" that can be used to explain the change in the odds ratio associated with a one-unit change in the predictor variable, holding other variables constant. Values greater than 1 indicate that, as the predictor variable (*e.g.,* job experience) increases, the odds of the outcome (*e.g.,* hired) increase. If the value is less than 1, then as the predictor variable increases, the predicted probability declines (*i.e.,* the variable has a negative effect on the outcome variable). For example, if the Exp(B) value for an experience factor (coded 1-3, indicating between 1 and 3 years' experience) is 2.5, this would indicate that every single year of experience translates to an applicant being 2.5 times more likely to be hired (holding all other variables constant). It is important to note, however, that a change in the Exp(B) value does not correspond to a constant change in the probability of that event (*e.g.,* hire) occurring.

- **Wald Chi-Square Statistic**: This value shows the unique contribution of each predictor in the model in the context of the other predictors (*i.e.,* the relative strength of each predictor, eliminating any overlap between predictors).

- **Hosmer and Lemeshow Goodness-of-Fit Test:** This test divides the subjects in the analysis into deciles based on predicted probabilities, then computes a chi-square from observed and expected frequencies. The resulting p-value of this test should be non-significant (*i.e., p-values* of > .05 are desirable), which indicates that the researcher fails to reject the null hypothesis that there is no difference, implying that the model's estimates fit the data at an acceptable level. When considering this test, if there are many "tied values," it may be desirable to use 6, 8, 10 and possibly 12 levels to see if they are consistent in giving a Chi Square p-value of greater than .05 which would indicate that the model was, in fact a good fit – even if the standard Hosmer and Lemeshow test appears to indicate that the model does not fit.

- **Nagelkerke R-Square:** This value constitutes a "pseudo R-square" value that provides a practical way for estimating the *proportion of variance* explained by the predictors in the model. For example, a Nagelkerke R-Square value of

.20 would indicate that the combined set of predictors in the model explains about 20% of the reasons/factors going into the hiring or promotion decision.

With this background provided, the steps for completing an LR using a statistical program (*e.g.,* SPSS) are provided below.

Analysis Preparation

Step 1: Verify data coding.

Step 2: Generate frequency tables to examine each variable for missing data and to ensure that dichotomous variables are actually dichotomous.

Step 3: Recode variables as necessary. For example, education can be coded 1 = high school, 2 = AA degree, 3 = BA/BS degree, 4 = master's degree, 5 = doctoral degree. In some instances (*e.g.,* where non-linear but significant correlations are observed), consider transforming continuous variables (*i.e.,* by either squaring, using cubic splines, or fractional polynomials). Transformation techniques should only be used when there is clear evidence that the data requires such transformations for the model to interpret valid results.

Model Development

Step 1: Conduct univariate analyses of each predictor variable and its relationship to the dichotomous dependent variable (*e.g.,* hires). Identify those predictors with B coefficients that are statistically significant at the p <= .25 level to use as candidates in LR model development (a higher or lower threshold may be used – the key is making sure that there are practice or policy reasons for including the variable).

Step 2: Using the "Enter Method," enter the predictors into Block 1 of the equation. Enter the gender or race variable into Block 2. Generate the model and evaluate the Block 1 model summary to determine whether the Model, Block, and Step are statistically significant. If so, then proceed to Step 3.

Step 3: Evaluate the Hosmer and Lemeshow Test to determine the fit of the model. If this test is not statistically significant (*i.e.,* if the p-value is >.05), proceed to step 4.

Step 4: Compare the Classification Table for Block 0 (containing only the constant) to that for Block 1 to get a general idea about how much more accurate predictions are likely to be based on the model over just using the constant.

Step 5: Examine the variables entered into Block 1 of the equation to determine which variables are statistically significant based on the Wald test. Unless a predictor is verifiably practically important (*e.g.,* hiring managers were instructed to use, or reported having used, education when making hiring decisions), it should be discarded unless it is statistically significant.

Step 6: Evaluate the Block 2 model summary to determine whether the Model, Block and Step are statistically significant. If so, then proceed to Step 7. If Block 2 is not statistically significant, then gender or race did not provide statistically significant explanatory power. Verify this by looking at the gender or race variable in the "Variables Entered into the Equation" summary to verify that the p-value for this variable is not statistically significant. If this proves to be

23

the case, conclude that gender or race was not a significant predictor (indicating a fair, bias-free process).

Step 7: Evaluate the Hosmer and Lemeshow Test to determine the fit of the model. If this test is not statistically significant, proceed to Step 8.

Step 8: Examine the variables entered into Block 2 of the equation to determine which variables are statistically significant. If the gender or race variable (which must be evaluated one model at a time – *i.e.*, one model for race, one model for gender) is statistically significant

Step 9: Evaluate the difference in the Nagelkerke R-Square between Block 1 and Block 2. If the increase here is not substantial, gender or race played only a minor role (if any) in the hiring or promotion decision process (even if they were statistically significant). For example, if the value for Block 1 (which included only job-related qualification factors) is 20% and the value for Block 2 is 21%, it can be estimated that the addition of gender or race contributed only 1% of predictive/explanatory power over the combined job factors.

Model Refinement

Step 1: Through an iterative process of including additional predictors (evaluating the effect of including that variable on the other variables as well as on the standard error, the Nagelkirke R-Square, and the classification table), include those variables that tend to maximize the variance accounted for, and the accuracy, as indicated by the classification table.

If including a practically important predictor (which is not statistically significant) has a deleterious effect on the other predictors (making them non-significant when they originally were) or if it causes the standard error to increase significantly, do not include the predictor.

Step 2: Examine the data for possible interactions with gender or race. For example, if gender is a statistically significant predictor and years of experience is a statistically significant predictor, multiply gender by years of experience and include this interaction in the equation to see if, accounting for the interaction of gender with years of experience, gender alone is a statistically significant predictor. Advanced steps need to be taken to interpret any interaction effects (if they are statistically significant).

Examining Assumptions

Step 1: Evaluate collinearity using the standard linear regression collinearity diagnostics. Look for the following as "hints" of potential collinearity:

- Eigenvalues near 0
- Standardized regression coefficients attain magnitudes of greater than 1
- Small Tolerance values (near .01) are observed

Step 2: Consider eliminating those variables with very small Tolerance values because it indicates that the variable shares a large proportion of variance with another predictor.

Step 3: Examine the effect of these eliminations on the model, its fit, and its effectiveness.

Step 4: Consider reducing or eliminating collinearity by standardizing each predictor and adding them together to create a new variable.

Interpretation

Step 1: Evaluate the correlation direction of the job qualification factors to be sure that all job qualification factors included in the final model are correlated in a direction that is consistent with the hiring/interview process. For example, if "Relevant Work Experience" is a job qualification factor in Block 1 and higher values are associated with higher levels of qualification (and hiring decision is coded as 1 = hired, 0 = not hired), then a positive correlation is expected.

Step 2: If gender is a statistically significant predictor in the equation, evaluate the Exp(B) output. If gender is coded 0 and male is coded 1, an Exp(B) of 1.25 would indicate that males have a 25% greater odds of being hired than females after controlling for job qualification factors.

Step 3: (Optional): Develop an LR model using only the job qualification factors for the reference group (*e.g.*, males, if females are the focal group of interest). Then use the resulting model weights to compute the number of predicted hires or promotions for the focal group (*e.g.*, women). For example, if the male-only LR output included the following values: Constant: -4.19, Predictor 1 B coefficient (education): .46, and Predictor 2 B coefficient (experience): .71, use these values in the steps and formulae below to compute *predicted hire values* for women:

> Step 1: Compute "A" as: A = Sum (-4.19+(Education*.46)+ (Experience*.71))
> Step 2: Compute "B" by computing the *exponentiated* value of A (*e.g.*, Exp(A)).
> Step 3: Compute "C" using: (B/(1+B))

After using this formula to compute predicted values for each woman, sum the predicted values and compare this value to the actual number of female hires to compare the actual shortfall.

Notes

[1] The EEOC filed 710,928 Title VII charges against various employers between 1992 and 2003. These charges resulted in $1.16 billion in monetary benefits to plaintiffs. While only about 5% of Title VII cases are based on adverse impact claims, the 1 billion estimate should still be regarded as conservative because it does not include monetary benefits obtained through litigation, cases filed by private law firms, and the costs associated with defending against such lawsuits. In fact, the author's consulting firm has worked on over 175 EEO cases since 1974; and the cases directly relating to adverse impact claims exceed the 200 million mark (when combining plaintiff and defense costs).

[2] The Uniform Guidelines on Employee Selection Procedures and the related Questions & Answers can be found at www.uniformguidelines.com.

[3] DeGroot, M. H., Fienberg, S. E., Kadane, J. B. (1985), *Statistics and the Law*, New York, NY: John Wiley & Sons (p. 30).

[4] Personal communication (August, 2004) with Richard E. Biddle, member of the subcommittee on Guidelines Preparation, and Mary Tenopyr, Special Consultant to TACT.

[5] For example, compare Harper, (1981), *Statistics as Evidence of Age Discrimination, 32* Hastings L.J. 1347, 1355 & n. 65 with Kaye, D. (1982), *The Numbers Game: Statistical Inference in Discrimination Cases*, 80 Mich.L.Rev. 833, 841.

[6] The "Pooled Two-Sample Z-Score" test specified in Chapter 3 of OFCCP's Compliance Manual (October 13, 2004 on-line Internet version) outputs a Z-score value that is a two-tail Z value.

[7] Title VII protects everyone from discrimination, which is why a two-tail test has been determined to be more appropriate.

[8] See Finkelstein, M. O., & Levin, B. (2001), *Statistics for Lawyers* (2nd ed.). New York, NY: Springer (p. 237).

[9] The Mantel-Haenszel technique was originally developed for aggregating data sets for cancer research. See Mantel, N. & Haenszel, W. (1959), Statistical aspects of the analysis of data from retrospective studies of disease. *Journal of National Cancer Institute, 22*, 719-748.

[10] At the time of this writing, only one commercially-available software program is available for calculating the exact version of the Mantel-Haenszel: StatXact from Cytel Software Corporation (Version 4.0 and higher).

[11] A correction to a discrete probability distribution to approximate a continuous probability distribution. This correction adjusts the estimator formula to better approximate the exact probability value. Correction values typically range between 0 and 0.5.

[12] A statistically significant finding on a Selection Rate Comparison analysis does not necessarily automatically constitute adverse impact either. Practical significance should usually be considered as well.

[13] A more commonly applied technique is called a "gross under-representation" or "gross disparity" which evaluates the gap between focal and reference group representation using the statistical significance tests described herein for the Availability Comparison analysis.

[14] See Agresti, A. & Gottard, A. (2007). Nonconservative exact small-sample inference for discrete data, *Computational Statistics and Data Analysis*; Armitage, P., Berry, G., Matthews, J. N. S. (2001). *Statistical Methods in Medical Research* (4th ed.). Wiley-Blackwell; and Simonoff, J.S. (2003). *Analyzing Categorical Data* (1st ed.). Springer.

[15] If the target position is not underutilized when compared to the relevant feeder position(s), yet the relevant feeder position(s) is underutilized when compared to those with the requisite skills in the relevant labor area (called an "outside proxy group"), it can be argued that the proxy group can be used to compare to the target position. This process is referred to as a "barriers analysis."

[16] See <u>Donnel v. General Motors Corp</u>. (576 F2d 1292, 8th Cir 1978); <u>Dothard v. Rawlinson</u> (433 U.S. 321, 1977); <u>Williams v. Owens-Illinois, Inc.</u> (665 F2d 918, 9th Cir.; Cert. denied, 459 U.S. 971, 1982).

[17] 1991 Civil Rights Act (42 U.S.C. §2000e-2[k][ii][B]).

[18] Gastwirth, J.L. & Greenhouse, S.W. (1987), Estimating a common relative risk: Application in equal employment. *Journal of the American Statistical Association, 82*, 38-45.

[19] Logistic and probit regression are very similar, with the primary difference being that LR seeks to predict the logit, or log odds of an event occurring, whereas probit regression outputs the probability value (as a Z score) of an event occurring. Probit analyses can also be applied when the frequency of the outcome for the dependent variable is more than one for a given case (*e.g.,* multiple promotions).

Chapter 2 - Selection Procedure Development and Validation

While many types of selection procedures are frequently litigated, none are as vulnerable as the infamous written test. There are at least two reasons for this. First, written tests typically have higher levels of adverse impact against minorities (Sackett, 2001; Neisser, 1996) than other types of selection procedures, making them eligible for civil rights litigation. Second, they are sometimes only theoretically related to the job, or not sufficiently related to the job. Despite these drawbacks, written tests are frequently valid predictors of job success and are typically not biased against minorities (SIOP Principles, 2003, p. 32).

For these reasons, employers should complete validation studies on written tests. Completing a thorough validation process helps insure that the test used for selection or promotion is sufficiently related to the job (and includes only test items that Job Experts have deemed fair and effective) and generates documentation that can be used as evidence should the test ever be challenged in an arbitration or civil rights litigation setting.

It would be difficult if not impossible to create a step-by-step instruction guide for developing and validating all of the different types of written tests that are commonly used by employers. Because test content varies, based on the *types* of KSAPCs (knowledges, skills, abilities, and personal characteristics) being measured, the *level* at which they are being measured (*e.g.,* entry-level testing versus promotional), and the *purpose* of the test (*e.g.,* employment, licensing, credentialing, etc.), this becomes an even more difficult task.

This Chapter is not written to take the weight of this burden. Rather, it is designed to provide a basic outline of steps that can be followed for developing and validating some of the most commonly used tests by employers, such as:

- Mechanical ability
- Cognitive ability
- Situational judgment
- Reading comprehension
- Math skills
- Job knowledge
- Problem solving/decision making skills

This Chapter assumes that the reader will be using a conventional written test format (*e.g.,* multiple choice questions) to measure KSAPCs that are necessary for entry-level or promotional testing purposes. While some of the content herein is relevant for educational and/or credentialing or licensure tests, it is not designed to specifically address these testing situations.

Validation Defined

There are three definitions to understand before beginning the validation process. They are the practical, the legal, and the academic definitions of validity.

Practically speaking, a valid selection procedure is one that measures the actual requirements of the job in a fair and reliable way. A valid selection procedure is one that "hits the mark" and does so consistently, with the "mark" being the core, essential requirements for a given position that are targeted by the selection procedure. A valid selection procedure effectively measures the net qualifications that are really needed for the job, and not much more or less.

In the legal realm, a selection procedure is valid if it can be proven by an employer in litigation that it is ". . . *job related for the position in question and consistent with business necessity*" (to address the requirements of the 1991 Civil Rights Act, Section 703[k][1][A][i]). This standard is usually met (or not) by arguing how the selection procedure first addresses the Uniform Guidelines[1] (1978), followed by professional standards (*i.e.,* the Standards and Principles, discussed below), then by parallel or lower courts that have applied the standard in various settings.

Academically, the Principles (2003) and Standards (1999) have adopted the same definition for validity: "The degree to which accumulated evidence and theory support specific interpretations of test scores entailed by proposed uses of a test" (p. 184).

Overview of the Mechanics of Content and Criterion-related Validity

Subsequent chapters in this book describe in detail how to validate various selection procedures, so only a cursory overview of validation mechanics is provided here, and this is provided only as a primer to the subsequent, more advanced discussions.

How is a content validation study conducted? What are the mechanistic parts involved? What are the basic elements of a criterion-related validity study? Mechanically speaking, content and criterion-related validity are very different. Let's take a look at how they differ based on how they are constructed.

A content validity study is conducted by *linking* the essential parts of a job analysis (the job duties and/or knowledges, skills, and abilities) to the selection procedure. Thus, content validity is formed by creating a *nexus* between the job and the selection procedure. It relies on a process that requires Job Experts (incumbents or immediate supervisors) to provide judgments (usually by providing ratings on surveys) regarding *if* and *how well* the selection procedure represents and measures the important parts of the job.

A word-processing test that measures skills in using word-processing software to edit and format business correspondence would likely be content valid for a clerical worker's job if they perform these functions. An entry-level physical ability test measuring fire scene physical performance uses a content validity approach for the position of firefighter.

Criterion-related validity is statistical. This type of validity is achieved when a selection procedure is statistically correlated with important aspects of job performance at a level that is "statistically significant" (with a probability value of less than .05). One interesting benefit of this type of validity is that the employer is not pressed to define exactly what the selection procedure is measuring. While it is always a very good idea to know and describe to applicants the KSAPCs that are being measured by a selection procedure, it is not a requirement to do so because the selection procedure is scientifically related to job performance. By contrast, content validity has specific requirements for the employer to show and describe exactly what KSAPCs are being measured by the selection procedure, and how they relate to the job (see 15C4 - 5 of the Uniform Guidelines).

Criterion-related validity can be achieved by correlating selection procedure scores to several different types of job performance measures, including both subjective and objective measures. The most typical subjective performance measures include supervisor ratings and/or peer ratings of work products (quality and/or quantity) or job performance, and performance review scores.[2] Objective measures can include quantifiable work output measures (*e.g.*, number of widgets produced per hour), quality-related measures (*e.g.*, number of widgets returned because of defects), absenteeism, turnover, disciplinary actions, safety incidents, and other aspects of performance that are gathered and recorded in a uniform and consistent manner.

Benefits of the Validation Process

Now that validation has been briefly defined, what is its value to the employer? Why validate selection procedures? "Validation is expensive" and "We are only required to validate a selection procedure if it has adverse impact" (a true statement) are typical of statements that personnel consultants hear frequently. With formal validation studies sometimes costing in the tens of thousands of dollars, these are legitimate concerns.

Validation generates two major benefits for the employer. First, validation helps insure that the selection process is measuring key and relevant job requirements in a reliable and consistent manner. This, of course, helps select better workers into the workforce. Even if the validation process increases the effectiveness of a selection process only slightly, the results over years and hundreds of applicants can sometimes be astounding. Second, the validation process generates evidence (in the event of litigation) that the selection procedures are ". . . job related for the position in question and consistent with business necessity" (to address the requirements of the 1991 Civil Rights Act, Section 703[k][1][A][i]).

Related to the latter benefit, validated selection procedures can also dissuade potential plaintiffs from even beginning the lawsuit process if the relationship between the selection procedure and the job is sometimes self-evident (called "face validity"). Applicants are much less likely to challenge a selection procedure if it "smells and looks like the actual job." Likewise, plaintiff attorneys will be discouraged to gamble the time and money necessary to wage a "validation war" if the employer has conducted good-faith validation studies.

Professional Standards for Validation

In the early 1950s, three different aspects of validity were discussed – content, criterion-related, and construct (Principles, 2003, p. 5). From the 1950s to the publication of the 1978 Uniform Guidelines, these three remained as the concrete, "tried and true" validation strategies (especially in litigation settings). While the

Uniform Guidelines set down these validation ground rules in 1978, the government anticipated that the educational and personnel testing fields would continue to advance the science and art of validation. It, therefore, included the following provision for considering future development in framing the criteria that will be used for validating selection procedures:

> For the purposes of satisfying these guidelines, users may rely upon criterion-related validity studies, content validity studies or construct validity studies, in accordance with the standards set forth in the technical standards of these guidelines, section 14 of this part. *New strategies for showing the validity of selection procedures will be evaluated as they become accepted* by the psychological profession (Section 5A) [emphasis added].

Fulfilling this expectation, the psychological community authored the 1985 version of the *Standards for Educational and Psychological Testing* (also known as the Joint Standards, published by the American Educational Research Association, the American Psychological Association, and the National Council on Measurement in Education) and Division 14 of the American Psychological Association (the Society for Industrial and Organizational Psychology, or SIOP) published the *Principles for the Validation and Use of Personnel Selection Procedures* (also known as the SIOP Principles) (1987).

   These two documents advanced the testing field to the current state of validation at that time. Fourteen years later (in 1999), the Joint Standards were substantially updated. Following suit, the Principles received a major update 16 years later in 2003. While published by different associations, the Principles and Standards are virtually in agreement regarding the key aspects of validity (Principles, 2003, p. 4). Part of the motivating factor behind the publication of the new Principles was to provide an update to the earlier (1987) version based on the newly published Standards (1999).

   At the heart of these two documents is how they define validity. Both the Standards and the Principles have moved from defining validity in terms of the three conventional types of validity (like those discussed in the Uniform Guidelines, below), but as moving towards a definition of ". . . validity as a *unitary concept* with different sources of evidence contributing to an understanding of the inferences that can be drawn from a selection procedure" (Principles, 2003, p. 4).

   The Standards and Principles allow five different "sources of evidence" to generate validity evidence under this "unitary concept" umbrella:

1. Relationships between predictor scores and other variables, such as selection procedure-criterion relationships;
2. Content (meaning the questions, tasks, format, and wording of questions, response formats, and guidelines regarding administration and scoring of the selection procedure. Evidence based on selection procedure content may include logical or empirical analyses that compare the adequacy of the match

between selection procedure content and work content, worker requirements, or outcomes of the job);

3. Internal structure of the selection procedure (*e.g.,* how well items on a test cluster together);

4. Response processes (examples given in the Principles include (a) questioning test takers about their response strategies, (b) analyzing examinee response times on computerized assessments, or (c) conducting experimental studies where the response set is manipulated); and,

5. Consequences of testing (Principles, 2003, p. 5).

The Principles explain that these five "sources of evidence" (used for showing validity under the unitary validity concept) are not distinct types of validity, but that "... each provides information that may be highly relevant to some proposed interpretations of scores, and less relevant, or even irrelevant to others" (p. 5).

Uniform Guidelines Requirements for Validation

The current government treatise for validation is the 1978 Uniform Guidelines. This document was assembled by a mutual effort by the U.S. Equal Employment Opportunity Commission (EEOC), Civil Service Commission, Department of Labor, and Department of Justice. The goal of publishing the Uniform Guidelines was to provide an objective standard by which testing and adverse impact concepts could be defined and used for government enforcement, arbitration, and litigation. Numerous earlier texts and enforcement guidelines existed prior to the Uniform Guidelines, but it is safe to say that the Uniform Guidelines constituted the most definitive treatise at the time of its publication. The Uniform Guidelines remain mostly unchanged (a few minor updates are pending at the time of this writing, which will constitute the first change since their original publication).

Three primary forms of validation are presented in the Uniform Guidelines: content, criterion-related, and construct-related (listed in the order most frequently used by employers):

Content validity. Demonstrated by data showing that the content of a selection procedure is representative of important aspects of performance on the job. See section 5B and section 14C.

Criterion-related validity. Demonstrated by empirical data showing that the selection procedure is predictive of or significantly correlated with important elements of work behavior. See sections 5B and 14B.

Construct validity. Demonstrated by data showing that the selection procedure measures the degree to which candidates have identifiable characteristics which have been determined to be important for successful job performance. See section 5B and section 14D.

Blending the Professional and Government Validation Standards into Practice

How are the professional standards different from the government standards? How are they similar? All three types of validation described in the Uniform Guidelines are also contained in the professional standards (the Principles and Standards):

- The *content validity* described in the Uniform Guidelines is similar to the "validation evidence" source #2 and #5 (to a limited degree) of the professional standards.
- The *criterion-related validity* described in the Uniform Guidelines is similar to #1 and #5 of the professional standards.
- The *construct validity* described in the Uniform Guidelines is similar to #1, #3, and #5 of the professional standards.

When conducting a validation study, which set of standards should a practitioner be most concerned about – the Principles? the Standards? or the Uniform Guidelines? The conservative answer is all three, but if one had to choose a "primary set" of criteria, here are a few reasons to consider for choosing the Uniform Guidelines:

- They have the backing of the U.S. government (the EEOC, OFCCP, Department of Labor, Department of Justice, and nearly every state fair employment office).
- They are regularly used as the set of criteria for weighing validity studies during enforcement audits conducted by the OFCCP and numerous other state fair employment offices.
- They have been afforded "great deference" by the courts and have consistently been used as the measuring stick by the courts for assessing the merit of validity studies.
- They have been referenced thousands of times in judicial documents. By contrast, as of the year 2000, the Principles have only been referenced in 13 federal court cases and the Standards in ten, the former of which was also cited as "less than instructive" (Lanning, 1999).[3]
- They inherently include the key elements of the Standards and Principles, while the reciprocal is only true for some "sources of validation evidence" espoused by the professional standards.

Notwithstanding the endorsement above, it is important to note that the Principles and Standards offer more guidelines and regulations than the Uniform Guidelines, and provide more complete guidance for many unique situations that emerge in testing situations. Nonetheless, for the reasons stated above, the Uniform Guidelines are the primary set of criteria that will be addressed throughout this text as the standard for completing validation studies.

Of the three validation types proposed in the Uniform Guidelines, only content and criterion-related validity will be reviewed. Construct validity will not be discussed further for a few key reasons. First, the author is not aware of any EEO-related case where a judge has endorsed a validation study based solely on construct validity. Because the concept is highly academic and theoretical, it is difficult for even advanced practitioners to build selection procedures based solely on construct validity. With this being the case, expert witnesses will find themselves hard-pressed to explain such concepts to a judge! Second, if one were to ask 100 validation experts to define construct validity, almost as many unique definitions would emerge, several even contradicting each other! Third, most forms of construct validity require some type of criterion-related validity evidence. All of this simply begs the question: *Why not just use criterion-related validity in the first place?* For these reasons, the reader is referred to other texts if they desire to review the concept in more depth (see Cascio, 1998, pp. 108-111; Gatewood & Feild, 1994, pp. 220-221).

Steps for Completing a Content Validation Study

There are four steps for conducting a conventional content validation study: job analysis, selection plan, selection procedure development, and selection procedure validation. The first two steps form the essential foundation of a professionally-conducted content validation study, and are the same regardless of the type of selection procedure that will be validated (*e.g.*, a written test, physical ability test, interview, etc.). The steps and requirements for completing the last two steps are highly contingent on the type of selection procedure used.

A job analysis consists of a thorough analysis of the job duties and knowledges, skills, abilities, and personal characteristics (KSAPCs) required for a position. A selection plan extracts from the job analysis the key, essential KSAPCs and/or job duties that should be measured by the selection process. The steps for completing each are provided below in this Chapter. The process of developing and validating content valid selection procedures that can be linked back to the job analysis and selection plan components are discussed in following chapters.

Eight Steps for Completing a Job Analysis

Developing a thorough and accurate job analysis is as important to a content validation study (or criterion-related validity, but less so) as the foundation is to a house. There are numerous ways to build a solid job analysis. The following "blueprint" is adopted from the Guidelines Oriented Job Analysis® (GOJA®) Process, which has been supported in numerous EEO cases[4] and reviewed in several textbooks and articles.[5] (GOJA is now available online at http://www.AutoGOJA.com).

Step 1: Assemble and train a panel of qualified Job Experts

Job Experts are qualified job incumbents who perform or supervise the target position. The following criteria are presented as guidelines for selecting the members of the panel. The Job Experts chosen should:

1. Collectively represent the demographics of the employee population (with respect to gender, age, race, years of experience, etc.). It is a good idea to slightly over-sample gender and ethnic groups to insure adequate representation in the job analysis process;[6]

2. Be experienced and active in the position they represent (*e.g.,* Job Experts should not be on probationary status or temporarily assigned to the position). While seasoned Job Experts will often have a good understanding of the position, it is also beneficial to include relatively inexperienced Job Experts to integrate the "newcomer's" perspective. However, at least one year of job experience should be a baseline requirement for Job Experts selected for the panel;

3. Represent the various "functional areas" and/or shifts of the position. Many positions have more than one division or "work area" or even different shifts, where job duties and KSAPCs may differ; and,

4. Include between 10 and 20% supervisors for a given position. For example, if a 7-10 person Job Expert panel is assembled, include 1-2 supervisors on the panel.

How many Job Experts are necessary to include in the job analysis process to produce reliable results? Some courts have relied on as few as 7-10 Job Experts[7] for providing judgments and ratings about job and selection procedure characteristics. Figure 2-1 provides some guidance regarding the number of Job Experts necessary to obtain a statistically reliable and accurate estimate regarding job information.

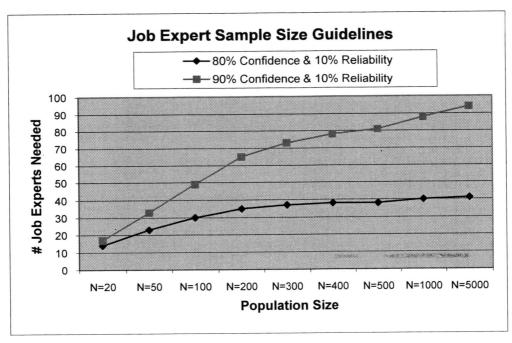

Figure 2-1 Job Expert Sample Size Guidelines

In the example above, if there are currently 200 employees in a position and the employer desires to be 80% confident (with 10% "margin of error") that the collective opinions of a Job Expert panel will accurately represent the larger population of 200 employees, about 35 Job Experts are required. Using a 90% confidence level requires about 65 Job Experts.[8] However, using just 10 Job Experts provides about a 66%

confidence level (with 10% margin). While this figure and some court cases have provided guidance on this issue, practical judgment and workforce availability should be considered when assembling a panel of Job Experts.

It should be noted that there is a large "diminishing effect" that can be observed on the chart above. For example, including 80 Job Experts in a population of 400 yields very similar levels of accuracy when compared to including 100 Job Experts for a population of 5,000! The time and money that can be saved by using a "smart" rather than "huge" sampling strategy is very significant. It is not uncommon to find situations where employers unnecessarily involve hundreds of "extra" subjects in a survey when a much smaller sample would have provided nearly identical results!

It should be noted that the GOJA Process described herein involves conducting a workshop with a Job Expert panel including 7-10 employees who currently hold the job. Based on the experience level of the researcher, the nature and type of the position being studied, and the Job Experts who are available, other job analysis methods may also be very useful. These include conducting structured interviews (of individual Job Experts or Job Expert panels), reviewing diaries, logs, or other work records, conducting time/study analyses, administering questionnaires, or using checklists.

After designating the Job Experts who will participate in the job analysis, they should be trained on the overall process and be informed that their responses should be both *independent* and *confidential* (*i.e.,* not disclosed to anyone outside the job analysis Job Expert panel). Because each Job Expert's opinion should be counted equally regardless of rank or functional job area, it is often useful to explain to the Job Experts that the job analysis workshop is a meeting "without rank." It is also useful for the group to be made aware of the limitations of possible "group think" and to be encouraged to think independently.

Step 2: Job Experts write Job Duties

In this step, Job Experts independently write job duties performed in the target position without providing any ratings (*e.g.,* frequency, importance). Having Job Experts independently identify duties is an important first step in the job analysis process. This independent work – without a group or "paired" discussion – helps insure that the final combined list of duties (which is the next step) is as complete as possible. Job duties should usually begin with an action word, include the process (tasks) for completing the duty, and include the work product or outcome of the duty. For example: "Prepare correspondence using word processing software, and reference documents and deliver to clients using email."

Allowing multiple, independent opinions typically allows a final duty list to be created that, after being consolidated, includes 2-3 times the number of duties that any individual Job Expert recorded. Depending on the complexity of the job, providing Job Experts with 1-2 hours to record their job duties is usually sufficient.

Step 3: Consolidate Job Duties into a master Job Duty list

After the Job Experts have independently recorded the duties of the target position, a facilitator should convene the panel to consolidate a master list that reflects the majority opinion of the group. Using a 70% consensus rule (*e.g.,* 7 out of 10) for this step is suggested. A lower ratio may be used if the job analysis results will be sent in survey form to a larger Job Expert sample. At this step, job duties from pre-existing job descriptions and other suggestions or data from management should be integrated into the discussion and added to the master list if the majority of the Job Experts agree.

Step 4: Write KSAPCs, Physical Requirements, Tools & Equipment, Other Requirements, and Standards

Have the Job Experts repeat the process described in Step 2, but for the KSAPCs, Physical Requirements, Tools & Equipment, Other Requirements, and Standards. The following definitions can be helpful for this step:

- Knowledges: A body of information applied directly to the performance of a duty. For example: Knowledge of construction standards, codes, laws, and regulations.
- Skill: A present, observable competence to perform a learned physical duty. For example: Skill to build basic wood furniture such as bookcases, tables, and benches from raw lumber, following written design specifications.
- Ability: A present competence to perform an observable duty or to perform a non-observable duty that results in a product. For example: Training ability to effectively present complex technical information to students in a formal classroom setting, using a variety of approaches as needed to maximize student learning.
- Personal Characteristics: These are characteristics that are not as *concrete* as individual knowledges, skills, or abilities. Examples include "dependability," "conscientiousness," and "stress tolerance." The Uniform Guidelines do not permit measuring *abstract traits* in content-validated selection process (see Section 14C1) unless they are clearly *operationally defined* in terms of observable aspects of job behavior.[9] For example, while the characteristic "dependability" (if left undefined) is too abstract to directly measure in a selection process, it can be defined as "promptness and regularity of attendance," which *is* an observable work behavior, and can be measured. "Stress tolerance," if not clearly operationally defined, is also too abstract for inclusion in a selection process under a content validity approach. However, defining it as "the ability to complete job duties in a timely and efficient manner while enduring stressful or adverse working conditions" converts it into an essential work ability that is readily observable on the job, and measurable. Therefore, personal characteristics can be included in the selection process but must first be converted from abstract ideas into observable and measurable skills and abilities.

Physical Requirements, Other Requirements, and Standards will vary greatly between jobs. Several existing taxonomies are available – see the GOJA System for several examples of each (available at http://www.AutoGOJA.com).

Step 5: Consolidate KSAPCs, Physical Requirements, Tools & Equipment, Other Requirements, and Standards into a master list

For this step, the Job Experts repeat the process described in Step 3, but for the KSAPCs, Physical Requirements, Tools & Equipment, Other Requirements, and Standards. As in Step 3, the KSAPCs, Physical Requirements, Tools & Equipment, Other Requirements, and Standards from pre-existing job descriptions and other suggestions or data from management can be included in the process.

Step 6: Have Job Experts provide ratings for Duties, KSAPCs, and Physical Requirements

At this point, the Job Experts and supervisors can now provide ratings for the final list of duties and KSAPCs. For Job Duties, Job Experts can provide the following ratings (see AutoGOJA for sample rating scales):

- Frequency of performance: How frequently is the Job Duty performed? Daily? Weekly? This is not a requirement under the Uniform Guidelines for *content validity*, but it is useful for several practical reasons (note, however that *it is required* for criterion-related validity studies!). One of the useful purposes for this rating is for determining which job duties constitute *essential functions* under the Americans with Disabilities Act (Section 1630.2[n][3][iii]).
- Importance: How important is competent performance of the Job Duty? What are the consequences if it is not done or done poorly? The importance rating is perhaps one of the most critical ratings that Job Experts provide. Section 14C2 of the Uniform Guidelines states that the duties selected for a selection procedure (*e.g.,* a work sample test) ". . . should be *critical* work behavior(s) and/or *important* work behavior(s) *constituting most of the job.*" Thus, the Uniform Guidelines are clear that when using content validity for a work sample test, the selection procedure can be linked to a single critical duty ("critical" is later defined by the Uniform Guidelines as "necessary"), or several important duties that constitute most of the job.

For KSAPCs and Physical Requirements, Job Experts can rate:

- Links to Duties: Where is this KSAPC/Physical Requirement actually applied on the job? What are the Job Duties (by duty number) where it is used? This step is crucial in establishing content validity evidence. By linking the duties to the KSAPCs and Physical Requirements, a nexus is created showing where actual job skills (for example) are actually applied on the job. Completing this step addresses Section 14C4 of the Uniform Guidelines.
- Frequency: How often is this KSAPC/Physical Requirement applied on the job? While it is a good idea to obtain a direct rating from Job Experts on this factor, this question can also be answered by determining the Job Duty with the highest frequency rating to which the KSAPC/Physical Requirement is linked.
- Importance: How important is the KSAPC/Physical Requirement to competent job performance? This is perhaps the most important rating in a

content validity study because the Uniform Guidelines require that a selection procedure measuring a KSAPC/Physical Requirement should be shown to be a "necessary prerequisite" of "critical or important work behaviors . . .used in the performance of those duties" (Sections 14C4 and 15C5). Because the Uniform Guidelines make this clear distinction between *only* "important" and "critical or necessary," the importance rating scale should take this into consideration by making a clear demarcation in the progression of importance levels between *important* and *critical*. A selection procedure measuring KSAPCs/Physical Requirements should be linked to critical and/or important work duties, and should be rated as "critical" or "necessary" by Job Experts.

All Job Experts who participated in the job analysis process can provide ratings; however, in Step 7, using only two supervisors is sufficient for providing the supervisor ratings. Calculating inter-rater reliability and removing outliers[10] from the data set can be a useful step for insuring that the raters are providing valid ratings.

After all ratings are collected, they should be reviewed for accuracy and completeness, and then averages for each Job Duty and KSAPC rating should be calculated. This should be performed before proceeding further because supervisors will consider the rating averages in subsequent steps.

Optional step for positions with a large numbers of incumbents: Distribute a Job Analysis Survey (JAS) to additional Job Experts for ratings

Completing the six steps above results in a completed job analysis that represents the collective and majority opinions of the 7-10 Job Experts included in the process. While including 7-10 Job Experts in the process is likely to provide accurate and reliable information about a position for many employers, increasing the Job Expert sample size will increase the accuracy and reliability of the information about the position (if there are more than ten Job Experts in the position).

Obtaining the opinions of additional Job Experts can be completed using a Job Analysis Survey (JAS). A JAS can be prepared by providing the duties, KSAPCs, and Physical Requirements in survey form to the Job Experts and having the Job Experts rate the "content" of each, in addition to all other standard "job-holder ratings." For example, Job Experts can use the following scale in a JAS for rating each duty:

This duty is (select one option from below) a duty that I perform.

1. not at all similar to (does not describe)
2. somewhat similar to (some of the objects listed and actions described in the duty are somewhat similar to the objects and actions in the duty performed in your job)
3. similar to (most of the objects listed and actions described in the duty are similar to the objects and actions in the duty performed in your job)
4. the same as (extremely similar or exactly like)

Job Experts can use the following scale to rate each KSAPCs and Physical Requirements:

This KSAPC / Physical Requirement is (select one option from below) a KSAPC / Physical Requirement I apply on the job.

1. not at all similar to (does not closely describe)
2. somewhat similar to (somewhat describes)
3. similar to (closely describes)
4. the same as (very accurately describes)

One potential benefit of providing the additional Job Expert group with a JAS is that the additional Job Experts may know of other legitimate Job Duties, KSAPCs, or Physical Requirements that are required for the position, but were not identified by the original Job Expert group. It is suggested to provide extra space on the JAS where the additional Job Experts can record and rate additional duties, KSAPCs, and/or Physical Requirements they identify while completing the JAS.

It is recommended to use 3.0 as the minimum average-rating criteria for these two ratings when deciding whether to include a duty or KSAPC/Physical Requirement in a final job analysis.

Step 7: Have two supervisors review the completed job analysis and assign supervisor ratings

After the final job duties, KSAPCs, and Physical Requirements have been rated by the Job Experts and the ratings have been averaged, convene two supervisors (these supervisors may have participated in the first six steps of the process, or can be new to the AutoGOJA Process) to assign the "Supervisor Only" job analysis ratings. The ratings that supervisors should provide for Job Duties include:

- Percentage of Time: When considering all Job Duties, what percentage of a typical incumbent's time is spent performing this Job Duty? Evaluating the percentage of time that incumbents spend on a particular duty is one of several factors that should be considered when making essential function determinations under the 1990 Americans with Disabilities Act (Section 1630.2[n][3][iii]). While helpful, it is not absolutely required for content validation studies.

- Best Worker: What Job Duties distinguish the "minimal" from the "best" worker? Job Duties that are rated high on the Best Worker rating are those that, when performed above the "bare minimum," distinguish the "best" performers from the "minimal." For example, lifting boxes and occasionally helping guests with luggage may be necessary for a hotel receptionist position. However, performing these job duties at a level "above the minimum" will not likely make any difference in a person's overall job performance. It would likely be other Job Duties such as "greeting hotel guests and completing check-in/check-out procedures in a timely and friendly fashion" that would distinguish between the "minimal" and the "best" workers for this job. The average rating on this scale can provide guidance for using a *work sample* type of content validity selection procedure on a pass/fail, ranking, or banding basis (see Section 14C9 of the Uniform Guidelines). It is not necessary to obtain this rating for Job Duties unless the employer desires to validate a work sample type of selection procedure (*i.e.,* a selection procedure that relies on linkages to Job Duties and not necessarily KSAPCs).

- Fundamental: How fundamental is this Job Duty to the purpose of the job? Would the position be fundamentally different if this Job Duty was not required for performance? Handcuffing suspects is fundamental to the job of Police Officer. Rescuing victims is fundamental to the firefighter job. Fundamental Job Duties are duties that constitute "essential functions" under the 1990 Americans with Disabilities Act (this rating is helpful, but not necessary for validation). A Job Duty may be considered fundamental to the job in any of the following ways:
    - o The duty is frequently performed (check the Frequency rating) and/or the proportion of work time spent on it is significant (check the average Percentage of Time rating), or
    - o The consequence to the purpose of the job is severe if the Job Duty is not performed or if it is performed poorly (check the average Importance rating), or
    - o Removing the Job Duty would fundamentally change the job. In other words, the duty is fundamental because the reason the job exists is to perform the duty, or
    - o There are a limited number of employees available among whom the performance of this Job Duty can be distributed, or
    - o The duty is so highly specialized that the incumbent was placed in the job because of their expertise or ability to perform this particular Job Duty.
- Assignable (Assignable to Others): Can this Job Duty be readily assigned to another incumbent without changing the fundamental nature of the position? In such instances, the Job Duty should not be considered as an "essential function" under the 1990 Americans with Disabilities Act. For example, a Job Duty is determined to be fundamental (using the "fundamental duty" rating) and hence also "essential" under the ADA; however, if such Job Duty can be *readily assigned to another employee* without changing the fundamental nature of the job, the Job Duty can be re-designated as not essential. Job Duties which are frequently performed or which take up a large proportion of work time and which are important or critical, probably are not easily assigned to others. Duties which occur infrequently and/or which require a small percentage of work time can sometimes be assumed by others, regardless of how important or unimportant they are.

For KSAPCs and Physical Requirements, supervisors can rate:

- Minimum v. Helpful Qualifications: Is this KSAPC/Physical Requirement a necessity for the position? While possibly helpful to the performance of the job, is it an absolute requirement? This rating can help determine which KSAPCs/Physical Requirements should be included in a selection process.

Minimum qualifications are those that the applicant or candidate must have prior to entry into the position; helpful qualifications can still be included in the selection process (if they meet the other requirements discussed herein), but are not absolute necessities prior to entry.

- Level Needed for Success (for Job Knowledges Only). What level of this job knowledge is required on the first day of the job? Total, complete mastery? General familiarity? The data from these ratings is useful for choosing the job knowledges that should be included in a written job knowledge test (see Section 14C4 of the Uniform Guidelines for specific requirements for measuring job knowledge in a selection process).

- Level Needed Upon Entry: How much of this KSAPC/Physical Requirement will be required on the first day of the job? All? Some? None? Will some on-the-job training be provided, or will candidates be required to bring all of this KSAPC/Physical Requirement with them on the first day of the job, with no additional levels attained after hire? This rating provides direction on which KSAPCs/Physical Requirements to include in a selection process. This is a requirement of the Uniform Guidelines (Section 14C1).

- Best Worker: Which KSAPC/Physical Requirements distinguish the "minimal" from the "best" worker? KSAPC/Physical Requirements that are rated high on the Best Worker rating are those that, when possessed above the "bare minimum" levels required for the job, distinguish the "best" performers from the "minimal." The average rating on this scale can provide guidance for using a selection procedure measuring KSAPC/Physical Requirements on a pass/fail, ranking, or banding basis (see Section 14C9 of the Uniform Guidelines).

Step 8: Prepare final job analysis document, including descriptive statistics for ratings

After compiling the Job Expert and supervisor rating data, a report should be compiled that provides descriptive statistics (*e.g.,* means and standard deviations) for each rated item. The final data (*e.g.,* Job Duties, KSAPCs, etc.) can be entered directly into the job analysis document, along with the means and standard deviations that accompany each, to compile a final job analysis for a position.

Developing a Selection Plan

Now that a thorough job analysis has been developed, a Selection Plan is the next step in the content validation process. Completing a Selection Plan is the step in the validation process where the key, measurable KSAPCs and Physical Requirements are laid out as targets to be assessed by the selection process. A Selection Plan distills the complete list of KSAPCs and Physical Requirements into only those that can and should be tested by one or more selection procedures in the overall selection process. This is accomplished by reviewing every KSAPC/Physical Requirement according to the "Selection Plan screening process" as shown below:

1. Importance: Select only the KSAPCs/Physical Requirements that are above a certain level on the Importance rating scale. It is usually sufficient to draw the

line at one-half (0.5) a rating point above the level on the rating scale that distinguished between the "important" versus "critical and necessary" (*e.g.,* require an average rating of 3.5 if 3.0 is "important" and 4.0 is "critical"). This is important because the KSAPCs/Physical Requirements selected for measurement should be those that are most critical for success on the job (see Section 14C4 of the Uniform Guidelines). It is possible to develop a valid selection procedure for measuring only "important" (not necessary) KSAPCs if they "constitute most of the job" (see Section 14C4 of the Uniform Guidelines).

2. Level Needed Upon Entry: Select only the KSAPCs/Physical Requirements that are above a certain level on this rating scale. Establish the criteria the point on the rating scale where more than one-half (51% +) of the level needed is required on the first day of the job. This step is important because the KSAPCs/Physical Requirements selected for measurement should be those that needed upon entry to the job (see Sections 5F and 14C1 of the Uniform Guidelines).

3. Level Needed (Knowledges only): Select only the Job Knowledges that are required (on the first day of the job) at a "working" or "mastery" level. This step helps avoid measuring job knowledges that are not critical for job success, or can easily be looked up without a negative impact on the job. This step is only required if job knowledge tests will be included in the selection process, and is required to address Section 14C4 of the Uniform Guidelines.

4. Minimum/Helpful Qualification (MQ/HQ): While it is possible to measure KSAPCs/Physical Requirements that are Helpful Qualifications and not absolutely "minimum" (if they meet the other steps above), it is typically a good idea to focus primarily on those that are absolutely necessary for the job (*i.e.,* are MQs).

5. Best Worker: Rank order the remaining KSAPCs/Physical Requirements (*i.e.,* those that met the criteria above) from highest to lowest, using the average Best Worker rating. This will place the "best predictors" for selecting the best workers at the top of the list.

After this five-step process has been used to distil the complete list of KSAPCs/Physical Requirements, meet with the Job Experts and the Supervision/ Management staff to discuss the selection procedures that have been used in previous selection processes as well as those that can possibly be used for future selection processes. From this discussion, choose which selection procedures will be used in the next selection process and how each will be used (pass/fail, ranked, or weighted and combined with other selection procedures – see Chapter Eight for a discussion of the various criteria for each). At a minimum, rank only on those selection procedures that are among the highest on the Best Worker ratings, or those that received absolute ratings that were sufficiently high to justify ranking.

The following factors should be discussed when deciding which selection procedures to use, and how to use them (listed in priority order):

1. Which selection procedures in the past have been most effective in selecting the most qualified incumbents? While a criterion-related validity study is required to answer this question definitively, management judgment can be used in most situations. Which proposed (but not yet used) selection procedures are believed to be most likely to select the best workers? What have similar employers used successfully? The reliability of the selection procedures can also be considered at this step (see Chapter Three for a discussion on reliability).

2. What degree of adverse impact did the previous selection procedures have against women and minorities? How does this weigh against the perceived level of effectiveness of these selection procedures? Are there alternatives that would have less adverse impact, but be substantially equally valid? (Section 3B of the Uniform Guidelines requires that employers make this consideration when using a selection procedure that has adverse impact).

3. Which selection procedures are easiest to administer? Which take the longest time to complete and score? For example, a written test can be administered to 1,000 applicants with much less time and administrative effort than an interview involving multiple rater panels.

4. What are the costs of the selection procedures? Notice that this factor is last on the list. When making selection decisions that impact the overall performance of an employer, the careers and livelihoods of individuals, and impact the social community as a whole, other factors should be considered above cost whenever possible.

Table 2-1 provides an example of what this five-step process will produce.

Selection Plan Example									
KSAPC/ Physical Req.	**KSAPC/Physical Requirement Rating**					**Selection Procedure & Use (Pass/Fail, Rank, or Combine*)**			
Knowledge, Skill, Ability, Personal Characteristic, or Physical Requirement	**Best Worker (1-5)**	**Level Needed Upon Entry (1-4)**	**Level Needed (Knowledges only) (1-4)**	**Importance (1-5)**	**Minimum/Helpful Qualification (MQ/HQ)**	**Application Form**	**Written Test**	**Structured Interview**	**Background Check**
Interpersonal & team working skills	4.2	3.2	N/A	4	MQ			R	
Verbal communication skills	3.9	3.5	N/A	3.7	MQ			R	
Knowledge of State vehicle code	2.6	3.5	3.4	3.9	MQ		P/F		
Upper body strength	1.9	3.9	N/A	3.4	MQ				
Basic math skills	1.4	3.5	N/A	3.1	MQ				

* The score from this selection procedure will be combined with scores from other selection procedures in the selection process.

Table 2-1 Selection Plan Example

Notice that the KSAPCs in Table 2-1 are ranked from top to bottom based on their average Best Worker rating assigned by Job Experts. Reproducing all of the relevant KSAPC ratings allows management to make informed decisions on *if* and *how* each will be assessed in the selection process.

Content Validation Requirements for Various Types of Selection Procedures

The Uniform Guidelines present different criteria for validating "work sample" tests (*i.e.,* tests that attempt to directly mirror or replicate one or more job duties) and KSAPC tests (*i.e.,* tests that measure KSAPC without necessarily directly mirroring or replicating the job). Table 2-2 shows these requirements by type of test:

Content Validity Requirements for Work Sample and KSAPC Tests	
Requirements for Work Sample Tests	**Requirements for KSAPC Tests**
Test must be a **representative sample** of the **behavior** measured, or of a **work product** of the job.	Knowledges (K) must be **operationally defined** as a body of learned information which is (1) used in, and (2) a necessary prerequisite for, observable aspects of work behavior. Skills, Abilities, and Personal Characteristics (SAPCs) must be **defined in terms of observable aspects of work behavior**.
The **manner** of the test should **closely approximate** the work situation.	Show that the **test measures the intended KSAPC.**
The **setting** of the test should **closely approximate** the work situation.	Show that the test is a **representative sample** of the KSAPC.
The **level of complexity** of the test should **closely approximate** the work situation.	Show that the KSAPC measured is **used in the performance** of a critical or important work behavior(s).
	Show that the KSAPC measured is a **necessary prerequisite** to performance of critical or important work behavior(s).
	For SAPCs, the SAPC should either **closely approximate** an observable work behavior, or its product should closely approximate an observable work product.

Table 2-2 Content Validity Requirements for Work Sample and KSAPC Tests

Section 14C1 of the Uniform Guidelines states:

> Selection procedures which purport to measure knowledges, skills, or abilities may in certain circumstances be justified by content validity, although they may not be representative samples, if the knowledge, skill, or ability measured by the selection procedure can be operationally defined as provided in paragraph 14C(4) of this section, and if that knowledge, skill, or ability is a necessary prerequisite to successful job performance.

This clarification is needed because sometimes content-valid selection procedures that measure KSAPCs do not necessary resemble or "closely approximate" the job. Consider reading ability, for example. Reading ability might be a critical, "needed-on-day-one" requirement for the position of Police Officer, but reading ability can be measured in a valid way without having the applicant read and take a written test on police-related information. For instance, the reading ability of applicants applying for the police department could be measured by having the applicants read a 10-page narrative (written at a grade level needed for success as a police officer) about how to clean windows, and answer questions to demonstrate adequate comprehension. While cleaning windows has absolutely nothing to do with the job of police officer, consider how such a test sizes up to the KSAPC test requirements shown in Table 2-2.

Does the reading comprehension test about cleaning windows:

1. Measure an ability (reading) that is defined in terms of observable aspects of work behavior? Yes, *provided that* the reading ability in the Job Analysis (to which this test is linked) is linked to job duties that are observable.
2. Measure the intended KSAPC (reading ability)? Yes, *provided that* the test measures reading ability at the level necessary for the job.
3. A representative sample of the KSAPC (reading ability)? Yes, *provided that* the sentence structure and readily level are similar. Police officers are likely to read 10 pages or less with certain levels of comprehension necessary.
4. Measure a KSAPC that is used in the performance of a critical or important work behavior(s)? Yes, *provided that* reading ability is linked to critical or important Job Duties.
5. Measure a necessary prerequisite to performance of critical or important work behavior(s)? Yes, *provided that* reading ability has been rated sufficiently high on the importance scale used.
6. Closely approximate an observable work behavior, or does its product closely approximate an observable work product? Yes, a police officer can be observed reading and studying new laws, bulletins, etc.

The example above is provided for illustration purposes only. In the case of a *real* ability test, it is recommended to use content that is similar to that found on the job. The more closely the content of the test represents the job, the better. This adds to the face validity of the process and helps improve applicants' perception of the fairness of the process as a whole. For instance, a test that includes materials such as sample police policies and procedures, vehicle codes, and traffic bulletins would not only measure reading ability for the position of Police Officer, but might also benefit from the psychological processes involved in comprehending this type of material as compared to reading materials about window washing (*e.g.,* especially if one type was more or less abstract or concrete than the other).

Next, consider a test event commonly found in physical ability tests for the position of firefighter called a "Dry Hose Advance." This event is one of several events in a test used to screen applicants for the position of entry-level firefighter. To take the test, applicants are required to wear firefighter protective clothing (including pants, coat, gloves, and a 20-pound breathing apparatus) since this is how the event is performed on the job. This event measures the applicant's ability to take a dry (not charged with water) 1-1/2 inch fire attack hose line from a fire truck and extend the hose 150-feet (which simulates taking the hose line from the truck and deploying it to the position where it will be used to attack the fire).

Does this test event mimic the job? Yes – almost exactly (and as best as can be hoped for without lighting an actual fire). When linking this event back to the Job Analysis (to complete the essential nexus necessary for content validity), where does it fit? Is this a *work sample* or a *KSAPC* test? It is clearly a work sample test. Consider how this test fares when running it through the criteria shown in Table 2-2 for work sample tests. Is the Dry Hose Advance test:

1. A *representative sample* of the behavior measured, or of a work product of the job? Yes, clearly. Firefighters perform this exact same event, even for a similar distance, while performing it on the job. The only difference on the job is the fire and the smoke that may be present.
2. Conducted in a *manner that closely approximates* the work situation? Yes, the physical movements and actions in this test event are done in a way that very closely approximates the work situation, and does not require specialized training.
3. Conducted in a way that the *setting* of the test *closely approximates* the work situation? Yes, both the test and the actual job duty it simulates are done outside, by one person, using a "transverse hose bed" and are done in a way where speed is of the essence.
4. Conducted in a way that the *level of complexity* of the test *closely approximates* the work situation? Yes, the test is not too difficult or easy compared to the job. It is about the same.

This example is intended to show that work sample tests – more so than KSAPC tests – need to be specific about such factors as "how long," "how heavy," "how far," "how difficult," etc.

Criterion-related Validity

Overview

The Uniform Guidelines define criterion-related validity as, "Data showing that a selection procedure is predictive of, or significantly correlated with, important elements of job performance." Let us start by discussing the advantages of criterion-related validity over content-related validity.

The Uniform Guidelines state that a content validity strategy is " . . . not appropriate for demonstrating the validity of selection procedures which purport to measure traits or constructs such as intelligence, aptitude, personality, common sense, judgment, leadership, and spatial ability" (Section 14C1). It has been mentioned previously that content validity can, in fact, be used to measure some of these "more abstract traits" if they are operationally defined in terms of observable aspects of the job (see Section 14C4 and Uniform Guidelines Questions & Answers Supplement #75). That is, if they are converted from "generic abstracts" into concrete, measurable characteristics that are defined in ways they can be observed on the job, they are fair game for measurement under a content validation strategy.

But what if they cannot be converted in this way? Is it permissible to measure these traits *at all*? Yes, and this is where criterion-related validity comes in. Hypothetically speaking, an employer defending a selection procedure that is based on criterion-related validity could stand up in court and say:

> Your honor, I don't know exactly what this test is measuring, but I do know it works. Applicants who score high on this test typically turn out to be our best workers, and applicants who score low typically do not. We know this because we conducted a study where we correlated

test scores to job performance ratings and the study showed a correlation of .35, which is statistically significant at the .01 level – meaning that we are highly assured that the relationship between test scores and job performance is well beyond what we would expect by chance alone.[11]

It would be nice if the defense of a selection procedure based on criterion-related validity was this simple! This "simple defense," however, is in fact true *in concept*. Content validity battles in litigation are always much more involved, with experts fighting over the complex nuances of what constitutes a "defensible content validity study" that addresses government and professional standards. This is because criterion-related validity is by nature empirical – the employer either has a statistically significant correlation, or does not. With content validation, the end decision regarding its merit is typically based on a judgment call regarding the relative degree of content validity evidence that exists based on a job analysis of the remaining parts of the study.

Criterion-related validity studies can be conducted in one of two ways: using a *predictive* model or a *concurrent* model. A predictive model is conducted when applicant test scores are correlated to subsequent measures of job performance (*e.g.,* six months after the tested applicants are hired). A concurrent model is conducted by giving a selection procedure to incumbents who are currently on the job and then correlating these scores to current measures of job performance (*e.g.,* performance review scores, supervisor ratings, etc.).

Before going into detail regarding the mechanics on how to complete a criterion-related validity study using either of these two methods, a brief caution is provided first. Completing a criterion-related validity study is a gamble. If an employer has been using a written test for years, and has never completed any type of study to evaluate its validity, a criterion-related validity study would be the easiest type of validation study to conduct. Gather selection procedure scores for applicants who have been hired over the past several years, enter them into a column in a spreadsheet next to another column containing their average performance ratings, use the = PEARSON command in Microsoft® Excel® to correlate the two columns, and presto! Instant validity. Or not.

If the resulting correlation value from the Pearson command is statistically significant, good news: your selection procedure is valid (providing that a host of other issues are addressed!) But what if the correlation value is a big, round zero (meaning no validity whatsoever)? Even worse, what if the correlation is negative (indicating the best test takers are the worst job performers)?

If this type of "quick correlation study" is conducted, and the employer had a sufficient sample size (see discussion below on statistical power), they just invalidated their selection procedure! The drawback? The employer is now open for lawsuits if the information is exposed, or negative information is now available if a lawsuit is currently pending. The benefit? Now the employer can discontinue using the invalid selection procedure and replace it with something much better. This dilemma is referred to among personnel researchers as the "validator's gamble."

Steps for completing a criterion-related validity study

Before reviewing the steps to complete a criterion-related validity study, a brief discussion on statistical power and reliability is necessary. Without these two ingredients, the rest of the recipe does not matter! Conducting a criterion-related validity study without sufficiently high statistical power and reliability is like trying to bake bread without yeast.

Statistical power

Statistical power is the ability of a statistical test (in this case, a Pearson Correlation) to detect a statistically significant result *if it exists to be found*. In the case of correlations, statistical power highly depends on the size of the correlation coefficient the researcher expects to find in the population being sampled. If the researcher suspects that there is a (decent sized) correlation coefficient of .30 in the sample being researched (and they suspect that this correlation can only be in the favorable direction – positive – which requires a one-tail statistical test), 64 subjects are necessary to be 80% confident (*i.e.,* to have 80% power) that the study will result in a statistically significant finding at the .05 level (if it is exists in the population). If the researcher suspects a smaller, but still significant correlation of .20 exists in the population, 150 subjects are necessary for the same levels of power.

To avoid a gamble, use at least 200. Using a large sample will provide the researcher with high levels of power to find a statistically significant finding if it exists and will provide assurance that if the study did not result in a statistically significant finding that it was not because the sample was too small (but rather because such a finding just did not exist in the first place!).

Criterion and selection procedure reliability

It is noted in the steps below that both the criterion measures (*e.g.,* supervisor ratings) and selection procedures (*e.g.,* a written test in the study) should have sufficiently high levels of reliability (at least .60 for the criterion measures and .70 or higher for the selection procedures). The reason for this can be explained with a simple rational explanation, followed by some easy math.

The rational reason why an unreliable measure (*i.e.,* the criterion measure or the selection procedure) can spoil a criterion-related validation study is this: if a measure is inconsistent (unreliable) by itself, it will also be inconsistent when asked to (mathematically) cooperate with another variable (as in the case of the correlation required for criterion-related validity). A selection procedure that is not sure about what it is measuring by itself will not be any more sure about what its measuring related to another variable (like the criterion measure)!

Mathematically, this is explained with a concept called the "theoretical maximum" which states that the maximum correlation that two variables can produce is limited by the square root of the product of their reliability coefficients. How does this work out practically? Consider a selection procedure with a reliability of .80 and a criterion measure with a low reliability of .40. The maximum correlation one can expect given the unreliability of these two variables (especially the criterion measure) is .57. If the reliabilities are .50 and .60, the maximum correlation that can be obtained is .55. With reliabilities of .90 and .60, a maximum of .73 is possible. With this caution, be sure that the criterion measure and the selection procedure have sufficiently high levels of reliability! A researcher will be quite disappointed to go through the steps for completing a criterion-related validation process, only to find out that the study did not stand a chance in the first place of resulting with significant findings!

So, assuming that the researcher has a sufficiently large sample (power), and reliable criterion measures and selection procedures, the following steps can be completed to conduct a *predictive* criterion-related validity study:

1. Conduct a job analysis (see previous section) *or* a "review of job information." Unlike content validity, a complete A to Z job analysis is not necessary for a criterion-related validity study (see Sections 14B3 and 15B3 of the Uniform Guidelines).

2. Develop one or more criterion measures by developing subjective (*e.g.,* rating scales) or objective measures (*e.g.,* absenteeism, work output levels) of critical areas from the job analysis or job information review. A subjectively rated criterion can only consist of performance on a job duty (or group of duties). It cannot consist of a supervisor or peer's rating on the incumbent's level of KSAPCs (a requirement based on Section 15B5 of the Uniform Guidelines). It is critical that these measures have sufficiently high reliability (at least .60 or higher is preferred).

3. Work with Job Experts and supervisors, trainers, other management staff, and the Job Analysis data to form solid speculations ("hypotheses") regarding which KSAPCs "really make a difference" in the high/low scores of such job performance measures (above). Important: if the Job Analysis for the position included Best Worker ratings, these should provide a good indicator regarding the KSAPCs that distinguish job performance in a meaningful way. These ratings can be used to key in on the prime KSAPCs that are most likely to result in a significant correlation with job performance measures.

4. Develop selection procedures that are *reliable* measures of those KSAPCs. Choosing selection procedures that have reliability of .70 or higher is preferred.

5. After a period of time has passed and criterion data has been gathered (*e.g.,* 3-12 months), correlate each of the selection procedures to the criterion measures using the PEARSON command in Microsoft® Excel® and evaluate the results.[12]

To complete a *concurrent* criterion-related validation study, complete steps 1-4 above and replace Step 5 by administering the selection procedure to the *current incumbent population* and correlating the selection procedure scores to current measures of job performance.

Let's now assume your study produced one or more significant correlations. How can these be interpreted? The U.S. Department of Labor (2000, p. 3-10) has provided the following reasonable guidelines for interpreting correlation coefficients.

Guidelines for Interpreting Correlations	
Coefficient Value	Interpretation
Above .35	Very beneficial
.21 - .35	Likely to be useful
.11 - .20	Depends on circumstances
Below .11	Unlikely to be useful

Table 2-3 Guidelines for Interpreting Correlations

Advanced criterion-related validity topics

This text is designed to provide a fundamental overview of the key components of a criterion-related validity study. Because this type of validation is statistical in nature, there is a practically endless variety of tools, calculations, and issues related to this topic. Some of these are outlined below:

- Expectancy tables *and charts*. Once a statistically significant correlation has been identified, there are a vast number of calculations that can be used to practically evaluate the impact of using the validated selection procedure in a selection process. Expectancy tables can show, with mathematical accuracy, the expected increase in job performance that can be obtained by ratcheting up (or down) the cutoff used for the selection procedure. For example, a selection procedure with a high correlation to job performance might show that if the employer uses a cutoff of 65% on the selection procedure that expected job performance levels would be a "6.0" (on a scale of 1-9); whereas a cutoff of 80% might equate to a 7.0, etc. The reader is referred to a statistical program titled "Theoretical Expectancy Calculator" by Personnel Decisions International Corporation for a useful tool for making these (and other related) calculations.

- Cross validation. This is another important concept related to criterion-related validity studies. Cross validation is a useful tool for determining the transportability or "generalizability" of one study's findings to another setting. This can be done mathematically using formulas that adjust the correlation coefficient found in one study, or empirically by taking the selection procedure to that other setting and evaluating the correlation coefficient found in the new setting. It should be noted that correlation values almost always get smaller when this process is done, due to the fact that the correlation values obtained in a single sample are often inflated due to the unique characteristics of that employer, selection procedure, and the combination thereof.

- Corrections. Statistical correlations are typically repressed (*i.e.,* smaller than they could be) because of a phenomena called *range restriction* (that occurs on the selection procedure and/or criterion measures) and because of the unreliability of the criterion and/or the selection procedure. Range restriction occurs on the selection procedure when some of the applicant scores are not included in the study (because they failed the selection procedure). Range restriction occurs on the criterion measure when some of the job incumbents self-select out of the sample (*e.g.,* by finding another job) or are terminated. Range restriction reduces the amount of variance in the correlation study, which lowers the power of the study (an ideal study is one that includes both the low- and high-end of test takers and job performers). Corrections can also be made to adjust for the unreliability of the criterion measure, *but corrections should not be made to the selection procedure* (because this is a real limitation that is present in both the study and in the future use of the selection procedure). Formulas to correct for range restriction and unreliability can be found in Guion, 1998; Cascio, 1998; and Hubert & Feild, 1994.

- <u>Bias</u>. If an adequate sample exists for minorities and/or women (typically a minimum rule of 30 are necessary), a study of bias can be conducted to assess whether the selection procedure is a fair and accurate predictor for both majority and minority groups. The procedures for conducting a bias study can be found in Chapter Seven.

Challenges to Using a Validity Generalization Defense in Title VII Enforcement

Introduction

The 1991 Civil Rights Act requires that employers justify tests that have adverse impact by demonstrating they are sufficiently "job related for the position in question and consistent with business necessity." Framing a defense in such situations requires that employers address the federal Uniform Guidelines on Employee Selection Procedures (1978), professional standards, and relevant court precedence. With the growing popularity of Validity Generalization (VG) techniques, some practitioners may be tempted to rely wholly on using VG to defend employment tests that have come under Title VII scrutiny rather than conducting local validation studies. Such approaches will possibly lead to disappointing outcomes in litigation because Title VII and the courts have generally required that employers demonstrate *local and specific* validation evidence where there is *local and specific* evidence of adverse impact.

As of August 24, 2006, it has been four decades since federal EEO regulations[13] first began requiring that employers validate tests that have "adverse impact," the effect that occurs when two groups have substantially different passing rates on a test. While the methodology for satisfying this requirement has evolved along with the growing EEO field, the basic necessity of providing "job relatedness" evidence for the test causing adverse impact has been set in stone since the famous <u>U.S. Supreme Court Griggs v. Duke Power</u> (1971) case.[14] Many essential elements from *Griggs* were encapsulated into the federal treatise to enforce Title VII (the Uniform Guidelines on Employee Selection Procedures, 1978).

With the Uniform Guidelines remaining unchanged since 1978, the courts have continued to maintain one highly common requirement: when an employer uses a specific test for a particular job, and such test has adverse impact against a certain group, the employer must justify the use of the test by demonstrating a "manifest relationship" between the test and the job. This is because Title VII requires employers to bolster a specific justification for both the test itself as well as how it is being *used* (*e.g.,* ranked, banded, used with a minimum cutoff, or weighted with other selection procedures) in specific situations where adverse impact exists. Further, the 1991 Civil Rights Act allows plaintiff groups to prevail in Title VII litigation if they can demonstrate that other suitable alternatives are (or were) available that have less adverse impact, but would have served the "legitimate business interests"[15] of the employer with less adverse impact.

Though the 1991 Civil Rights Act requires showing *specific and local validity evidence* to justify tests with adverse impact, some practitioners and testifying experts have attempted to justify personnel tests by using "Validity Generalization" ("VG" hereafter) studies which base their results on similar tests used for similar positions. VG studies are typically conducted by combining criterion-related validity studies, correcting for statistical artifacts such as criterion unreliability and range restriction,[16] and drawing general conclusions about the validity of a particular test or types of tests, both for the positions within the study and similar positions outside the study.

Such studies are preferred by some practitioners because they can provide a generalized defense for a wide variety of various personnel testing situations as well as avoid tedious and costly validation studies which can require large sample sizes to draw accurate results. Instead, dozens of studies conducted elsewhere can be combined, corrected for statistical artifacts, and used to form the basis for a validity claim in virtually every similar situation. Without using VG, practitioners are left with more situational types of validity studies such as content or criterion-related validity strategies to defend tests in Title VII situations.

Content validity strategies usually involve an in-depth job analysis study, extensive test development activities to measure key competencies that are necessary on the first day of hire, and a link-up study to connect the test elements to the core competencies identified in the job analysis. Criterion-related validity studies are conducted using either a predictive strategy where applicant test scores are correlated to some future measure of job performance (*e.g.,* supervisor ratings) or a concurrent strategy where current job incumbents are tested and rated on some relevant job performance metric. Under either strategy, statistically significant correlations between test scores and job performance can usually translate into worthy validation evidence in Title VII situations (see some limitations discussed herein).

While the usefulness of VG as a practical research tool is not denied here, it is argued that practitioners should be cautioned against over-relying on VG studies to make *universal* or *automatic* validity inferences to justify tests that exhibit adverse impact. The challenges that are likely to arise when such positions are taken in either Title VII or government enforcement situations will be reviewed in the following sections, as well as the standards relevant to VG contained in the federal validation standards (the Uniform Guidelines) and the professional standards, which include the Standards for Educational and Psychological Testing (1999) and the Principles for the Validation and Use of Personnel Selection Procedures (2003). Guidelines and recommendations are also provided for practitioners who may wish to supplement a localized validation defense using VG when their testing practices are scrutinized.

Overview of Validity Generalization

Schmidt & Hunter (1977) began a new era in personnel psychology with the application of meta-analysis techniques to the field of personnel testing. Meta-analysis is a statistical technique used to combine the results of several related research studies to form general theories about relationships between variables across different situations. When these techniques are applied to personnel testing, it has generally been referred to as VG. Prior to 1977, meta-analyses in the personnel testing and psychological literature were few and far between. Since that time, the application of meta-analysis techniques to evaluate the validity of employment tests has grown considerably.

While the steps and mechanics involved in conducting a VG study vary (Johnson, Mullen, & Salas, 1995), the purpose for conducting VG studies in an employment setting is to evaluate the effectiveness (*i.e.,* validity) of a personnel test or particular type of test (*e.g.,* cognitive ability, conscientiousness) and to describe what the findings mean in a broader sense (Murphy, 2003). To accomplish this investigation, the selected validation studies are combined and then various corrections are made to determine the overall operational validity of the test or type of test. Such corrections can range from making basic corrections (by correcting only for sampling error) to correcting for test and criteria unreliability, as well as range restriction.

While these "corrected" VG studies can often offer researchers useful insights into the strength of the relationship between the test and job performance in the studies included in the VG analysis, there is no guarantee that the level of validity promised by a VG study will be found if a study was performed in a new local setting. This is primarily because a host of situational factors exist in each and every new situation that may impact the validity of a test (see discussion and tables to follow). In addition, there are a number of limitations with typical VG studies that may further limit their relevance and reliability when evaluating test validity in new situations.

Validity Generalization and Title VII

Back to the Beginning: "Generic Validity" Versus "Job Specific Validity" in Griggs v. Duke Power

Adverse impact and test validation intersected for the very first time in U.S. Supreme Court history in the 1971 *Griggs v. Duke Power case*. In *Griggs*, the Duke Power Company required all employees who desired employment in any division outside the general labor department to obtain satisfactory scores on the Wonderlic Personnel Test (which purported to measure general intelligence) and the Bennett Mechanical Comprehension test, as well as possess a high school education. These requirements were not intended to measure the ability to directly perform a *particular job or category of jobs*, and the court ruled that the requirements failed to "bear a demonstrable relationship to successful performance of the jobs for which they were used. Both tests were adopted, as the Court of Appeals noted, *without meaningful study of their relationship to job-performance ability*" [emphasis added]. Further, a vice president of the Company testified that the requirements were instituted on the Company's judgment that they ". . . generally would improve the overall quality of the workforce." The court ruled, "What Congress has commanded (citing then-current EEO law) is that any tests used must *measure the person for the job and not the person in the abstract* . . . The touchstone is business necessity. If an employment practice which operates to exclude Blacks cannot be shown to be related to job performance, the practice is prohibited" (*Griggs*, 1971).

Duke Power continued the use of these tests, despite the fact that they had high levels of adverse impact against minorities, arguing that the subgroup differences exhibited by the tests were commensurate with differences that existed between groups on job performance. The court ruled, however, in their 8-0 decision, that the tests needed to measure abilities that had a demonstrated, proven relationship to the specific requirements of the specific job, rather than to the person in the abstract.

Validity Generalization and the Sixth Circuit EEOC v. Atlas Paper Case

The Sixth Circuit Court of Appeals re-affirmed *specific* versus *generic* validity requirements when it ruled that VG, *as a matter of law*, could not be used to justify testing practices that had adverse impact (EEOC v. Atlas Paper, 1989). In *Atlas*, the Sixth Circuit rejected the use of VG to justify a test (the Wonderlic) purporting to measure general intelligence, which had adverse impact when used for selecting clerical employees. Without conducting a local validity study, an expert testified that the generalized validity of the challenged test was as "valid for all clerical jobs" as it would be for "lemon pickers." The lower District Court had previously approved Atlas' use of the Wonderlic test, but the Court of Appeals reversed this decision and rejected the use of VG evidence as a basis for justifying the use of the test by stating:

> We note in respect to a remand in this case that the expert failed to visit and inspect the Atlas office and never studied the nature and content of the Atlas clerical and office jobs involved. The validity of the generalization theory utilized by Atlas with respect to this expert testimony under these circumstances is not appropriate. Linkage or similarity of jobs in dispute in this case must be shown by such on site investigation to justify application of such a theory.

Note that the requirement mandated above is exactly what is currently required by the Uniform Guidelines for transporting validity evidence into a new situation (Section 7B) – both require that a job comparability study be done between the job in the original validation study and the new local situation. In fact, even the original VG article published in the I-O field advocated conducting a job analysis in the new local situation for transporting validity evidence (Schmidt & Hunter, 1977, p. 530). The Sixth Circuit decision in *Atlas* offered even a more direct critique of VG by stating:

> The premise of the validity generalization theory, as advocated by Atlas' expert, is that intelligence tests are always valid. The first major problem with a validity generalization approach is that it is radically at odds with Albemarle Paper v. Moody, Griggs v. Duke Power, relevant case law within this circuit, and the EEOC Guidelines, all of which require a showing that a test is actually predictive of performance at a

specific job. The validity generalization approach simply dispenses with that similarity or manifest relationship requirement. Albemarle and Griggs are particularly important precedents since each of them involved the Wonderlic Test . . . Thus, the Supreme Court concluded that specific findings relating to the validity of one test cannot be generalized from that of others" (EEOC v. Atlas Paper, 868 F.2d. at 1499).

Based upon the applicability of the findings from *Albemarle* regarding the *situational specific* validity requirements. The judge issues a factual conclusion and rule of law, stating:

> The kind of potentially Kafkaesque result, which would occur if intelligence tests were always assumed to be valid, was discussed in Van Aken v. Young (451 F.Supp. 448, 454, E.D. Mich. 1982, aff'd 750 F.2d. 43, 6th Cir. 1984). These potential absurdities were exactly what the Supreme Court in Griggs and Albemarle sought to avoid by requiring a detailed job analysis in validation studies. As a matter law . . . validity generalization theory is totally unacceptable under the relevant case law and professional standards (EEOC v. Atlas Paper, 868 F.2d. at 1499).

Atlas demonstrates the likely result of relying solely on VG evidence when testing practices exhibit adverse impact. In fact, some practitioners have stated that, even if the Uniform Guidelines were changed to adopt a more open stance toward VG, a constitutional challenge would likely follow because ". . . they would then be at odds with established law – in particular the Sixth Circuit *Atlas* case that dismisses VG as inconsistent with Albemarle and impermissible as a matter of law" (Landy, 2003, p. 191).

Conducting Uniform Guidelines-style "transportability" studies to address Section 7B offers much higher levels of defensibility. Conducting a local validation study perhaps offers even higher levels of defensibility because it amasses local and specific evidence that the test was related to job performance in the given situation. The 5th Circuit Appellate court has accepted such validation evidence (based on job comparability evidence, as required by the Uniform Guidelines) in at least two cases (Cormier v. PPG Industries, 1983 and Bernard v. Gulf Oil Corp., 1989). However, because these cases pre-date the 1991 Civil Rights Act and the latter was tried under the less-stringent Wards Cove v. Atonio (1989) standards, they have little applicability at the time of this writing because the 1991 Civil Rights Act reinstated the more stringent *Griggs* standard, which requires employers to demonstrate that the test is job related *for the position in question* and consistent with business necessity (Gutman, 2005, p. 43). Rather than allowing a "generalized inference" of validity for a test, the 1991 Civil Rights Act requires a demonstration of job-relatedness for the specific position in question, not for an entire, sweeping category of employment tests (*e.g.,* those measuring cognitive abilities).

The very principle that tests must be proven to be job related and consistent with business necessity was unanimously framed in *Griggs* and was subsequently endorsed by Congress when it passed the Equal Employment Opportunity Act of 1972, amending Title VII of the Civil Rights Act of 1964. The passage of the 1991 Civil Rights Act – which overturned the U.S. Supreme Court on this specific issue – indicates that the requirement will endure subsequent challenges.

Test Validity and Legal Defensibility under the Uniform Guidelines and Professional Standards

Testing-related lawsuits can come from either enforcement agencies (*e.g.,* the U.S. Equal Employment Opportunity Commission, Department of Justice, Department of Labor via the Office of Federal Contract Compliance Programs, State Equal Opportunity Commissions) or through private plaintiff attorneys. In these situations, practitioners will need to demonstrate validity under previous case law, the Uniform Guidelines, and professional standards (the Principles and Standards). Because the relevance of previous case law varies greatly by the type of test (*e.g.,* cognitive ability, physical ability, etc.), the at-issue position (*e.g.,* public safety), and how the test is used (*e.g.,* ranked or banded), only the Uniform Guidelines and Professional Standards will be discussed below.

Uniform Guidelines

The Uniform Guidelines on Employee Selection Procedures was cooperatively authored in 1978 by the U.S. Equal Employment Opportunity Commission, Civil Service Commission, Department of Labor, and Department of Justice. The Uniform Guidelines are designed to aid in the achievement of our nation's goal of equal employment opportunity without discrimination on the grounds of race, color, sex, religion or national origin, and were adopted by the Federal agencies to provide a uniform set of principles governing use of employee selection procedures (Uniform Guidelines Questions & Answers Supplement #1). The Uniform Guidelines define their "basic principal" as:

> A selection process which has an adverse impact on the employment opportunities of members of a race, color, religion, sex, or national origin group . . . and thus disproportionately screens them out is unlawfully discriminatory unless the process or its component procedures have been validated in accord with the Guidelines, or the user otherwise justifies them in accord with Federal law . . . This principle was adopted by the Supreme Court unanimously in <u>Griggs v. Duke Power Co</u>. (401 U.S. 424), and was ratified and endorsed by the Congress when it passed the Equal Employment Opportunity Act of 1972, which amended Title VII of the Civil Rights Act of 1964 (Uniform Guidelines Questions & Answers Supplement #2).

Except for the "Questions & Answers Supplement" that was published on May 2, 1980, the Uniform Guidelines have remained unchanged since their original publication in 1978 because they are inherently tied to the statutory requirements of the 1964 Civil Rights Act and are based on the 1971 *Griggs* standard. As such, a change to the Civil Rights Act would likely be necessary to trigger corresponding changes to the Uniform Guidelines. While a change did occur to the Civil Rights Act when Congress passed the 1991 Civil Rights Act to overturn eight U.S. Supreme Court cases (one of which was *Wards Cove*, which attempted to lower the validity standard originally set up in *Griggs*), the Uniform Guidelines continue to be "entitled to great deference" when it comes to establishing test validity in litigation settings. This "great deference" endorsement provided by the U.S. Supreme Court in *Albemarle* has subsequently been similarly recognized in at least 20 additional federal cases. In some cases they have been adopted verbatim as a "legal standard" (*e.g.,* Brown v. Chicago, 1998). The Uniform Guidelines have also been cited and used as standards in hundreds of court cases at all levels.

By way of contrast, the SIOP Principles have been cited fewer than 20 times,[17] and sometimes with less than favorable results when they are found to be at odds with the Title VII *Griggs* standard that has been adopted by the Uniform Guidelines. For example, in Lanning v. Southeastern Pennsylvania Transportation Authority (1999), the court stated: "The District Court seems to have derived this standard from the Principles for the Validation and Use of Personnel Selection Procedures ('SIOP Principles') ... *To the extent that the SIOP Principles are inconsistent with the mission of Griggs and the business necessity standard adopted by the Act, they are not instructive*" [emphasis added].[18]

In addition to the three primary types of validation evidence which are presented (content, criterion-related, and construct), the Uniform Guidelines allow a limited form of VG evidence (called "transportability") to be used when justifying testing practices becomes necessary (see Section 7B, discussed below). They also provide criteria for inferring validity evidence based on studies conducted elsewhere (see Section 15E, also discussed below).

Professional Standards: Joint Standards and SIOP Principles

The National Council on Measurement in Education (NCME), American Psychological Association (APA), and the American Educational Research Association (AERA) cooperatively released the Standards (also known as the Joint Standards) in 1999. The purpose of the Joint Standards was to ". . . provide criteria for the evaluation of tests, testing practices, and test use" for professional test developers, sponsors, publishers, and users that adopt Standards (p. 2). One of the fifteen chapters (Chapter 14) is devoted exclusively to testing in the areas of employment and credentialing. The remaining chapters include recommended standards for developing, administering, and using various tests.

The Society for Industrial and Organizational Psychology (Division 14 of the American Psychological Association) released an updated version of the Principles (the SIOP Principles) in 2003. This document is offered by SIOP as an official policy statement, and was also approved as policy by the APA Council of Representatives in August 2003. Because both sets of standards are endorsed by the same major professional body (the APA), they share a high degree of overlap.

There are very important distinctions between the Uniform Guidelines and these two sets of professional standards. The primary difference is that the express purpose of the Uniform Guidelines is to weigh validity evidence in situations where adverse impact is present – *i.e.,* the Uniform Guidelines constitute the "rule book" for weighing "job relatedness and business necessity" evidence when adverse impact is on the other side of the justice scale. Absent sufficient validity evidence, a ruling of "adverse impact discrimination" will be handed down in government audit or litigation settings. However, the Uniform Guidelines are not designed to be a state-of-the-art manual on testing or psychometric theory. They provide only the most basic elements for showing validity.

The Joint Standards and SIOP Principles are not designed to enforce Title VII, nor do they have the statutory or governmental backing to do so. Rather, the Joint Standards and SIOP Principles are designed as widely applicable advisory sources, compared to the narrowly-tailored Uniform Guidelines which are designed to enforce the mission of *Griggs*. Both professional standards offer a far more exhaustive set of guidelines and regulations than the Uniform Guidelines, and they cover a much broader scope of testing issues than the Uniform Guidelines.

By way of comparison, the Uniform Guidelines are only 27 pages long; whereas the Joint Standards and SIOP Principles include 194 and 73 pages, respectively. The terms "adverse impact,"[19] "Uniform Guidelines," and "Title VII" are not mentioned a single time in either the Joint Standards or SIOP Principles. This is not because the framers were not concerned about the legal defensibility of tests, but rather because the professional standards *were not developed primarily as guidelines for evaluating testing practices in light of Title VII.* The Uniform Guidelines were, however, designed for this express purpose.

Validity Generalization, the Uniform Guidelines, Joint Standards, and SIOP Principles

Validity Generalization and the Uniform Guidelines
The Uniform Guidelines include clear provisions for *transporting* validity evidence from an existing validation study into a new local situation. The discussion on this topic is confined to three sections: 7B, 15E1, and Question & Answer #66. The latter provides an express answer regarding the circumstances in which the validity of a given test can be moved to a new local situation:

> *Question*: Under what circumstances can a selection procedure be supported (on other than an interim basis) by a criterion-related validity study done elsewhere?

> *Answer*: A validity study done elsewhere may provide sufficient evidence if four conditions are met (Sec. 7B):

>> 1. The evidence from the other studies clearly demonstrates that the procedure was valid in its use elsewhere.
>> 2. The job(s) for which the selection procedure will be used closely matches the job(s) in the original study as shown by a comparison of major work behaviors as shown by the job analyses in both contexts.
>> 3. Evidence of fairness from the other studies is considered for those groups constituting a significant factor in the user's labor market.

Section 7B(3). Where the evidence is not available the user should conduct an internal study of test fairness, if technically feasible. Section 7B(3).

4. Proper account is taken of variables which might affect the applicability of the study in the new setting, such as performance standards, work methods, representativeness of the sample in terms of experience or other relevant factors, and the currency of the study.

It is likely that HR professionals would want answers to these pertinent questions prior to implementing a new testing practice at their location as they are tied to both business *and* social concerns (*i.e.,* knowing when to justify a test when adverse impact is present).

Similar to part 4 of Questions & Answers #66, Section 7 of the Uniform Guidelines also includes the caveat that, when transporting validity evidence from other studies, specific attention should be given to "variables that are likely to affect validity significantly" (called "moderators" in the context of VG studies) and if such variables exist, the user may not rely on the studies, but will be expected to instead conduct an internal validity study in their local situation. This same advice is offered in this paper, along with a list of variables that may significantly affect validity (see Tables 2-6 to 2-8). Fortunately, the Joint Standards, SIOP Principles, and recent VG research have elaborated on just which variables are, in fact, likely to moderate validity significantly between the original studies and new local situations.

Section 15E1 of the Uniform Guidelines provides additional guidance regarding transporting validity evidence from existing studies into new situations. Like Section 7B, this section includes elements that are likely to be concerns shared by both HR and testing professionals that pertain to the utility and effectiveness of the test and the mitigation of risk that is gained by using a test that has validity evidence for their local positions. Making sure that the adopted test is a good "fit" for the target position is addressed by Section 15E1(a); insuring that the criteria predicted by the test in the original setting is also relevant in the new setting is covered in Section 15E1[b]; and screening out any extraneous variables that may operate in a way that negatively impacts test validity is specified in Section 15E1[c]. Finally, considering how the test is used (*e.g.,* ranked, banded, or used with a cutoff) also has significant impact on the utility and diversity outcomes of the employer (Section 15E1[d]). Practitioners and researchers alike place weight on each of these factors when making decisions regarding test development and validation.

Addressing the requirements of the Uniform Guidelines when conducting validation research can actually help assure testing professionals that their testing practices select high-quality applicants. In fact, all four sections of 15E1(a-d) are *employer-relevant* objectives – they are not just "government requirements" surrounding EEO compliance.

Validity Generalization and the Joint Standards
The Joint Standards include a one-page preamble (p. 15) and two standards (along with comments) surrounding VG. While the complex issue of VG is given only a 2-page treatment in the entire 194-page book, the discussion is compact and to the point. The two standards that deal with the subject (Standard 1.20 and 1.21) advise test users

and test publishers regarding the conditions under which validity evidence can be inferred into a new situation based on evidence from other studies. Note that these two standards (1.20 and 1.21) are specifically tailored around the use of modern VG and meta-analysis techniques (whereas the Uniform Guidelines cover some of these same issues, but more generally).

> *Standard 1.20.* When a meta-analysis is used as evidence of the strength of a test criterion relationship, the test and the criterion variables in the local situation should be comparable with those in the studies summarized. If relevant research includes credible evidence that any other features of the testing application may influence the strength of the test-criterion relationship, the correspondence between those features in the local situation and in the meta-analysis should be reported. Any significant disparities that might limit the applicability of the meta-analytic findings to the local situation should be noted explicitly.

> *Standard 1.21.* Any meta-analytic evidence used to support an intended test use should be clearly described, including methodological choices in identifying and coding studies, correcting for artifacts, and examining potential moderator variables. Assumptions made in correcting for artifacts such as criterion unreliability and range restriction should be presented, and the consequences of these assumptions made clear.

Validity Generalization and the SIOP Principles

The SIOP Principles provide a more extensive discussion on VG than the Joint Standards. Most of the discussion relevant to VG provided by the SIOP Principles is contained within pages 8-10 and 27-30, which outline three strategies that are neither mutually exclusive nor exhaustive: (a) transportability, (b) synthetic validity/job component validity, and (c) meta-analytic validity generalization (p. 27).

Compared to the previous two types of generalized validity evidence, the SIOP Principles provide the most detailed requirements regarding the use of meta-analysis for generalizing validity evidence. The essential extracts are provided below:

1. "Professional judgment in interpreting and applying the results of meta-analytic research is important" (p. 28).
2. "Researchers should consider the meta-analytic methods used and their underlying assumptions, the tenability of the assumptions, and artifacts that may influence the results" (p. 29).
3. "In evaluating meta-analytic evidence, the researcher should be concerned with potential moderators to the extent that such moderators would affect conclusions about the presence and generalizability of validity. In such cases, researchers should consider both statistical power to detect such moderators and/or the precision of estimation with respect to such moderators" (p. 29).
4. Consideration should be given to both Type I and Type II decision errors (p. 29).

5. The research reports used in the meta-analysis should be identified and made available (p. 29).
6. The relevant literature should be consulted to ensure that the meta-analytic strategies used are (a) sound, (b) have been properly applied, (c) the appropriate procedures for estimating predictor-criterion relationships on the basis of cumulative evidence have been followed, (d) the conditions for the application of meta-analytic results have been met, and (e) the application of meta-analytic conclusions is appropriate for the work and settings studied (p. 29).
7. All study characteristics that may possibly impact the study results should be reported, including (a) the rules by which the researchers categorized the work and jobs studied, (b) the selection procedures used, (c) the definitions of what the selection procedure is measuring, (d) the job performance criteria used, (e) the quality of the individual research studies (p. 29).
8. "Meta-analytic methods for demonstrating generalized validity are still evolving. Researchers should be aware of continuing research and critiques that may provide further refinement of the techniques as well as a broader range of predictor-criterion relationships to which meta-analysis has been applied" (p. 29).
9. Important conditions in the "operational setting should be represented in the meta-analysis" (*e.g.,* the local setting involves a managerial job and the meta-analytic database is limited to entry-level jobs) or a "local individual study may be more accurate than the average predictor-criterion relationship reported in a meta-analytic study" (p. 29).
10. Significant attention should be paid to the similarity of the constructs measured by the selection procedures include in the meta-analysis and those in the local situation (p. 30).
11. Interpretational difficulties can arise when researchers attempt to generalize about selection procedures within the meta-analysis, or the situation into which validity will be transported, when the selection procedures differ based upon the development process, content, or ways in which they are scored (p. 30).
12. Researchers wanting to assemble validity evidence for a position with a small population are encouraged to rely upon a validity generalization strategy if extensive cumulative evidence exists for the predictor-criterion relationship in similar situations (p. 41).

There are two major sets of factors that should be considered when attempting to address the various requirements presented by the Uniform Guidelines, Joint Standards, and SIOP Principles. The first set relates to the *internal quality* of the VG study itself. This includes factors such as study design features, similarity of the tests, jobs, and criteria used in the study, and the number of studies included. Table 2-4 shows these factors as defined by the Uniform Guidelines and professional standards. The second set pertains to the factors regarding the *comparability between the VG study and the new local situation,* which are also addressed by the Uniform Guidelines and professional standards as outlined in Table 2-4.

Federal and Professional Standards for Evaluating the Internal Quality of a VG Study				
Factor #	Requirement	Uniform Guidelines	Joint Standards	SIOP Principles
1	Identification and availability of original studies (published and unpublished)	15E1(D), Q&A #66	p. 15	p. 29
2	Sample size/statistical power	-1	p. 15	p. 10, 29
3	Test fairness (*i.e.,* lack of bias)	7B(3)		
4	Investigation of "moderator variables" that may impact the validity coefficient	Q&A #43, #66	Stds. 1.20, 1.21	p. 9, 28, 29
5	Application of appropriate statistics			p. 29
6	Appropriate procedures for estimating predictor-criterion relationships	-1		p. 29
7	Conditions for the application of meta-analytic study results	.		p. 29
8	Appropriateness of the application of conclusions (for work and work setting)	-1		p. 29
9	Report rules used for coding/ categorizing the work/jobs studied, similarity of tests, construct definitions, criteria, and other study characteristics		Std. 1.21	p. 29
10	Number of studies included		p. 15	p. 29, 30
11	Reporting subsets of studies that vary by situational features		Std. 1.20	
12	Methodological choices, assumptions, and consequences regarding correcting for artifacts (e.g., criterion unreliability and range restriction) in the VG study	-1	p. 15, Std. 1.21	p. 28-29
13	Similarity of content of selection procedures in studies			p. 30
14	Similarity of structure of selection procedures (e.g., structured vs. unstructured interviews) in studies		p. 15	p. 30
15	Similarity of scoring of selection procedures in studies		p. 15	p. 30

Note. (1) The Uniform Guidelines provide specific requirements for a single validation study (which may include multiple samples or settings) in Sections 14B and 15B that are in fact relevant to VG-related research. They do not, however, provide specific parameters for evaluating the internal quality of a VG study beyond what is listed in this table.

Table 2-4 Standards for Evaluating the Internal Quality of a VG Study

Table 2-4 displays the similarities and differences between the Uniform Guidelines, the Joint Standards, and the Principles regarding the factors that should be considered when evaluating the internal quality of a VG study. The Uniform Guidelines have only limited discussion of the factors that should be considered, and while the Joint Standards and SIOP Principles cover the majority of the 15 factors listed, there is a notable lack of overlap between the two (with the Principles providing the majority of discrete factors).

The Uniform Guidelines appear to have the fewest requirements regarding the factors relating to evaluating the robustness of a VG study. One major clarification, however, should be made regarding this observation. The Uniform Guidelines include very specific criteria for establishing criterion-related validity evidence for a single location (which also apply to a cooperative study) in Sections 14B and 15B, but these sections do not offer guidelines for importing such validity evidence into a new situation because these are addressed elsewhere in the Uniform Guidelines.

Evaluating the comparability between the VG study and the new local situation is just as critical as evaluating the internal quality of the VG study. Some of these factors include the comparability between the test in the VG study and the local situation, the similarities between the criterion variable(s) in the VG study and the local situation (*e.g.,* turnover versus job performance), the types of jobs involved, organizational-level factors such as job context, and characteristics of the applicant population.

VG studies that include validation research on different types of tests, positions, or applicant populations will have a hard time addressing Title VII when they are used in new local situations, and the extent to which validity evidence can be bridged between the VG study and the new local situation depends highly on the degree of similarity on these factors. Table 2-5 shows these factors as defined by the Uniform Guidelines and professional standards.

	Federal and Professional Standards for Evaluating the Similarity Between the VG Study and the Local Situation			
Factor #	**Requirement**	**Uniform Guidelines**	**Joint Standards**	**SIOP Principles**
1	Comparability between the test in the VG study and the local situation	7B1, 15E1(A), Q&A #43, #66	Std. 1.20 (see also p. 15)	p. 30
2	Comparability between criterion variable(s) in the VG study and the local situation	Q&A #43, #66	Std. 1.20	p. 30
3	Investigation of factors that may moderate the strength of the validity coefficient in the new situation	7D, 15E1(C), Q&A #43, #66	Stds. 1.20, 1.21	p. 9, 28, 29
4	Types of jobs	Q&A #43, #66	Std. 1.20 (see also p. 15)	p. 9, 27, 29, 30
5	Types of criteria	Q&A #43, #66	p. 15	p. 9, 29, 30
6	Organizational-level factors (job context)		p. 15	p. 9, 27, 29
7	Characteristics of test takers (e.g., base rate)	15E1(C), Q&A #43, #66	Std. 1.20 (see also p.15)	p. 9, p. 27
8	Characteristics of test takers (*i.e.*, race/ethnicity, gender)	15E1(C)		
9	Time interval separating collection of test and criterion measures	Q&A #66	Std. 1.20 (see also p. 15)	
10	How selection procedure is used (e.g., ranking, banding, cutoff, etc.)	15E1(D)	Std. 1.21	p. 29
11	Methodological choices, assumptions, and consequences regarding correcting for artifacts (e.g., criterion unreliability and range restriction) and the extent to which they may differ between the original study and new situation	-1	Std. 1.21 (see also p.15)	p. 28-29
12	Professional judgment in interpreting and applying VG related research			p. 28

Note. (1) The Uniform Guidelines provide specific requirements in Sections 14B and 15B, but in the context of a single validation study (which may include multiple samples or settings).

Table 2-5 Evaluating the VG Study and the Local Situation

Table 2-5 shows the overlapping criteria in these various standards regarding making a comparison between the studies included in the VG study (*e.g.,* types of tests, types of positions, etc.) and those in the new local situation. Notice that some of the requirements overlap between the Uniform Guidelines, Joint Standards, and SIOP Principles, with the highest degree of overlap occurring between the Joint Standards and SIOP Principles.

There are additional considerations necessary that pertain to the *assumptions* that must be made when "importing" validity evidence into a new local situation without conducting a local study. This is important because when courts evaluate the validity of a test that is potentially discriminatory against a certain group (which occurs when adverse impact is not justified by validity), *they typically do not like to rely on assumptions* (Berger, 2000). Rather, they have consistently required *situational-specific evidence regarding the job relatedness of a particular test and its relationship with accurately and specifically defined job requirements.*[20]

As discussed above, the U.S. Supreme Court (*Griggs* and *Albemarle*) and the Appellate Courts (*Atlas*) have indicated a clear and consistent disfavor towards employers using testing practices to hire applicants for generalized traits (*e.g.,* "hiring smart and educated people" as in *Griggs*). Rather, they prefer to evaluate how the specific test has a "manifest" (the term used in *Griggs*) or "demonstrated" (the term used in the 1991 Civil Rights Act) relationship to the clearly-defined needs of the specific "position in question" (the other requirement in the 1991 Civil Rights Act). The next section will review the types of assumptions made when importing validity evidence into a new situation using VG.

Assumptions Made When Importing Validity Evidence from VG Studies into a New Local Situation

Consider a hypothetical VG study that combines 20 validation studies for a certain test used for similar positions at different employers. Then consider a new local situation (called "Site 21") which uses the same test for a position that is similar to those included in the other 20 studies, but is challenged in a federal Title VII case because the test exhibits adverse impact. What factors could possibly influence the level of validity that would be found at Site 21 if a local study was to be conducted? Should validity be automatically assumed at Site 21 if the test was found valid overall at the 20 previous sites when combined into a VG study involving similar jobs?

Practitioners should be aware that these issues are of utmost interest to a federal court because, before using the VG study to infer that a *sufficient level of validity* (adequate to justify the adverse impact) exists at Site 21, numerous assumptions must be made. Some of the obvious assumptions include the similarity between jobs, consistent and reliable administration of the test, the base rate of the applicants (the percentage of applicants who possess the qualifications for the job), and the cutoff score used for the test. Each of these factors (along with others shown in Tables 2-6 to 2-8) would have a major impact on the level of validity that could be found at Site 21.

The reasons for this are quite obvious. If the target position at Site 21 is significantly different in some way from the positions in the VG study (*e.g.,* different supervisory structure, performance criteria, etc.), a corresponding impact can occur on the results of a local study. If the test is administered at Site 21 with a different time limit, or an inconsistent proctor, even more complications could arise that will impact test validity. If the base rate of the applicants at Site 21 is much higher or lower than the applicant populations included in the VG study, another major impact is possible.[21] If Site 21 requires a college degree, or tests applicants using other measures before they take the CAT, this can also impact the level of validity. While testing professionals can sometimes distinguish between legitimate moderators of validity and artifacts that work to suppress the real levels of validity that may be present in a study, federal judges just want to know the "bottom-line" validity number.

The following situational factors represent a variety of factors that can influence the strength of the test-criterion relationship in the local situation. These factors can be broken down into three major categories: those related to the applicant pool (see Table 2-6), the test itself (see Table 2-7), and characteristics about the job (see Table 2-8).

Situational Factors Pertaining to the Applicant Pool that can Influence the Results of a Local Validation Study		
Factor #	Factor	Possible Impact
1	Sample Size	The statistical power of the study can lead to Type I or Type II errors.
2	Base Rate (% of applicants who "show up qualified")	Impacts the strength of the validity coefficient (with respect to both statistical significance and practical significance, or utility, of the test).
3	Competitive Environment	Job desirability and the competitive element for the position can impact the range and distribution characteristics of applicant scores.
4	Other Selection Procedures Used Before/After the Test (range restriction)	Range restriction has a suppressive effect on test validity because only the highest scorers are subsequently hired (and later rated on job performance criteria). Thus, tests that are used before and after the target test will restrict the qualification levels of the applicants.

Table 2-6 Applicant Pool Situational Factors that Influence a Local Validation Study

Situational Factors Pertaining to the Test that can Influence the Results of a Local Validation Study		
Factor #	Factor	Possible Impact
1	Test Content	The content of the test is one of the most relevant factors when considering the transportability of validity evidence into a new situation. While different tests may measure similar constructs, their underlying content and statistical qualities may differ substantially. Using various test versions across locations also introduces an additional form of unreliability.
2	Test Administration Conditions (proctoring, time limits, etc.)	Test results include true variance around the construct being measured, random error variance, and systematic error variance. The consistency, or lack thereof, of a test administration can have a significant impact on test validity because it impacts the error variance introduced into the test scores.
3	Test Administration Modality (e.g., written vs. online)	The mode (or method) in which a test is given can have an impact on applicant scores and test validity.
4	Test Use (ranked, banded, cutoffs used)	The way in which test scores are used defines the test distribution characteristics, and the extent to which test scores can relate to other variables (e.g., job performance criteria).
5	Test Reliability (internal consistency)	The reliability of a test has a very significant impact on the validity of a test (it sets the maximum validity threshold of a test-criteria relationship).
6	Test Bias (e.g., culturally-loaded content)	Test bias can introduce error into the testing process and thus impact the level of validity obtained in a local study.

Table 2-7 Test Situational Factors that Influence a Local Validation Study

Situational Factors Pertaining to the Job that can Influence the Results of a Local Validation Study		
Factor #	Factor	Possible Impact
1	Job Content Comparability	The similarity between the job(s) included in the original validation study and the new setting is a key factor in validity being found in the new situation. Even jobs that share similar titles may, in actuality, perform vastly different job duties (Uniform Guidelines, 7B-1). Even jobs that have *identical* duties can spend different amounts of time on each and can vary in the importance level of similar duties (Uniform Guidelines, Q&A #51).
2	Job Performance Criteria	The comparability between the job performance criteria used in the original study and those used in the local study (e.g., objective, subjective, production, sales, turnover, etc.) can have a substantial impact on validity level that would likely be found in the new local situation.
3	Reliability of Job Performance Criteria	The reliability level of job performance criteria has a very significant impact on the validity of a test (like test reliability, it sets a maximum validity threshold) and a variety of factors can impact rater reliability. (Landy & Farr, 1983, pp. 120-122).
4	Rating Bias on Job Performance Criteria	Rating bias has been extensively discussed in the personnel testing literature and can have a substantial impact on test validity in a new local situation (Stauffer & Buckley, 2005; Landy & Farr, 1983, pp. 120-122).
5	Range Restriction on Job Performance Criteria	Range restriction on the criteria occurs when less than 100% of the applicants tested and hired are available to receive job performance ratings (this has a suppressive effect on test validity).
6	Level of Supervision/Autonomy	The level of supervision or autonomy in the jobs in the original validation study and the new situation can possibly have an impact on test validity (Morgeson, Delaney-Klinger, Hemingway, 2005; Barrick & Mount, 1993).
7	Level/Quality of Training/Coaching Provided	Employees can often "rise and fall" in organizations based on the level of training and coaching they receive, which obviously can have an impact on job performance ratings (Ellinger, Ellinger, & Keller, 2003). For example, types and amounts of feedback have been shown to increase performance by 8% - 26% (Landy & Farr, 1983, pp. 264-265).
8	Organizational- and Unit-level Demands and Constraints	These factors can have a wide degree of impact on both individual-level job performance and job performance ratings.
9	Job Satisfaction	Job satisfaction can have a significant influence on job performance (Judge, Thoresen, Bono, Patton, 2001; Schleicher, Watt, & Greguras, 2004).
10	Management and Leadership Styles and Role Clarity	The leader-member exchange (LMX) literature has suggested that significant relationships exist between LMX and several job performance factors, as well as satisfaction with supervision, overall satisfaction, member competence, and turnover. Interactions between leaders and members are strongly related to supervisory ratings of performance, which could in turn impact test validity (Gerstner & Day, 1997; Podsakoff, MacKenzie, & Bommer, 1996). Role ambiguity can also have a significant impact on job performance ratings (Tubre & Collins, 2000).

11	Reward Structures and Processes	Employee incentive systems can vary greatly between various organizations and positions and can have an extensive impact on job performance (Jenkins, Mitra, Gupta, Shaw, 1998; Pritchard, Jones, Roth, Stuebing, & Ekeberg, 1988).
12	Organizational Citizenship, Morale, and Commitment of the General Workforce	The effects of organizational citizenship behaviors, morale, and perceived organizational support have a significant impact on individual- and organizational-level performance. (Allen & Rush, 1998; Rhoades & Eisenberger, 2002).
13	Organizational Culture, Norms, Beliefs, Values	These factors can have a wide impact on individual/team level performance (Meglino, Ravlin, & Adkins, 1989; Brown & Leigh, 1996; Heck, 1995).
14	Organizational Socialization Strategies for New Employees	How new employees are introduced and acculturated into the workforce can have an impact on employee performance and job ratings (Steel, Shane, & Kennedy, 1990; Chao, O'Leary-Kelly, Wolf, Klein, Gardner, 1994).
15	Formal and Informal Communication (e.g., style, levels, and networks)	Communication between supervisors, employees, and work units can obviously have a highly significant impact on employee performance and job ratings (Kacmar, Witt, Zivnuska, & Gully, 2003; Alexander, Helms, & Wilkins, 1989; Pincus, 1986; Abraham, 1996).
16	Centralization and Formalization of Decision-Making	An organization's decision-making characteristics and structure can play a major role in employee performance and job ratings (Judge & Ferris, 1993; Steel, Shane, & Kennedy, 1990; Sagie, 1994).
17	Organization Size	Organization size can impact a wide array of factors that can have an impact on test validity. For example, Weiner (1997) found that employee turnover (often a criterion in validity studies) and perceived problems were found to vary as a function of agency size. Smaller agencies reported lower turnover rates and indicated that traits (KSAs) play a relatively greater role in employee turnover than did larger agencies.
18	Physical Environment (lighting, heating, privacy)	These factors have been studied (sometimes controversially) for decades in I-O psychology, and sometimes have mixed results. Nonetheless, these are some factors that can obviously have an impact on employee performance and job ratings (Peters, O'Conner, & Rudolf, 1980).

Table 2-8 Job Situational Factors that can Influence a Local Validation Study

Theoretically, each of the 28 factors listed in Tables 2-6 to 2-8 can impact the validity of a test in a new situation.[22] In fact, these factors are so critical that it is entirely possible that a test from a job/employer with high validity based on some criteria, such as supervisory ratings, could yield *completely different validity results* in a new local setting due to the impact of *any one of these factors*. Personnel psychology literature is full of study results that substantiate the *complex interaction* that occurs between human performance, tests, and job performance (*e.g.,* Murphy & Shiarella, 1997). Making accurate and reliable predictions of human behavior – which is essentially the core focus of validity studies – is difficult at best because of the plethora of factors that can reduce and/or suppress the complex relationship between tests and job performance.

There is overlap between the factors that impact the internal quality of a VG study (see Table 2-4), the factors pertaining to the similarity between the VG study and the local situation (Table 2-5), and the complete list of factors that will ultimately determine the level of validity found in a new local situation (Tables 2-6 to 2-8). Because some of these factors are more widely known to affect validity studies than others, they have been incorporated into the federal and professional standards (*e.g.,* factors 1 and 4 in Table 2-6; factors 1, 4, and 5 in Table 2-7; and factors 1-3 and 5 in Table 2-8). Further, several factors listed in Table 2-8 could be classified as "moderators," which are consistently mentioned in both sets of professional standards (*e.g.,* Standards 1.20 and 1.21 in the Joint Standards and pages 9, 28, and 29 of the SIOP Principles).

Modern VG procedures have mechanics for detecting moderators that seek to limit validity generalization inferences into new local situations.[23] Currently, however, there is no way to determine *if* and *to what extent* the factors in Table 2-8 would inhibit validity existing and/or being found if a study was conducted in the new local situation. Thus, without conducting a local study, there is ultimately no way of *knowing* if, and to what extent, validity would be found. Even if the VG study showed a near perfect correlation in 20 previous studies, one cannot really *know* if validity would be found in a new local situation because of how the factors outlined in Tables 2-6 to 2-8 may come into play.

Even though VG techniques do have some safeguards for detecting moderators, the factors discussed above can remove and/or completely obstruct validation evidence from existing at a new local situation where such evidence is required in a Title VII action. This is why the Uniform Guidelines includes Questions &Answers #43 and #66 to clarify that, while tests can be valid predictors of performance on a job in a certain location, the same test may be invalid for predicting success on a different job or the same job in a different location because of legitimate and real differences in work behaviors, criterion measures, study samples, or other factors. This is also why the Uniform Guidelines require that specified standards be satisfied before a user may rely on findings of validity in another situation (*i.e.,* through a 7B transportability study). It should also be noted that, while these factors can work to suppress validity in a new local situation, the reason that validity evidence is sometimes not found in a local study is because the test has no relationship to job performance.

In addition to these limitations, it will be especially difficult to argue in a litigation setting exactly what the *actual correlation value* "would have been" based upon the VG evidence if a local study had been conducted. VG techniques include the "90% credibility statistic"[24] and other similar tools that are designed to provide confidence boundaries around what the actual correlation value *might be* in studies outside the VG study. Ultimately however, it is still an *assumed value* rather than an *actual value* that is derived from a local study.

Because of these limitations, practitioners may be challenged in Title VII situations to effectively argue that none of these factors *did* (during the past use of the test), *would* (in the present), or *will* (to justify use of the test in the future) come into play in a local situation, and that the validity results observed in the VG study will just "fit right into" the specific unique situation – complete with a validity coefficient large enough to justify all the adverse impact exhibited by the test. In a Title VII situation, it is the user's burden to prove these factors did not (or would not) hinder the test from being valid in the local situation (and hence it will likely be the plaintiff's strategy to show how they did or would).

Some of the factors listed in Tables 2-6 to 2-8 are statistical characteristics that serve to suppress the true validity of the test (*e.g.,* range restriction). Other factors, such as the sample size involved in a statistical study, lower the statistical power of a correlational comparison and reduce the study's ability to uncover the actual correlation value that may be present. Correction formulas can adjust for some of these factors. Other factors, however, are not of this nature and constitute real characteristics that may lower the actual level of test-criteria relationship in the study (*e.g.,* test reliability, applicant base rate, etc.).

To a certain extent, however, all of these factors are relevant in Title VII matters because ultimately a court will want to know the validity level in a local situation (see several cases examples discussed below). Experts can argue about which corrections should be used or not, given the particular circumstances at hand, but there is no argument stronger than a statistically significant correlation coefficient found at a local situation. In Title VII situations, a court will likely desire to know the bottom-line validity irrespective of *if and how* each one of these factors came into play.

Experts can also argue about the extent to which the factors discussed above can affect a test's validity in a new local situation. The reality, however, is that, for a test to show validity in a new situation, each one of these factors must not substantially hinder the "statistical cooperation" between the test and criterion. The fact that each of these factors could have an impact in the local setting is not even the substantial issue in a Title VII situation; the major issue is that they *could* have an impact and the practitioner that chooses to solely rely on outside validity evidence using only VG is making the assumption that these factors would not, in fact, have an impact on the validity of the test. It may be possible to find validation studies where each of these factors (see Tables 2-6 to 2-8) manifested in a way that inhibited test validity. But even beyond an academic research level, certainly experienced workers can identify with each of these factors and how they have worked both at an individual level and at an organization, division, or work group level for positions they have personally held.

If researchers were hypothetically allowed to arrange the conditions of a validation study to maximize their chances of finding the highest correlation, it is very likely that every one of the factors outlined in Tables 2-6 to 2-8 would be manipulated. For example, assume a researcher wanted to conduct a validation study on a cognitive ability test and a personality test that measured conscientiousness. Assume that VG studies conducted on the specific tests of interest showed that average validity coefficients were .30 and .20 respectively for these two tests for positions similar to the target situation. If hypothetically allowed to go through every factor on Tables 2-6 to 2-8 and dictate the conditions for each,[25] rather than leaving each one to chance, experienced practitioners would manipulate each to maximize the chances of finding high validity. This is because each of these factors can in fact operate to maximize or suppress validity. In fact, experts in each respective area (cognitive ability testing and personality testing) might even want to design a local situation differently for each type of test.

The significance of these factors has been noted by the Uniform Guidelines, Joint Standards, and SIOP Principles. Many have been specifically included in these documents because they constitute key considerations both within a VG-style meta-analysis and when seeking to externalize from them (*i.e.,* infer validity into a new situation). Between all three documents, the Uniform Guidelines offer the least restrictive guidelines for transporting validity from other validation studies into new local situations when compared to the collection provided in the professional standards (see Tables 2-4 and 2-5).

The Elements of a Criterion-Related Validity Study that are Typically Evaluated in Title VII Situations

When the courts evaluate criterion-related validity evidence, which is the type of evidence of validity that can be included in statistical VG studies, four basic elements are typically brought under inspection: Statistical significance, practical significance, the type and relevance of the job criteria, and evidence available to support the specific use of the testing practice. If any of these elements are missing or do not meet certain standards, courts often infer that discrimination has taken place because adverse impact is not justified without validity evidence. Each of these elements is discussed in more detail below.

Statistical significance. The courts, Uniform Guidelines, and professional standards are in agreement when it comes to the issue of statistical significance thresholds and criterion-related validity. The .05 threshold is used on both sides of adverse impact litigation for determining statistically significant adverse impact (using hypergeometric probability distributions for testing cases) as well as determining the statistical significance of the correlation coefficient obtained in the validation study.

Practical significance. Just like statistical significance, the concept of practical significance has also been applied to both the adverse impact and validity side of Title VII cases. In the realm of adverse impact, the courts have sometimes evaluated the practical significance or "stability" and effect size of the adverse impact.[26] This is typically done by evaluating what happens to the statistical significance finding when two applicants are hypothetically changed from failing to passing status on the selection procedure that exhibited adverse impact. If this changes the statistically significant finding from "significant" (<.05) to "non-significant" (>.05), the finding is not practically significant.

In the realm of criterion-related validity studies, practical significance relates to the strength of the validity coefficient (*i.e.,* its raw value and actual utility in the specific setting). This is important in litigation settings because the square of the validity coefficient represents the percentage of variance explained on the criterion used in the study. For example, a validity coefficient of .15 explains only 2.3% of the criterion variance, whereas coefficients of .25 and .35 explain 6.3% and 12.3% respectively. Some cases have included lengthy deliberations about these "squared coefficient" values to argue the extent to which the test validity is practically significant. A few examples are provided below.

- Dickerson v. U. S. Steel Corporation (1978): A validity study was inadequate where the correlation level was less than .30, the adverse impact on minorities from the use of the selection procedure was severe, and no evidence was presented regarding the evaluation of alternative selection procedures. Regarding the validity coefficients in the case, the judge noted, "a low coefficient, even though statistically significant, may indicate a low practical utility," and further stated, ". . . one can readily see that even on the statistically significant correlations of .30 or so, only 9% of the success on the job is attributable to success on the (test) batteries. This is a very low level, which does not justify use of these batteries, where correlations are all below .30. In conclusion, based upon the guidelines and statistical analysis . . . *the Court cannot find that these tests have any real practical utility*. The Guidelines do not permit a finding of job-relatedness where *statistical but not practical significance is shown*. On this final ground as well, therefore, the test batteries must be rejected" [emphasis added].

- NAACP Ensley Branch v. Seibels (1980): Judge Pointer rejected statistically significant correlations of .21, because they were too small to be meaningful.
- EEOC v. Atlas Paper (1989): The judge weighed the decision heavily based on the strength of the validity coefficient: "There are other problems with Hunter's theory which further highlight the invalidity of the Atlas argument. Petty computed the average correlation for the studies to be .25 when concurrent and .15 when predictive. A correlation of .25 means that a test explains only 5% to 6% of job performance. Yet, Courts generally accept correlation coefficients above .30 as reliable . . . This Court need not rule at this juncture on the figure that it will adopt as the bare minimum correlation. Nonetheless, the Court also notes that higher correlations are often sought when there is great adverse impact (Clady v. County of Los Angeles, id; Guardians Assn. of New York City v. Civil Service, 630 F.2d at 105-06). Thus, despite the great adverse impact here, the correlations fall significantly below those generally accepted (FN24)."
- U.S. v. City of Garland (2004): The court debated the level of the validity coefficients extensively: "As discussed supra at n. 25, whether the correlation between the Alert (test) and performance should be characterized as 'low' or 'moderate' is a matter of earnest contention between the parties" (See D.I. 302 at p. 11, 35-40). In a standard statistical text cited at trial, correlations of .1 are described as "low" and correlations of .30 described as "moderate."

In addition to the courts, the Uniform Guidelines (15B6), U.S. Department of Labor (2000, p. 3-10), and SIOP Principles (p. 48) are in concert regarding the importance of taking the strength of the validity coefficient into practical consideration.

Type and relevance of the job criteria. There are many cases that have deliberated the type and relevance of the job criteria included as part of a validity study, including *Garland, Lanning*, and others cited herein. The Uniform Guidelines (15B5) and SIOP Principles (p. 16) also include discussion on this topic. Tests that have significant correlations with job criteria that are reliable and constitute critical aspects of the job will obviously be given higher weight when evaluated.

Considering the validity coefficient level and the specific use of the testing practice. Some cases have set minimum thresholds for validity coefficients that are necessary to justify the particular *use* of a test (*e.g.*, ranking versus using a pass/fail cutoff). Conceptually speaking, tests that have high levels of reliability (*i.e.*, accuracy in defining true ability levels of applicants) and have high validity can be used at a higher degree of specificity than tests that do not have such characteristics (*e.g.*, Guardians Association of the New York City Police Dept. v. Civil Service Commission, 1981). When tests are used as ranking devices, they are typically subjected to a stricter validity standard than when pass/fail cutoffs are used. The cases below placed minimum thresholds on the validity coefficient necessary for strict rank ordering on a test:

- Brunet v. City of Columbus (1993): This case involved an entry-level firefighter Physical Capacities Test (PCT) that had adverse impact against women. The court stated: "The correlation coefficient for the overall PCT is .29. Other courts have found such correlation coefficients to be predictive of job performance, thus indicating the appropriateness of ranking where the correlation coefficient value is .30 or better."
- Boston Chapter, NAACP Inc. v. Beecher (1974): This case involved an entry-level written test for firefighters. Regarding the correlation values, the court stated: "The objective portion of the study produced several correlations that were statistically significant (likely to occur by chance in fewer than five of one hundred similar cases) and practically significant (correlation of .30 or higher, thus explaining more than 9% or more of the observed variation)."
- Clady v. County of Los Angeles (1985): This case involved an entry-level written test for firefighters. The court stated: "In conclusion, the County's validation studies demonstrate legally sufficient correlation to success at the Academy and performance on the job. Courts generally accept correlation coefficients above .30 as reliable … As a general principle, the greater the test's adverse impact, the higher the correlation which will be required."
- Zamlen v. City of Cleveland (1988): This case involved several different entry-level firefighter physical ability tests that had various correlation coefficients with job performance. The judge noted, "Correlation coefficients of .30 or greater are considered high by industrial psychologists" and set a criteria of .30 to endorse the City's option of using the physical ability test as a ranking device.

The Uniform Guidelines (3B, 5G, and 15B6) and SIOP Principles (p. 49) also advise taking the level of validity into consideration when considering how to *use* a test in a selection process. Test usage is such a critical consideration because validity has to do with the *interpretation of individual scores*. Tests, per se, are not necessarily generally valid; rather, specific scores may or may not be valid given consideration of how closely they are aligned with the true needs of the job. A keyboarding speed and accuracy test may be valid for both the positions of a personnel psychologist and a legal secretary; but the cutoff of 85 words per minute is certainly more valid for the legal secretary position than it is for the personnel psychologist position.

In the event of a Title VII case, practitioners who rely solely on a VG study to infer validity evidence into a new situation will not have information on these four critical factors to provide the court. Because VG relies essentially on inferring validity based on other studies, there is no way to tell if a local study would result in a validity coefficient that is *statistically significant*, if such validity coefficient would be *practically significant*, if the *job criteria predicted was relevant* given the needs of the particular position, or if the validity coefficient would sufficiently *justify the specific use* of the testing practice. This presents a challenge when opting to deploy a VG-only defense in Title VII situations. Each of these is discussed in more detail below.

By relying solely on a VG study, there is no way to determine whether a validity coefficient would be statistically significant in a local situation because no local validity coefficients were ever calculated. While VG studies can generate estimated population validity coefficients (with various types of corrections), it is not possible to determine if such validity coefficient would be obtained in the local situation, and (more importantly), whether it would exceed the court-required level needed for statistical significance (<.05). Even if one considers the population validity coefficient calculated from a VG study at face value (*e.g.,* r = .25), calculating the statistical significance level requires also knowing the sample size included in the study, which is another unknown unless a local study is in fact conducted. For example, a coefficient of .20 is significant with a sample of 69 (p = .0496 using a one-tail test for significance), but is not significant with a sample of 68 (p = .051). The first can be argued as defensible under Title VII; the other *is not*.

Without knowing what the actual validity coefficient would be in a local situation, it is also not possible to evaluate its practical significance in the local job context. While contemporary VG techniques include the 90% credibility interval to forecast the minimum size the validity coefficient is likely to be in similar situations outside the VG study, one must still guess what the validity actually *would have been* in the specific situation. In some circumstances, judges may be more inclined to make determinations whether the test would "survive scrutiny" in light of the situational factors of the case only after being given the *actual validity number* (see several such cases above).

The exact level of adverse impact is always known in Title VII situations because that is what brought the suit/audit in the first place. It is typically reported in standard deviation units reflecting the statistical probability level of the finding. How will judges handle situations where the adverse impact level is known, but the *level of correlation (validity)* in that same situation is not? Some cases include lengthy discussions regarding the strength of the validity evidence (*e.g., Dickerson, Garland, and Zamlen*). VG studies often include a wide mix of various job criteria predicted by a test and, without conducting a local study, there is no way to tell if the test would in fact be correlated to the job criteria of the position in the local setting that would be sufficiently important to the overall job. The Uniform Guidelines offer a caution on this issue: "Sole reliance upon a single selection instrument which is related to only one of many job duties or aspects of job performance will also be subject to close review" (Section 14B6).

Finally, regarding the "specific use" criteria, the cases discussed above provide several examples of litigation settings where defendants have been required to weigh their validity evidence to support the *specific use* of the test under scrutiny (with ranking being the most highly scrutinized). The Uniform Guidelines advise that tests should be evaluated to insure its appropriateness for operational use, including setting cutoff scores or rank ordering (Section 15B6). Only local validity studies reveal the actual validity level of a test in a certain situation. While provisions exist in the Uniform Guidelines for justifying test use in various circumstances, local validity studies offer the added benefit of producing the known validity level of a test.

Recommendations

In the past 30 years, VG and its related tools, techniques, and research results have contributed greatly to the understanding of the overall effectiveness and utility of a wide range of selection procedures (*e.g.,* Hunter & Hunter, 1984; Schmidt & Hunter, 1998). It has also generated years of debate (Sackett, Schmitt, Tenopyr, Kehoe, & Zedeck, 1985). Perhaps the most effective and least controversial application of VG is to identify the types of tests that have been previously shown to be the most effective for particular job classifications (and for specific types of criteria). After such tests have been identified, they can be adopted and used either under a transportability model by addressing 7B of the Uniform Guidelines in a local study if technically feasible. These steps will be especially important when the tests have adverse impact, in which case the use of VG – as with any other source of validity evidence (*e.g.,* content validity) – should follow conservative guidelines when being used to provide job-relatedness evidence in Title VII situations. Guidelines for this are suggested below:

When VG evidence is prepared for use in a Title VII situation, practitioners should:

1. Address the evaluation criteria provided by the Uniform Guidelines, Joint Standards, and SIOP Principles regarding the evaluation of the *internal quality* of the VG study (see the 15 factors listed in Table 2-4). This will help insure that the VG study itself can be relied upon for drawing inferences.
2. Address the evaluation criteria provided by the Uniform Guidelines, Joint Standards, and SIOP Principles regarding the *similarity between the VG study and the local situation* (see the 12 factors listed in Table 2-5). These will help insure that the VG study itself can be relied upon and the research is in fact relevant to the local situation (*e.g.,* similarities between tests, jobs, job criteria, etc.). Perhaps the most critical factor evaluated by courts when considering VG types of evidence in litigation settings is the similarity between jobs in the VG study and the local situation (see also 7B of the Uniform Guidelines). VG evidence is the strongest where there is clear evidence that the work behaviors between the target position and those in the positions in the VG study are highly similar as shown by a job analysis in both situations (as suggested by Schmidt & Hunter, 1977).
3. Only use VG evidence to *supplement* other sources of validity evidence (*e.g.,* content validity or local criterion-related validation studies) rather than being the sole source. Supplementing a local criterion-related validity study with evidence from a VG study may be useful if evidence exists that statistical artifacts (not situational moderators) suppressed the observed validity of the

test in the local situation. Further, if only limited subjects are available to include in a local criterion-related validity study (*i.e.,* the study has low statistical power – see Schmidt, Hunter, & Urry, 1975), it may be beneficial to supplement local validation research with VG evidence, provided that the local study demonstrates at least minimal levels of validity with respect to statistical significance, practical significance, the use of relevant criteria, and that the test is used appropriately given this evidence and the levels of adverse impact observed.

For example, a practitioner wishes to supplement the validity evidence of a test and has only 70 subjects available to conduct a local validation study. The study returns only a moderate (but significant) correlation between test scores and relevant job performance criteria and it is likely that this moderate result is due to sampling error, criterion unreliability, and range restriction (rather than situational moderators). In these circumstances, it may be useful to draw inferences from professionally conducted VG studies that may show what validity levels can be expected after accounting for these three statistical suppressors.

4. Evaluate the test fairness evidence from studies included in the VG study using the methods outlined by the Uniform Guidelines, Joint Standards, and SIOP Principles when technically feasible.

5. Evaluate and consider using "alternate employment practices" that are "substantially equally valid" as required by the 1991 Civil Rights Act Section 2000e-2[k][1][A][ii] and Section 3B of the Uniform Guidelines.

While these recommendations may prove useful for integrating VG evidence into new local settings, perhaps the most effective way to introduce validity evidence from outside sources is to conduct a Uniform Guidelines-style transportability study (to address Section 7B). This method is especially useful for employers that may have limited budgets or lack ready access to the necessary expertise for conducting other types of validity studies. The process for completing such a study is relatively straightforward, and requires only acceptable validation evidence from an outside study (or studies), a job analysis in both the new local situation and the original study, a comparability study between the two, and evidence of test fairness. From a practical, business point-of-view, this technique has tremendous advantages.

Notes

[1] While the Uniform Guidelines do not formally constitute a set of legal requirements, they have consistently been awarded "great deference" starting as early as the Griggs v. Duke Power Company (401 U.S. 424, 1971) case. They have also been unilaterally adopted verbatim as a legal standard in several cases – e.g., Brown v. Chicago (WL 354922, N.D. III, 1998).

[2] It is important to note that the Uniform Guidelines require that criterion measures consist of *actual job performance*, not ratings of the overall knowledge, skill, or abilities of the incumbents (see Section 15B).

[3] For example, in Lanning v. Southeastern Pennsylvania Transportation Authority (181 F.3d 478, 80 FEPC., BNA, 221, 76 EPD P 46,160 3rd Cir.(Pa.) Jun 29, 1999 (NO. 98-1644, 98-1755), the court stated: "The District Court seems to have derived this standard from the Principles for the Validation and Use of Personnel Selection Procedures ("SIOP Principles") . . . To the extent that the SIOP Principles are inconsistent with the mission of Griggs and the business necessity standard adopted by the Act, they are not instructive" (FN20).

[4] Some of these cases include: Forsberg v. Pacific Northwest Bell Telephone (840 F2d 1409, CA-9 1988; Gilbert v. East Bay Municipal Utility District (DC CA, 19 EPD 9061, 1979); Martinez v. City of Salinas (DC CA, No. C-78-2608 SW (S.J.); Parks v. City of Long Beach (DC CA, No. 84-1611 DWW [Px]); Sanchez v. City of Santa Ana (DC CA, No. CV-79-1818 KN); Simmons v. City of Kansas City (DC KS, No. 88-2603-0); and U.S. v. City of Torrance (DC CA, No. 93-4142-MRP [RMCx]).

[5] Buford, J. A. (1991), *Personnel Management and Human Resources in Local Government.* Center for Governmental Services, Auburn University. Gatewood, R. S. & Feild, H. S. (1986), *Human Resource Selection.* Drydan Press; Buford, J. A. (1985), *Recruiting and Selection: Concepts and Techniques for Local Government.* Alabama Cooperative Extension Service, Auburn University; Schuler, R. S. (1981), *Personnel and Human Resource Management.* West Publishing Company; Bemis, S. E., Belenky, A. H., & Soder, D. A. (1984), *Job Analysis: An Effective Management Tool.* Bureau of National Affairs: Washington D.C.; Campbell, T. (July, 1982), Entry-Level Exam Examined in Court. *The Western Fire Journal*; Sturn, R. D. (September, 1979), Mass Validation: The Key to Effectively Analyzing an Employer's Job Classifications. *Public Personnel Management.*

[6] Employers who have been challenged in court for employment discrimination and who have included only majority group members in the job analysis or validation process typically have a difficult time defending themselves in court.

[7] Contreras v. City of Los Angeles (656 F.2d 1267. 9th Cir. 1981) and U.S. v. South Carolina (434 U.S. 1026, 1978).

[8] Arkin, H., & Colton, R. R. (1950), *Tables for Statisticians.* New York: Barnes & Noble, Inc. Technical note: other sampling techniques can be useful for estimating the sample sizes necessary for estimating the average ratings for the job analysis rating scales; however, because most of the (somewhat continuous) scales are used in a dichotomous fashion (and further because the population standard deviations are unknown in each job analysis study), the population proportion formula was used for estimating these sample size requirements.

[9] See Section 14C1 and 14C4 of the Uniform Guidelines and Questions & Answers # 75.

[10] Eliminating ratings (not raters, but only their ratings that have been identified as outliers) using a 1.645 standard deviation rule (all ratings that are 1.645 standard deviations above or below the mean are deleted) is one way of completing this step. Using this criteria will serve to "trim" the average ratings that are in the upper or lower 5% of the distribution.

[11] This hypothetical example, of course, assumes that the employer adequately addressed all of the nuances required for defensible criterion-related validity studies.

[12] The reader is cautioned against making too many correlational comparisons because doing so increases the odds of finding statistically significant correlations that are due to chance alone.

[13] The EEOC Guidelines on Employment Testing Procedures were issued on August 24, 1966 and interpreted "professionally developed ability test" to mean: ". . . a test which fairly measures the knowledge or skills required by the particular job or class of jobs which the applicant seeks, or which fairly affords the employer a chance to measure the applicant's ability to perform a particular job or class of jobs." The EEOC position was later superseded by the Guidelines on Employee Selection Procedures, 29 CFR 1607, 35 Fed. Reg. 12333 (Aug. 1, 1970), which required that employers using tests have available "data demonstrating that the test is predictive of or significantly correlated with important elements of work behavior which comprise or are relevant to the job or jobs for which candidates are being evaluated" [1607.4(c)]. These were replaced by the 1978 Uniform Guidelines on Employee Selection Procedures, which have remained unchanged to the date of this writing.

[14] With the exception of the two year period between 1989 and 1991 where the Wards Cove v. Atonio (1989) case, lowered the standard for employers to "producing a business justification" for the test because this case was overturned by the passage of the 1991 Civil Rights Act.

[15] The adverse impact discrimination section of the 1991 Civil Rights Act first describes the classic type of adverse impact discrimination (adverse impact absent validity), which is followed by an "OR" that allows an adverse impact ruling to also occur if "the complaining party makes the demonstration described in subparagraph (C) with respect to an alternate employment practice, and the respondent refuses to adopt such alternative employment practice" (Section 2000e-2[k][1][A][ii]). In passing the 1991 Act, Congress was specifically refuting the *Wards Cove* interpretation of the "alternate employment practice" (which emphasized "equally effective" and "cost or other burdens" on the proposed alternative employment practice) and was reverting the alternate employment practice requirement to its status before *Wards Cove*, which was framed by the U.S. Supreme Court in <u>Watson v. Fort Worth Bank & Trust</u> (487 U.S., 1988), that required the plaintiff to "show that other tests or selection devices, without a similarly undesirable racial effect, would also serve the employer's legitimate interest in efficient and trustworthy workmanship" (a requirement which originated in *Albemarle*).

[16] Criterion unreliability and range restriction suppress observed validity coefficients. Criterion reliability sets an *upper threshold* on the maximum correlation that can be obtained between test scores and job performance. Correcting for criterion unreliability allows the researcher to evaluate what the correlation may have been if the criterion was perfectly reliable. Range restriction occurs when less than the entire applicant group is hired, which suppresses the validity coefficient because only part of the ability range (*i.e.,* those who passed the cutoff) is subsequently rated on job performance.

[17] Based on search conducted on Westlaw in May, 2006.

[18] However, see U.S. v. City of Erie (PA 411 F. Supp. 2d 524 W.D. Pa., 2005, FN 18), which placed a caveat to this criticism stating that the Lanning court did not "throw out" or otherwise invalidate the SIOP Principles in their entirety when making this statement.

[19] While the Joint Standards and SIOP Principles do, however, discuss subgroup differences in testing, they do not discuss the technical determination of adverse impact because it is a legal term of art.

[20] Such situationally-specific evidence does not need to take the form of a local criterion-related validity study, but can be accomplished by using a link-up study as described in Section 7B and/or 15E of the Uniform Guidelines, or other source of validity evidence (e.g., content validity).

[21] Test validity is highly impacted by the base rate of applicants, and is typically maximized when the base rate in the mid-range, rather than extremely low or high because there is more variance available to interact with the job criteria in the study.

[22] This section does not argue that each one of these factors always has an influence on the outcome of validity studies. The point being stressed here is that they *can* – even while some factors are more likely than others to have such impact. If one relies wholly on VG studies of validity evidence in a Title VII situation (without conducting some type of a local study) one will never know what impact these factors would have in fact had on the validity in the new local situation.

[23] For example, the 75% rule can be used to evaluate if at least 75% of the between-study variance is likely due to sampling error (rather than moderators). This rule, however, has not been without controversy [see for example, Algera, J. A., Jansen, P. G., Roe, R. A., & Vijn, P. (1984). Validity generalization: Some critical remarks on the Schmidt-Hunter procedure. *Journal of Occupational Psychology, 57,* 197-210]. Also see the 90% credibility interval, noted below.

[24] The 90% credibility interval provides the threshold where 90% of the correlation values in the distribution of "true validities" lie. Some VG practitioners use this value as a "90% assurance" that the validity in a situation similar to those included in the VG study will be at least this large [Hunter, J.E. & Schmidt, F. (1996). Cumulative research knowledge and social policy formulation: the critical role of meta-analysis. *Psychology, Public Policy, and Law, 2* (2), 324-347].

[25] For example, select a large sample, medium base rate, low range restriction, low test cutoff to allow wide variance on the criterion measures, test content perfectly like the original in the study, perfect test administration conditions, job criteria that was both job and test construct relevant, no rating bias, supervisory ratings offered by at least two trained raters, supervision levels that allowed individual abilities wide variance in job performance, etc.

[26] For example, Contreras v. City of Los Angeles (656 F.2d 1267, 9th Cir., 1981), U.S. v. Commonwealth of Virginia (569 F2d 1300, CA-4 1978, 454 F. Supp. 1077), Waisome v. Port Authority (948 F.2d 1370, 1376, 2d Cir., 1991).

Chapter 3 - Developing, Validating, and Analyzing Written Tests

Written Test Development Steps

The following steps can be followed to develop and validate most written tests that will measure KSAPCs needed for the job.

Step 1: Determine the KSAPCs to be measured by the test

The Selection Plan described in Chapter Two can be used for selecting the KSAPCs that can be measured by the written test. If a Selection Plan has not been completed, consider using the criteria below (as baselines). The KSAPCs selected for the written test should be:

1. "Needed day one" on the job;
2. Important or critical (necessary) for the performance of the job;[1]
3. Linked to one or more critical (necessary) job duties; and
4. *For job knowledges only,* rated sufficiently high on the "Level Needed for Success" rating (see the Job Analysis Section in Chapter Two). This is necessary for insuring that the job knowledge domains measured by the test are needed (on the first day of hire) at a level that requires the applicant to have the information in memory (written tests should not measure aspects of a job knowledge that can simply be looked up or referenced by incumbents on the job without serious impacting job performance).

It is important to note the KSAPC selected for measurement on the written test should meet these criteria both *generally* (*i.e.,* as defined in the job analysis) and *specifically* (*i.e.,* the *separate facets or aspects* of the selected KSAPCs should also meet these criteria). For example, if "basic math" is required for a job and it meets the criteria above, test items should not be developed for measuring *advanced* math skills.

Step 2: Develop a test plan for measuring the selected KSAPCs

There are three areas that should be addressed for developing a solid written test plan:

- *General components* of a test plan;
- Choosing the *number* of test items; and
- Choosing the *types* of test items.

Each of these areas is discussed below.

General components of a test plan

The elements and steps necessary for a written test plan will vary based on the types of KSAPCs measured by the test. The components below should therefore be regarded as general requirements:

- What is the purpose of the test? Will it be used to qualify only those who possess mastery levels of the KSAPC? Advanced levels? Baseline levels?
- Will the test be scored in a multiple hurdle or compensatory fashion? Multiple hurdle tests require applicants to obtain a passing score on each section of the written test. Compensatory tests allow an applicant's high score in one area to compensate for an area in which they scored low. A multiple hurdle strategy should be used if certain baseline levels of proficiency are required for each KSAPC measured by the test; a compensatory approach can be used if the developer will allow higher levels of one KSAPC to compensate for another on the test. Evaluating how the KSAPCs are required and used on the job is a key consideration for making this decision.
- What is the target population being tested? Has the applicant population been pre-screened using minimum qualification requirements?
- Will the test be a *speeded* test or a *power* test? A test is considered a speeded test when time is considered an element of measurement on the test (for reasons that are related to the job) and it is not necessary to allow the vast majority of applicants to complete the test within the time limit (some tests based on criterion-related validity are designed with speed as an essential component of the test). A power test allows at least 95% of the applicants to complete the test within the allotted time. Most written tests are administered as power tests.
- What reading level will be used for the test? Most word processing programs include features for checking the grade reading level of the test, which should be slightly below the reading level required at entry to the job.
- What will the delivery mode be for the test (*e.g.,* paper/pencil, oral, computer-based testing)?
- What scoring processes and procedures will be used?
- Will a test preparation or study guide be provided to applicants? Test preparation and study guides can be developed at many levels, ranging from a cursory overview of the test and its contents to an explicit description of the KSAPCs that will be measured.
- Will test preparation sessions be offered to the applicants?

Choosing the number of test items

Some of the key considerations regarding selecting the number of items to include on the written test are:

- Making an *adequate* sampling of the KSAPC measured. A sufficient number of items should be developed to effectively measure each KSAPC at the desired level. Note that some KSAPCs will require more items than others for making a "sufficiently deep" assessment of the levels held by the applicants.

Be sure that the important aspects of each KSAPC are included in the test plan.

- Making a *proportional* sampling of the KSAPCs. This pertains to the number of items measuring each KSAPC compared with others. The test should be internally weighted in a way that insures a robust measurement of the relevant KSAPCs (this is discussed in detail below). Special consideration should be given to this proportional sampling requirement when developing job knowledge tests (see the TVAP® User Manual in the Evaluation CD for a sample test plan for job knowledge tests).
- Including a sufficient number of items to generate high test reliability. While there are numerous factors that impact test reliability, perhaps the single most important factor is the number of test items per relevant KSAPC and in the test overall.

There are no hard-and-fast rules regarding the number of items to include for measuring a KSAPC. A developer can have few or many test items for any "testable KSAPC" (those that meet the criteria above); however, some rational or empirical process for internally weighting the written test is helpful and usually makes the test more effective. Here are some guidelines to consider:

- Some KSAPCs are more complex or broad than others, and thus may require more test items for adequate measurement. For example, finding out how much an applicant knows about advanced physics may require more items than would be adequate for assessing their simple multiplication skills.
- If several discrete KSAPCs will be measured on the same written test, be sure that they are not *divergent*. If they are, put them on separate tests (or on the same test as a subscale that is scored separately). If the test will be scored and used as one overall assessment (*i.e.,* with one final score for each applicant), the various KSAPCs on the test will need to be *homogeneous* (*i.e.,* having similar types of variance because they are based on similar or inter-related content and items of similar difficulty levels). If one KSAPC is substantially different from others on the same test, the test items will be working against each other and will decrease the overall reliability (making the interpretation of a single score for the test inaccurate).
- As a general rule, do not measure a discrete KSAPC with fewer than 20 items, and be sure that the overall test includes at least 60 items if measuring more than one KSAPC. This will help insure that the test will have sufficiently high reliability.

One of the factors for choosing the number of items to include on the test (and from which KSAPCs) is to internally weight the test in a way that is relevant to the requirements of the job. One effective system for developing internal weights for a test is to have Job Experts assign point values to the various sections of the test. For example, if there are five different KSAPCs measured by the test, the Job Expert panel can be asked to assign 100 points among the five KSAPCs to come up with a final weighting scheme for the test.

The drawback to using this approach is that the items will now require *polytomous weighting* (*e.g.,* 0.8 points for the items measuring Skill A, 1.2 points for each item measuring Skill B, etc.). This can be avoided by simply adding or removing the number of items to each section as necessary to match the test weighting provided by Job Experts, being careful not to have too few items on any given section.

Choosing the type of test items

What type of test items should be included on the test to measure the KSAPCs? Complex? Easy? Difficult? When measuring job knowledge domains, should items be included that measure the difficult, complex, evaluative aspects of the knowledge, or just the simple facts and definitions? The key consideration regarding selecting the type of items for a test is making sure that the KSAPCs are measured in a *relevant* way using items that are appropriately geared to the level of the KSAPC that is required on the job.

One helpful tool for making item type considerations is Bloom's Taxonomy (1956), which can be adopted as a model for developing written test items that measure the intended KSAPC at various levels.

Bloom's Taxonomy for Item Writing		
Level	**Skill Demonstrated**	**Test Item Stem**
1 - Knowledge	Recall factual information	List the three major…
	Knowledge of dates, events, places	Define the four parts of…
	Terminology	What is the definition of…?
	Basic knowledge of major ideas	Which author…?
	Major classifications and categories	Who was responsible for…?
2 - Comprehension	Grasp key meanings	What is the difference between…?
	Apply knowledge to a different context	Which of the following would occur…?
	Infer causation	Summarize the major…
	Compare/contrast	Use the following to estimate…
	Determine sequences	How are these two similar…?
3 - Application	Use information to solve problems	Apply the concept of X to solve for Y…
	Apply methods, theories, or calculations	What are the steps for completing…?
	Diagnose to possible outcomes	Calculate the X of Y…
	Reduce to most plausible best answer	Complete the following by using…
	Analyze within a concrete framework	Which of the following best describes…?
4 - Analysis	Detect patterns	Analyze and determine…
	Comprehend in-depth meanings	Which of the following would not…?
	Evaluate organization of multiple parts	What are the key differences between…?
	Break down complex system into parts	Explain the difference between…
	Diagnose complete systems	What are the key similarities between…?
5 - Synthesis	Make abstractions	Which of the following would occur…?
	Make generalizations from a set of facts	What would be the necessary steps to…?
	Make likely predictions	What would need to be substituted…?
	Draw conclusions based on ideas	Order the following by importance…
	Make logical inferences	How could X be rebuilt if Y…?
6 - Evaluation	Discriminate between theories or ideas	Which of the following is the best…?
	Argue to a conclusion	Rank order the proposed solutions…
	Detect biases or faulty conclusions	Which of the following would…?
	Make critical judgments using inferences	Assess and select the best…
	Diagnose the most effective solutions	What would likely happen if…?

Table 3-1 Bloom's Taxonomy for Item Writing

Test developers can use this Taxonomy (or an abbreviated version) to provide guidance for developing items that are at an appropriate level for the job (considering how the KSAPC is applied on the job – *e.g.,* factual recall, application, analysis, etc.).

Another factor to consider regarding the item type is the format of the item. Common formats include multiple choice, true/false, open-ended, or essay. Multiple choice is perhaps the most common format used for fixed-response items (items with only a limited number of alternatives), and for a good reason. Applicants have a 50% likelihood of guessing the correct answer for true/false items, and only 25% likelihood for multiple choice items with four alternatives (or 20% likelihood for items with five alternatives).

Open-ended and essay formats require subjective scoring, which can be timely and costly. Another drawback with these formats is that another type of unreliability enters into the equation when the tests are scored: inter-scorer reliability. Inter-scorer reliability relates to the consistency between scorers who subjectively grade the tests. While there is nothing wrong with these types of item formats (in fact they are the best item formats to use for the higher level of Bloom's Taxonomy), they will not be discussed further in this text for the reasons stated above.

Step 3: Develop the test content

Test items can be developed by personnel professionals and/or Job Experts. If Job Experts are used, begin at Step 1; if experienced test developers are used, begin at Step 6:

1. Select a panel of 4-10 Job Experts who are truly experts in the content area and are diverse in terms of ethnicity, gender, geography, seniority (use a minimum of one year of experience), and "functional areas" of the target position. Supervisors and trainers can also be included.
2. Review the Selection Plan (see Chapter Two), test plan (see above), and Validation Surveys (discussed below) that will be used to validate the test. This step is critical because the Job Experts should be very well informed regarding the KSAPCs measured by the test (and their affiliated job duties), and the number and types of items to be included on the test.
3. Have each Job Expert review and sign a confidentiality agreement. Along with this agreement, create an atmosphere of confidentiality and request that no documents or notes be taken out of the workshop room. Lock the doors when taking breaks.
4. Conduct a training session on item writing (various guidelines are available for this, including one provided in the TVAP® User Manual included on the Evaluation CD).
5. The training should conclude with an opportunity for Job Experts to write sample test items and then exchange and critique the items using the techniques learned in the training.
6. Write test items following the Selection Plan and test plan. Be sure that item writers reference the Validation Survey that will be used by the validation panel to be sure that the items will address the criteria used by this panel for validating the items. When determining the number of items to write

according to the test plan, double the number of items that are slated for measuring each KSAPC. This is necessary because the validation process will screen out some of the items. Additional items can also be used to replace items that show poor item statistics. A Test Item Form should be used by item writers to record the KSAPC measured, correct answer, textual reference including distractor references (for job knowledge items), and other useful information for each draft item.

7. Have the item writers exchange and critique items, paying careful attention to:

- Grammar, style, and consistency;
- Selection Plan and test plan requirements; and,
- Criteria on the Validation Survey.

8. Do not be afraid to delete a poor item early in the development/validation process. Keep only the best items at this phase in the process.

9. Create a final version of the draft test that is ready for review by the validation panel. This version of the test should include the item, KSAPC measured, correct answer, and textual reference with distractor references (for job knowledge items).

Step 4: Validate the test

Validating a written test requires convening a group of qualified Job Experts (see criteria above for selecting these individuals) and having them review and rate the written test using several factors. Some of these factors include the quality of the test items, fairness, relationship to the job, and proficiency level required. A suggested list of rating questions that can be used is provided below (see the TVAP® software in the Evaluation CD for a Validation Survey that includes these survey questions):

1. Regarding the *quality* of the test item, does it:
   a. Read well? Is it clear and understandable?
   b. Provide sufficient information to answer correctly?
   c. Contain distractors that are similar in difficulty? Distinct? Incorrect, yet plausible? Similar in length? Correctly matching to the stem?
   d. Have an answer key that is correct in all circumstances?[2]
   e. Provide clues to other items on the test?
   f. Ask the question in a way that is free from unnecessary complexities?
   g. Ask the question in a way that is fair to all groups?
2. Regarding the job-relatedness of the item, does it:
   a. Linked to an important or critical KSAPC that is needed the first day of the job?
   b. Linked to an important or critical job duty (Job Experts should identify this using Job Duty numbers from the Job Analysis) (Note: if the KSAPCs measured by the test have been linked to essential Job Duties, this step is not required, but can be helpful).
3. Regarding the proficiency level required for the KSAPC measured by the item, what percent of minimally-qualified applicants would Job Experts

expect to answer this item correctly? (This data can be used for setting validated cutoff scores – see Chapter Eight).
4.   For job knowledge tests:
    a.   Is the item based on current information?
    b.   Does it measure an aspect of job knowledge that must be memorized?
    c.   How serious are the consequences if the applicant does not possess the knowledge required to answer this item correctly?

Validation criteria for test items

There are no firm minimum criteria that specifically apply to any of the key validation factors offered in the Uniform Guidelines or in the professional standards. In fact, it is quite possible to have a written test that could be considered as an "overall valid" selection procedure, but that includes several items that would be rated negatively on the ratings proposed above. However, the goal is to have every item address these criteria.

There are a few seminal court cases that can provide guidance on some of these key validation criteria. Two of these high-level court cases are Contreras v. City of Los Angeles (1981) and U.S. v. South Carolina (1978). Because of the transportable concepts regarding written test validation that have been argued and decided in these cases, they have also been frequently referenced in other cases involving written tests. Because the judges in each of these cases ended up supporting the development and validation work surrounding the tests involved, they are worth discussing briefly here.

In the Contreras case, a three-phase process was used to develop and validate an examination for an Auditor position. In the final validation phase, where the Job Experts were asked to identify a knowledge, skill, or ability that was measured by the test item, a "5 out of 7" rule (71%) was used to screen items for inclusion on the final test. After extensive litigation, the Ninth Circuit approved the validation process of constructing a written test using this process.

In the *South Carolina* case, Job Experts were convened into ten-member panels and asked to provide certain judgments to evaluate whether each item on the tests (which included 19 subtests on a National Teacher Exam used in the state) involved subject matter that was a part of the curriculum at the teacher training institution, and therefore appropriate for testing. These review panels determined that between 63% and 98% of the items on the various tests were content valid and relevant for use in South Carolina. The U.S. Supreme Court endorsed this process as "sufficiently valid."

These two cases provide useful guidance for establishing the minimum thresholds (71% and 63% respectively) necessary for Job Expert endorsement necessary (at least on the job-relatedness questions) for screening test items for inclusion on a final test. It is important to note that in both of these cases at least an "obvious majority" of the Job Experts was required to justify that the items were sufficiently related to the job to be selected for the final test. The TVAP® Software and User Manual in the Evaluation CD include specific criteria that are proposed for each validation standard above, along with rating scales to be used for gathering Job Expert ratings.

Step 5: Score and analyze the test

The important part of progression is breaking down the theoretical into something that the average practitioner can actually use in every day work. It is the intention of this section to achieve this goal. While there is no escaping the fact that test analysis requires the use of advanced statistical tools, some of these can be automated by software tools. Many of them can be completed in common spreadsheet programs. The purpose of this section is to equip the reader with a basic knowledge regarding some of the fundamental, essential components of test analysis, and (most importantly) *interpretation rules* that can be applied to look for problem areas. Most of the test analysis concepts and functions discussed below are included in the TVAP® Software on the Evaluation CD.

Classical test analysis[3] (conducted after a test has been administered) can be broken down into two primary categories: item-level analyses and test-level analyses. Item-level analyses investigate the statistical properties of each item as they relate to other items and to the overall test. Test-level analyses focus on how the test is working at an overall level. Because the trees make up the forest, the item-level analyses will be reviewed first.

Item-level analyses

While there are numerous item analysis techniques available, only three of the most essential are reviewed here: Item-test correlations (called "point biserial" correlations), item difficulty, and Differential Item Functioning (DIF). Item *discrimination indices* are also useful for conducting item-level analyses, but are not discussed in this text.

Point biserials: Point biserial calculations result in values between -1.0 and +1.0 that reveal the correlation between the item and the overall test score. Items that have negative values are typically either poor items (with respect to what they are measuring or how they are worded, or both) or are good items that are simply mis-keyed. Values between 0.0 and +0.2 indicate that the item is functioning somewhat effectively, but is not contributing to the overall reliability of the test in a meaningful way. Values of +0.2 and higher indicate that the item is functioning in an effective way, and is contributing to the overall reliability of the test. For this reason, the single best way to increase the reliability of the overall test is to remove items with low (or negative) point biserials.

The point biserial of a test item can be calculated by simply correlating the applicant scores on the test item (coded 0 for incorrect, 1 for correct) to the total scores for each applicant on the overall test used the = PEARSON formula in Microsoft® Excel®. When the total number of items on the test is fewer than 30, a corrected version of this calculation can be done by removing the score of each item from the total score calculation (*e.g.*, when calculating a point biserial for item 1, correlate item 1 to the total score on the test using items 2-30; for item 2, include only items 1 and 3-30 for the total score).

Item difficulty: Item difficulties show the percentage of applicants who answered the item correctly. Items that are excessively difficult or easy (where a very high proportion of test takers are either missing the item or answering it correctly) are typically the items that do not contribute significantly to the overall reliability of the test, and should be considered for removal. Typically, items that provide the highest contribution to the overall reliability of the test are in the mid-range of difficulty (*e.g.,* 40% to 60%).

Differential Item Functioning (DIF): DIF analyses detect items that are not functioning in similar ways between the focal and reference groups. The Standards (1999), explain that DIF "…occurs when different groups of applicants with similar overall ability, or similar status on an appropriate criterion, have, on average, systematically different responses to a particular item" (p. 13). In some instances, DIF analyses can reveal items that are biased against certain groups (test bias can be defined as any quality of the test item, or the test, that offends or unnecessarily penalizes the applicants on the basis of personal characteristics such as ethnicity, gender, etc.).

It should be noted that there is a very significant difference between simply reviewing the *average item score differences* between groups (*e.g.,* men and women) and DIF analyses. One might be tempted to simply evaluate the proportion of men who answered the item correctly (say 80%) versus the proportion of women (say 60%) and then note the size of the difference (20%) when compared to other items on the test with more or less spread between groups.

What is wrong with this approach? There is one major flaw: it fails to take group ability levels into account. What if men simply have a 20% higher ability level than women on the KSAPC measured by the test? Does this make the test, or the items with this level of difference "unfair" or "biased." Certainly not. In fact, this "simple difference" approach was used in one court case, but received an outcry of disagreement from the professional testing community.

The case was <u>Golden Rule Life Insurance Company v. Mathias</u> (1980) and involved the Educational Testing Service (ETS) and the Illinois Insurance Licensure Examination. In a consent decree related to this case, the parties agreed that test items could be divided into categories (and some items removed) based only on black-white average item score differences on individual items. This practice did not consider or statistically control for the overall ability differences between groups on the test, and was subsequently abandoned after the president of ETS renounced the practice, stating:

> . . . the practice was a mistake . . . it has been used to justify legislative proposals that go far beyond the very limited terms of the original agreement . . . We recognized that the settlement compromise was not based on an appropriate 'bias prevention' methodology for tests generally. What was to become known as the 'Golden Rule' procedure is based on the premise – which ETS did not and does not share – that group differences in performance on test questions primarily are caused by 'bias.' The procedure ignores the possibility that differences in performance may validly reflect real differences in knowledge or skill (Anrig, 1987).

The criteria used in the Golden Rule case also sparked dissention in the professional testing community:

> The final settlement of the case was based on a comparison of group differences in sheer percentage of persons passing an item, with no effort to equate groups in any measure of the ability the test was designed to assess, nor any consideration of the validity of items for the intended purpose of the test. The decision was clearly in complete violation of the concept of differential item functioning and would be likely to eliminate the very items that were the best predictors of job performance (Anastasi, 1997).

So, it is safe to say that the professional testing community sufficiently rebuked the idea of just simply comparing group differences on items or tests overall. This is precisely where DIF analyses provide a significant contribution to test analyses. Because DIF analyses are different than simple average item score differences between groups and take *overall group ability* into consideration when detecting potentially bias items, some courts have specifically approved of using DIF analyses for the review and refinement of personnel tests.[4]

Because DIF analyses function in this way, it is possible that even if 20% of minority group members could answer a particular item correctly and 50% of the whites could answer the item correctly (a large, 30% score gap between the two groups) the item might still escape a "DIF" designation. A DIF designation, however, would occur if the minority group and whites scored closely overall as a group (for example, 55% and 60% respectively), but scored so divergently on the test item.

Consider a 50-item word problem test that measured basic math skills. Assume it was administered to 100 men and 100 women, and that the men and women scored about equally overall on the test (*i.e.*, their overall averages were about the same). Forty-nine (49) of the 50 items measure math skills using common, every-day situations encountered by men and women alike. One of the items, however, measures math skills using a football example:

> You are the quarterback on a football team. It is 4th down with 11 yards to go and you are on your own 41-yard line. You were about to throw a 30-yard pass to a receiver who would have been tackled immediately, but instead you were sacked on the 32-yard line. What is the difference between the yardage that you could have gained (had your pass been caught) versus how much you actually lost?

Does this test item measure some level of basic math? Yes, however, to arrive at the correct answer (39 yards), a test taker needs to use *both* math skills and football knowledge. Unless football knowledge is related to the job for which this test is being used, this item would probably show bias (via the DIF analysis) against individuals who are not familiar with football.

There are numerous methodologies available for conducting DIF analyses. These methods vary in statistical power (*i.e.*, the ability to detect a DIF item should it exist), calculation complexity, and sample size requirements. Perhaps the most widely used method is known as the Mantel-Haenszel method, which is known as one of the more robust and classical methods for evaluating DIF.[5]

DIF analyses, because they rely heavily on inferential statistics, are very dependent on sample size. As such, items flagged as DIF based on large sample sizes (*e.g.,* more than 500 applicants) are more reliable than those based on small sample sizes (*e.g.,* less than 100 or so). While the testing literature provides various suggestions and guidelines for sample size requirements for these types of analyses,[6] a good baseline number of test takers for conducting DIF analyses is more than 200 applicants in the reference group (whites or men) and at least 30 in the focal group (*i.e.,* the minority group of interest).

DIF analyses provide the most accurate results on tests that measure the *same* or *highly related* KSAPCs (*i.e.,* tests with high reliability). For example, if a 50-item test contains 25 items measuring math skills and 25 items measuring interpersonal abilities and, because these two test areas might not be highly inter-related, the test has low reliability, DIF analyses on such a test would be unreliable and possibly inaccurate. In these circumstances, it would be best to separate the two test areas and conduct separate DIF analyses.

Most DIF analyses (including the analysis used in the TVAP® Software on the Evaluation CD), output standardized statistical values that can be used to assess varying degrees of DIF (sometimes called Z values). For example, a test item with a Z value of 1.5 would constitute a lesser degree of DIF than a Z value of 3.0, etc.

When should test items be removed based on DIF analyses? There is no firm set of rules for removing items based on DIF analyses, so this practice should be approached with caution. Before removing any item from the test based on DIF analyses, the following considerations should be made:

- The level of DIF: The minimum level of DIF that should be considered "meaningful" is a Z value of 1.645 (such values are statistically significant at the .10 level). Values exceeding 2.58 (significant at the .01 level) are even more substantial. Items that have DIF levels that exceed this value should be more closely scrutinized than items with lower levels of DIF. Items that have only marginal levels of DIF should be carefully evaluated in subsequent test administrations.

- The point biserial of the item: If the item has a very high point biserial (*e.g.,* .30 or higher), but is flagged as DIF, one should be cautious before removing the item. Items with high point biserials contribute to the overall reliability of the test, and if removing the item based on a DIF analysis significantly lowers the reliability of the test, the psychometric quality of the test will be decreased.

- The item-criterion correlation (if available): If the test is based on a criterion-related validity study (where test scores have been statistically related to job performance), evaluate the correlation between the particular item and the measure of job performance. For example, assume a test consisting of 30 items that has an overall correlation to job performance of .30. Then consider that one of these items is flagged as DIF when administered to an applicant pool of several hundred applicants, and this specific item has a 0 (or perhaps even a negative) correlation with job performance when evaluated based on the original validation study. Such an item may be a candidate for removal (when considered along with the other guidelines herein).[7]

- Qualitative reasons why the item could be flagged as DIF: Items that are sometimes flagged as DIF contain certain words, phrases, or comparisons that require culturally- or group-loaded content or knowledge (which is unrelated to the KSAPC of interest) to provide an adequate response (see the football-based math test item example above). It is sometimes useful to evaluate the item alternative that the DIF group selected over the majority group (*e.g.,* if one group selected option A with high frequency and the other option C).

- The Job Expert validation ratings for the item: Is the specific aspect of the KSAPC measured by the item (not just the general KSAPC to which the item is linked) necessary for the job? Did this item receive clear, positive validation ratings from the Job Expert panel? If the item had an unusual number of red flags when compared to the other items that were included on the test, it may be a candidate for removal.

- The DIF values "for" *or* "against" other groups: If an item shows high levels of DIF against one group, but "reverse DIF" for another group, caution should be used before removing the item. However, if the group showing the high levels of DIF is based on a much larger sample size than the group with reverse DIF, a greater weight should be given to the group with the larger sample size.

- How groups scored on the subscales of the test: DIF analyses assume that the test is measuring a single attribute or dimension (or multiple dimensions that are highly correlated). However, sometimes groups score differently on various subscales on a test, and these differences can be the reason that items are flagged DIF (*i.e.,* rather than the item itself being DIF against the group, it may only be flagged as DIF because it is part of a subscale on which subgroups significantly differ). For example, consider a test with the following characteristics: high overall internal consistency (reliability of .90), and two subscales: Scale A and Scale B. Assume that the average score for men is 65% on Scale A, 75% on Scale B, and 70% overall. The average score for Women is score 70% overall, but they have opposite scale scores compared to men (75% on Scale A and 65% on Scale B). Then assume that a DIF analysis with all items included showed that one item on Scale B was DIF against women. In this case, it would be useful to remove all items from Scale A and re-run the DIF analysis with only Scale B items included to determine if the item was still DIF against women. This process effectively controls for the advantage that women had on the overall test because of their higher score on Scale A.

Test-level analyses

There are essentially two types of overall, test-level analyses: descriptive and psychometric. Descriptive analyses pertain to the overall statistical characteristics of the test, such as the average (mean), dispersion of scores (standard deviation), and others. The psychometric analyses evaluate whether the test is working effectively (e.g., test reliability). Each of these is discussed below.

Descriptive test analyses: The two primary descriptive types of test analyses are the mean (mathematical average) and standard deviation (average dispersion – or spread – of the test scores around the mean). Only a very brief mention of these two concepts will be provided here.

The test mean shows the average score level of the applicants who took the test. Note that this does not have any bearing whatsoever on whether the applicant pool is qualified (at least the mean by itself does not). While the mean can be a useful statistic for evaluating the overall test results, it should be given less consideration when evaluating mastery-based or certification/licensing tests (because certain score levels are needed for passing the test, irrespective of the fluctuation in score averages based on various applicant groups).

The standard deviation of the test is a statistical unit showing the average score dispersion of the overall test scores, and is also useful for understanding the characteristics of the applicant pool. Typically, 68% of applicant scores will be contained within one standard deviation above and below the test mean, 95% will be contained within two, and 99% within three. The standard deviation can be used to evaluate whether the applicants, as a whole, are scoring too high or low on the test (hence the test is losing out on valuable information about test takers because they are magnetized to one extreme of the distribution).

The mean and standard deviation are sometimes inappropriately used for setting cutoff scores.[8] Test developers are encouraged to use these two statistics for mostly informative, rather than instructive, purposes.

Psychometric analyses: Like item-level analyses, numerous analyses can be done to evaluate the quality of the overall test. This discussion will be limited to the most frequently used, essential analyses for written tests, which include common forms of test reliability and the Standard Error of Measurement (SEM). Two other advanced psychometric concepts that pertain mostly to mastery-based tests (tests used with a pass/fail cutoff based on a pre-set level of proficiency required for the job) will also be discussed at the end of this section: Decision Consistency Reliability (DCR) and Kappa Coefficients.

Test reliability

Test reliability pertains to the consistency of applicant scores. A highly reliable test is one that measures a one-dimensional or inter-related KSAPC in a consistent way. There are several factors that can have a significant impact on the reliability of a written test, however, the most important factor is whether the items on the test "hang together" statistically. The items on a test need to be highly inter-correlated for a test to have high overall reliability. The Uniform Guidelines and professional standards provide no minimum thresholds for what constitutes acceptable levels of reliability. The U.S. Department of Labor (2000, p. 3-3), has provided some general guidelines.

Guidelines for Interpreting Test Reliability	
Reliability Value	**Interpretation**
.90 and up	Excellent
.80 - .89	Good
.70 - .79	Adequate
Below .70	May have limited applicability

Table 3-2 Guidelines for Interpreting Test Reliability

Perhaps the most common type of reliability analysis used for written tests is Cronbach's Alpha. This method is widely used by statistical and psychometric software because it provides a highly accurate measure regarding the *consistency* of applicant scores. The Kuder-Richardson 20 (KR-20) formula is very similar to the Cronbach's Alpha, but can be used for dichotomously-scored items only (*i.e.,* items that have only two possible outcomes: correct or incorrect). Cronbach's Alpha, however, can be used for polytomous items (*i.e.,* items that have more than one point value).

The Kuder-Richardson 21 (KR-21) formula is another method for evaluating the overall consistency of the test. It is typically more conservative than Cronbach's Alpha, and is calculated by considering only each applicant's total score (whereas the Cronbach's Alpha method takes item-level data into consideration).

Standard Error of Measurement (SEM)

To a certain extent, test reliability exists so that the Standard Error of Measurement (SEM) can be calculated. The two go hand-in-hand. The (traditional) SEM can be easily calculated by multiplying the Standard Deviation of the test by the square root of one minus the reliability of the test. This can be calculated in Microsoft® Excel® as: = SD*(SQRT(1-Reliability)), where *SD* is the standard deviation of applicant overall test scores and *Reliability* is the test reliability (using Cronbach's Alpha, KR-20, or the KR-21 formula, etc.).

The SEM provides a *confidence interval* of an applicant's "true score" around their "obtained score." An applicant's true score represents their true, actual ability level on the overall test, whereas an applicant's obtained score represents the score that they "just happened to obtain on the day the test was given." SEMs help testing professionals understand that if the applicant *as much as sneezes* during a hypothetical second test administration of an equally difficult test, their score could be lower than obtained on the first administration. Likewise, if the applicant had a better night's sleep for the second administration, their score would possibly be higher than the first administration.

How this concept translates into testing is relatively straightforward. After the SEM has been calculated, it can be used *to install boundaries for where each applicant's true abilities lie on the test.* Assume the SEM for a written test is 3.0. This means that an applicant who scores 50 on the test most likely (with 68% confidence) has a "true score" on the test ranging between 47 and 53 (1 SEM, or 3.0 points, above and below their obtained score). Using 2 SEMs (or 6 points above and below their obtained score) provides a 95% likelihood of including a score that represents their true ability level. Using 3 SEMs provides 99% confidence.

There is one small limitation with the traditional SEM discussed above (the one calculated using the formula above). This limitation is due to the fact that a test's reliability typically changes throughout the distribution. In other words, the reliability of the highest scorers on the test is sometimes different than the average, and from the lowest scorers. This is where the *Conditional SEM* comes in.

Conditional Standard Error of Measurement

The Standards (1999) require the consideration of the Conditional Standard Error of Measurement when setting cutoff scores (as opposed to the traditional Standard Error of Measurement) (see pages 27, 29, 30 and Standard 2.2, 2.14, and 2.15 of the Standards).

The traditional SEM represents the standard deviation of an applicant's true score (the score that represents the applicant's actual ability level) around his or her obtained (or actual) score. The traditional SEM considers the *entire range of test scores* when calculated. Because the traditional SEM considers the entire range of scores, its accuracy and relevance are limited when evaluating the reliability and consistency of test scores within a certain range of the score distribution.

Most test score distributions have scores bunched in the middle and spread out through the low and high range of the distribution. Those applicants who score in the lowest range of the distribution lower the overall test reliability (hence affecting the size of the SEM) by adding chance variance caused by guessing and not by possessing levels of the measured KSAPC that are high enough to contribute to the true score variance of the test. High scorers can also lower the overall reliability (and similarly affect the size of the SEM) because high-scoring applicants possess exceedingly high levels of the KSAPC being measured, which can also reduce the true variance included in the test score range. Figure 3-1 shows how the SEM is not constant throughout a score distribution (this chart is derived from data provided in Lord, 1984).

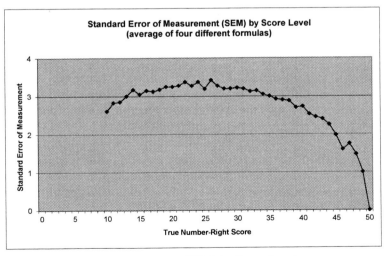

Figure 3-1 Standard Error of Measurement (SEM) by Score Level

Because the SEM considers the *average reliability* of scores throughout the *entire range* of scores, it is less precise when considering the scores of a particular section of the score distribution. When tests are used for human resource decisions, the entire score range is almost never the central concern. Typically in human resource settings, only a certain range of scores are considered (*i.e.*, those scores at or near the cutoff score, or the scores that will be included in a banding or ranking procedure).

The Conditional SEM attempts to avoid the limitations of the SEM by considering only the *score range of interest* when calculating its value. By only considering the scores around the critical score value, the Conditional SEM is the most accurate estimate of the reliability dynamics of the test that exist around the critical score.

In addition to the psychometric reasons behind the curved slope of the Conditional SEM (as displayed by Figure 3-1), there are intuitive reasons behind the phenomena. A person who obtains a "perfect" or "near-perfect score" (95% - 100%) on a multiple-choice knowledge test will almost always repeat such a score if retested. Their high ability level will almost always be reflected on the test, because their "true score" is naturally very high. Such a person has a very tight level of precision around their score and will likely repeat such a score if the test were hypothetically administered numerous times. However, someone who scores in the middle of a distribution knows some concepts measured by the test, but not others. If this person repeatedly takes the test, a greater degree of score variation will occur. This person's score will be marked by some guessing, some concepts they do not know well, some they do know well, and some concepts they know very well. The person who scores low on the test (at or slightly above the "chance score" of the test that could be obtained by merely guessing) would hypothetically repeat scores on the test that vary widely, with some total scores being more lucky than others, but with every total score being driven more by chance than true ability level.

These three hypothetical examples – the high scoring, middle scoring, and low scoring test takers – reflect why the Conditional SEM is smallest in the high score range, moderately-sized in the mid-test range, and typically largest in the lowest parts of the score distribution.

Several methods are available for calculating the Conditional SEM. The recommended procedure is described in Appendix B.

Psychometric analyses for mastery-based tests
Tests that require pre-determined levels of proficiency that are based on some job-related requirements are mastery-based tests. Mastery-based tests are used to classify applicants as "masters" or "non-masters," or those who "have enough competency" or "do not have enough competency" with respect to the KSAPCs being measured by the test (see Chapter Two) and Standard 14.15 of the Standards (1999). Two helpful statistics for mastery-based tests are Decision Consistency reliability (DCR) and Kappa Coefficients.

Decision Consistency Reliability (DCR): DCR is perhaps the most important type of reliability to consider when interpreting reliability and cutoff score effectiveness for mastery-based tests. DCR attempts to answer the following question regarding a mastery-level cutoff on a test: "If the test was hypothetically administered to the same group of applicants a second time, how *consistently* would the applicants who passed the first time (classified as 'masters') pass the test again if they took it a second time?"

Similarly, DCR attempts to answer: "How consistently would the applicants who *failed* the test the first time (classified as 'non-masters') fail the test if they took it a second time?" This type of reliability is different than internal consistency reliability (*e.g.,* Cronbach's Alpha, KR-21), which considers the consistency of the test internally, without respect to the consistency with which the cutoff classifies applicants as masters and non-masters.

One very important characteristic about DCR reliability is that it is inherently different than the other forms of reliability discussed above (*i.e.,* Cronbach's Alpha, KR-20, KR-21). Because DCR pertains to the consistency of classification of the test, which is an *action* of the test (rather than an *internal characteristic* of the test which is what the other reliability types reveal), its value cannot be used in the classical SEM formula.

Calculating DCR is beyond the built-in commands available in most spreadsheet programs, but can be calculated using the methods described in Subkoviak (1988) and Peng & Subkoviak (1980). (The TVAP® Software in the Evaluation CD includes these calculations built into Microsoft® Excel® using calculations and embedded programming.) DCR values between .75 and .84 can be considered "limited"; values between .85 and .90 considered "good"; and values higher than .90 considered "excellent" (Subkoviak, 1988).

Kappa Coefficients: A Kappa Coefficient explains how consistently the test classifies "masters" and "non-masters" beyond what could be expected by chance. This is essentially a measure of utility for the test. Calculating Kappa Coefficients also requires advanced statistical software or programming. For mastery-based tests, Kappa Coefficients exceeding .31 indicate adequate levels of effectiveness, and levels of .42 and higher are good (Subkoviak, 1988).

Steps for Developing a Content Valid Job Knowledge Written Test

By Stacy L. Bell, M.S.

Job knowledge can be defined as, "...the cumulation of facts, principles, concepts and other pieces of information that are considered important in the performance of one's job" (Dye, Reck, & McDaniel, 1993, p. 153).[9] As applied to written tests in the personnel setting, knowledge can be categorized as: *declarative knowledge* – knowledge of technical information; or *procedural knowledge* – knowledge of the processes and judgmental criteria required to perform correctly and efficiently on the job (Hunter, 1984; Dye et al., 1993).[10]

    While job knowledge is not typically critical for many entry-level positions, it clearly has its place in many supervisory positions where having a command of certain knowledge areas is essential for job performance. For example, if a Fire Captain, responsible for instructing firefighters who have been deployed to extinguish a house fire, does not possess a mastery-level of knowledge required for the task, the safety of the firefighters and the public could be in jeopardy. It is not feasible to require a Fire Captain in this position to refer to textbooks and determine the best course of action, but rather he or she must have the particular knowledge memorized.

    As described previously in this Chapter, there are a variety of steps that should be followed to ensure that a job knowledge written test is developed and utilized properly. Depending upon the size and type of the employer, they may be faced with litigation from the EEOC, the DOJ, the OFCCP (under DOL), or a private plaintiff attorney. Each year, employers accused of utilizing tests that have adverse impact spend millions of dollars defending litigated promotional processes.[11]

    An unlawful employment practice based on adverse impact may be established by an employee under the 1991 Civil Rights Act only if:

> A(i) a complaining party demonstrates that a respondent uses a particular employment practice that causes a disparate impact on the basis of race, color, religion, sex, or national origin, and the respondent fails to demonstrate that the challenged practice is job-related for the position in question and consistent with business necessity; or,

> A(ii) the complaining party makes the demonstration described in subparagraph (C) with respect to an alternate employment practice, and the respondent refuses to adopt such alternative employment practice (Section 2000e-2[k][1][A])

    In litigation settings, addressing these standards is typically conducted by completing a validation study (using any of the acceptable types of validity). This section outlines seven steps for developing a job-related and court-defensible process for creating a *content*-valid, job knowledge, written test used for hiring or promoting employees.

The seven steps below are designed to address the essential requirements based on the Uniform Guidelines (1978), the Principles (2003), and the Standards (1999) [12]:

1. Conduct a job analysis;
2. Develop a selection plan;
3. Identify test plan goals;
4. Develop the test content;
5. Validate the test;
6. Compile the test; and,
7. Conduct post-administration analyses.

Step 1: Conduct a job analysis

The foundational requirement for developing a content-valid, job knowledge written test is a current and thorough job analysis for the target position. Brief 1-2 page "job descriptions" are almost never sufficient for showing validation under the Uniform Guidelines unless, at a bare minimum, they include:

- Job Expert input and/or review;
- Job duties and KSAPCs that are essential for the job;
- Operationally defined KSAPCs.

In practice, where validity is required, updated job analyses typically need to be developed. Ideally, creating a Uniform Guidelines-style job analysis would include the following ratings for **job duties** (see Chapter Two for a complete discussion on completing job analyses).

Frequency (Uniform Guidelines, Section 15B3; 14D4) [13]
This duty is performed *(Select one option from below)* by me or other active (<u>target position</u>) in my department.

1. **annually** or less often
2. **semi-annually** (approx. 2 times/year)
3. **quarterly** (approx. 4 times/year)
4. **monthly** (approx. 1 time/month)
5. **bi-weekly** (approx. every 2 weeks)
6. **weekly** (approx. 1 time/week)
7. **semi-weekly** (approx. 2 to 6 times/week)
8. **daily/infrequently** (approx. 1 to 6 times/day)
9. **daily/frequently** (approx. 7 or more times/day)

Importance (Uniform Guidelines, Section 14C1, 2, 4; 14D2, 3; 15C3, 4, 5; 15D3)
Competent performance of this duty is *(Select one option from below)* for the job of (<u>target position</u>) in my department.

1. **not important: Minor** significance to the performance of the job.

2. **of some importance: Somewhat useful and/or** meaningful to the performance of the job.
   - Improper performance may result in slight negative consequences
3. **important: Useful and/or meaningful** to the performance of the job.
   - Improper performance may result in **moderate** negative consequences
4. **critical: Necessary** for the performance of the job.
   - Improper performance may result in **serious** negative consequences
5. **very critical: Necessary** for the performance of the job, and with more extreme consequences.
   - Improper performance may result in **very serious** negative consequences

Ideally, creating a Uniform Guidelines-style job analysis requires that each **KSAPC** has the following ratings:

Frequency (Uniform Guidelines, Section 15B3; 14D4) [16]
This KSAPC is performed *(Select one option from below)* by me or other active (target position) in my department.

1. **annually** or less often
2. **semi-annually** (approx. 2 times/year)
3. **quarterly** (approx. 4 times/year)
4. **monthly** (approx. 1 time/month)
5. **bi-weekly** (approx. every 2 weeks)
6. **weekly** (approx. 1 time/week)
7. **semi-weekly** (approx. 2 to 6 times/week)
8. **daily/infrequently** (approx. 1 to 6 times/day)
9. **daily/frequently** (approx. 7 or more times/day)

Importance (Uniform Guidelines, Section 14C1, 2, 4; 14D2, 3; 15C3, 4, 5; 15D3)
This KSAPC is *(Select one option from below)* for the job of (target position) in my department.

1. **not important: Minor** significance to the performance of the job.
2. **of some importance: Somewhat useful and/or** meaningful to the performance of the job.
   - Not possessing adequate levels of this KSAPC may result in **slight** negative consequences
3. **important: Useful and/or meaningful** to the performance of the job.
   - Not possessing adequate levels of this KSAPC may result in **moderate** negative consequences
4. **critical: Necessary** for the performance of the job.
   - Not possessing adequate levels of this KSAPC may result in **serious** negative consequences

5. **very critical: Necessary** for the performance of the job, and with more extreme consequences
   - Not possessing adequate levels of this KSAPC may result in **very serious** negative consequences

Differentiating "Best Worker" Ratings (Uniform Guidelines, Section 14C9)
Possessing above-minimum levels of this KSAPC makes *(Select one option from below)* difference in <u>overall</u> job performance.

1. no
2. little
3. some
4. a significant
5. a very significant

Note: Obtaining ratings on the "Best Worker" scale is not necessary if the job knowledge written test will be used only on a pass/fail basis (rather than ranking final test results).

When Needed (Uniform Guidelines, Section 5F; 14C1)
Possessing *(Select one option from below)* of this KSAPC is needed <u>upon entry to the job</u> for the (<u>target position</u>) position in your department.

1. none or very little
2. some (less than half)
3. most (more than half)
4. all or almost all

In addition to these four KSAPC rating scales, it is recommended that a **mastery level** scale be used when validating written job knowledge tests. The data from these ratings are useful for choosing the job knowledges that should be included in a written job knowledge test, and are useful for addressing Section 14C4 of the Uniform Guidelines, which require that job knowledges measured on a test be ". . . operationally defined as that body of learned information which is used in and is a necessary prerequisite for observable aspects of work behavior of the job." It is recommended to use an average rating threshold of 3.0 on the mastery-level scale for selecting which job knowledges to include on job knowledge tests. A sample mastery level scale is listed below:

Mastery Level (Uniform Guidelines, Section 14C4)
A *(Select one option from below)* level of this job knowledge is necessary for successful job performance.

1 - **low**: none or only a few general concepts or specifics available in memory in none or only a few circumstances without referencing materials or asking questions.

2 - **familiarity**: have <u>some</u> general concepts and <u>some</u> specifics available in memory in <u>some</u> circumstances without referencing materials or asking questions.

3 - **working knowledge**: have <u>most</u> general concepts and <u>most</u> specifics available in memory in <u>most</u> circumstances without referencing materials or asking questions.

4 - **mastery**: have <u>almost all</u> general concepts and <u>almost all</u> specifics available in memory in <u>almost all</u> circumstances without referencing materials or asking questions.

Finally, a duty/KSAPC **linkage scale** should be used to ensure that the KSAPCs are necessary to the performance of important job duties. A sample duty/KSAPC linkage scale is provided below:

Duty/KSAPC Linkages (Uniform Guidelines, Section 14C4)
This KSAPC is _____ to the performance of this duty.

1. not important
2. of minor importance
3. important
4. of major importance
5. critically important

When Job Experts identify KSAPCs necessary for the job, it is helpful if they are written in a way that maximizes the likelihood of job duty linkages. When KSAPCs fail to provide enough content to link to job duties, their inclusion in a job analysis is limited. Listed below are examples of a poorly written and a well written KSAPC from a firefighter job analysis:

Example of a **poorly-written** KSAPC:

Knowledge of ventilation practices.

Example of a **well-written** KSAPC:

Knowledge of ventilation practices and techniques to release contained heat, smoke, and gases in order to enter a building. Includes application of appropriate fire suppression techniques and equipment (including manual and power tools and ventilation fans).

Step 2: Develop A Selection Plan
The first step in developing a selection plan is to review the KSAPCs from the job analysis and design a plan for measuring the essential KSAPCs using various selection

procedures (particularly, knowledge areas). Refer to the Selection Plan section in Chapter Two for specific criteria for selecting KSAPCs for the selection process. At a minimum, the knowledge areas selected for the test should be important, necessary on the first day of the job, required at some level of mastery (rather than easily looked up without hindrance on the job), and appropriately measured using a written test format. Job knowledges that meet these criteria are selected for inclusion in the "Test Plan" below.

Step 3: Identify Test Plan Goals

Once the KSAPCs which will be measured on the test have been identified, the test sources relevant for the knowledges should be identified. Review relevant job-related materials and discuss the target job in considerable detail with Job Experts. This will focus attention on job specific information for the job under analysis. Review the knowledges that meet the necessary criteria and determine which sources and/or textbooks are best suited to measure the various knowledges. It is imperative that the selected sources do not contradict one another in content.

Once the test sources have been identified, determine whether or not preparatory materials will be offered to the applicants. If preparatory materials are used, ensure that the materials are current, specific, and released to all applicants taking the test. In addition to preparatory materials, determine if preparatory sessions will be offered to the applicants.

Use of preparatory sessions appears to be beneficial to both minority and non-minority applicants, although they do not consistently reduce adverse impact (Sackett, Schmitt, Ellingson, & Kabin, 2001).[14] If study sessions are conducted, make every attempt to schedule study sessions at a location that is geographically convenient to all applicants and is offered at a reasonable time of day. Invite all applicants to attend and provide plenty of notice of the date and time.

Following the identification of the knowledge areas and source materials that will be used to develop the job knowledge written test, identify the number of test items that will be included on the test. Be sure to include enough items to ensure high test reliability. Typically, job knowledge tests that are made up of similar job knowledge domains will generate reliability levels in the high .80s to the low .90s when they include 80 items or more.

Consider using Job Expert input to determine *internal weights* for the written test. Provide Job Experts with the list of knowledges to be measured and ask experts to distribute 100 points among the knowledges to obtain a balanced written test. See Table 3-3 for a sample of a knowledge weighting survey used to develop a written test used for certifying firefighters (this type of test would be used by fire departments that hire only pre-trained firefighters into entry-level positions).

Firefighter Certification Test Development Survey	
Job Expert Name: _____ **Date:**	
Instructions: Assume that you have $100 to "buy" the perfect firefighter for your department (based only on job knowledge qualifications - assume other important areas such as physical abilities and interpersonal skills have already been tested). How much money would you spend in the following areas to ensure that you have bought the most qualified firefighter for your department? Be sure that your allocations equal exactly $100.	
Knowledge Sources to Choose From	**Amount of Dollars You Would Spend to "Buy" the Perfect Firefighter**
Pumping Apparatus Driver/Operator Handbook (1st ed.)	
Principles of Vehicle Extrication (2nd ed.)	
Fire Department Company Officer (3rd ed.)	
Fire and Emergency Services Instructor (6th ed.)	
Aerial Apparatus Driver/Operator Handbook (1st ed.)	
Essentials of Firefighting (4th ed.)	
Rapid Intervention Teams	
The Source Book for Fire Company Training Evolutions (92nd ed.)	
Fire Inspection and Code Enforcement (6th ed.)	
Hazardous Materials (2nd ed.)	
Ability to Compute Hydraulic Equations	
TOTAL (must equal $100)	

Table 3-3 Firefighter Certification Test Development Survey

Attempt to obtain *adequate sampling* of the various knowledges and ensure that there are a sufficient number of items developed to effectively measure each knowledge at the desired level. Note that some knowledges will require more items than others for making a "sufficiently deep" assessment. The test should be internally weighted in a way that ensures a sufficient measurement of the relevant knowledge areas.

Following the determination of the length of the test and the number of items to be derived from each source, determine the *types* of items that will be included on the test. One helpful tool is a process-by-content matrix to ensure adequate sampling of job knowledge content areas and problem-solving processes. Problem-solving levels include:

- *Knowledge* of terminology
- *Understanding* of principles
- *Application* of knowledge to new situations

While knowledge of terminology is important, the *understanding* and *application* of principles may be considered of primary importance. The job knowledge written test should include test items that ensure the applicants can define important terms related to the job *and* apply their knowledge to answer more complex questions. Job Experts should consider how the knowledge is applied on the job (*e.g.,* factual recall, application, etc.) when determining the types of items to be included on the final test form (see Table 3-4 for a sample process-by-content matrix for a police sergeant written test).

Process-by-Content Matrix: Police Sergeant				
Source	Definition	Principle	Application	Total
1. Essentials of Modern Police Work	4	10	20	34
2. Community Policing	3	7	13	23
3. Rules of Evidence	3	10	17	30
4. Department Rules & Regulations	1	3	6	10
5. State Criminal Code	4	5	9	18
6. State Vehicle Code	4	6	10	20
7. City Ordinances	2	2	6	10
8. Performance Appraisal Guidelines	0	1	1	2
9. Labor Agreement with the City	0	1	2	3
Total	21	45	84	150

Table 3-4 Process-by-Content Matrix: Police Sergeant

Step 4: Develop the Test Content

After the number and types of test items to be developed has been determined, select a diverse panel of four to ten Job Experts (who have a <u>minimum</u> of one year experience) to review the test plan to ensure compliance with the parameters. Have each Job Expert sign a "Confidentiality Form." If the Job Experts are going to write the test items, provide item-writing training (see Attachment C in the TVAP® User Manual on the Evaluation CD for item-writing guidelines) and have Job Experts peer review the items.

Once the Job Experts have written the items to be included in the test bank, ensure proper grammar, style, and consistency. Additionally, make certain that the test plan requirements are met. Ensure that the items address the criteria on the TVAP Survey (see the Evaluation CD for the TVAP Software and corresponding survey for rating/validating test items). Assume that 20-30% of the test items will not meet the requirements of the TVAP Survey and account for this attrition by developing a surplus of test items. Once the bank of test items has been created, provide the final test version to the panel of Job Experts for the validation process (the next step).

Step 5: Validate The Test

Use the TVAP Survey to have Job Experts assign various ratings to the items in the test bank. Additionally, have the Job Experts identify an appropriate time limit. A common rule-of-thumb used by practitioners to determine a written test cutoff time is to allow one minute per test item plus thirty additional minutes (*e.g.,* a 150-item test would yield a three hour time limit).[15] A reasonable time limit would allow for at least 95% of the applicants to complete the test within the time limit.

Step 6: Compile The Test

Evaluate the Job Expert ratings on the TVAP Survey and discard those items that do not meet the criteria (see TVAP User Manual). Once the Job Experts have assigned the various ratings to each of the test items, analyze the "Angoff" ratings identified by Job Experts. Discard raters whose ratings are statistically different from other raters by evaluating rater reliability and high/low rater bias. Calculate the difficulty level of the test (called the *pre-administration cutoff percentage*).

Step 7: Post-Administration Analyses

Following the administration of the job knowledge written test, conduct an item-level analysis of the test results to evaluate the item-level qualities (such as the point-biserial, difficulty level, and Differential Item Functioning [DIF] of each item). Use the guidelines in Chapter Three for deciding which items to keep or remove for this administration (or improve for later administrations). In addition to the guidelines proposed in Chapter Three for evaluating when to discard an item due to DIF, consider the following excerpt from Hearn v. City of Jackson (Aug. 7, 2003)[14] where DIF was being considered for a job knowledge test:

> Plaintiffs suggest in their post-trial memorandum that the test is subject to challenge on the basis that they failed to perform a DIF analysis to determine whether, and if so on which items, blacks performed more poorly than whites, so that an effort could have been made to reduce adverse impact by eliminating those items on which blacks performed more poorly. . . Dr. Landy testified that the consensus of professional opinion is that DIF modification of tests is not a good idea because it reduces the validity of the examination. . . Dr. Landy explained: The problem with [DIF] is suppose one of those items is a knowledge item and has to do with an issue like Miranda or an issue in the preservation of evidence or a hostage situation. You're going to take that item out only because whites answer it more correctly than blacks do, in spite of the fact that you'd really want a sergeant to know this [issue] because the sergeant is going to supervise. A police officer is going to count on that officer to tell him or her what to do. So you're reducing the validity of the exam just for the sake of making sure that there are no items in which whites and blacks do differentially, or DIF, and he's assuming that the reason that 65 percent of the blacks got it right and 70 percent of the whites got it right was that it's an unfair item rather than, hey, maybe two or three whites or two or three blacks studied more or less that section of general orders.

Certainly this excerpt provides some good arguments against discarding items based only on DIF analyses. These issues and the guidelines discussed in Chapter Three should be carefully considered before removing items from a test.

After conducting the item-level analysis and removing items that do not comply with acceptable ranges, conduct a test-level analysis to assess descriptive and psychometric statistics (*e.g.,* reliability, standard deviation, etc.). Adjust the unmodified Angoff by using the Standard Error of Measurement or the Conditional Standard Error of Measurement where applicable (see Chapter Eight for a complete discussion on this subject).

In summary, developing a content valid job knowledge written test for hiring/promoting employees (where the job requires testing for critical job knowledge areas) is the safest route to avoid potential litigation. If the test has adverse impact – validate. Pay particular attention in addressing the Uniform Guidelines, Principles, and Standards (in that order, based on the weight they are typically given in court), and remember that a house is only as strong as its foundation. Be sure to base everything on a solid job analysis.

Steps for Developing a Personality Test Using Criterion-related Validity

By Daniel A. Biddle, Ph.D.

This section outlines the basic steps for developing and validating a low-adverse impact personality assessment for organizations that have at least 250 job incumbents in a specific job title or job group.

One of the most important human performance factors is personality. People's overall job performance can suffer due to personality traits such as lack of drive, initiative, focus, determination, conscientiousness, or other characteristics that are separate and distinct from intelligence or ability. Workers who are lacking in some of these factors will often fall short in a variety of job performance areas, such as maintaining productive professional relationships, effectively solving interpersonal conflict issues that arise with other co-workers or clients, staying focused on completing projects, or completing quality work.

How can HR professionals identify these personality factors in the hiring and selection process? Conducting in-depth interviews can provide some insight into these areas as well as evaluating work history and patterns, but these types of investigations often require more time than HR professionals have. Further, HR professionals in mid- to large-sized organizations would need to screen hundreds and sometimes thousands of job candidates, making such in-depth investigations less than feasible. This is where written personality assessments play an integral role in the hiring process. Many personality measures are brief, to-the-point, and effective. But which traits are needed for the jobs in your organization? How can a valid personality test be developed for your organization? These questions and others will be answered in this brief "how-to" guide for developing validated personality tests.

Before unpacking the development recipe, however, two issues should be stated. First, personality measures are a great way to lower adverse impact in most hiring processes. Because personality tests typically have *less than half* of the adverse impact[16] commonly generated by cognitive ability tests, they are one of several effective ways to reduce adverse impact in your organization's hiring process. Having said that, cognitive ability tests are often solid predictors of job success and should not be removed from a hiring process for the sole reason of avoiding possible adverse impact.

The ideal selection process is one that *proportionately measures* most of the key qualification factors needed for success – with cognitive ability and personality factors being just two such components. Second, personality tests come by a dozen different names. Sometimes they are called "work style" tests; sometimes they are referred to as "profiles"; and sometimes just "personality measures." This section focuses on true, inherent personality factors, rather than on attitudes and values that are sometimes more changeable over time.

By way of a disclaimer, test development is technical work. It requires statistical, psychological, and measurement knowledge and skills. Therefore, the following steps should be completed with great diligence, caution, thoroughness, and oversight.

Step 1: Research the Personality Traits that Underlie Job Performance

Literature searches can be conducted for the specific positions and the existing personality tools and traits that have successfully predicted job success. For example, if the targeted personality area is "customer service orientation," the existing tools that measure this trait can be reviewed and their technical manuals reviewed to provide insight to what specific personality dimensions may translate to job success (copyright cautions are duly noted for this step). The personnel psychology literature should also be consulted to investigate the specific aspects of customer service orientation that have been associated with job success. Such research might identify that several aspects of customer service orientation should be targeted for test development, such as sociability, extroversion, tactfulness, being cooperative, flexibility, openness, non-judgmental, optimism, and reliability.

At a minimum, the "Big Five" personality traits (Barrick & Mount, 1991) should be evaluated and relevant aspects included. The "Big Five" personality model includes five broad factors, or dimensions, of personality. Developed through years of study, it is considered to be the most comprehensive empirical or data-driven framework of personality. The five factors are Openness, Conscientiousness, Extroversion, Agreeableness, and Neuroticism (the Neuroticism factor is sometimes referred to as Emotional Stability). Careful research may identify that some levels of one or more of these traits may be relevant for your targeted position(s).

Step 2: Develop a Bank of Test Items that Measure the Targeted Traits

Items should consist of short, behaviorally-based statements that are rated by the candidates on four levels of endorsement (1 = Strongly Disagree, 2 = Disagree, 3 = Agree, and 4 = Strongly Agree). For example, statements such as, "I am always prepared," "I like order," and "I pay attention to details" are examples of items that measure conscientiousness. In addition to positively-framed items (*i.e.*, where higher endorsements mean they are more likely to possess the targeted trait), negatively-framed items should also be included to make the construct of interest more obscure to the applicants who tend to "fake good" on personality tests. For measuring conscientiousness, this might mean including items such as, "I leave my belongings around," or "Sometimes wrapping up the little details of a project is just a waste of time." In other words, measuring the *inverse* of a targeted trait is a discreet way to attempt to insure that the applicant is less able to fake their way on a personality test. For example, if one is developing a personality test for a Public Relations position and extroversion is thought to be a correlate of job success, measure *introversion*. Ultimately, the goal is to generate an item pool that is representative of both the low- and high-levels of each targeted trait. After the items have been developed, have them critiqued by an expert and reduced to a useable number (between 100 and 200, with at least 20 measuring each targeted trait or dimension of that trait).

At this stage, it may also be beneficial to consider integrating items and/or scales from existing personality tests (*e.g.,* one or more of the Big Five personality scales). Some test publishers are likely to negotiate license arrangements that will allow this.

Step 3: Develop a Lie Scale to Detect and Screen Out Faking and/or Random Responders

In nearly every criterion validation project, "random," "dishonest," and "illegitimate" responders can occur. These can wreak havoc in a validation study. To prevent this from happening, develop 10-15 "lie scale" items to be used for detecting and eliminating such responders. Lie scale items can be contrasting sets where the statement is first worded, "I like dogs more than cats," and subsequently worded, "I like cats more than dogs" (for actual test items, use trait-relevant content). These sets can then be checked during the data build process and the non-matching responders excluded. There are several ways for completing this process; this is just one possible strategy.

Step 4: Develop a Job Performance Rating Survey (JPRS)

This is perhaps the most important part of the process because this is where the "target" (job performance) is fashioned for the "arrows" (test items) to be cast. Without a clear target, all else is wasted. The Job Performance Rating Survey (JPRS) should be developed by working with job experts and reviewing the job description (or even better, a job analysis) to determine the important aspects of job behavior that are key for success in the target position. Select between 10 and 20 different aspects of work behavior that are observable, rather than abstract "traits" or "abilities." Be sure not to double-up in the same areas – it is better that each rating domain is as unique as possible.

To help maximize the likelihood of study success, use a rating scale for each rating dimension that forces a distribution of the job incumbents to be rated by supervisors. For example, the rating scale and instructions can advise the raters to divide their employees into ten (relatively) equal categories, with about 10% of the employees in each. Raters should be encouraged that assigning some of their employees to the lower 10%, 20%, or 30% categories does not mean that they are incompetent performers, but rather that this is where they stand, relevant to the rest of the staff that they supervise in this single performance area. Completing a rating process in this way helps maximize the range of ratings obtained in the study, which will allow the test items with greater levels of variance with which to correlate. Not completing the study in this fashion and using, for example, readily available annual performance review scores, can translate to dismal failure of the research project. This is because such performance criteria can sometimes be influenced by political factors rather than specific observations that are relevant to the job performance areas of the personality test in the study. They are also sometimes too universal to be detected by the specific areas measured by the test. When selecting job performance criteria to include in the study, it is best to be *specific* as well as *accurate* (which means obtaining honest, candid, and widely varying job performance ratings).

Step 5: Convene the Supervisory Staff to Complete the JPRS on at least 250 Target Incumbents

Be sure to conduct training and/or provide clear rating instructions to the supervisors explaining that the ratings will be used exclusively for test development purposes, and will not be revealed to any outside agency. Caution: it is recommended to first convince employee Unions of the value (*i.e.,* selecting in qualified, well-rounded workers) and confines (with individual performance data and ratings being kept completely confidential and used for the study purposes only) of this study before attempting this process. It is absolutely critical that the raters are encouraged to provide extremely candid and honest ratings through this process If possible, have at least two supervisors rate each employee.[17] Employees should only be rated if they have at least one month of on-the-job experience, and have been directly observed by the raters on each performance aspect they rate.

Step 6: Administer the Personality Items to the Job Incumbents

This step is relatively straightforward. The job incumbents should be informed that they are participating in a validation study that will be used for developing an assessment for selecting qualified workers (in the future), and that their test results will in no way be used for evaluating their own personal job performance or pay status.

Step 7: Choose a Strategic Test Building Strategy

At this point, there are three possible strategies that can be used for evaluating the validity of the items included in the study and developing the test. The first (and most recommended) strategy is to use a two-step ("calibrate" and then "validate") process that is completed by dividing the total sample in half, building the best possible test based on the item-JPRS correlations observed in the Calibration sample, and then trying this test out on the Validation sample. This is the process described in the remainder of this section. But first, two alternative methods are highlighted:

1. Factor analysis can be used on the entire sample of test takers to build test scales that can be correlated to the JPRS dimensions to evaluate statistically significant correlations. Either factor scoring (where each item is proportionally and positively/negatively weighted by its correlation to the factor) or manual item-factor weighting can be used to evaluate the correlation of test scales. Manual weighting can be done by identifying items that are above a certain item-factor correlation threshold (*e.g.,* .20) and assigning them point values according to their correlation strength to the factor (*e.g.,* items with correlations >.30 are weighted 2X, above .20 weighted 1X, items with <.-30 weighted -2X, items with <.20 weighted -1X).
2. Test items can be sorted into their *a priori* trait categories (*e.g.,* by grouping the conscientiousness items together, the extroversion items together, etc.) and evaluated for validity against the entire sample using a one-tailed test for significance (because they are based on a *directional hypothesis* for the correlation).

There are several caveats, conditions, and strengths/limitations with each of these strategies. The reader is advised to seek guidance where necessary. The following steps only discuss the "Split Half, Calibration/Validation" study design.

Step 8: Setup a Database for Conducting Correlational Analyses using a "Split Half, Calibration/Validation" Study Design

First, evaluate and remove study participants who are deemed illegitimate using the Lie Scale described above (judgment must be used for determining just how many subjects to screen out and which decision rules to be used). Then, join the two data files into a single database that contains each person's (raw, unscored) response on the test items and their ratings given by supervisors. Next, randomly divide the entire sample of 250+ incumbents into two equal data sets. One data set will be used to build the test (called the "Calibration" sample); the other will be used to validate the test (called the "Validation" sample).

Step 9: Create the "Optimal Test" Using the Calibration Sample Only

Using the Calibration sample only, run correlations between each test item and each of the 10-20 dimensions on the JPRS. Look for correlational trends and patterns. If the JPRS has several divergent areas (as might be shown through a factor analysis), some items may correlate with certain aspects of job performance, but not others. This is where the "art" of test development comes in, and advice from seasoned professionals certainly becomes valuable.

After determining the items and dimensions on the JPRS that exhibit the strongest correlational trends, assign point values to the items that somewhat mirror their correlation strength. *Important note:* For this step, it is not necessary to select items that are only statistically significant. If an item demonstrates a positive correlational trend (say, >.20 or so) to one or more JPRS dimensions of interest, it should be selected for inclusion on the test and weighted appropriately. For example, if some items are found that exhibit high correlations across most JPRS dimensions, these items can be double weighted. If items are negatively correlated with job performance, reverse score them for keying purposes (also double weighting the strongest items). This process will likely reduce the item pool by more than half.

After the new test form has been constructed, assess the reliability to be sure that the test overall (or each separate, scored subscale) has internal reliability that exceeds .70.[18] Because this process capitalizes on the sample-specific nuances that were inherent with this Calibration sample, the total test will show an inflated correlation to the job performance dimensions, and will probably exceed correlation values of .30 or .40. These values will not constitute the actual validity of the test; rather they are inflated estimates. The actual test validity cannot be known until the next step has been completed.

Step 10: Evaluate the Validity of the Test by Correlating it to the JPRS Dimensions on the "Hold Out" Validation Sample

Using only the Validation Sample (the other half of the data set that was not used for building the test in the step above), correlate the test to the JPRS dimensions. Correlations observed that exceed statistical significance levels should be flagged for the remaining steps that follow. Caution should be taken against trying too many correlations, or hanging on to correlations that are "barely" significant, especially if they have adverse impact. In addition, an iterative process of going back-and-forth between the Calibration and Validation sample and "data mining" are strongly discouraged.

Step 11: Conduct a Fairness Study to Evaluate Whether the Test is an Adequate Predictor of Job Success for Various Subgroups

Section 14B8 of the Uniform Guidelines requires conducting a fairness study whenever it is *technically feasible* to do so. Generally, this means that whenever a study includes at least 30 minorities or women, a fairness study should be conducted, which requires using Moderated Multiple Regression (MMR) to test for slope and intercept differences observed in the regression equations for the subgroups included. (Contact BCG for a copy of a step-by-step guide for using MMR to evaluate test fairness.). In addition to using MMR to evaluate the overall fairness of the test, Differential Item Function (DIF) analyses can be used for evaluating test fairness at the *test item* level (BCG also maintains the recommended steps, procedures, and tools for conducting DIF analyses which are available at no charge).

Step 12: Assemble the Test and Determine the Appropriate Use in the Hiring Process

How the test is used in the hiring process (*e.g.,* pass/fail, ranked, banded, or weighted and combined with other tests) should be based upon the validity, reliability, and adverse impact levels exhibited. Because personality tests typically have moderate levels of validity (high teens to mid-twenties) as well as reliability (hovering in the seventies/eighties), but typically have lower levels of adverse impact (when compared to say, cognitive ability tests), banding is a good place to start (it is recommended to use the *conditional* Standard Error of Difference when setting score bands[19]). In addition, it is useful to add a warning to the test introductory page to help discourage applicant faking, such as: "It is important that you answer these questions as honestly and openly as possible. Failure to do so will likely result in incorrect answers and a lower overall score. Some questions are worth more than one point, and some questions are scored in ways that would not be expected. Intentional deception is likely to result in lower overall performance."

Step 13: Complete a Criterion-related Validation Report to Address Section 15B of the Uniform Guidelines

Completing a report that addresses the federal Uniform Guidelines provides three great benefits: (1) It provides a ready, off-the-shelf document that can be used in litigation situations, (2) it documents the key (complicated) steps that were followed to build the test, and (3) it gives the test shelf life. Tests that have no such pedigree can be minimized or disregarded over time, especially if the key personnel involved in their creation have left the organization. Tests that have a pedigree will maintain their value through time and turnover.

In summary, including a good personality test in your organization's hiring process is a great idea. The returns can be enormous anytime HR professionals can add validity and utility into their hiring process *while reducing adverse impact*. Following the key steps described above demonstrate how relatively easy it is to develop such an asset.

Notes

[1] If the test will be used to rank applicants, or a pass/fail cutoff that is above minimum competency levels will be used, the "Best Worker" rating should also be used as a minimum criteria, with a minimum level set for selecting KSAPCs for the test (see Chapter Eight).

[2] The developer may prefer to not allow Job Experts to review the test answer key because in some situations doing so can have an impact on their "minimum passing" ratings. Nonetheless, the answer key should always be verified by at least two people.

[3] Classical test analysis refers to the test analysis techniques that use conventional analysis concepts and methods. More modern test theories exist (e.g., Item Response Theory), but are not discussed in this text.

[4] See, for example: Edwards v. City of Houston, 78 F.3d 983, 995 (5th Cir., 1996) and Houston Chapter of the International Association of Black Professional Firefighters v. City of Houston, No. H 86 3553, U.S. Dist. Ct. S.D. Texas (May 3, 1991).

[5] Narayanan, P, & Swaminathan, H. (1995). *Performance of the Mantel-Haenszel and simultaneous item bias procedures for detecting differential item functioning*. Applied Psychological Measurement, *18*, 315-328.

[6] See: Mazor, K. M., Clauser, B. E., & Hambleton, R. K. (1992), The effect of sample size on the functioning of the Mantel-Haenszel statistic. *Educational and Psychological Measurement*, *52*, 443-451; Narayanan, P. & Swaminathan, H. (1995), Performance of the Mantel-Haenszel and simultaneous item bias procedures for detecting differential item functioning. *Applied Psychological Measurement*, *18*, 315-328; and Swaminathan, H. & Rogers, H. J. (1990), Detecting differential item functioning using logistic regression procedures. *Journal of Educational Measurement*, *27*, 361-370.

[7] In any given criterion-related validity study, it is not likely that all items on the test will be statistically related to job performance (this is not the requirement for tests based on criterion-related validity, but rather that only the overall test is sufficiently correlated). However, if there is no *specific evidence* that the test item is related to job performance, while simultaneously there is *specific evidence* that the item could possibly be unfair against a certain group, it is justifiable to consider the item for removal (the other factors listed should also be considered).

[8] See for example Evans v. City of Evanston (881 F.2d 382, 7th Cir., 1989).

[9] Dye, D. A., Reck, M., & McDaniel, M. A. (1993, July). The validity of job knowledge measures. *International Journal of Selection and Assessment*, *1* (3), 153-157.

[10] Hunter, J.E. (1983). A causal analysis of cognitive ability, job knowledge, job performance and supervisory ratings. In F. Landy and S. Zedeck and J. Cleveland (Eds.), *Performance measurement theory* (pp. 257-266). Hillsdale, NJ: Erlbaum.

[11] For example, see Bouman v. Block (940 F2d 1211, 9th Cir 1991); Hearn v. City of Jackson, Miss. (110 Fed. 242, 5th Cir 2004); Isabel v. City of Memphis (F.Supp.2d 2003, 6th Cir 2003); Paige v. State of California (102 F.3d 1035, 1040, 9th Cir 1996).

[12] The steps outlined in this Chapter are based on the requirements outlined by the Uniform Guidelines (1978), the Principles (2003), and the Standards (1999). The proposed model is not a one-size-fits-all process, but rather a generic template which could be employed in an ideal setting. While it is not *guaranteed* that by following these steps litigation will be avoided, implementing the practices outlined in this Chapter will greatly increase the likelihood of success in the event of a challenge to a written testing process.

[13] The Uniform Guidelines do not require frequency ratings for content validity; however, obtaining frequency ratings provides useful information for addressing the 1990 Americans with Disabilities Act (ADA) and can also help when developing a test using content validity.

[14] Sackett, P. R., Schmitt, N., Ellingson, J. E., & Kabin, M. B. (2001). High-stakes testing in employment, credentialing, and higher education: Prospects in a post-affirmative-action world. *American Psychologist, 56*(4), 302-318.

[15] This rule-of-thumb time limit is only applicable for conventional multiple-choice tests. Where many calculations are needed for each test item (*e.g.,* hydraulic items on a Fire Engineer test), obtain input from Job Experts to ensure an appropriate time limit.

[16] In a meta-analysis conducted by Schmitt, Clause and Pulakos (1996), the mean standardized difference was -.09 for personality measures compared to -.83 for general cognitive ability. Various traits, however, will produce different subgroup gaps.

[17] This is an invaluable step because having two raters rate (at least a subset) of the employees will allow rater reliability to be evaluated, which will allow statistical corrections to be made to estimate the true (adjusted) levels of validity identified in the study.

[18] Because personality factors are necessarily complex and "slippery" statistically, conducting a test-retest study is often the only way to ascertain the true reliability.

[19] See, for example, Biddle, D. Kuang, D. C.Y., & Higgins, J. (2007, March). Test use: ranking, banding, cutoffs, and weighting. Paper presented at the Personnel Testing Council of Northern California, Sacramento. See also Biddle, D. & Feldt, L. (2011). A new method for personnel score banding using the conditional standard error of measurement. Unpublished manuscript.

Chapter 4 - Developing, Validating, and Analyzing Structured Interviews

The purpose of any selection interview is to provide an applicant with a fair opportunity to demonstrate the KSAPCs and experiences that qualify them for the position. While the interview is the most commonly used component of selection systems, it can also be the most misunderstood and misapplied. Handled poorly, an interview can not only be ineffective, but may also have unintended adverse impact. Otherwise qualified applicants may be eliminated if the many variables contributing to a successful interview are not implemented properly.

Because an interview, by nature, will not measure characteristics of the entire applicant, it should be used in conjunction with the other selection procedures. A structured interview can serve as a useful supplement to the other selection procedures to allow the employer to gain valuable insight regarding certain aspects of an applicant's KSAPCs. It is different from unstructured interviews in that the same questions are asked of every applicant in the same way to ensure that all applicants are assessed using the same criteria.

Methods for Improving the Interview Process

There are ways of improving a typical interview that can improve the process and help ensure that the interview is as job related as possible. The following observations are based upon research into past characteristics of typical interviews, and include some suggestions to improve the validity of the process:

- How valid and reliable the interview is may be highly specific to both the *situation* and to the *rater*.
- The interview should be used to evaluate factors that are not typically better measured by other means.
- The use of the interview is best accomplished if a standardized, or structured, approach is followed. In an unstructured interview, material is not consistently covered.
- The rater should be skilled (*i.e.,* trained) in eliciting full and complete responses from the applicant and synthesizing all of the information obtained.
- Even when a panel of raters obtains the same information, each panel member can interpret or weigh the information differently. It is best to use mechanically combined scoring systems that consider several dimensions (rather than broad sweeping holistic judgments or ratings).
- The form of the question(s) affects the answer(s) obtained.
- The raters' attitudes affect their interpretations of what the applicant says.
- Raters appear to be influenced more by unfavorable than by favorable information.
- Rapport, or the lack thereof, between rater and the applicant is a situational variable that can unduly influence the interview's effectiveness.

- Structured or patterned interviews show stronger inter-rater reliabilities, meaning that there is generally a greater agreement across different raters when a standardized interview is used.
- Raters typically develop stereotypes of a good/poor applicant and seek to match applicants with stereotypes.
- Biases are established by raters early in the interview and these tend to be followed by a bias-matching favorable or unfavorable decision.
- Raters seek data to support or deny their own personal hypotheses and, when satisfied, may turn their attention elsewhere and miss important information. This means raters can weigh heavily on a small amount of information that supports their preconceived notions about applicants. Sometimes this also means that raters can dismiss any disconfirming information that does not coincide with their preconceived notions.

While many of the characteristics about interviews are unfortunately beyond the control of the practitioner, two variables can be controlled: the amount of *structure* provided for the interview and the *content* of the interview. A structured interview is controlled by three factors:

1. The interview questions asked (content);
2. The way the rater controls the actual interview situation (structure); and,
3. The standardized scoring of the interviews.

The remaining section will explain the various question types that can be included in an interview, and a detailed, step-by-step process for developing and administering effective, valid, structured interviews.

Types of Questions to Include in Structured Interviews

There is an entire landscape of question types that can be asked legally and effectively during an interview process. Some are more effective than others and, as a general rule, the more time and preparation work invested in developing the question set, the better the questions. This Chapter covers three basic question types: situational, behavioral, and competency-based.

Situational questions

Situational questions ask applicants: "What would you do if . . .?" These questions are based on events that have previously occurred on the job (or would be likely to occur) and ask the applicant to explain how they would handle the situation (limited, of course, by not having job experience in the position for which they are applying). Situational types of questions typically have good validity coefficients when correlated to measures of job performance (typically .30 to .46) and solid reliability (inter-rater reliability estimates are typically between .76 and .87) (Gatewood & Feild, 1994, p. 537) (see also Cascio, 1998, p. 198). These questions can be powerful selection tools because they immediately place the applicant in a tough job situation and demand that they adequately address the situation. Consider the following example from an electrical trade position:

Workers at XYZ company have a practice of checking tools for proper operation prior to leaving the shop to go to a job site. This allows workers to be assured that tools will work properly at the job site. Your supervisor asks you to work with three helpers to collect and test the tools that will be brought to the next job site. After the helpers assist you in gathering and testing the tools, the tools are loaded in the truck and brought to the work site. After starting work at the site, your supervisor finds that one of the tools that you and the three helpers loaded is not working properly. He gets angry at you and demands that you drive all the way back to the shop to obtain a new tool. You know which one of the helpers gave you the faulty tool. What would you do in this situation? What would you expect to accomplish by taking these steps?

Typically for situational questions of this type, scoring guidelines and anchors are developed that provide raters benchmarks for high, acceptable, and low levels of applicant responses.

Behavioral questions

Behavioral questions ask applicants: "What have you done when . . .?" These questions are based on the (reasonable) assumption that the best predictor of future behavior is past behavior. As such, these questions ask applicants to explain how they have handled difficult or complex situations in previous settings. Generally speaking, these questions are the most limited type of interview questions since they can sometimes be "faked" with information the interviewer has no way of confirming. Below is an example of a behavioral question:

It is sometimes necessary to work as part of a team to accomplish a project. Can you tell me about a time during a job or school project where you were part of a team and one or more of the members were difficult to work with? Please explain how you handled this situation. What was the outcome? Would you do anything differently now?

Competency-based questions

Competency-based questions ask applicants: "Explain how you would . . ." These questions drill deep into the applicant's knowledge and skill set in a way that leaves little room for impression management or faking. When properly developed, administered, and scored, these questions are one of the most powerful selection tools for complex jobs that require high levels of knowledge and skill upon entry. A well-designed, competency-based question is one that simply cannot be faked by the applicant.

Consider an Information Management (IT) position. IT managers need to possess good interpersonal and project management skills, but most importantly, they need to possess solid, mastery-level knowledge and skills relevant to the computer systems they will be managing. Asking only situational and behavioral types questions when interviewing IT managers is an almost certain recipe for disaster (unless the situational questions include competency-based characteristics). It is entirely possible during an interview that asks only situational and behavioral questions to *completely miss* whether the IT manager applicant possesses the mastery-level knowledge and skill necessary to *actually perform* the job.

While the situational and behavioral questions can help evaluate how the applicant will likely work with people and handle projects, such questions may completely overlook the depth and breadth of an applicant's true computer-related knowledge and skill. Including some solid competency-based questions into the mix of other questions quickly addresses this problem.

The best competency-based question is one that the applicant *cannot possibly answer* without possessing the desired level of knowledge and skill. For example, a competency-based question for the IT manager position might be:

> Our company has 35 employees and we use Microsoft® Mail Server version XX.0 for our email services. If Microsoft released a new version of the Mail Server program next month, what steps would you take to migrate our company to the new version? Please be specific and be sure to describe each step you would take and why. Feel free to take your time to prepare your response before answering.

After the applicant has provided their complete response, follow up with questions (to be asked of every applicant) such as:

- How would you notify staff of the change?
- What backup plans would you have in place before starting the work?
- When would you start the project?
- What problems have you had with Mail Server Version XYZ.0?
- What strengths do you like about Mail Server Version XYZ.0?
- What steps would you follow to set up a new employee's mail account?
- What books or reference sources would you consult before or during the migration process?

Because these questions require applicants to apply very specific knowledge and skill sets, they pose a difficult barrier for unqualified applicants to overcome (especially when coupled with follow-up questions and scored by IT professionals who are familiar with the topics covered in the interview). Competency-based questions and follow-ups can be even more specific than the example above (generally speaking, more specific questions are better, provided that the question does not measure knowledge that will be trained on the job). The best competency-based question is one that absolutely requires the applicant to respond with mastery-level competencies that demonstrate that they currently possess the levels of the KSAPC needed on the first day of the job.

Steps for Developing Situational Questions

The following is a detailed description of the steps necessary for developing validated situational questions for a structured interview.

1. Complete a job analysis for the target position. Be sure that the job analysis includes (at a minimum), duties, KSAPCs, linkages between the duties and KSAPCs (required to address Section 14C4 of the Guidelines), and "Best Worker" ratings (see the Job Analysis ratings discussed in Chapter Two). Each of these steps should be performed before proceeding further in the development process.

2. Select the KSAPCs to measure on the interview by following the steps for completing a Selection Plan outlined in Chapter Two. Be sure that the KSAPCs that are selected for the interview can be appropriately measured in an interview format (for example, KSAPCs such as reading ability, math, and "hands-on" type of skills cannot usually be properly assessed by an interview and are typically better assessed using other methods). Also be sure that the KSAPCs selected for the interview are those that are rated highest on the "Best Worker" rating scale (*i.e.,* are performance differentiating). This is helpful, especially if the interview will be used as the final, ranked, or banded selection procedure.

3. Prepare for a one-day workshop with Job Experts by compiling a final list of the selected KSAPCs and create a "Situational Interview Question" form that provides space for the Job Experts to record a "critical incident" (see below) that has occurred on the job (or is very likely to occur), the KSAPC that is related to the incident, and the least effective, acceptable, and most effective responses to the situation.

4. Convene 7-10 Job Experts for the one-day workshop to generate draft situational questions for the interview. Start the workshop by explaining the work completed so far (*e.g.,* the job analysis, selecting KSAPCs for the interview), the benefits of using a job-related interview process (it helps to specifically mention that the end goal of the process is to effectively select new employees for the job who will be excellent co-workers), and the final product (a valid structured interview).

5. Break the Job Experts into 2-3 teams (each having at least two individuals) with each team having relatively the same number of KSAPCs (*e.g.,* if there are 12 KSAPCs that survived the Selection Plan screening process above, and divide the Job Experts into four teams with each having three KSAPCs). Have each team review their set of KSAPCs and the duties to which they are linked. This will re-familiarize the Job Experts with the KSAPCs and how they are specifically applied on the job.

6. Define and review the concept of *critical incidents* with the Job Experts. Spend some time with the concept, asking for group input and examples of critical incidents that have recently occurred on the job (this can be a fun process as the group recalls their own blunders and/or successes as well as those of their co-workers!). When discussing the concept of critical incidents, define them as:

Events or a set of circumstances on the job that presented an *opportunity* for job incumbents to 'rise to the occasion' by demonstrating stellar performance, or *not*, by making less-than-effective choices.

The critical incidents should not include common, everyday events or circumstances that merely provide an opportunity for incumbents to make "average" or "just enough" reactions to sufficiently address the situation. The best critical incident is one where the words and actions of the incumbent directly translated to a positive or negative outcome on an important aspect of the job.

7. Prepare the panel for developing situational questions based on these critical incidents by reviewing the criteria presented below. The situational question should:

    a. Not measure KSAPCs that an employee will be expected to learn on the job, or can be trained in a brief orientation (*i.e.*, avoid "tricks of the trade").

    b. Provide sufficient content and complexity to stimulate a response from the applicant that would allow raters to provide an adequate assessment of the applicant. Situations that have simple solutions or present only absolute alternatives should be avoided.

    c. Be job-related (*i.e.*, it should represent an incident that has occurred, or is very likely to occur on the job).

    d. Not require job-specific knowledge to provide an adequate response. That is, the question should not penalize applicants who have a high level of the KSAPC being measured by the question, but are unable to respond with much information to the question because they do not have experience in the target position. The question should allow applicants to relate the situation to their past life experiences to provide a response.

    e. Not be too easy or too difficult.

    f. Be culturally and politically sensitive and appropriate. In other words, it should present a situation that allows qualified applicants of various socio-ethnic backgrounds to provide an ample response relevant to the job.

8. Ask the individual team members to independently develop critical incidents that relate to their assigned KSAPCs. Remind them that critical incidents can include situations that have occurred on the job (to them or someone else) or would be very likely to occur. Ask the Job Experts to record these incidents on the Situational Interview Question Form. Be sure they complete all parts of the survey. It sometimes helps to do the first one as an example with the overall group. Allow ample time for this process. Ask each Job Expert to come up with at least four incidents.

9. Have the Job Experts exchange their completed forms and ask each team to refine the incidents within their team and select the best ones. So, if there are three team members and each Job Expert developed four incidents (12 total), the team might select a final set of eight of their "best incidents."

10. Have the Job Experts submit the incidents and read each one (anonymously without revealing the author of the incident) to the entire group. Have the group informally grade each one "A," "B," or "C."

11. Keep the incidents that were graded A or B by the group. Work with the entire team to *convert the incidents into final situational questions* by following three steps:

   a. Convert the incidents into question form to be asked directly of the applicant (*e.g.,* "Assume you are a clerical worker at XYZ corporation and the following event occurs . . .").

   b. Refine the possible responses (least effective, acceptable, and most effective) to include typical responses that applicants are likely to provide during the interview. This step is important because these response guidelines will be used in the interview scoring process.

   c. Develop customized follow-up questions for each situational question. These follow-up questions are useful for escalating the situation (in a standardized format) for applicants who initially provide superficial or "pat" answers for how they would address the situation.

12. Develop a final interview package that includes the final situational questions along with standardized rating forms and scoring summary forms (to be used to compile scores from individual raters to the panel as whole). Because practical judgment, decision making, and verbal communication are measured inclusively along with each situational question, they can be scored for each situational question or in terms of the overall performance of the applicant (after answering all questions).

13. It is possible to conclude at this step with a set of situational questions that are highly job related and will effectively screen applicants for relevant KSAPCs. However, an additional step can be included in the process at this point that will have two benefits: (1) it will generate validation evidence and documentation should the interview ever be challenged, and (2) it can refine the final set of questions to be even better than the initial set. This step involves convening a Job Expert team of 7-10 members who have not yet seen the final set of situational questions and having them review and provide validation ratings on the situational questions. This step is sometimes beneficial just from a practical standpoint because it serves to have a "fresh perspective" on the situational questions as the final product is reviewed by Job Experts who have never seen them. This step can be completed by having the new Job Expert team evaluate the set of situational questions using the following ratings:

   a. Is the question clear and understandable?

b.   Is the question written at an appropriate difficulty level?
c.   Does the question measure a KSAPC that is needed the first day of the job?
d.   Is this question fair to all groups of people?
e.   Is the question job related? (Does it represent a situation that has occurred or is very likely to occur on the job?)
f.   What KSAPC is measured by this question?
g.   Will applicants be able to provide a sufficient response without possessing job-specific (or employer specific) knowledge?

The court-endorsed rating guidelines presented in Chapter Three for written tests can be readily adopted as criteria for selecting a valid set of situational questions.

Administering and Scoring an Interview

The steps below can be followed to administer and score an interview in a fair and defensible manner:

1.   Select raters to serve on interview panels. Raters can be supervisors of the target position and/or human resource staff members. If high-level knowledge, competency-type questions will be used, knowledge of the subject matter is essential for raters (in many instances this will necessitate using only supervisors).
2.   Train the raters on the questions, scoring forms, and common rating errors. The following rating errors should be explained *and demonstrated* to raters:

Halo: Halo refers to the tendency of the rater to rate an applicant in about the same way on all domains because of a general, overall impression – whether favorable or unfavorable. This error usually results because the rater becomes impressed, either favorably or unfavorably, with one or two of the qualification areas and tends to base ratings in all qualification areas according to this initial impression.

Leniency: This error refers to the tendency of raters to place their ratings in the higher end of the scale for all applicants. A major reason for this error can be attributed to the fact that raters often feel that placing everyone in the top categories is helpful or kind. In actuality, it can render ratings useless.

Severity: This error refers to the tendency for raters to put a greater proportion of their ratings in categories below the average than in those above.

Central Tendency: This error is very common in the rating situation. It refers to the tendency of the rater to place all ratings at the center of the scale. This may occur because the rater is not entirely clear as to the meaning of the ratings or perhaps wishes to "play it safe" by giving no extreme ratings in either direction. Of course, this results in little or no variability between applicants and thus detracts from the objectives of the interview. This can also render the ratings useless.

Similar-to-me: This type of rating error occurs when certain characteristics about the applicant bias the scores high when they are similar to the rater and low when they are not.

It is typically a good practice to complete the rater training process by holding one or two mock interviews and having the raters complete and pass a brief rater training test. The critical factor regarding rater training is that raters should share a similar *frame of reference* for what constitutes a strong, mediocre, and low scoring applicant on each of the scales.

3. Assemble panels and randomly assign applicants to panels. Rating panels should consist of at least three members, and preferably no more than six. Two-member panels are also plausible, but detecting rater bias is limited when only two raters are used. Insure that the panels are diverse with respect to ethnicity and gender.

4. Administer and score the interview. After the scores are compiled, they should be double-checked for accuracy.

5. If multiple rater panels are used and each panel rates more than 20 applicants (or so), *standard score* each panel before combining all applicant scores onto the final score list. Standard scoring can be accomplished by creating a *Z score* for each applicant by subtracting each applicant's score from the average (mean) score of all applicants rated by the panel and dividing this value by the panel's standard deviation (of all applicant total scores on that panel). Only after completing this step for each panel should the applicant scores be combined and ranked on a final score list. This process statistically equates applicant scores between panel (sometimes rater panels have higher or lower averages for applicant scores and this process places them on the same level).[1]

Note

[1] Alternatively, Multiple-Response RASCH Modeling can be used for deriving a total score for each candidate (using FACETS software program). When RASCH method are used for analyzing rater data and scoring interviewees, raters should be "mixed" (randomly assigned to panels) and "linked." FACETS can also be useful for evaluating rater bias.

Chapter 5 - Developing and Validating Training, Education & Experience (TEE) Requirements

How many years of on-the-job experience should a police officer have before being eligible for promotion to sergeant? How many years' experience should a firefighter possess before becoming eligible for promotion to captain? What is the minimum number of years a person should be an apprentice in an industrial trade before becoming a licensed journey worker? How many years of flying experience should a pilot possess before being eligible to become a commercial airline pilot for a major airline? Should a person possess an undergraduate degree plus two years of experience before applying for a management position? A degree plus four years of experience? Five years?

Personnel and human resource professionals regularly struggle with these types of questions for both entry-level and promotional processes. When time-in-grade or other training, experience, and education (referred to hereafter as TEE) requirements are used and generate adverse impact, they instantly become subject to validation scrutiny if challenged in arbitration or legal settings.

Because TEE requirements are frequently established using nothing other than "best judgment" by executive and management staff, employers often find themselves in litigation situations explaining to the judge why they thought a five-year minimum time-in-grade requirement was better than a four-year requirement, or three and one-half years – down an endless slippery slope of subjectivity.

But this does not need to be the case. There are several defensible methods for validating TEE requirements. Some of these are discussed later in this Chapter. But first, a brief tour through the various government and professional standards and criteria surrounding TEE requirements will be provided.

The Uniform Guidelines and Principles (2003) provide very specific criteria for validating TEE requirements. Before reviewing these detailed requirements, first consider using the following questions as a checklist for insuring that a proposed TEE requirement rating or scoring system includes the necessary "basic elements."

Is the TEE requirement:

1. *Objective?* For example, rather than requiring that applicants possess a relevant degree from a "good or respectable school," simply require that they possess the degree from an accredited school or licensing program.
2. *Uniformly applied to all applicants?* Be sure that the rating structure and process used for the TEE requirement is standardized and applied consistently to all applicants.
3. *Likely to discriminate (distinguish between qualified and unqualified applicants)?* Be sure that the TEE requirement will actually distinguish unqualified from qualified applicants. Employers

sometimes spend needless time developing TEE requirements that are actually unnecessary, or ineffective, in the selection process.

4. *Clearly job related?* There should be a clear nexus between the TEE requirement and measurable KSAPCs from a job analysis (*i.e.,* KSAPCs that are definitely needed on the first day of the job – Section 14C1 and 5F of the Guidelines prohibit measuring KSAPCs that applicants will learn on the job, or those that can be trained in a "brief orientation").

5. *Provided in such a way that all applicants will have an equal opportunity to demonstrate that they possess the desired KSAPC?* Applicants should be directly asked whether they possess the TEE requirement. This is critical, because simply reviewing resumes to assess whether applicants meet the desired TEE requirements without specifically asking them to identify if they possess the TEE requirement can unfairly disqualify some applicants.

6. *Scored using a system that is consistent and reliable?* It is best to use two raters to score the TEE requirements (if they are scored and not just pass/fail) so that inter-rater reliability can be evaluated.

Several of the TEE validation requirements will be addressed by following the six criteria presented above. However, in some cases, special steps and consideration should be taken. One general limitation with TEE rating systems is that they depend on the applicant providing honest information about their background. Related to this, the accuracy of TEE rating systems depends on whether the employer chooses to verify the information provided. At the very least, employers should include a "lie warning" on TEE surveys that informs applicants that any information provided that turns out to be false will be immediate grounds for disqualification. Have the applicants acknowledge this warning by providing their signature on the survey.

Uniform Guidelines Criteria Regarding TEE Requirements

The Uniform Guidelines present a rather conservative set of criteria for validating TEE requirements:

> Prior training or experience: A requirement for, or evaluation of, specific prior training or experience based on content validity, including a specification of level or amount of training or experience, should be justified on the basis of the relationship between the content of the training or experience and the content of the job for which the training or experience is to be required or evaluated. The critical consideration is the resemblance between the specific behaviors, products, knowledges, skills, or abilities in the experience or training and the specific behaviors, products, knowledges, skills, or abilities required on the job, whether or not there is close resemblance between the experience or training as a whole and the job as a whole. (Section 14C6)

The subparts of this section require that at least two criteria be addressed when using a content validation strategy to support the use of TEE requirements (or ratings) in a selection process. These are: (1) specifying the *level* or *amount* of the TEE requirements (or rating systems), and (2) conducting some form of *linkage* to establish the resemblance between the content (and levels) of the TEE requirement and the content of the job itself.

Rather than using global, holistic Job Expert ratings to establish the "resemblance" between the TEE requirement and the job *in general*, the Uniform Guidelines require that the resemblance is evaluated at a *micro-level*, with specific attention to the behaviors (or duties, including their affiliated work products) and the KSAPCs of each.

While this section of the Uniform Guidelines requires that specific linkages are established between the TEE requirement and the job, the requirement is less stringent on the *inferential leap* (the level of inference being made between two areas, in this case the TEE requirement and the job) criteria of content validity that is required for other types of selection procedures.

This is because the last sentence in Section 14C6 (". . . whether or not there is *close resemblance* between the experience or training as a whole and the job as a whole") and Question #73 of the Uniform Guidelines (". . . users may justify a requirement for training, or for experience . . . on the basis of content validity, even though the prior training or experience *does not duplicate the job*").

Thus, these two sections leave some room for prior training, experience, or education to sufficiently meet the content validation requirements *even if they are not directly related to duties of the job*. For example, consider an employer in the food service industry who desires to use a TEE requirement of "at least two years supervisory experience." Should applicants who possess two years supervisory experience at a manufacturing plant be eligible to apply? Certainly, because the supervisory skills that are acquired at the manufacturing plan are likely to translate directly to the food services industry. Skills like holding employees accountable, team work, meeting deadlines, and performance evaluation is likely to be very similar and transportable between these two trades.

Professional Standards Regarding TEE Requirements

The Principles (2003) present a set of criteria that almost exactly match the Uniform Guidelines:

> A content-based selection procedure may also include evidence of specific prior training, experience, or achievement. This evidence is judged on the basis of the relationship between the content of the experience and the content of the work requiring that experience. To justify such relationships, more than a superficial resemblance between the content of the experience variables and the content of the work is required. For example, course titles and job titles may not give an adequate indication of the content of the course or the job or the level of proficiency an applicant has developed in some important area. What should be evaluated is the similarity between the

behaviors, activities, processes performed, or the KSAOs
[knowledges, skills, abilities, and other characteristics] required by
the work. (p. 23)

The contribution that the Principles provide above the Uniform Guidelines is
the requirement of having "more than a superficial resemblance" and the example of
"course titles and job titles may not give an adequate indication of the content of the
course or the job of proficiency an applicant has developed in some important area."

The criteria set forth in the Uniform Guidelines and Principles for validating
TEE requirements will not typically be addressed when employers simply arbitrarily
and subjectively determine TEE requirements. It is exactly this practice that often
brings employers to court to defend TEE requirements (which are often the most
difficult types of selection procedures to defend). So how can employers develop
validated TEE requirements in an efficient way? With so many detailed requirements
surrounding the validation of TEE requirements, it would appear that validating them
must be a challenging endeavor. Not necessarily.

The validation system described below provides steps and guidelines that will
work for many types of TEE requirements. While these recommendations are
designed to address the key validation criteria proposed in the Uniform Guidelines and
Principles, practitioners are advised to reference these documents when specific
questions arise.

Using TEE Requirements in Open Selection/Promotional Processes

Described below is a validated system for scoring and rating TEE requirements that
are used in selection or promotion processes where applicants from *outside the
employer* are allowed to apply (*i.e.*, "open systems"). This system is based on the
presumption that applicants can bring any combination of training, experience, and
education to the job and a "wide net" needs to be cast to capture those that are
specifically related to the requirements of the job.

Sometimes employers use simple "fixed checkbox" surveys for essential TEE
requirements where applicants simply check a box indicating whether they possess the
specified level of the KSAPC. Such surveys are simple to develop and require almost
no scoring (only sorting into qualified and unqualified stacks). However, there are
some serious drawbacks to using this strategy. Because applicants can obtain relevant
training, experience, and education qualifications in *so many different ways*, it is
almost impossible to build a one-sized-fits-all checklist where applicants individually
assess whether they meet certain specific requirements and then check the box
indicating "Yes" or "No."

There are virtually endless ways in which applicants can acquire competency
in the KSAPCs required for the job. Training and experience can be acquired through
on-the-job training, military training, rehabilitation programs, apprenticeship
programs, or self-employment. In fact, the Uniform Guidelines allow *volunteer
experience* to be counted toward meeting training and experience requirements for a
job (see Uniform Guidelines Questions & Answers Supplement #73). This presents a
serious challenge for a "one-size-fits-all" checkbox system.

Another limitation to these types of surveys is that they typically ignore the "level" of the KSAPC that is required (a requirement of Section 14C6 of the Uniform Guidelines). Just how much of the KSAPC training or experience is *enough*? Six months? Two years? How can this be predefined without knowing how frequently each applicant applied the relevant KSAPC during the two years of experience they claim to possess?

Developing the baseline minimum requirement for a simple checkbox system can be very challenging. Unless the developer is willing to pre-list every possible way for acquiring the level of KSAPC required, and is willing to take a firm stance on just *exactly how much* of each of these various ways in which the KSAPC can be attained, a scored system like the one proposed below should be used instead.

Steps for developing a valid TEE rating system for open selection/promotion processes

1. Conduct a job analysis that addresses the requirements of the Uniform Guidelines (see Chapter Two). It is especially important for this TEE requirement validation system that job knowledges are *operationally defined* as "that body of learned information which is used in and is a necessary prerequisite for observable aspects of work behavior of the job" and skills and abilities are operationally defined in terms of "observable aspects of work behavior of the job" (Section 14C4 of the Uniform Guidelines).

2. Identify KSAPCs that can be appropriately and effectively measured in a TEE rating process. Make sure to include at least eight KSAPCs if inter-scorer reliability will be calculated (see below).[1] Completing a Selection Plan is perhaps the best way of doing this. If a Selection Plan has not been completed, be sure to at least use the criteria described in Chapter Two for selecting KSAPCs that can be measured using a content validity process (*e.g.,* necessary the first day of the job, important or critical, and rated high on the Best Worker rating if the TEE system will be used to rank applicants or used with a cutoff above minimum competency levels). The following are examples of KSAPCs that *should not* be measured using a TEE rating system:

   - Math skills
   - Reasoning or problem solving
   - Verbal communication
   - Reading ability
   - Physical abilities
   - Personality characteristics
   - Interpersonal skills

These KSAPCs should not be measured in a TEE rating system for obvious reasons. Be careful about including KSAPCs that, while critical for the job, might be better measured using other methods.

3. Develop a TEE Survey that provides applicants with the necessary fields (with plenty of space) to describe their relevant training, experience, and education for each KSAPC selected. A sample TEE Survey is provided in Figure 5-1.

SAMPLE TEE SURVEY			
Knowledge, Skill, Ability, or Personal Characteristic	**Training** (including professional, military, or other)	**Experience** (professional or volunteer)	**Education** (list by course title)
(Provide KSAPC from Job Analysis Here)	**(Applicant completes)**	**(Applicant completes)**	**(Applicant completes)**
Did you receive any grades, awards, credentials, certificates, performance ratings, or commendations? If so, describe each.			
How long was the training, experience, or educational course?			
If applicable, what levels were attained? Entry-level? Advanced levels?			
When was it completed?			
Where was it completed (name of employer or institution)?			
Name and contact information of a person or institution that can verify this information.			

Figure 5-1 Sample TEE Survey

This sample survey has been compressed for printing purposes. The Survey should be printed using landscape format and should provide applicants with plenty of space to handwrite their responses.

4. Develop a scoring system for the TEE Survey. Each KSAPC on the Survey can be unit weighted (with each counting equally) or weighted based on the relative importance of each TEE requirement to the job. Weights for each KSAPC on the Survey can be developed by asking a panel of Job Experts to assign 100 points among the KSAPCs, and then averaging the results. The job analysis data should be considered by the Job Experts when assigning point values; however, it is not necessary that the point ratings are in agreement with the job analysis data.[2]

5. After the TEE Surveys have been completed and submitted by applicants, two raters score the TEE Surveys (*e.g.,* using a 1-5 rating system for each scored item). The raters should review the job analysis for the position before providing ratings, and should use a consistent scoring taxonomy for providing scores. See the example TEE Rating Guidelines provided in Figure 5-2 below.

TEE RATING GUIDELINES		
Criteria		**Explanation**
R	Relevancy	How relevant is the TEE description? How well is it linked to the target KSAPCs? How well does the TEE resemble the job requirements? If not, how transportable is it?
A	Achievement	What level of achievement or proficiency is indicated (if any)? Were any credentials or awards attained?
T	Time	How much time did the applicant spend completing the training, experience, or education? Months? Years? How frequently was the training or experience repeated?
E	Extent	To what extent was the TEE acquired? To what level? At only a baseline level? Mastery? Expert?
D	Date	When was the TEE acquired? How recently? Was it acquired recently enough to still be relevant?

Figure 5-2 TEE Rating Guidelines

The ratings for each KSAPC should be a holistic judgment based on the collection of training, experience, and education described by the applicant, with specific attention being given to each of the RATED factors.

6. The final score for each applicant should be calculated and placed on a final score list and used on a pass/fail, banding, or rank-ordered fashion based on the reliability of the two raters, adverse impact, and the other factors discussed in Chapter Eight.

Using TEE Requirements in Closed Selection/Promotional Processes

In some employment situations, promotional opportunities are closed to outside applicants and only applicants from inside the employer who meet certain seniority or work experience requirements are eligible to apply. While using work seniority in closed promotional systems has relaxed validation requirements under Title VII,[3] they should still be evaluated for objectivity, fairness, and validity. Provided that the seniority system is bona fide and is the result of a negotiated labor contract, a straight-line seniority can be used in close promotional processes with little liability exposure for the employer.

Developing minimum time-in-grade requirements

In some situations, there is only one "feeder" job that can promote into the target position and the employer desires to set a pre-defined "time-in-grade" experience requirement for promotion into the target job (*e.g.,* a police officer promoting to a police sergeant). Under these circumstances, a minimum time-in-grade requirement can be established by surveying Job Experts in the target position and their supervisor regarding the minimum amount of experience that is needed for being eligible to promote into the target position (*i.e.,* eligible to apply for the position and then compete on the remaining selection procedures).[4]

Using "number of hours" in this rating (rather than months or years of experience) can address the fact that there may be part-time workers in the feeder positions. Calculate the average of the minimum-hours ratings from Job Experts and supervisors and reduce this value by one Standard Error of the Mean (SEM) to help compensate for sampling error in the ratings (*e.g.,* average rating of 3,500 hours minus 1 SEM of 500 hours = 3,000 hours minimum required to apply for the promotional position). The SEM can be calculated by dividing the standard deviation of the Job Expert ratings by the square root of the number of Job Experts minus one (1).

Developing a valid Work History Evaluation (WHE) for a closed promotional process

Now consider a target promotional position that has several feeder jobs, or only one feeder position that includes numerous "functional areas" (sub-classifications of the same position based on work area or specialization) and the target position supervises any or all of these areas. An example of this is a police sergeant who supervises police officers who work in several different various functional roles such as investigation, patrol, training, or booking. Another example is a Foreman for a stevedoring industry who supervises various Longshore (dock) workers who work in different functional areas such as crane operator, loader, lasher, transport driver, and others.

In these circumstances, a promotional process can be developed that assigns weights to the various feeder positions and/or functional areas based on their value in preparing incumbents for the target position. Developing such a scoring system requires calculating a *relative importance* weight for each of the feeder positions/functional areas and a *minimum and maximum number of hours* in each to be used in a selection procedure for promotion called a Work History Evaluation (WHE). A WHE can be used with a pass/fail cutoff or weighted and combined with other selection procedures in the promotional process. The steps for developing a WHE are provided below.

1. Create a WHE development survey that includes two sections as described below:
   a. The first section should include a description of each of the feeder position(s)-functional area(s) that promote into the target position. Next to each should be a field for Job Experts to write the relative weight of the feeder position-functional area considering the extent to which experience in the position prepares incumbents to perform in the target position (Job Experts will distribute 100 points to each according to its relevant value).
   b. The second section should include a field for Job Experts to write a minimum and maximum number of hours next to each feeder position-functional area. These ratings will be used for determining a minimum amount of time that incumbents must possess in each before accruing points, and a maximum limit where excessive experience in an area is capped in the scoring system. The minimum hours rating is necessary because incumbents who work less than that in some feeder positions/functional areas are not likely to have developed sufficient

levels of the KSAPCs that are related to that feeder position-functional area that will help them perform the target position. In positions where low levels of training are required, a very low minimum will be expected. A maximum number of hours is necessary because incumbents who choose to remain in one feeder position-functional area for extended periods will not likely continue to accrue valuable levels of the KSAPC for the target position beyond a certain level (*i.e.,* there is a diminishing value for remaining in some positions for extended periods).

2. Convene a panel of Job Experts and supervisors of the target position. The number of panel members required for this step depends on the sampling confidence desired (see Figure 2-1). In many situations, a panel of 7-10 qualified and experienced panel members is sufficient.

3. Provide the panel members with the Job Analysis (including a description of the various feeder positions/functional areas that will be weighted in this process). Describe the purpose of the workshop (developing a validated WHE for promotion into the target position) and discuss how the WHE will be used.

4. Have Job Experts complete both sections of the survey and input, and double-check the data.

5. Calculate the average and standard deviation for each feeder position-functional area for each section of the survey. Discard Job Expert ratings that are 1.645 standard deviations above or below the average rating for each (this process helps remove outliers, or extreme data points, from the data set and helps insure that the majority opinions are used for making the final weighting values).

6. Calculate a final weight and minimum/maximum value for each feeder position-functional area and use these values for calculating points for applicants using the weight of each multiplied by the percentage of the minimum/maximum values. For example, assume position A is worth 10% of the overall weight (based on Section One of the survey) and Section Two of the survey revealed a "minimum hours" value of 250 and a maximum of 1,500 for this position. If an applicant worked 1,500 hours in this position, they would have worked 100% of the target range. If they worked only 249 hours, they would have worked 0% of the target range. Assume an applicant has worked 1,250 hours in this position. This is 80% of the target range – which is the total number of hours the applicant worked within the target range divided by the number of hours above the minimum, but below the maximum. So their points for this position would be calculated as: 10% [the position's relative weight from Section One] * (1,000 / 1,250), or 10% * 80% = 8%. Note that the numerator (1,000) hours was determined by summing the number of hours this applicant had *above the minimum* (*e.g.,* 1,250 - 250). The denominator (1,250) was determined by subtracting the maximum hours from the minimum (1,500 - 250). When combined with their scores on the other positions, a final score can be obtained for each applicant.

7. If applicants can possibly have work experience hours in a feeder position-functional area that has substantially changed over the years, a minimum recency factor can also be included in this process.

Notes

[1] TEE rating systems can also be applied to job duties. The KSAPC rating method is proposed here because having the applicants provide descriptions of their training, experience, or education as it relates to job duties can sometimes present problems with the TEE raters giving credit for areas that will be trained on the job and are not necessarily required upon job entry (which can be problematic according to Section 14C4 of the Uniform Guidelines). The proposed KSAPC rating method should avoid this problem if the KSAPCs selected for the TEE rating process are screened using the Selection Plan process described in Chapter Two.

[2] This is because Job Experts will view the importance level of KSAPCs differently *based on which ones are available to be weighted* on the selection device, or in a selection process overall. In addition, KSAPCs can receive more or less weight based simply on how broadly or specifically they are described on the Job Analysis. For example, if a major KSAPC is simply worded in an over-encompassing way on the Job Analysis, it may receive less weight during a weighting process than a KSAPC that is divided into two aspects and written twice on the Job Analysis, which provides it with twice the opportunity to be evaluated and weighted by Job Experts.

[3] Section 703(h) of Title VII states: "Notwithstanding any other provision of this Title, it shall not be an unlawful employment practice for an employer to apply different standards of compensation, or different terms, conditions, or privileges of employment pursuant to a bona fide seniority or merit system, or a system which measures earnings by quantity or quality of production or to employees who work in different locations, provided that such differences care not the result of an intention to discriminate because of race, color, religion, sex, or national origin . . ." Therefore, absent a showing of a deliberate intent to use a seniority system for discriminatory purposes, they are less susceptible to Title VII lawsuits than other types of selection procedures.

[4] Employers should use caution when establishing these requirements because many occupations have only recently received influx from women and minority incumbents.

Chapter 6 - Developing and Validating "Work Sample" Physical Ability Tests

By James E. Kuthy, Ph.D., Daniel A. Biddle, Ph.D. & Stacy L. Bell, M.S.

Many employment situations require workers to be physically "strong" and "fit," as well as many combinations between each. Many truck driver positions, for example, require drivers to exert substantial feats of strength (*e.g.*, installing heavy tire chains in the snow, strapping and securing a load, etc.) sporadically between hours of low cardiovascular exertion (*e.g.*, driving). Other positions (warehouse "order pickers" for example), may require workers to be both "strong" and "fit" while they maintain constant workloads that demand both strength and fitness for an entire shift.

Employers often struggle with installing robust and defensible testing instruments for these various conditions. For example, some employers install strict cardiovascular fitness tests that use stair climbing machines or stationary bicycles to estimate the applicant's maximum V02[1] threshold. Such tests may lead to disgruntled applicants who do not perceive a direct connection between the test and the requirements of the job (*i.e.*, they lack "face validity," which can lead to low perceptions of fairness). In addition, a test that measures an applicant's "physiological or biological responses to performance" is classified by the EEOC (under the Americans with Disabilities Act of 1990) as a medical examination, which means that it can only be administered after a contingent job offer has been made.[2] The scoring and use of this type of test becomes even more challenging because they typically require using gender and age in the scoring formulae,[3] which is a specific violation of the 1991 Civil Rights Act when it comes to employment testing.[4] A further limitation regarding using only VO2 maximum tests for physically-demanding jobs is that, in some instances, cardiovascular endurance is negatively correlated with injuries – indicating that (at least in some instances), the more physically-fit workers may, in fact, be *more* injury-prone due to their perceived levels of fitness than less-fit individuals, who may be more inclined to abide by safe and efficient working practices.

Other employers install only static strength tests that measure whether an applicant is capable of lifting or manipulating the weights that are routinely handled on the job, and leave stamina unmeasured in the hiring process. Still other employers do not install any form of testing, and leave it to chance as to whether applicants will be able to perform rigorous job requirements. Neither of these solutions alone will likely serve the employer's best interests when hiring for physically-demanding jobs.

In situations where the physical job demands are rigorous, the best way to insure that applicants are job-ready is to develop a work sample test that replicates and mirrors a "vital snapshot" of the job. In this way, whatever combination of strength and fitness that is required for the actual job is mirrored on the pre-employment test (as much of each that can feasibly be included on a pre-employment test). Research strongly suggests there will be fewer dissatisfied test takers if the content of a test is transparently similar to the content of the job, such that those who fail the test would realize that they would not successfully perform the job.

With that in mind, it is frequently helpful if the content and context of the physical ability and/or work sample test events mimic critical or important work behaviors that constitute most of the job. In the words of Section 14C4 of the federal *Uniform Guidelines*, "the closer the content and context of the selection procedure are to work samples or work behaviors, the stronger is the basis for showing content validity." The following is a description of a content-related validity strategy for validating a physical ability test.

Steps for Developing a Physical Ability Test Using Content Validity

1. Conduct a thorough job analysis that focuses on the physical aspects of the job.
2. Identify the parts of the job (*i.e.,* job duties, or sets of job duties) that are typically performed in rapid succession that collectively require *continuous physical exertion* for over 10 minutes. For some positions, this may be one job duty repeatedly performed where a rapid work pace is required on the job (*e.g.,* loading or unloading a truck). For other jobs (*e.g.,* firefighters), this may consist of a set of unrelated job duties where a rapid pace is required for physically-demanding job duties (*e.g.,* pulling hoses, then raising the fly section of a ladder).[5]
3. Work with supervisors and trainers to assemble a continuously-timed, multiple-event job simulation physical ability test (PAT). The PAT events included need to be those where a rapid (but safe) working pace is important.
   a. If you wish to use physical ability testing for parts of the job that are not typically performed in rapid succession, then work with supervisors and trainers to assemble discrete test events for measuring the ability to perform those parts of the job.
4. Run a representative sample of Job Experts (*e.g.,* 20-30) through the PAT and administer a validation survey that collects the following information from each:
   a. Actual PAT completion time. If you are using a continuously-timed, multiple-event job simulation PAT, then collect the time it takes each Job Expert to complete all of the events combined. If you are using a single-event PAT, or a series of single-event PATs, then collect the time it takes each Job Expert to complete each test event.
   b. Opinion time for a minimally-qualified applicant to complete the PAT (*e.g.,* Job Experts could be asked, "Given your time to complete the PAT, your current fitness level, and your level of job experience, what time should a minimally-qualified applicant score when taking this PAT?").
   c. Their Yes/No answer to the following questions:
      i. Does the PAT measure skills/abilities that are important/critical (essential for the performance of the job)?
      ii. Does the PAT measure skills/abilities that are necessary on the first day of the job (*i.e.,* before training)?

    iii.   Does the PAT replicate/simulate actual work behaviors in a manner, setting, and level of complexity similar to the job?

    iv.   Do the events in the PAT need to be completed on the job in a <u>rapid and safe</u> manner (*i.e.,* is speed important)?

    v.   Are the weights and distances involved in the PAT representative of the job?

    vi.   Is the duration that the objects/equipment are typically carried or handled in the PAT similar to what is required of a single person on the job?

    vii.   Is the PAT free from any "special techniques" that are learned on the job that allow current job incumbents to perform the PAT events better than an applicant could (that are not demonstrated to the applicants prior to taking the PAT)?

    viii.   Does the PAT require the same or less exertion of the applicant than is required on the job?

5. Analyze the Job Expert data gathered from Step 4:
   a. First, analyze the Yes/No ratings gathered from Step 4c (above). At least 70% of the Job Experts must answer "Yes" to each question. If this is not the case, go back to the drawing board and re-design the test as necessary. Then re-survey the Job Experts until at least 70% of the Job Experts endorse each.
   b. Next, compute the average of the opinion times gathered in Step 4b. Use the SEM computed in Step 6 below to adjust their average opinion time (by adding 1 or 2 SEMs) to be used as the final cutoff score (*i.e.,* the amount of time that is allowed to successfully complete the test event).
   c. Compute the average Job Expert PAT time (from 4a above) and add 1.645^6 Standard Errors of Difference (SEDs) to this average.[7] This score level constitutes the lowest score boundary of the "normal expectations of acceptable proficiency in the workforce" that is required when setting cutoff scores by the Uniform Guidelines (see Section 5H). Ideally, the final cutoff score (set using the adjusted opinion times above) should be close to this score level.

6. Conduct a test-retest study to determine the Standard Error of Measurement (SEM) of the PAT. This requires having 60+ applicants or incumbents taking the PAT twice (separated by 1-2 weeks), and correlating the two scores to obtain the test-retest reliability estimate (r_{xx}). This value is used along with the standard deviation of the sample to compute the SEM using the formula: $SEM = \sigma_x(1 - r_{xx})^{1/2}$ where σ_x is the standard deviation of test scores and r_{xx} is the test-retest reliability. For example, if the test-retest reliability is .84 and the standard deviation is 10, the SEM would be 4.0 (in Excel: = 10*(sqrt(1-.84)).

Any pace, distance, weights, or other limitations used during testing must be job-related (*i.e.,* related to actual pace, distances, weights, or other limitations that are required on the job). For example, if an employee on the job would have up to three minutes to move something from point A to point B, then the job candidate should not be required to perform this same task in less time during the test.[8] Similarly, if an employee is expected to carry an object a certain distance on the job, but is allowed to briefly place that object on the ground to rest and/or change their grip, the test taker should also be allowed to similarly rest and/or change their grip if required to carry an item during a test. In other words, the test should be similar in difficulty to the actual job, and should not require the test taker to carry more weight, move something a longer distance, or perform work that is substantially more difficult than on the actual job.

Test events that mimic work behaviors do not require a statistical examination of test performance and job performance to be conducted. Alternatively, test events that do not mimic work behaviors, but which are predictive of job performance, can be used if a statistically significant relationship can be shown between performance on the test and performance on the job. To use this type of testing, a relatively large number of job candidates or current employees (at least 130 is recommended, however, meaningful studies can be conducted with smaller samples if the relationship between the test and job performance is relatively strong) must take the test and their test scores be statistically compared to their work performance (this process utilizes a criterion-related validation strategy).

Steps for Developing a Physical Ability Test Using Criterion-related Validity

1. Complete Steps 1-3 outlined in the content validity section above.
2. If a *concurrent* criterion-related validation strategy (where the PAT will be administered to current job incumbents from the target position) will be used, administer the PAT to 130 current incumbents. The benefit of conducting a concurrent study is that it is fast – the researcher will find out quickly if the PAT is valid (*i.e.,* significantly correlated to job performance). The drawback is that concurrent studies sometimes have less "power" than the predictive studies (because of range restriction in the post-screened worker population involved in the study). This might result in a situation where the study does not reveal a significant correlation that actually exists in the greater population and would have shown up if a larger study had been conducted. Another drawback of a concurrent study is that it requires off-the-job time from incumbents to complete the PAT.
3. If a *predictive* criterion-related validation strategy (where the PAT will be administered to onboarding applicants and subsequently rated on job performance) will be used, administer the PAT to 130 applicants who are subsequently hired (*e.g., 500 tested, 130 hired*). One of the benefits of using a predictive study is that it may have higher power (increased likelihood of finding significance) because the employer is testing a broader ability range of applicants (compared to the post-tested employee group used in a concurrent study). Another advantage is that a predictive study is "passive" – it does not take existing employees off the job. The drawback is that it takes time to test and finally hire 130+ applicants who are subsequently rated on job performance.

4. Develop a Job Performance Rating Survey (JPRS) to be used for gathering job performance ratings from supervisors for each incumbent who completed the PAT. Several aspects of job performance (*e.g.,* 5-10) that are suspected of being related to the PAT scores should be included.
5. Administer the JPRS and collect the ratings.
6. Complete the statistical analyses and determine whether the PAT is significantly correlated to one or more job performance dimensions.
7. Set the cutoff at a level that represents the performance levels required for the job, being alert to any corresponding levels of adverse impact.

When using either a content- or criterion-related validation strategy, physical ability and work sample test events should be designed to be as simple as practical (unless the job analysis shows that a minimally-qualified employee on the first day of the job prior to training would need to be able to learn complex work-related tasks in a short period of time and then be able to perform those tasks they just learned). In other words, each event should include as few steps and/or procedures for the job candidate to follow as possible, unless more complexity is justified by the job analysis. Simplicity of the test events helps minimize confusion and aides with scoring. If possible, longer or more complex events should be broken into shorter, separate parts. Also, the amount of time and information that a candidate is provided to learn how to perform the event (and is allowed to practice and ask questions about that event) should increase as the complexity of the event increases.

Administering the Test

Test administrators should be trained about the testing process prior to their being permitted to administer the test. Furthermore, it is recommended that, if testing will take place over any period of time or uses multiple administrators, a lead administrator is appointed to oversee the test's administration to insure continuity between testing sessions. In addition, test administrators should faithfully follow the test event description plan that has been developed for the administration and scoring of each event. Deviating from the plan can result in increased potential liability to the employer.

Prior to the administration of each test event, candidates should be informed of the contents of that event. To help insure standardization, which is fundamental for fair and valid testing, it is best if the administrator reads from a script word-for-word, or plays a recording, that describes each event before job candidates attempt those events. The administrator should also demonstrate (or show a video demonstrating) each event (including the different techniques that may be used for successfully performing the required task during each event).

In general, if a candidate appears confused or frustrated when taking the test, the administrator should ask, "Do you need me to repeat the instructions?" If the candidate says "Yes," or if a candidate directly asks for additional instructions, the administrator should provide appropriate information. An exception to this would be if the ability to follow instructions is part of the testing criteria of the test being administered. If that is the case, have a plan in place for how to address this issue in a job-related fashion (based on the job analysis and input from the job experts) in advance of testing.

Since many of the job candidates will be performing the events required during testing for the first time, it would make sense (in most situations) that they be given a longer amount of time, or allowed greater flexibility, to perform the task than if they were being performed by someone who has been performing the job for a relatively long period of time. Similarly, the number of attempts to complete an event should be a realistic number that could be used to determine whether that job candidate could successfully perform a similar task on the job. In the interest of fairness, test takers should generally be allowed more than one attempt to complete an event, unless it is obvious that injury or harm would occur to the test taker (or others), and/or expensive or non-replaceable company property would be seriously damaged if another attempt was allowed. If testing is stopped because of the likelihood that injury or harm would occur if another attempt was allowed, this should be documented in detail.

In some instances, it might be acceptable to deduct points if instructions need to be provided to the test taker more than once during this type of test. However, deducting points or other penalties for this type of activity must be job-related and justified in relationship to how the job is actually performed. For example, if there is no penalty on the job if an employee asks questions or clarifications when learning to perform a task on the job, there should not be any penalty for this behavior during the test. Conversely, if the job requires that an employee learn a task and perform that task on the job without additional instructions, then taking this into consideration during testing may be justified.

When administering the physical ability and/or work-sample test to candidates, the paramount concern should be the safety of each candidate. Safety can be promoted by ensuring that each candidate is shown the proper way(s) to perform each event prior to their taking the test, and by carefully observing the test takers during the events when appropriate.

Also, if relevant, the administrator should stress the importance of safety to the test taker before the test is administered. In addition, it might be helpful to provide a demonstration of how the test taker could safely use, maneuver, lift, carry, and/or move the materials during testing. To minimize potential injuries or problems during testing, it is strongly recommended that the test taker be allowed a reasonable period of time to practice lifting and/or carrying the materials/devices to be handled during each event. Administrators should also explain to the candidate that, since safety is a primary concern, they will be disqualified if they do not follow the safety rules and/or safe working practices that have been explained to them. It might be helpful to provide a printed copy of any safety rules or safe work practices that will be used as disqualifications during the test to the job candidates in advance of the test. However, even if a printed copy of the safety rules and safe work practices are given to the candidates in advance, those rules should again be read, explained, and/or demonstrated to the candidates at the time of testing.[9] Employers should consider that any actions they take during recruitment and testing sends a message to potential employees about the culture of the organization.

Testing should be immediately stopped if a candidate fails to follow a safety rule and/or safe working practice. Explain to that candidate again how the task should be safely performed and, if appropriate, provide another demonstration. Allow the candidate to continue testing unless it is obvious that injury or harm would occur to the test taker (or others), and/or company property would be seriously damaged, in which case another attempt should not be allowed. Again, if the testing process is stopped because of the likelihood that injury or serious damage would occur if the test was continued, this should be documented in detail.

If a candidate violates a safety rule or if, during the physical ability or work sample task event, they perform the task in a way that the administrator feels demonstrates that they do not possess the level of safety-related knowledge that a minimally-qualified, entry-level employee should possess, a complete and accurate description of that violation or unsafe work behavior should be presented to a panel of target-job experts (and/or supervisors and/or trainers of the target job) or safety-committee members for evaluation.[10] Those experts shall determine whether the violation or unsafe work practice indicated that the candidate does not possess the level of safety-related knowledge or ability that a minimally-qualified, entry-level employee should possess. The job candidate will be disqualified if it is determined by the panel that their performance indicated they do not possess the level of safety-related knowledge or ability that a minimally-qualified, entry-level employee for the target job should possess prior to any training or on-the-job experience with the employer who is doing the testing.

Suggestion: If the test requires any physical activity or stress:

- It is recommended that candidates should be required to sign a waiver of liability.
  - The liability release form should be completed and signed before a candidate is allowed to take the test.
  - The liability release form should include a description of the test so that the candidate can make an intelligent waiver.
- If the employer so decides, candidates may also be required to obtain a medical release prior to testing.
- If appropriate, first aid and/or medical assistance should be available at the testing site and/or readily available.

If a candidate appears to be injured during testing, stop the test and ask them, "Are you injured?" If the candidate says "Yes" and/or it is obvious to the test administrator that they have injured themselves, stop the event and obtain assistance immediately. Develop a plan in advance as to how to respond to injuries that may occur during testing and make certain all test administrators are aware of the emergency response plan if an injury should occur.

The starting and ending points for each event, and/or the path that the test taker should take during testing, should be clearly marked for the test taker to see. For example, if the candidate can be penalized for traveling outside of a certain path during a test event, (1) the path limits should be clearly marked so the test taker knows their limits when performing a test event, and (2) the limits should be based upon solid, job-related reasons (for instance, the narrow path that must be followed when the job is actually performed which travels between two pieces of closely-aligned equipment; or that an employee or another person might be injured on the job if a certain path was not carefully followed). It is helpful to photograph the test course to document that these steps have been taken.

In general, spectators during testing should not be allowed. However, even if there are no spectators, the candidates themselves will be observing each other perform the events. All observers and candidates should be instructed not to cheer, jeer, whistle, yell, signal, or in any way interfere with a fellow candidate's performance of an event. That being said, the test administrator is encouraged to provide a moderate, consistent level of encouragement, support, and/or instructions to all candidates.

If the testing requires strenuous physical activity, it is recommended that candidates be asked to remain at the testing site until they have sufficiently recovered from the testing process. This could potentially reduce claims related to testing.

In general, candidates should not be permitted to leave the testing process until:

1. They have correctly performed the test events (administrators should make notes of any observable deficiencies).
2. The candidate says they wish to stop the test or cannot complete the event; the candidate is then disqualified.
3. The candidate has attempted, but did not successfully complete the event or test; the candidate is then disqualified.

Candidates who wish to leave prior to any of these three conditions should be asked, if possible, to sign a document indicating they have voluntarily withdrawn from the selection process. The administrator should carefully document the circumstances if the candidate refuses to sign such a document before leaving.

Scoring Physical Ability Tests

Scoring accuracy and fairness to all candidates can be promoted by implementing a standardized approach for the administration and scoring of each event (*i.e.,* sending all candidates through the same events, in the same sequence, and with the same instructions) and, if possible, utilizing multiple scorers (*e.g.,* two individuals with stop watches). Also, clear and unambiguous, observable criteria must be used when determining whether someone passes or fails the test event in the same way for scoring each and every test taker. Ambiguous criteria, such as whether the test taker "appeared to be struggling," "was breathing hard," or "had to stand on the tips of their toes when performing the task," are not acceptable for scoring purposes.

The final decision must be made as to whether the test taker successfully completed the task required or not, within the defined observable criteria (such as being able to carry an object which weighs the same or less than the weight carried on the job; a job-related distance that is the same or less distance than on the job; or within a job-related amount of time that is the same or more than the amount of time in which the task must be performed on the job).

The amount of time a test taker uses to perform the test events should be carefully measured and recorded. To increase the reliability of time measurements, it is recommended that two administrators should time the test events whenever possible. The use of timers, where the candidate presses a button to begin the test event and presses the same button when they have completed the event, is also helpful.

Administrators should ensure that test results and information are recorded on the appropriate form(s). To minimize potential conflict later, it might help if the scoring form is signed by both the test administrator and the job candidate at the end of testing. However, this is not generally required for a testing process to be considered valid.

The Americans with Disabilities Act and Physical Ability Testing

As mentioned previously, testing that measures the test takers' physiological signs (such as heart or breathing rate) would be considered "medically-based" testing under the Americans with Disabilities Act. Medically-based tests can only be given after a bona-fide offer of employment has been extended to the job candidate. Furthermore, the Americans with Disabilities Act specifies that applicants be required to perform the "essential" work functions with or without reasonable accommodations, that these be clearly described to applicants prior to job entry, and may be represented and measured on pre-employment tests. The EEOC indicates that "essential functions are the basic job duties that an employee must be able to perform, with or without reasonable accommodation." A job function may be considered essential for any of the several reasons, including but not limited to the following:

- The function may be essential because the reason the position exists is to perform the function;
- The function may be essential because of the limited number of employees available among whom the performance of that job function can be distributed; and/or
- The function may be highly specialized so that the incumbent in the position is hired for their expertise or ability to perform the particular function.

Evidence of whether a particular function is essential includes, but is not limited to:

- The employer's judgment as to which function is essential;
- Written job descriptions prepared before the advertising or interviewing applicants for a job;
- The amount of time spent on the job performing the function;
- The consequences of not requiring the incumbent to perform that function;
- The terms of a collective bargaining agreement;
- The work experience of past incumbents in the job; and/or
- The current work experience of incumbents in similar jobs.[11]

While it may seem counterintuitive, an employer must provide reasonable accommodation to an applicant with a disability during testing *even if* that same employer knows they will be unable to provide this individual with a reasonable accommodation on the job (due to "undue hardship" which the employer must be prepared to prove). The Equal Employment Opportunity Commission warns employers to assess the need for accommodations for the application process separately from those that may be needed to perform the job.[12]

The next section of this Chapter provides an example of a physically-challenging test event that has been successfully used for determining if firefighter job candidates can perform one part of the job of a firefighter if they were hired. This shows the level of detail that is advised for developing and administering physical ability testing that would most likely survive a challenge.

Sample Test Event Description: Ladder Removal/Carry

Description: Candidate removes a 24-foot aluminum extension ladder from mounted hooks, carries the ladder a minimum of a total of 60 feet (around a diamond shaped course, the boundaries of which are marked on the ground for them to follow), and replaces the ladder on to the same mounted hooks within three (3) minutes.

Specifications:

- The 24-foot aluminum extension ladder should weigh 41 pounds.
- The mounted hooks should be positioned so that the top portion of the ladder is located 48 inches from the ground.

Demonstration to Candidates: Information that should be given to candidates during the demonstration:

There are three methods that may be used when completing this event: (1) the High Shoulder Carry, the (2) Low Shoulder Carry, and (3) the Suitcase Carry. With all methods, candidates should begin by finding the balance point of the ladder. Rungs in the middle of the ladder, which should provide the best balance point, will be marked.

1. High Shoulder Carry:
   In the high shoulder, carry the entire ladder sits on the top of the candidate's shoulder. Candidates may place the ladder directly on their shoulder from the mounted hooks and proceed around the designated area, replacing the ladder to the hooks directly from the shoulder.
2. Low Shoulder Carry:
   In the low shoulder carry, the top beam of the ladder sits on the top of the candidate's shoulder. Candidates may place the ladder directly on their shoulder from the mounted hooks and proceed around the designated area, replacing the ladder to the hooks directly from the shoulder.
3. Suitcase Carry:
   In this method, the top beam of the ladder is held in one arm like a suitcase.

If, in the administrator's opinion, the candidate loses control of the ladder while carrying it around the designated area, the administrator may intervene. The administrator will take the ladder from the candidate, placing it on the ground at the place where the test taker lost control. The candidate can then pick the ladder up (in any fashion) and continue.

When replacing the ladder, both ends of the ladder must be in control of the test taker and off of the ground.

The ladder must be replaced on the hooks in the original position. There will be rungs painted on the ladder to assist candidates in this process. If the ladder is not replaced in the original position, candidates will be required to remove the ladder and replace it in the proper position.

Scoring: While performing this event, candidates are allowed two penalties before failing. A penalty should be given for any of the following:

- If the candidate drops the ladder, or if it touches the ground;
- If the candidate loses control of the ladder and the administrator must step in and assist;
- If the candidate must place the ladder on the ground to gain stability;
- If the ladder falls over the neck of the candidate, with the candidate's neck between ladder rungs. (In this case, the proctor should immediately assist in the removal and grounding of the ladder);
- If the candidate steps outside of the marked boundary path; and lastly,
- If the candidate fails to follow instructions when performing the test event.
  - If the candidate fails to follow instructions when performing a test event, immediately stop testing and timing the event. Explain again how the event should be performed and, if appropriate, provide an additional demonstration. Ask the candidate to acknowledge that they understand the instructions on how to properly perform the test event before allowing the candidate to continue (or start again, depending on the circumstances). This should be allowed twice. If the candidate still does not follow the instructions after testing begins a third time, the candidate automatically fails this event and testing for that candidate should be discontinued.

Pass/Fail Criteria: The candidate will be automatically disqualified (*i.e.,* fail) if a third penalty occurs or if the event is not successfully completed within three (3) minutes.

Candidates should also be evaluated for their ability to work safely and/or follow safe working practices during the physical ability testing process. The administrator should carefully document any of the following:

- If candidates fail to follow the safety rules and/or procedures of which they had been made aware;
- If candidates ignore potential safety hazards that should have been obvious to a minimally-qualified, entry-level employee the first day on the job prior to training; or
- If, during the event, candidates perform in a way that is in violation of safety protocols that should have been obvious to a minimally-qualified, entry-level employee the first day on the job prior to training.

Methods shown to candidates:

- Safe lifting techniques (*e.g.,* bend knees when lifting)
- Finding the balance point of the ladder
- Placing ladder directly on shoulder from mounted hooks
- High shoulder carry
- Low shoulder carry
- Suitcase carry
- Properly replacing the ladder (with both ends off of the ground and in the appropriate position)

Notes

[1] VO2 maximum refers to the highest rate of oxygen consumption attainable during maximal or exhaustive exercise.

[2] The U.S. Equal Employment Opportunity Commission, Notice Number 915.002 (Date 10/10/95). See (http://www.eeoc.gov/policy/docs/preemp.html).

[3] Siconolfi, S. F., Garber, C. E., Lasater, T. M., & Carleton, R. A. (1985). A simple, valid step test for estimating maximal oxygen uptake in epidemiologic studies. *American Journal of Epidemiology, 121*, 382-390.

[4] Section 703 of the Civil Rights Act of 1964 (42 U.S.C. 2000e-2) (as amended by section 105) states: "It shall be an unlawful employment practice for a respondent, in connection with the selection or referral of applicants or candidates for employment or promotion, to adjust the scores, use different cutoff scores for, or otherwise alter the results of, employment related tests on the basis of race, color, religion, sex, or national origin."

[5] In some job situations where time is not an issue, the correct question may instead be the number of repetitions, the amount of weight, or the distance carried. For example, the candidate may be given five minutes to put together small parts and then asked "how many small parts should a minimally-qualified applicant be able to put together within five minutes?" or "how many sets of items should a minimally-qualified applicant be able to move within 15 minutes?"

[6] Alternatively, 1.96 SEDs can be used, which provides 97.5% confidence.

[7] The SED is computed by multiplying the SEM by the square root of 2.

[8] *EEOC v. Dial Corp.*, 469 F.3d 735 (8th Cir. 2006). A major company lost a 3.4 million-dollar court case due to the fact that, during testing, job candidates were required to not only perform a work-related task at a faster pace than required to be performed on the job, but also without the short breaks between efforts that are allowed on the job.

[9] This will help to emphasize to the candidate the importance of safety on the job and will also help minimize potential grievances that might allege the safety rules and/or safe working practices were not explained sufficiently.

[10] Test takers frequently do not accurately recall how well they performed during testing. For this reason video- and/or audio-recording of test events will often enhance an employer's ability to successfully defend the elimination of an unqualified job candidate. As with all test-related documents, recordings should be retained in the event of challenge by job candidates, which can sometimes occur years after testing has taken place. In addition, recordings of job candidates should only be used for selection purposes.

[11] See the 1990 *Americans with Disabilities Act*, Section 1630.2(n).

[12] See Question #13 in the EEOC's *Enforcement Guidance: Reasonable Accommodation and Undue Hardship Under the Americans with Disabilities Act document* at http://www.eeoc.gov/policy/docs/accommodation.html for more details.

Chapter 7 - Investigating Test Bias
By Gregory M. Hurtz, Ph.D.

The Uniform Guidelines categorize a test as "unfair" whenever "…members of one race, sex, or ethnic group characteristically obtain lower scores on a selection procedure than members of another group, and the differences in scores are not reflected in differences in a measure of job performance" (Section 8A). This section continues to explain that tests that meet this definition of unfairness "may unfairly deny opportunities to members of the group that obtains the lower scores."

Since the framing of the Uniform Guidelines, most practitioners have used an earlier conceptualization of test fairness called the "Cleary Rule." This rule was developed by Cleary in 1968 where she stated that test bias can be evaluated by testing two hypotheses with respect to the linear relation between test scores and a criterion measure: (1) Equality of slopes, and then (2) equality of intercepts (given that slopes are equal). Cleary used the mathematics of the Analysis of Covariance (ANCOVA) to test these hypotheses.

ANCOVA tests for group differences on a criterion variable after partialling out a covariate. For the test bias analysis, the "criterion" variable is a measure of job performance, the "covariate" is the test score, and the "groups" (e.g., male vs. female) are represented by a dummy variable (*e.g.,* men coded using 1; women coded using 0). An assumption of ANCOVA is that the slope of the line from regressing the criterion onto the covariate is equivalent across the groups. Stated another way, it is assumed that there is no group-by-covariate interaction, meaning that the covariate is related to the criterion to equivalent degrees across the groups. Thus, by Cleary's example, first test whether there are slope differences across groups. If there are slope differences, then one cannot test for intercept differences for the same reasons that ANCOVA holds the homogeneity of regression lines assumption (but see Lautenschlager & Mendoza, 1986 discussion, below); if there are no slope differences, then proceed to testing for intercept differences by looking for covariate-adjusted group mean differences in ANCOVA. These mean differences *are* the intercept differences. If there are no such group differences, then the regression of the criterion (*i.e.,* job performance) on the covariate (*i.e.,* test scores) is equivalent across groups, and the conclusion is that there is no bias.

Later writings on the Cleary Rule have framed it within the context of moderated multiple regression (MMR) analysis in the Cohen and Cohen (1975) tradition, but this is identical to the ANCOVA approach because the moderator is a dummy variable. Thus, test for slope differences with a test-by-group product term, and intercept differences with the group dummy code. Following Cleary's example, test for the interaction first (later named "slope bias") and, if there is no interaction, then test for intercept differences (later named "intercept bias"). In absence of either type of difference, the conclusion is there is no bias.

Lautenschlager and Mendoza's Reframing of Test Bias Analysis

Lautenschlager and Mendoza (1986) discuss testing for test bias via regression analysis as either a "step up" or "step down" process. They suggest that Cleary, or at least later users of the Cleary method who followed the Cohen and Cohen (1975) tradition for MMR, followed a "step up" process where, in essence, intercept differences were tested first, before slope differences. Bias was tested by adding terms to the regression equation and testing for significance, rather than starting with a complete interaction model and dropping terms to test for significance. The description of the Cleary Rule in Nunnally and Bernstein (1994) is evidence of this claim, as it clearly describes a "step up" approach.

Lautenschlager and Mendoza (1986) suggested that a "step down" procedure should be used that begins with the full interaction model. In concept, this is actually consistent with what Cleary had suggested from the start (*i.e.,* testing slope differences, and then testing intercept differences if there are no slope differences). However, Lautenschlager and Mendoza's approach does not start with an isolated test of slope differences followed by an isolated test of intercept differences; it starts with an omnibus test of whether there are slope *and/or* intercept differences. Due to the reduction in the sum of squared error for the test, they suggest this test will have more power to detect bias than will separate tests of slope and intercept differences. Thus, there will be less likelihood of making a Type II error when concluding that no bias is present.

Carrying Out Lautenschlager and Mendoza's Approach in SPSS

In order to carry out Lautenschlager and Mendoza's (1986) process in SPSS, the following steps should be taken which follow the flowchart presented in their article.

1. Create a dummy code for the group variable (*e.g.,* gender, ethnicity).
2. Create a product term by multiplying test scores by the dummy code (using the COMPUTE procedure).
3. Enter the performance criterion as the dependent variable in the regression analysis
4. <u>Conduct the omnibus test:</u> In Block 1 enter test scores, and in Block 2 enter the dummy code and the product term together (see screenshots below). Click the "Statistics" button, and select the "R-Squared change" option to provide the significance test of the change in R^2.

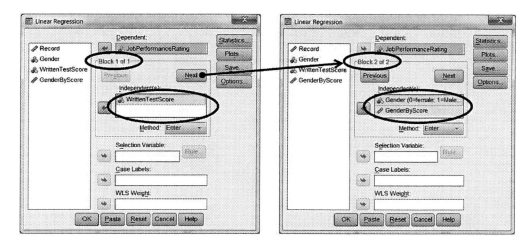

a. If the change in R^2 between Block 1 and Block 2 is <u>NOT</u> significant, this suggests no test bias; there are no slope or intercept differences. The analysis stops.

b. If the difference in R^2 between Block 1 and Block 2 <u>IS</u> significant (as in the sample output below), this suggests either slope or intercept bias is present (or perhaps both). If this answer is good enough, the analysis can stop. However, in order to understand the nature of the bias, further exploration is needed into whether slopes, intercepts, or both differ.

Model Summary

Model	R	R Square	Adjusted R Square	Std. Error of the Estimate	R Square Change	F Change	df1	df2	Sig. F Change
					Change Statistics				
1	.335a	.113	.103	1.833	.113	12.423	1	98	.001
2	.440b	.194	.169	1.765	.081	4.848	2	96	.010

a. Predictors: (Constant), Written Test Score (0-100)

b. Predictors: (Constant), Written Test Score (0-100), Gender (0=female; 1=Male), GenderByScore

> Significant; therefore, there is some form of bias.

Figure 7-1 Model Summary with Significant Difference in R^2

5. <u>Test for slope differences.</u> This is basically Cleary's first step. To run this test, move the group dummy code from Block 2 to Block 1 in the SPSS screens. So, test scores and the dummy code should now be in Block 1, and the product term alone in Block 2 (see screenshots below). Rerun the analysis. Now the test for the change in R^2 tests for the presence of slope differences alone. The next step depends on whether or not there are slope differences at this stage.

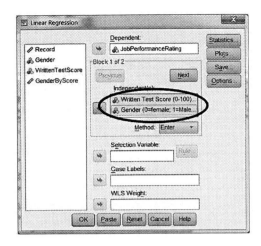 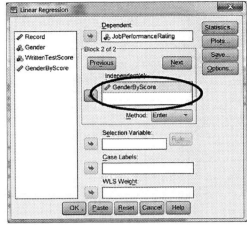

a. If there are **no** slope differences (*i.e.,* the change in R^2 is non-significant), test for intercept differences alone.

6. <u>Test for intercept differences</u>. Drop the product term from the analysis, and move the dummy code to Block 2 (see screenshots below). With test scores in Block 1 and the dummy code alone in Block 2, the change R^2 will now test for the presence of intercept differences.

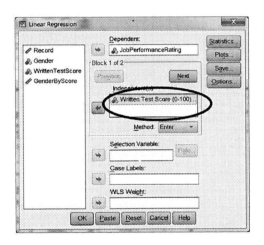 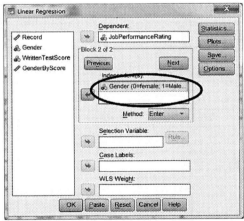

a. If there <u>ARE</u> intercept differences here (*i.e.,* the change in R^2 is significant), evaluate the effect size (*i.e.,* the change in R^2) and the practical significance of the score differences in terms of observed score units before making a firm conclusion of bias.

b. If there are <u>NO</u> intercept differences here (*i.e.,* the change in R^2 is non-significant), this contradicts the omnibus test. This is an unlikely event; however, given the suggestion that the omnibus test has more power it probably would not be wise to conclude no bias at this stage. Instead, it should be concluded that bias of an unknown form exists.

Analysis of the R^2 values may give some insight into where the bias lies even if the significance test did not pinpoint it.

7. Back to the test of slope differences - if there are slope differences (*i.e.,* the change in R^2 is significant), test for the presence of simultaneously occurring intercept differences. In Block 1, enter test scores and the product term. In Block 2, enter the dummy code. Now, the change in R^2 statistic tests for intercept differences in the presence of the slope differences.

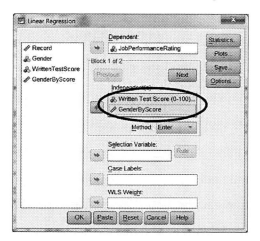 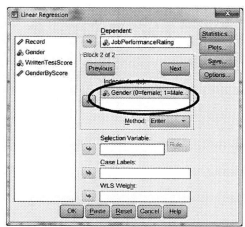

a. If there ARE intercept differences here (*i.e.,* the change in R^2 is significant), then the conclusion is that both slope bias and intercept bias is present. Evaluate the effect size and practical significance of the score differences in terms of observed score units before crying "bias" too loudly.

b. If there are NO intercept differences (*i.e.,* the change in R^2 is non-significant), then there is only slope bias. Evaluate the effect size and practical significance of the score differences in terms of observed score units before crying "bias" too loudly.

Subgroup Scatterplots

If any differences are found, it will probably be useful to view the subgroup scatterplots and regression lines to visualize the differences. Following is a demonstration of how to obtain either stacked or side-by-side scatterplots for each group in SPSS. Use what are now called "legacy graphs" in SPSS in order to be backwards-compatible to many previous versions of SPSS. In older version of SPSS, click on the Graphs menu, then select Scatter/Dot. In newer versions (at least as of version 18), this Scatter/Dot option is embedded in a submenu called "Legacy Dialogs" so select it from there.

Choose the Simple Scatter option and click Define (see screenshots below). Move the performance criterion measure into the Y Axis box, and the test score variable into the X axis box. For stacked scatterplots, move the group variable (*e.g.,* gender) into the Rows box in the "Panel by" area. For side-by-side scatterplots, put the group variable in the Columns box instead. The choice is aesthetic, although generally the stacked graphs will probably look better because they generally display a longer X axis and short Y axis, which most likely better reflects the nature of the X and Y variables (the "X" test scores are often scored on a wider range of values while the "Y" performance ratings are often on a restricted scale).

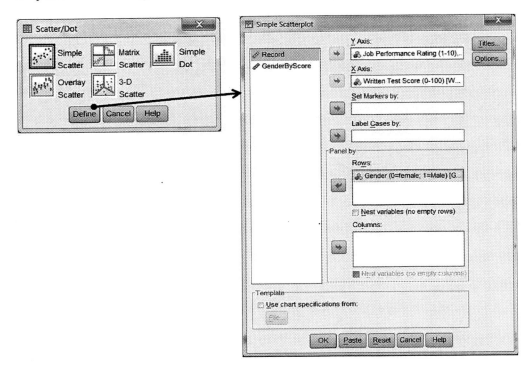

Click OK to generate the graph, and then double-click the graph to open the chart editor. Under the "Elements" menu, select Fit Line at Total to place the regression lines for each group on the scatterplots. This will also add a legend with the R^2 values for each subgroup (the square roots of these values are the typical Pearson correlations between test scores and performance for each subgroup). The stacked subgroup scatterplot based on the current example is shown next.

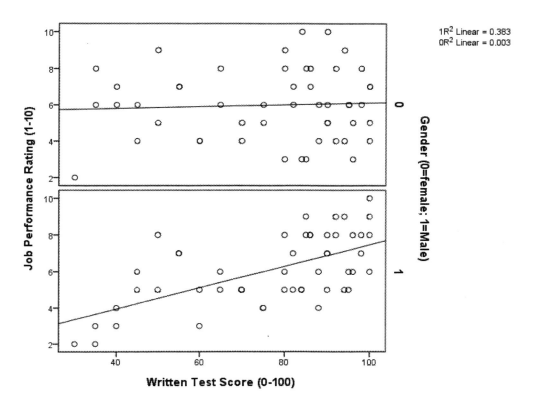

Figure 7-2 Stacked Subgroup Scatterplot

Relation to Other Tests

It should be noted that Lautenschlager and Mendoza's (1986) initial omnibus test is the identical F test as that derived by Chow (1960), commonly referred to as "the Chow test." Serlin and Levin (1980) also provide an identical F test for the same purpose; to determine whether slopes, intercepts, or both differ across a set of groups. The omnibus test is therefore well-documented.

Lautenschlager and Mendoza (1986) also suggest that follow-up analyses exploring regions of significance may be fruitful in determining whether the regressions differ within the range of test scores where decisions are to be made. It may be the case that the lines differ at the low end of the continuum, but do not differ appreciably in the upper end where hiring/promotion/etc. decisions are made. If the regions of significance calculations suggest this situation to be true, then the apparent bias may not ever influence any decisions. This could be valuable information in the defense of a test. Serlin and Levin (1980) discuss alternative methods of calculating regions of significance.

Chapter 8 - Using Selection Procedures: Cutoffs, Banding, and Ranking

A perfectly valid selection procedure can be *invalidated* through improper use. Validation has to do with the *interpretation of scores*. A valid selection procedure produces scores that can be informative in both absolute and relative terms. A person who scores 90% on a written test absolutely answered about 9 out of each set of 10 questions correctly. In an absolute sense, they answered just about every test item correctly. But what if they scored in the lowest 10% of all test takers (*i.e.,* about 90% of the applicants scored higher)? This paints a completely different picture. Relative to the other applicants, they scored very low. Interpretation at this point can be difficult: was it the test, was it the relative abilities of the test takers, or are there other factors at play?

Scores on a selection procedure should be used in such a fashion that the validation evidence supports the way the selection procedure interpreted them. If classifying applicants into two groups – qualified and unqualified – is the end goal, the test should be used on a pass/fail basis (*i.e.,* an absolute classification based on achieving a certain level on the selection procedure). If the objective is to make relative distinctions between substantially equally qualified applicants, then banding is the approach that should be used. Ranking should be used if the goal is to make decisions on an applicant-by-applicant basis (making sure that the requirements for ranking discussed in this Chapter are addressed). If an overall picture of each applicant's combined mix of KSAPCs is desired, then a weighted and combined selection process should be used.

For each of these procedures, different types of validation evidence should be gathered to justify the corresponding manner in which the scores will be interpreted. This Chapter will explain steps that can be taken to develop and justify each procedure.

Developing Valid Cutoff Scores

Few things can be as frustrating as being the applicant who scored 69.9% on a test with a cutoff of 70%! Actually, there *is* one thing worse: finding out that the employer elected to use 70% as a cutoff on the basis that 70% *seemed* like a good, fair place to set the cutoff. (After all, 70% is the usual standard for a "C" in school, and a grade of C means "satisfactory," correct?)

Or consider being a patient on an operating table where the chief surgeon missed 30% of the qualifying test items on their written board exams? One would certainly hope that the items they missed had nothing to do with the surgery they were about to perform. Arbitrary cutoffs simply do not make sense, either academically or practically. Further, they can incense applicants who might come to realize that a meaningless standard in the selection process has been used to make very *meaningful decisions* about their lives and careers.

For these reasons, and because the U.S. courts have so frequently rejected arbitrary cutoff that have adverse impact, it is essential that practitioners use *best practices* when developing cutoffs. And, when it comes to best practices for developing cutoffs, there is perhaps none better than the *modified Angoff method.*[1]

The Angoff (1971) method makes good practical sense, Job Experts can readily understand it, applicants can be convinced of its validity, the courts have regularly endorsed it,[2] and it stands up to academic scrutiny. Here is a quick overview of how it works:

Job Experts review each item on a written test and provide their "best estimate" on the percentage of minimally-qualified applicants they believe would answer the item correctly (*i.e.,* each item is assigned a percentage value). These ratings are averaged and a valid cutoff for the test can be developed. The *modified* Angoff method adds a slight variation: After the test has been administered, the cutoff level set using the method above is lowered by 1, 2, or 3 Conditional Standard Errors of Measurement (SEMs) to adjust for the unreliability of the test (see Chapter Three for a discussion related to the SEM).

The Uniform Guidelines require that pass/fail cutoffs should be ". . . set so as to be reasonable and consistent with the normal expectations of acceptable proficiency in the workforce" (Section 5H). The modified Angoff method addresses this requirement on an item-by-item basis.

The modified Angoff method can be used for several types of selection procedures, but is perhaps most widely used for written tests. The complete process for developing a cutoff using this method is described below.

Steps for developing and using the modified Angoff cutoff

The following steps are offered to develop and use a cutoff for a written test with the modified Angoff method. (It is critical that all test items have been validated before completing these steps – see Chapter Three for the steps required for validating written test items).

1. Select a panel of 4-12[3] Job Experts who are truly experts in the content area and are diverse in terms of ethnicity, gender, geography, seniority (use a minimum of one year's experience and a maximum of five years[4]), and "functional areas" of the target position. Supervisors and trainers can also be included.
2. Provide a copy of the Job Analysis for each Job Expert. Be sure that the Job Analysis itemizes the various job duties and KSAPCs that are important or critical to the job.
3. Make a copy of the test for each Job Expert and stamp all tests and keys with a numbered control stamp (so that each Job Expert is assigned a numbered test and key). The answer key may also be provided to Job Experts, however, they should be urged to assess the difficulty level of the item without readily referencing the key. In some situations, masking the answer key from the Job Experts can help reduce the potential for upward rating bias.[5]
4. Explain the confidential nature of the workshop, the overall goals and outcomes, and ask the Job Experts to sign confidentiality agreements. Also explain the overall test development and validation steps, including which steps that have been completed so far and which still remain to be completed.

5. Review the mechanics of a test item with the Job Expert panel, including the item "stem" (the part of the item that asks the question), alternates (all choices including the key), distractors (incorrect alternatives), and answer key. Also review any source linkage documentation for the items (*i.e.,* for job knowledge tests where the correct answers are located in a book or manual).

6. Facilitate a discussion with the Job Expert panel to clarify and define the concept of a "minimally-qualified applicant." This is perhaps the most important part of this process, because it will set the stage for the remaining steps that will ultimately "calibrate" the test. The definition should be limited to *an applicant who possesses the necessary, baseline levels of the KSAPC measured by the test item to successfully perform the first day (before training) on the job*. It is sometimes useful to ask the Job Experts to imagine 100 minimally-qualified applicants in the room (in the various states that an applicant can be) and ask, "How many of the 100 applicants do you believe will answer this item correctly?"

7. Ask Job Experts to provide their ratings regarding the percentage of minimally-qualified applicants they believe will answer the test item correctly. Warn them against providing ratings below a "chance score" (50% for true/false items; 25% for multiple choice items with four alternatives; 20% for items with five). In addition, Job Experts should not assign ratings of 100% because this rating assumes that *every* minimally-qualified applicant was having a "perfect day" on the testing day, and allows no room for error.

8. Allow the Job Experts to continue rating the first five test items and then stop. Select one of the first five test items as a "group discussion" item. Ask each of the Job Experts to share their percentage ratings for the item. Allow the Job Experts to debate over their ratings. This will help centralize the panel and "rein in" any extreme outliers before they rate the remaining items. It is acceptable to stimulate the Job Experts by discussing and contrasting their ratings, though the facilitator should not require nor coerce any Job Expert to make any changes. The facilitator and the Job Experts can argue, discuss, and challenge any individual Job Expert rating during group discussion; however, in the end, each Job Expert should cast their own vote after discussion.

9. Collect all rating surveys and remind Job Experts of the confidential nature of their workshop participation.

10. Input and double-check all Job Expert ratings.

11. Detect and remove outlier Job Experts from the data set. Experience shows that one or more outliers exist in almost every Job Expert panel. Outliers are raters who purposefully rated items too low (*i.e.,* were interested in lowering the standard), too high (wanted to raise the standard), or just plain randomly. Statistical control processes should be used to detect each of these potential rating biases, and the identified Job Expert's data set should be removed before the final cutoff level is set. While a variety of techniques are available to accomplish this goal, here are two that can be readily computed using spreadsheet programs as described below:

   a. To check for a Job Expert whose ratings are systematically too low or
       too high compared to the rest of the panel, calculate the average and
       standard deviation of the Job Expert averages for all items on the test
       (yes, an average of their averages). Then remove any Job Expert
       whose average ratings are 1.645[6] standard deviations above or below
       the average of all Job Experts.
   b. To detect Job Experts who provided random responses, or responses
       that were not congruent (to an extent) with the ratings of the other
       Job Experts, create an inter-correlation matrix (using the =
       PEARSON command in Excel) for all Job Experts on the panel.
       Look for Job Experts who were (a) not correlated with their peers (or
       less correlated than most other raters), and/or (b) not correlated with
       the average rating of all raters (by averaging the ratings for each item
       across all raters), and remove them from the data set (judgment will
       need to be used at this step to make considerations for the number of
       Job Experts, number of items rated, statistical power, etc.).

Because removing Job Experts using Step *a* or *b* above will change the data
set (possibly creating new problems with the remaining data), it is
recommended to only complete this iteration once, and to be sure to complete
the steps in order (*a* first, then *b*).

12. Calculate a *pre-administration cutoff percentage* (also called an "unmodified
    Angoff score" because it has not yet been reduced using the Conditional
    SEM) with the remaining data. The pre-administration cutoff percentage
    score is the *average of the Job Expert panels' average ratings for each item*
    on the final test. Each item's average percentage rating receives equal weight
    in the calculation of this score – if only two Job Experts rated an item, the
    item's average is only based on two values but the item is given equal weight
    to the item rated by the entire panel.

13. Administer the test and remove any items (if necessary) based on item- or
    test-level analyses. If items are removed from the test, also remove that
    item's average percentage rating from the calculation of the pre-
    administration cutoff percentage.

14. Calculate the three *post-administration cutoff raw score options* by (1)
    multiplying the pre-administration cutoff percentage by the number of items
    in the test (*e.g.,* 76.7% * 90 items = 69.03 of the 90 items answered
    correctly), (2) identifying the Estimated True Score (ETS – see Appendix B)
    associated with this raw score, using the formula: $ETS = ((X-M)* r_{xx} + M)$
    where X is the score, M is the average test score of all examinees, and r_{xx} is
    the reliability of the test, (3) "flooring" this score to the lowest value
    (because test takers cannot achieve fraction scores on written tests), and
    finally (4) reducing this value by 1, 2, or 3 Conditional SEMs (see the
    Appendix B for CSEM computations). For example, using the example
    above and a test with a mean of 60 and reliability of .90, the ETS would be
    68.127, which is floored to a score of 68. If the CSEM at the score of 68 was
    3.5, the three cutoff score options (A, B, C) would be option A: 64 (68 - 3.5

= 64.5, which floors to 64), option B: 61 (68 - (3.5 * 2 = 7), option C: 57 (68 - (3.5 * 3 = 10.5) = 57.5, which floors to 57.

This process provides three viable cutoff score options for the test. In the U.S. Supreme Court decision made in <u>U.S. v. South Carolina</u> (1978) five statistical and human factors were considered when deciding whether to use 1, 2, or 3 SEMs when setting the final cutoff score:

- *Size of the SEM.* As discussed in Chapter Three, using the Conditional SEM is recommended over the traditional SEM because it considers the error variance (unreliability) only for test takers around the cutoff score, which is the area of decision-making interest. Large SEMs indicate low test reliability and/or high levels of variance in the applicant pool.
- *Possibility of sampling error in the study* (this relates to the number of Job Experts who served on the cutoff development panel). Panels with only a few Job Experts raise concern based on this factor (especially if there are a large number of incumbents in the workforce – see the Job Expert sample size discussion in Chapter Two).
- *Consistency of the results (internal comparisons of the panel results).* Panels that included bias Job Experts raise concern here (only if they were not removed using the proposed steps above).
- *Supply and demand for teachers in each specialty field* (this pertains to the demand for workers needed in the work force).
- *Racial composition of the teacher force* (the levels of adverse impact on each of the three cutoff options should be considered).

While these factors were based upon the specific needs and circumstances in <u>U.S. v. South Carolina</u>, they provide some useful considerations for employers when setting cutoff scores.

An additional (optional) step can be taken to further evaluate and possibly refine the final cutoff score. This step has to do with an evaluation of the possible *upward rating bias* that sometimes occurs with Job Expert rating panels. This step is useful because in some situations, Job Expert panels set the bar too high. This "upward bias" tendency that is sometimes observed does not (of course) rule out the opposite, where a rater panel underestimates the idea minimum competency level. However, it has been our experience that rating biases of the overestimation type are more common than those of the underestimation nature.

While there are several viable theories that may explain why this phenomenon may occur with rating panels, one particular theory seems to provide a practical explanation. The conscious competence theory (which is sometimes also called the "Four Stages of Learning" theory) was originally posited by psychologist Abraham Maslow in the 1940s. This theory provides an explanation of how people learn in four progressive stages:

(1) Unconscious Incompetence (you do not know that you do not know something), to
(2) Conscious Incompetence (you are now aware that you are incompetent at something), to
(3) Conscious Competence (you develop a skill in that area but have to think about it), to the final stage
(4) Unconscious Competence (you are good at it and it now comes naturally).

These four "learning stages" have been widely adopted in both theory and practice in educational, psychology, and organizational behavior fields since their inception. It is the fourth stage (unconsciously skilled) that may cause some of the upward bias sometimes observed in rating panels. This is because individuals who have had so much practice with a particular skill – to the point where it becomes "second nature" and can be performed easily without intense concentration – can sometimes underestimate how long it took them to master the skill when they first started in the position, which may cause them to overestimate the percentage of qualified applicants who may be able to answer the test question on the first day of the job.

Common examples of skills that can be attained at this fourth level include driving, sports activities, typing, manual dexterity tasks, listening, and communicating. For example, performing a "Y turn" is second nature to most people who have been driving for several years. In fact, many experienced drivers may not even recall ever having to acquire this skill, but in actuality, many experienced drivers had to initially work hard at this skill until mastered.

This issue can create an upward bias when applying minimum passing score recommendations. Some raters might now be able to teach others in the target skill, although after some time of being unconsciously competent, the person might actually have difficulty in explaining exactly how they perform a particular skill because the skill has become largely instinctual. This arguably gives rise to the need for long-standing unconscious competence to be checked periodically against new standards.

Fortunately, the extent to which this possible bias may exist can be evaluated statistically. This can be completed by statistically comparing how the rating panels' recommended cutoff score related to the scores of the test takers who scored *in the region of the recommended cutoff score*.[7] Specifically, an item-by-item comparison can be made between each item's difficulty level (the percentage of test takers in the critical score range who answered the item correctly) and the item's average Angoff rating. For example, if the item difficulty (based on applicants in the critical score zone) of a particular item is 55%, but the average Angoff rating from the Job Expert panel is 80%, a 25% "potential overestimate gap" exists. The opposite would, of course, suggest a potential underestimate made by the Job Expert panel. And, if this trend ensues throughout the majority of items, an overall "upward rating bias" may exist.

One way to investigate whether there is a trend of overestimates is to evaluate the distribution skew of the gaps between item difficulties and Angoff ratings. Skew is a statistical indicator that reflects whether the distribution of the data is symmetrical (*i.e.,* uniformly distributed with an equal number of values above and below the average of the distribution). The skew statistic can be computed in Excel by applying the = skew formula to the column containing the difference values between the Angoff ratings and item difficulties. If the skewness statistic is zero (0), the data are perfectly symmetrical. As a general guideline, if the skewness statistic is less than −1 or greater than +1, the distribution is highly skewed. If skewness is between −1 and −½ or between +½ and +1, the distribution is moderately skewed. If skewness is between −½ and +½, the distribution is approximately symmetric. This skewness statistic can be applied to the difference values computed by obtaining the difference between Angoff ratings and the item difficulties. If the Angoff rating is subtracted from the item difficulties, positive skew values would reveal that there are a disproportionately high number of test items with positive values (*i.e.,* items that were potentially over-rated by the raters). Negative skew values indicate the opposite.

The standard error of the skew can then be computed (using the formula = sqrt(6/N) where N is the number of difference values). Then multiply this value by 2. If the resulting value exceeds 2.0, the skewness is significant[8] and an adjustment to the Critical Score should be made.

There are two types of possible adjustments that can be made to the Critical Score if the skewness test is significant. The first adjustment can be made by reducing each over-rated item's Angoff rating to the lower confidence boundary of the item's Angoff rating by multiplying the standard error of the mean (SE Mean) Angoff rating[9] by 1.96 for each over-rated item. For example, if the average Angoff rating for an item is 85% and the SE Mean is 3%, multiply 3% by 1.96 (5.88%) and subtract this value from 85% to arrive at the new Angoff rating for that item (79.12%).

If the Skewness Test results exceed 3.0, consider using a more robust adjustment that can be computed by reducing the Critical Score to the lower confidence boundary of the raters' overall Critical Score. This can be accomplished by multiplying the Standard Error of Difference of the rater panel[10] by 1.96 and subtracting this value from the Critical Score.

Setting cutoffs that are higher than the "minimum level" established by the modified Angoff method

What should be done if the employer cannot feasibly process all applicants who pass the validated cutoff score? Theoretically speaking, all applicants who pass the modified Angoff cutoff are qualified; however, if the employer simply cannot process the number of applicants who pass the given cutoff, two options are available.

The first option is to use a cutoff that is *higher* than the three cutoff options calculated above. If this option is used, the Uniform Guidelines are clear that the degree of adverse impact should be considered (see Section 3B and 5H). One method for setting a higher cutoff is to subtract one Standard Error of Difference (SED) (see the Banding section below for a discussion of the SED) from the highest score in the distribution, and passing all applicants in this score band. Using the SED in this process helps insure that all applicants within the band are substantially equally qualified. Additional bands can be created by subtracting one SED from the score immediately below the band for the next group, and repeating this process until the first cutoff score option is reached (*i.e.,* one Conditional SEM below the cutoff score).

This represents the distinguishing line between the qualified and unqualified applicants.

While this option may be useful for obtaining a smaller group of applicants who pass the cutoff score and are substantially equally qualified, a second option is strict rank ordering. However, strict rank ordering is not typically advised on written tests because of the high levels of adverse impact that are likely to result. To hire or promote applicants in strict rank order on a score list, the employer should be careful to insure that the criteria discussed in the Ranking section are sufficiently addressed.

Banding

In some circumstances, applicants are rank-ordered on a selection procedure and hiring decisions between applicants are based upon score differences at the one-hundredth or one-thousandth decimal place (*e.g.,* applicant A who scored 89.189 is hired before applicant B who scored 89.188, etc.). The troubling issue with this practice is that, if the selection procedure were administered a second time, it is just as possible that applicants A and B could very likely change places. In fact, if the reliability of the selection procedure was low and the standard deviation was large, these two applicants could, in fact, be separated by several whole points rather than mere fractions.

Banding addresses this issue by using the Standard Error of Difference (SED) to group applicants into "substantially equally qualified" score bands. The SED is a tool that can be used by practitioners for setting a confidence interval around scores that are substantially equal. Viewed another way, it can be used for determining scores in a distribution that represent *meaningfully different* levels of the KSAPCs measured by the selection procedure.

For example, assume a selection procedure with a possible score range of 0 to 100 and a SED of 4. If the highest scoring applicant obtained a score of 99, subtracting 1 SED from this score (99 - 4) arrives at a score of 95, which can be considered the first meaningful stopping place in the distribution of scores. That is, the applicant who scored 99 and the applicant who scored 94 have different ability levels, but the applicant who scored 99 and the applicant who scored 95 *do not*. Different band widths can be applied (by using 1, 2, or 3 SEDs) that provide different confidence levels surrounding the meaningful differences between scores. Note, however, that some banding techniques require a bi-directional consideration (*i.e.,* higher scorers and lower scorers) of the confidence intervals surrounding scores. See Appendix B for a complete description of defensible banding techniques

Banding has been a hotly debated issue in the personnel field.[11] Proponents of strict rank ordering argue that making hiring decisions in rank-order preserves meritocracy and ultimately insures a slightly more qualified workforce. Supporters of banding argue that, because tests cannot adequately distinguish between small score differences, practitioners should remain blind to miniscule score differences between applicants who are within the same band. They also argue that the practice of banding will almost always produce less adverse impact than strict rank ordering.[12] While these two perspectives may differ, various types of score banding procedures have been successfully litigated and supported in court[13] with one exception being the decision to band *after* a test has been administered, when the only reason for banding was to reduce adverse impact (Ricci, 2009). Otherwise, banding remains as an effective tool that can be used in most personnel situations.

Ranking

The idea of hiring applicants in strict order from the top of the list to the last applicant above the cutoff score is a practice that has roots back to the origins of the merit-based civil service system. The limitation with ranking, as discussed above, is that the practice can treat applicants whose scores are actually close to identical as if they were meaningfully different. The SEM shows the degree to which scores would likely shuffle if the selection procedure was hypothetically administered a second time.

Because of these limitations, the Uniform Guidelines and the courts have presented rather stringent requirements surrounding the practice of strict rank ordering. These requirements are provided below, along with some specific recommendations on the criteria to consider before using a selection procedure to rank order applicants.

Section 14C9 of the Uniform Guidelines states:

> If a user can show, by a job analysis or otherwise, that a higher score on a content valid selection procedure is likely to result in better job performance, the results may be used to rank persons who score above minimum levels. Where a selection procedure supported solely or primarily by content validity is used to rank job candidates, the selection procedure should measure those aspects of performance which differentiate among levels of job performance.

Performance-differentiating KSAPCs distinguish between acceptable and above-acceptable performance on the job. Differentiating KSAPCs can be identified either absolutely or relatively using the Best Worker rating discussed in Chapter Two. A strict rank ordering process should not be used on a selection procedure that measures KSAPCs that are only needed *at minimum levels* on the job and do not distinguish between acceptable and above-acceptable job performance (see Uniform Guidelines Questions & Answers Supplement #62).

Content validity evidence to support ranking can be established by linking the parts of a selection procedure to job duties and/or KSAPCs that are performance differentiating.[14] So, if a selection procedure is linked to a job duty and/or KSAPC that is "performance differentiating" either *absolutely* or *relatively* (*e.g.,* with an average Job Expert Best Worker rating that is 1.0 standard deviation above the average Best Worker rating or higher when compared to all other duties and/or KSAPCs), some support is provided for using the selection procedure as a ranking device.

While the Best Worker rating provides some support for using a selection procedure as a ranking device, some additional factors should be considered before making a decision to use a selection procedure in a strict rank-ordered fashion:

1. Is there adequate score dispersion in the distribution (or a "wide variance of scores")? Rank ordering is usually not preferred if the applicant scores are

"tightly bunched together"[15] because such scores are "tied" to an even a greater extent than if they were more evenly distributed. One way to evaluate the dispersion of scores is to use the Conditional SEM (see Appendix B). Using the Conditional SEM, the employer can evaluate if the score dispersion is adequately spread out within the relevant range of scores when compared to other parts of the score distribution. For example, if the Conditional SEM is very small (*e.g.*, 2.0) in the range of scores where the strict rank ordering will occur (*e.g.*, 95-100), but is very broad throughout the other parts of the score distribution (*e.g.*, double or triple the size), the score dispersion in the relevant range of interest (*e.g.*, 95-100) may not be sufficiently high to justify this criteria.

2. Does the selection procedure have high reliability? Typically, reliability coefficients should be .85 to .90 or higher for using the results in strict rank order.[16] If a selection procedure is not reliable (or "consistent") enough to "split apart" candidates based upon very small score differences, it should not be used in such a way that considers small differences between candidates as meaningful.

While the guidelines above should be considered when choosing a rank ordering or pass/fail strategy for a selection procedure, the extent to which the test measures KSAPCs and/or job duties[17] that are performance differentiating should be the *primary consideration*.

Employers using a selection procedure that is based on criterion-related validity evidence have more flexibility to use ranking than with selection procedures based on content validity. This is because criterion-related validity demonstrates scientifically what content validity can only speculate is occurring between the selection procedure and job performance. Criterion-related validity (see Chapter Three for a more detailed discussion) provides a correlation coefficient that represents the strength or degree of correlation relationship between some aspects of job performance and the selection procedure.

While the courts have regularly endorsed criterion-related validity studies, they have placed some minimum thresholds for the correlation value necessary (about .30 or higher) for strict rank ordering on a selection procedure based on criterion-related validity:

- Brunet v. City of Columbus (1993). This case involved an entry-level firefighter Physical Capacities Test (PCT) that had adverse impact against women. The court stated, "The correlation coefficient for the overall PCT is .29. Other courts have found such correlation coefficients to be predictive of job performance, thus indicating the appropriateness of ranking where the correlation coefficient value is .30 or better."

- Boston Chapter, NAACP Inc. v. Beecher (1974). This case involved an entry-level firefighter written test. Regarding the correlation values, the court stated, "The objective portion of the study produced several correlations that were statistically significant (likely to occur by chance in fewer than five of one hundred similar cases) and practically significant (correlation of +.3 or higher, thus explaining more than 9% or more of the observed variation)."

- Clady v. County of Los Angeles (1985). This case involved an entry-level firefighter written test. The court stated, "In conclusion, the County's validation studies demonstrate legally sufficient correlation to success at the Academy and performance on the job. Courts generally accept correlation coefficients above +.30 as reliable . . . As a general principle, the greater the test's adverse impact, the higher the correlation which will be required."

- Zamlen v. City of Cleveland (1988). This case involved several different entry-level firefighter physical ability tests that had various correlation coefficients with job performance. The judge noted that, "Correlation coefficients of .30 or greater are considered high by industrial psychologists" and set a criteria of .30 to endorse the City's option of using the physical ability test as a ranking device.

Weighting Selection Procedures into Combined Scores

Selection procedures can be weighted and combined into a composite score for each applicant. Typically, each selection procedure that is used to make the combined score is also used as a screening device (*i.e.,* with a pass/fail cutoff) before including scores from applicants into the composite score. Before using a selection procedure as a pass/fail device and as part of a weighted composite, the developer should evaluate whether the KSAPCs measured by the selection procedures are performance differentiating – especially if the weighted composite will be used for ranking applicants.

There are two critical factors to consider when weighting selection procedures into composite scores: determining the weights and standardizing the scores. Developing a reliability coefficient for the final list of composite scores[18] is also a critical final step if the final scores will be banded into groups of substantially equally qualified applicants. These steps are discussed below.

Determining a set of job-related weights to use when combining selection procedures can be a sophisticated and socially sensitive issue. Not only are the statistical mechanics often complicated, choosing one set of weights versus another can sometimes have very significant impact on the gender and ethnic composition of those who are hired from the final list. For these reasons, this topic should be approached with caution and developers should make decisions using informed judgment.

Generally speaking, weighting the selection procedures that will be combined into composite scores for each applicant can be accomplished using one of three methods: *unit weighting*, weighting based on *criterion-related validity* studies, and using *content validity* weighting methods.

Unit weighting is accomplished by simply allowing each selection procedure to share an equal weight in the combined score list. Surprisingly, sometimes unit weighting produces highly effective and valid results (see the Principles, 2003, p. 20). This is probably because each selection procedure is equally allowed to contribute into making the composite score, and no selection procedure is hampered by only contributing a small part to the final score. Using unit weighting, if there are two selection procedures, they are each weighted 50%. If there are five, each is allowed 20% weight.

If the employer is using selection procedures that are based on one or more criterion-related validity studies, the data from these studies can be used to calculate the weights for each. The steps for this method are outside the scope of this text and will not be discussed here.[19]

Using content validity methods to weight selection procedures is probably the most common practice. Sometimes practitioners get caught up in developing complicated and computationally-intensive methods for weighting selection procedures using job analysis data. Sometimes these procedures involve using complicated formulas that consider frequency and importance ratings for Job Duties and/or KSAPCs, and Job Duty/KSAPC linkages.

While this helps some practitioners feel at ease, these methods can produce misleading results. Not only that, there are easier methods available. For example, consider two KSAPCs that are equally important to the job. Now assume that one is more complex than the other, so it is divided into two KSAPCs on the job analysis and the other (equally important) KSAPC remains in a single slot on the Job Analysis. When it comes time to use multiplication formulas to determine weights for the selection procedures that are linked to these KSAPCs, one is likely to receive more weight *just because it was written twice on the Job Analysis*. The same problem exists if selection procedures are mechanically linked using job duties that have this issue.

What about just providing the list of KSAPCs to a panel of Job Experts and having them distribute 100 to indicate the relative to the importance of each? This method is fine, but can also present some limitations. Assume there are 20 KSAPCs and Job Experts assign importance points to each. Now assume that only 12 of these KSAPCs are actually tested by the set of selection procedures chosen for the weighted composite. Would the weight values turn out differently if the Job Experts were allowed to review the 12 remaining KSAPCs and were asked re-assign their weighting values? Most likely, yes, as illustrated in the example below:

Ask a friend to list their top ten favorite ice cream flavors in no certain order. Then ask them to distribute 100 points among the ten flavors, indicating the relative importance of each. Take away five ice cream flavors and have them distribute 100 points to the remaining five (not considering their original weighting). The weights they assign the second time to the five remaining ice cream flavors will likely be different than the weights that would be calculated by taking their original list of ten (along with the corresponding weights of each), removing the same five ice cream flavors, then recalculating the weights by dividing the original weight of each by the new total based on only the remaining five.

Another limitation with weighting selection procedures by evaluating their relative weight from job analysis data is that sometimes different selection procedures are linked to the same KSAPC (this can cause the weights for each selection procedure are no longer unique and become convoluted with other selection procedures). One final limitation is that sometimes selection procedures are linked to a KSAPC for collecting the weight determination, but they are weak measures of the KSAPC (while others are strong, relevant linkages). For these reasons, there is a "better way" as described in the next section.

Steps for weighting selection procedures using content validity methods

The following steps can be taken to develop content valid weights for selection procedures that are combined into single composite scores for each applicant:

1. Select a panel of 4-12 Job Experts who are truly experts in the content area and are diverse in terms of ethnicity, gender, geography, seniority (use a minimum of one year experience), and "functional areas" of the target position. Supervisors and trainers can also be included.
2. Provide a copy of the Job Analysis for each Job Expert. Be sure that the Job Analysis itemizes the various job duties and KSAPCs that are important or critical to the job.
3. Provide each Job Expert with a copy of each selection procedure (or a highly detailed description of the content of the selection procedure if confidentiality issues prohibit Job Experts from viewing actual copies). Make a copy of the selection procedure and key for each Job Expert and stamp with a numbered control stamp (so that each Job Expert is assigned a numbered set).
4. Explain the confidential nature of the workshop, the overall goals and outcomes, and ask the Job Experts to sign confidentiality agreements.
5. Discuss and review with Job Experts the content of each selection procedure and the KSAPCs measured by each. A Selection Plan is helpful for this step (see Chapter Two). Also discuss the extent to which certain selection procedures may be better measures of certain KSAPCs than others. Factors such as the vulnerability of certain selection procedures to fraud, reliability issues, and others should be discussed.
6. Provide a survey to Job Experts that asks them to distribute 100 points among the selection procedures that will be combined. Be sure that they consider the importance levels of the KSAPCs measured by the selection procedures, and the job duties to which they are linked, when completing this step.
7. Detect and remove outlier Job Experts from the data set (raters can be removed if their average weight rating is 1.645 standard deviations above or below the collective average).
8. Calculate the average weight for each selection procedure. These averages are the weights to use when combining the selection procedure into a composite score.

Standardizing scores

Before individual selection procedures can be weighted and combined, it is crucial that they be *standard scored.* This step is crucial! Standard scoring is a statistical process of *normalizing* scores and is a necessary step to place different selection procedures on a level playing field.

Assume a developer has two selection procedures: one with a score range of 0-10 and the other with a range of 0-50. What happens when these two selection procedures are combined? The one with a high score range will greatly overshadow the one with the smaller range. Even if two selection procedures have the same score range, they should still be standard scored. This is because if the selection procedures have different means and standard deviations they will produce inaccurate results when combined unless they are first standard scored.

Standard scoring selection procedures is a relatively simple practice. Converting raw scores into *Z scores* (a widely used form of standard scoring) can be done by simply subtracting each applicant's score from the average (mean) score of all applicants and dividing this value by the standard deviation (of all applicant total scores). After the scores for each selection procedure are standard scored, they can be multiplied by their respective weights and a final score for each applicant calculated. After this final score list has been compiled, the reliability of the new combined list can be calculated.[20]

Notes

[1] When tests are based on criterion-related validity studies, cutoffs can be calibrated and set based on empirical data and statistical projections that can also be very effective.

[2] For example U.S. v. South Carolina (434 U.S. 1026, 1978) and Bouman v. Block (940 F.2d 1211, C.A.9 Cal., 1991) and related consent decree.

[3] Various Job Expert sample sizes are suggested throughout this text. A minimum of four Job Experts is proposed in this Section (rather than the minimum of seven used elsewhere) because the exposure of confidential test information may be of high concern to the employer for completing this step.

[4] This "five year maximum" recommendation is made only to possibly help reduce the "upward rating bias" described later in this Chapter that sometimes occurs on rating panels. It is not an absolute requirement.

[5] See (for example) Cizek, G.J. & Sternberg, R.J. (2001). Setting Performance Standards: Theory and Applications (1st ed.). Routledge (pp. 145 and 361).

[6] This standard deviation will serve to "trim" the average ratings that are in the upper or lower 5% of the distribution.

[7] Using a confidence interval of +/- 1.645 Standard Errors of Difference, within the unadjusted critical score.

[8] Tabachnick, B. G., & Fidell, L. S. (1996). Using multivariate statistics (3rd ed.). New York: Harper Collins.

[9] The standard error of the mean Angoff rating for the item can be computed by first computing the standard deviation of the Angoff ratings, then dividing this value by the square root of the number of ratings – e.g., = 10/sqrt(12) in Excel.

[10] The SED of the rater panel can be computed by first computing the SEM of the rater panel (SD*(sqrt(1-the average rater reliability, or ICC) then multiplying this value by the square root of 2.

[11] For example, Schmidt, F. L. (1991). 'Why all banding procedures in personnel selection are logically flawed', *Human Performance*, 4, 265-278; Zedeck, S., Outtz, J., Cascio, W. F., and Goldstein, I. L. (1991), 'Why do "testing experts" have such limited vision?,' *Human Performance*, 4, 297-308.

[12] One clear support for using banding as a means of reducing adverse impact can be found in Section 3B of the Uniform Guidelines, which states: "Where two or more selection procedures are available which serve the user's legitimate interest in efficient and trustworthy workmanship, and which are *substantially equally valid* for a given purpose, the user should use the procedure which has been demonstrated to have the lesser adverse impact." Banding is one way of evaluating an alternate use of a selection procedure (*i.e.,* one band over another) that is "substantially equally valid."

[13] Officers for Justice v. Civil Service Commission (CA9, 1992, 979 F.2d 721, cert. denied, 61 U.S.L.W. 3667, 113 S. Ct. 1645, March 29th, 1993).

[14] See Section 14C4 of the Uniform Guidelines.

[15] Guardians v. CSC of New York (630 F.2d 79). One of the court's reasons for scrutinizing the use of rank ordering on a test was because 8,928 candidates (two-thirds of the entire testing population) was bunched between scores of 94 and 97 on the written test.

[16] Gatewood, R. D. & Feild, H.S. (1994), *Human Resource Selection* (3rd ed.) Fort Worth, TX: The Dryden Press (p. 184); Aiken, L.R. (1988). *Psychological Testing and Assessment* (2nd ed.). Boston: Allyn & Bacon (p. 100); Weiner, E. A. & Stewart, B. J. (1984). *Assessing Individuals.* Boston: Little, Brown. (p. 69).

[17] For selection procedures that are designed to directly mirror job duties (called "work sample tests"), only test-duty (and not test-KSAPC) linkages are required for a content validity study (see Section 14C4 of the Guidelines). In this case, the Best Worker ratings on the duties linked to the work sample test should be the primary consideration for evaluating its use (*i.e.,* ranking or pass/fail). For tests measuring KSAPCs (and not claiming to be direct "work sample tests"), the extent to which the selection procedure measures KSAPCs that are differentiating should be the primary consideration.

[18] See Mosier, C. I. (1943). On the reliability of a weighted composite. *Psychometrika, 8,* 161−168.

[19] See Uniform Guidelines Questions & Answers #47, the Principles (2003, p. 20, 47), and Cascio, W. (1998), *Applied Psychology in Human Resource Management,* Upper Saddle River, NJ: Prentice-Hall, Inc. for more information on this approach.

[20] See Feldt, L.S., & Brennan, R.L. (1989). *Reliability.* In R.L. Linn (Ed.), Educational Measurement (3rd ed.). New York, Macmillan. (pp. 105-146).

Chapter 9 - Using Multiple Regression to Examine Compensation Practices

By Jim Higgins, Ed.D.

Introduction

This Chapter presents an overview of an exceptionally powerful statistical technique that can be applied to determine whether significant differences exist among applicant or employee groups. Specifically, Multiple Regression (MR) will be reviewed and then shown how it can be applied for evaluating employee compensation for the purpose of determining whether males or whites are compensated more highly than females or minorities due to reasons that are not legitimately job related.

To fully appreciate the power and usefulness of MR for identifying significant differences that that cannot be explained by legitimate job-related factors, it is helpful to first review more basic statistical tools. The traditional, and most straightforward, approach that has been used to determine whether specific groups of employees (*i.e.,* whites or males) are differentially compensated when compared to other groups (*e.g., * specific minority groups or females) is to conduct a simple comparison of *average* compensation rates using an independent samples t-test (hereafter, *t-test*). T-tests are statistical tools that compare average scores between two groups (*e.g.,* test scores, compensation, job performance, etc.) to determine whether these differences are statistically significant. If a difference is statistically significant, it is said to be a real and reliable difference rather than a difference that is a "fluke" or chance event.

The advantage of using this approach was its conceptual simplicity. If, for example, males receive an average compensation that is statistically significantly higher than females, one might conclude that potential compensation bias exists in the way a company is paying these two groups.

The most significant problem with using a simple comparison of average salaries, however, is that there could be *legitimate reasons* for the two groups being compensated differently. For example, what if the job has been traditionally staffed by males and females have only recently begun to account for a significant proportion of the workforce? Under those circumstances, it might be safe to assume that, if the males have been employed in the job for a longer period of time, they would have had more time to work their way up the pay scale. If this is the case, then at least some portion of the difference between the salaries of males and females is due to a factor other than gender – time in job.

Clearly, the practice of making simple comparisons between the average salary of males and females or whites and minority groups is inadequate for developing a complete understanding of whether or not evidence exists for discrimination. What is needed is a statistical tool that allows a researcher to compare the average salaries of various groups of employees *while controlling for the legitimate job-related factors* that are also influencing employee pay. MR is a statistical tool that allows practitioners to do exactly that. Because MR is such a powerful tool for finding differences in compensation that cannot be explained by

181

legitimate job-related factors, it is the method of choice that has been used by the courts for decades, and has more recently been endorsed by the OFCCP.[1]

This Chapter provides an overview of a methodology that may be used to perform an MR analysis to determine whether reliable differences in compensation rates exist between males and females or whites and members of minority groups. A description of how to compute the analysis using both the SPSS® software package as well as Microsoft Excel® will be presented.

It is important to note that there are many features and reports in both SPSS and Excel that will not be discussed in this Chapter. This is not because they are not important. On the contrary, both of these programs offer MR tools and reports that are highly useful and important. However, to explain MR in this level of detail would require an entire book (and many books have been written specifically on this topic). Rather, this Chapter is devoted to running basic MR analyses and interpreting some of the key analysis outputs.

How Does Multiple Regression (MR) Work?

Conceptually speaking, MR is actually quite simple. In the realm of compensation analyses, MR uses two types of *variables*. A variable is any factor that can be used to differentiate people – that is, any factor on which people vary. Examples are time in job, compensation, and gender. All of these are variables because people vary in their length of time spent in their jobs, their amount or level of compensation, or the gender category to which they belong (male, female).

As far as MR is concerned, there are only two types of variables: *independent* and *dependent*. There is only one dependent variable that is always used in compensation-equity MR analyses, and that is compensation.[2] This is the "target" in any MR analysis because the goal is to determine whether compensation is based on fair and valid criteria. It is what one is trying to *predict* with the other variables – which are the independent variables. Sometimes independent variables are called "predictors" because they are used to predict the dependent variable – pay or other compensation factors.

Because the ultimate goal of using MR in compensation analyses is to find out whether gender or minority status is a significant independent variable, this variable should be added to the MR model *after* other job-related variables such as time in job, performance review scores, and others have *already had their opportunity* to predict pay. This procedure properly models the Title VII philosophy behind investigating disparities in pay – *i.e.,* allowing relevant job factors to "have the first shot" at explaining pay differences before entering the gender or minority variable into the model to see whether potential evidence of pay discrimination exists (by significantly adding to the model) – more on this discussion later.

MR analyses result in a series of statistical outputs that explain how well the independent variables predict compensation. The most basic and fundamental concept in MR analysis is the *correlation coefficient*. A correlation is simply a measure of relationship or association between two variables. Correlation coefficients can range between 0 and 1.0 (where two variables are positively related and higher values of one tend to correspond with higher values on the other – *e.g.,* height and weight) and -1.0 to 0 (where two variables are inversely related – *e.g.,* engine horsepower and fuel consumption). Correlations close to 0 are trivial; correlations closer to 1 (either positive or negative) indicate stronger relationships.

One of the other key outputs is called the "Multiple R-Squared" (reported as R^2) in multiple regression (MR) analysis). This value is important because it indicates the *explanatory power* of the model (*i.e.,* the set of independent variables in the MR analyses that attempt to "model" or predict pay). For example, an R^2 of .30 shows that 30% of the amount of overall differences among employees' pay rates can be explained by the independent variables in the MR analyses.

Another key output is called the "R^2 Change." This output is useful because it shows if the MR model is significantly better (or more explanatory) by the addition of each additional variable included in the model. For example, one might include four relevant job factors such as *time in job, performance evaluation scores, outside experience,* and *educational level* as independent variables in the model, and then add gender in a separate block (or "layer") in the MR model to see if the addition of gender significantly improves the model; in other words, to determine whether a 4% increase from 30% to 34% explanatory power *was statistically significant.*

Correlations between independent variables, the R^2 value, and the R^2 Change all have corresponding probability values (called "*p-values*") that allow the researcher to determine if they are "statistically significant," which occurs when they have *p-values* less than .05 (or 5%). This applies to *p-values* for correlations between variables and for the overall MR model (*i.e.,* the p-value of the R^2 or R^2 Change values). It is not necessary that *each* job factor used as an independent variable in the MR model be statistically significant when used to predict compensation. However, when the gender or minority status variable is statistically significant *even after* accounting for all other variables, a "red flag" occurs.

For example, assume a researcher builds an MR model that includes the following four independent variables that have the noted *p-values: time in job* (.03), *performance evaluation scores* (.10), *outside experience* (.14), and *educational level* (.01). Note that only *time in job* and *education* are statistically significant because they fall below the .05 threshold. *Performance evaluation scores* and *outside experience,* however, are approaching significance, but are not quite below the .05 "magic threshold" needed for statistical significance. These two factors, however, may nonetheless be *practically relevant* factors to this employer's pay system (as may be evidenced by the employer's pay policies or practices, and to some extent by the *p-values* that are "*leaning*" toward significance).

This can possibly present a slippery slope because it is not advisable to include independent variables into a MR analysis that are *neither statistically or practically relevant* to an employer's pay system. Including excessive and/or irrelevant factors in a MR model could possibly leave no room for gender or minority status to show up as statistically significant *even if it really is.* One must be careful to not overshadow such possible relationships with a cloud of irrelevant independent variables. The philosophy is to create the most "parsimonious" model (*i.e.,* one that best predicts compensation with the least number of variables) in multiple regression analysis.

Steps for Conducting Multiple Regression (MR) Analysis

The steps below describe a general process for conducting MR analyses. However, because MR analyses can be highly complicated and technical, these steps should be regarded as guidelines only. Also, many of these steps can turn from a linear to a circular process due to the dynamic nature of MR analyses.

These steps can also vary based on *why* the employer is conducting the study. For example, MR analyses that are completed on a *proactive basis* (*i.e.,* without any pressure from a government agency or pending litigation) can utilize employee grouping variables that are readily available (*e.g.,* job title). However, employers that are under scrutiny will need to carefully create analysis groupings (see "SSEGs" below) before conducting MR analyses because the results of the MR analyses will be more impacted by the employee groupings than *any other step* a researcher can complete.

Step 1 - Identify And Review Available Data

The first step that must be completed prior to attempting any statistical analysis is to review the contents of the data set (*i.e.,* spreadsheet). In so doing, one should develop a solid understanding of every relevant variable and verify that it is formatted in a manner that facilitates analysis in SPSS, Microsoft Excel, or other statistical software packages. Typical variables that are useful when using MR to determine whether reliable differences in compensation exist include:

- Employee ID;
- Job grouping variables such as job title, job group, and Similarly Situated Employee Groups (SSEGs);
- Race/Ethnicity (White, Black, Hispanic, Asian/Pacific Islander, American Indian/Alaskan Native);
- Gender;
- Date of last degree earned;
- Highest degree earned (and type and degree area);
- Date of birth (this information is frequently used as a substitute, or proxy, for overall work experience);[3]
- Time with company or date of hire;
- Time in current position or date of last change in grade/title;
- Current annual salary or hourly wage;
- Part-time vs. full-time status;
- Exempt vs. non-exempt status;
- Job title;
- Grade level or salary band classification;
- Employee location (if not housed at the facility);
- Prior experience data (can take a variety of forms); and,
- Job performance ratings.

When considering *which* of these variables to use and *how* to use them, try to fit them into the MR model in a manner that *mirrors the way in which compensation decisions are actually made* on the job (this is difficult, but sometimes produces very accurate MR results). For example, if education is treated on the job as simply an "either/or" factor when directly or indirectly determining pay (where those with Bachelor's degrees receive more pay, but higher degrees do not necessarily matter), then consider "dummy coding" education using 1s and 0s (see dummy coding discussion below). If, however, education is (directly or indirectly) a *continuous* factor for compensation decisions (where increasingly higher levels of education may factor into increasingly higher levels of pay), then treat education as a continuous variable in the MR model (*e.g.,* using "12" for high school education, "14" for Associates degree, "16" for Bachelors, "18" for Masters, and "20" for doctorate level degrees). How to mechanically include these variables into the MR analysis will now be discussed.

Excel typically creates variables using what it calls a "General" format. While Excel is able to handle these variables appropriately, other software packages (*e.g.,* SPSS) may or may not import these data correctly. This is especially true with "date" variables. SPSS may also tend to import numbers as "text" if they are in Excel's "general" format. To prevent complications surrounding these issues in Excel, *right click* on the column label (*e.g.,* "A", "B", etc.), click on "Format Cells" and verify column format. If the column contains:

- text values, select the "text" format;
- date values, select the format that displays dates as 3/14/2001;
- number values, select the "number" format and adjust the number of decimals appropriately; or,
- currency values (*e.g.,* Total Compensation), select the format that displays currency as $1,234.10.

Step 2 - Create And Verify Variable Coding

It is critical that variables are coded correctly when running any statistical analysis. MR may only be used on numeric variables and therefore it is necessary to confirm that each variable to be included in a MR-based compensation analysis be coded appropriately. Each of the following steps should be completed prior to attempting any actual analyses.

Recode the independent variables, as necessary. This is especially important for the variables of Gender and Ethnicity. For the purposes of clarity and consistency, it is recommended that the variables of gender and ethnicity be coded as follows:

Gender: Recode gender so that males = 0 and females = 1
Ethnicity: Recode ethnicity into a "minority/non-minority" variable with whites = 0 and the minorities = 1. If the compensation of a specific minority group (*e.g.,* African Americans) is of primary concern, whites should be coded as "0" and African Americans would be coded with a "1."

The process of converting categorical data (like gender and minority status) into 1s and 0s is called "dummy coding." The dummy coding protocols above have been provided as suggestions only – it really makes no difference which group is coded 1s or 0s – it only changes the *direction* in which the correlations will be interpreted (*i.e.,* either positively or negatively). By following the coding procedures recommended above, the researcher will need to look for *negative correlations* on the gender/minority status variable – indicating that the effect of being a woman or minority is negatively, or inversely, correlated with compensation.

Step 3 - Conduct Preliminary Data Analysis

Prior to conducting an MR analysis, it is important to begin with a preliminary exploration of the data set. The primary goal of this process is to confirm that the data are valid and to examine the interactions or relationships between variables – particularly the independent variables that will be used to model compensation practices.

By generating a correlation matrix, it is possible to determine the extent to which each of the independent variables is related to compensation. Large and significant correlations mean strong relationships exist between the variables and that each significantly correlating variable by itself has a strong ability to explain or account for why employees receive the compensation they do. Statistical programs like SPSS have menu-driven programs for calculating correlation matrices to evaluate the relationships between the variables in the MR model. To calculate a correlation matrix in Microsoft Excel, follow these steps:

1. Click on the "Tools" menu option;
2. Click on "Data Analysis";
3. Select "Correlation" from the list of available statistical procedures;
4. Click "OK";
5. Select the data to be included in the analysis (including column names if any are being used. However, if column names are included, make sure the Column Labels checkbox is checked);
6. Click "OK"; then,
7. Review the correlation matrix and consider the following questions:
   - Is there a statistically significant correlation (either positive or negative) between gender or minority status and compensation? While these results by no means represent definitive tests, they do reveal where the employer stands before taking job factors into account.
   - What other variables are correlated with compensation?
   - Are there any very large correlations that are statistically significant between any of the predictor variables (*e.g.,* age and time in job)? If there are any very large correlations between predictors, this could result in a problem with multicolinearity which may lead to errors in the model (see later in this Chapter for a complete discussion on multicollinearity).

Note that because this exploratory analysis was conducted before splitting the employees into their relevant job grouping variable (*e.g.,* job title or SSEG), the results are useful only for informative purposes. As such, this step is helpful for gaining an understanding of which variables are showing correlation tendencies with other variables, including pay.

Step 4 - Create Groups Of Employees For Analyses

Dividing the employees into groups is the most contentious issue in the realm of MR analyses when compensation is the target of the study. This is because, at least in litigation settings, MR analyses will almost always show fewer "hot spots" (jobs where the gender or minority status variable is statistically significant, even after taking job factors into account) where employees are divided into *smaller groups*. Plaintiff groups, on the other hand, generally desire to group employees into the largest groups possible because this maximizes their chances of unveiling "hot spots."

With these two extremes at odds, how does a researcher divide employees into analysis groups? Proponents of both extremes will have heated debates about exactly how to divide employees for analysis. For purposes of this discussion, however, the attempt will be to "split the middle" with the following guidelines.

The first and primary consideration is to create employee groups that are *similarly situated* with respect to four primary factors:

1. Similarity of the work they perform;
2. Levels of responsibility required in their position(s);
3. Skills needed to perform their jobs; and,
4. Qualifications needed to perform their jobs.

Employers that have thousands of employees may find this task daunting. In actuality, however, creating SSEGs is a manageable project when knowledgeable professionals are involved. Seasoned veterans who work in the employer's compensation or HR department can readily start chipping away at the thousands of employees by placing them into SSEG groups based on these four factors. Usually, grouping the first 30-50% of an employer's workforce goes quickly when professionals who are intimately familiar with the jobs are involved. The remaining portions of the workforce take more time as the odd jobs are combined together for analysis purposes.

Job analysis and/or job descriptions are almost always the most telling resources that can be consulted for grouping employees based on these criteria. Content-specific job titles can also provide very clean classification groups with respect to these factors. Combining employee groups across locations can also be done, provided that the pay systems are similar and geographical pay differentials are taken into consideration.

The second consideration surrounds the issue of *statistical power*.[4] Put simply, statistical power is the ability of a statistical test (*i.e.,* MR) to *detect a statistically significant finding if it exists to be found*. Larger sample sizes will always yield higher statistical power; while smaller sample sizes have lower statistical power. For example, when conducting an MR analysis with three variables (if a researcher is looking for what's called a "medium effect size," or a modest R^2 value of about .13), the researcher can be 80% confident of finding a statistically significant correlation *if it exists to be found* when a sample of about 80 employees is included in a single analysis group (*e.g.,* a SSEG).

While this value is based on a *calculated* power analysis that takes the number of variables (3), the desired effect size (.13), and the desired power level (80% confidence) into consideration, there are other "rules of thumb" that can be considered. One such general guideline is to have *no less than 50 subjects* (employees in our case) for an MR analysis,[5] with the number increasing with larger numbers of independent variables by multiplying the number of independent variables by 8. For example, if using three independent variables calculate the minimum number needed by adding 50 to 8 X 3 = 24, or 74 subjects.

Two additional rules of thumb are available. Where five or fewer independent variables are included in the MR analyses, just exceed the number of independent variables by at least 50 subjects (*i.e.,* the total number of subjects equals the number of independent variables plus 50).[6] Another rule of thumb for MR analyses (that include six or more independent variables), is to simply include a minimum of 10 subjects per independent variable.

However, when discussing the minimum *overall* sample size, one important factor should also be considered: the *minimum number of men/women and whites/minorities* in the analysis sample (*e.g.,* SSEG). Some have recommended using five as a minimum sample for women or minority groups. This certainly seems to be a reasonable threshold.

These guidelines should be regarded as minimums for statistical power. In practice, however, researchers must deal with the realistic constraints of grouping employees that are similarly situated, and this sometimes dictates conducting MR analyses on smaller groups than what might be ideal under statistical power considerations. It is never recommended to combine dissimilar employees simply in the quest for statistical power.

Here is why statistical power is so important for MR analyses: If a researcher has a large sample in an MR analysis (*e.g.,* a SSEG with 300 employees and three independent "job factor" variables) and the analysis results show that gender or minority status is *not* statistically significant, the researcher can rest assured that the employer has no evidence of pay discrimination for this SSEG. This is because the analysis had high levels of statistical power, yet it did not find statistical evidence attributed to gender or minority status.

Now consider an MR analysis that includes a SSEG that has only 15 employees with the same three independent variables, and it results in the same finding (*i.e.,* with no statistical evidence of pay discrimination). Under these circumstances one cannot be confident that the analyses resulted in meaningful statistical findings – because the sample size was *too small to yield a highly reliable evaluation* of the pay differences between groups. On the flipside, if one *does* find statistically significant results with such a small sample size, it cannot be regarded as a highly stable finding because it was based on such a small sample.

There is another important consideration that should be made about statistical power and MR analysis. Consider a situation where men earn $45,000/year and women earn $44,500 ($500 less than men). This $500 difference may not be statistically significant in an analysis group where 100 employees (50 men and 50 women) are being compared. However, when the sample size is increased to say 400 employees, with 200 men and 200 women, the $500 gap may become statistically significant – and this being *just a function of statistical power*.

Somewhere between the two competing goals of grouping employees based on the similarity of the work they perform, their responsibility level, and the skills and qualifications involved in their positions – yet still taking statistical power into consideration, lays the marriage between the art and science of MR analyses.

Step 5A1 - Conduct The Multiple Regression (MR) Analysis Using SPSS

To complete an MR analysis using SPSS, follow these steps:

1. Access the regression menu by clicking "Analyze," then "Regression," and then "Linear."
2. Select the Dependent Variable for analysis. This will be the variable that contains compensation information for all employees (*e.g.,* "Total Compensation" or "Base Annual Salary"). Be sure that the variable selected includes the same metric for all employees (*e.g.,* annual salary for all employees – not annual salary for some and the hourly equivalent for others). Also, be sure to remove any bonuses or commissions that are not part of the "typical" pay package from the total compensation amount, unless the reason that bonuses or commissions fluctuate is included as an independent variable in the MR model. For example, if a commission is based on the amount of product a sales person sells each year, then the amount of product sold by the sales person should be included as an independent variable in the MR model.
3. Select the Independent Variables for analysis. This is the heart of MR model development. Selecting these variables should be done using three steps:
   a. Enter the *practical factors* related to pay as independent variables. These are the variables for which there are policy and/or business practice reasons to include in the analysis because they are used to make compensation decisions, such as tenure on the job or performance ratings.
   b. Click on the "Next" button and enter the "gender" variable into Block 2 of the model. (Note: Gender and race/ethnicity analyses should be conducted separately. With that in mind, this step will be repeated on the minority/non-minority variable when developing a model to examine potential compensation disparities by minority status.)
   c. Make sure that the "Method" drop-down menu is set to "Enter."

Regression diagnostics and supplemental statistical procedures
SPSS will generate a range of additional statistics that will help evaluate the model developed as a result of the analyses. Follow these steps to obtain these supplemental reports:

1. Click on the "Statistics" button at the bottom of the linear regression menu/interface and select the following options:
   a. Click on the "Confidence Intervals" check box.

b. Click on the "R-Square Change" check box.
c. Click on the "Descriptives" check box.
d. Click on the "Colinearity Diagnostics" check box.
e. Click the "Continue" button.

Note: Advanced researchers will want to explore the "Casewise Diagnostics" option, which provides reports showing employees that are outside of their predicted pay levels. This feature is useful for identifying possible data entry errors, or employees that are significantly under- or over-paid based on the factors accounted for in the MR model.

2. Run the MR analysis and develop an initial model, then click "OK."

Step 5A2 - Interpret Initial Results

After the MR analysis has been run, the next step is to interpret the output. The steps below provide interpretive comments and guidelines for each part of the SPSS output.

Review the model summary

Several parts of the SPSS results shown in Figure 9-1 are of major interest. First, notice that the first column is called "Model," and that there are two models (*i.e.,* Model 1 and Model 2). Model 1 contains all of the predictors *except* the gender or minority/non-minority variable, which is entered in Block 2 when selecting the independent variables to be included in the analysis. Model 2 includes all of the independent variables found in Model 1, but also includes the gender or minority/non-minority variable.

Model Summary^c

Model	R	R Square	Adjusted R Square	Std. Error of the Estimate	R Square Change	F Change	df1	df2	Sig. F Change
					Change Statistics				
1	.659^a	.435	.343	$11,055.43949	.435	4.764	5	31	.002
2	.754^b	.569	.483	$9,812.28210	.134	9.353	1	30	.005

a. Predictors: (Constant), HighestDegree, YrsInGrade, Age, PerfCode, YrsOfService

b. Predictors: (Constant), HighestDegree, YrsInGrade, Age, PerfCode, YrsOfService, Gender

c. Dependent Variable: BaseSalary

Figure 9-1 SPSS Model Summary Report

The essential components of this report are explained below:

- The values under the "R" column represent the correlation between all of the predictors *taken together* and the dependent variable (pay). Higher values of "R" indicate stronger combined relationships and therefore the more explanatory the model.
- The "R-Square" (or R^2) column shows the percent of variation in the dependent variable (*i.e.,* compensation) that is accounted for by the information provided by the entire set of independent variables. In the example in Figure 9-1, the R^2 in Model 1 is .435 before taking gender into account, and .569 after gender is accounted for (see Model 2).
- The "R-Square Change" values show the increase in R^2 over Model 1 (*i.e.,* the percentage of additional variance that is explained by the inclusion of

the gender or minority status variable). Notice in Figure 9-1 that the R^2 increases from .435 to .569 after taking gender into account, and this increase (.134, or a "13.4% change") is statistically significant (see the Significant F Change discussed below). This implies that the addition of the gender variable significantly enhanced the explanatory power of the model (indicating possible pay discrimination). Small values that are not statistically significant contribute little to the explanatory power of the model.

- The "Significance of F Change" statistic for Model 2 shows the statistical significance of the *change* between Model 1 and Model 2. If the value is less than .05 in the Model 2 row, the change in R-Square was statistically significant. This suggests that even after accounting for the predictors in Model 1, gender/minority status still explains some of the remaining differences in compensation (in this case, gender accounts for 13.4% more than the job factors alone). If the change in R-Square was not statistically significant, the increase in R-Square, if there was any, may have simply been due to chance.

Review the ANOVA Report

The ANOVA Report provides the results of the Analysis of Variance test, which essentially reveals if the overall MR model was a "good fit."

ANOVA[c]

Model		Sum of Squares	df	Mean Square	F	Sig.
1	Regression	2911334329.63	5	582266865.9	4.764	.002[a]
	Residual	3788905011.55	31	122222742.3		
	Total	6700239341.18	36			
2	Regression	3811812942.53	6	635302157.1	6.598	.000[b]
	Residual	2888426398.65	30	96280879.96		
	Total	6700239341.18	36			

a. Predictors: (Constant), HighestDegree, YrsInGrade, Age, PerfCode, YrsOfService

b. Predictors: (Constant), HighestDegree, YrsInGrade, Age, PerfCode, YrsOfService, Gender

c. Dependent Variable: BaseSalary

Figure 9-2 SPSS ANOVA Report

The essential components of this report are explained below:

- The "Regression Sum of Squares" indicates the amount of variation that is explained by the model.
- The "Residual Sum of Squares" is a measure of how much variation is not explained by the model. Therefore, if the Regression Sum of Squares is large compared to the Residual Sum of Squares, this means that the model explains a large portion of the variance in compensation.
- This table is useful for comparing the Regression and Residual Sum of Squares in Model 1 and Model 2 to see whether each of the models has a

significant ANOVA value (meaning that the model is effective at explaining a statistically significant portion of the variance).

Review the Coefficients Report

The Coefficients Report provides the heart of the analysis results because it shows how well each independent variable worked to predict compensation. Note below that the report includes the independent variables for each model that was included in the analysis.

Coefficients[a]

Model		Unstandardized Coefficients		Standardized Coefficients	t	Sig.	Collinearity Statistics	
		B	Std. Error	Beta			Tolerance	VIF
1	(Constant)	31038.561	18694.132		1.660	.107		
	Age	371.211	240.275	.220	1.545	.133	.902	1.109
	PerfCode	-370.996	4297.297	-.012	-.086	.932	.875	1.143
	YrsOfService	2079.554	654.699	.460	3.176	.003	.871	1.148
	YrsInGrade	341.916	1059.453	.047	.323	.749	.848	1.179
	HighestDegree	9036.374	2472.815	.508	3.654	.001	.943	1.060
2	(Constant)	40645.955	16886.809		2.407	.022		
	Age	201.791	220.335	.119	.916	.367	.845	1.184
	PerfCode	52.133	3816.585	.002	.014	.989	.873	1.145
	YrsOfService	1575.253	604.024	.348	2.608	.014	.806	1.241
	YrsInGrade	144.362	942.536	.020	.153	.879	.844	1.185
	HighestDegree	6715.482	2322.258	.378	2.892	.007	.843	1.187
	Gender	12165.496	3977.985	.413	3.058	.005	.787	1.270

a. Dependent Variable: BaseSalary

Figure 9-3 SPSS Coefficient Report

The essential components of this report are explained below:

- The values in the "B" column under the "Unstandardized Coefficients" section show how much the dependent variable (*i.e.,* compensation) increases for each 1 unit increase in that particular independent variable while holding all of the other predictors constant. For example, each additional year of service translates to $2,079.55 in compensation (before gender is added in Model 2). Also notice the impact of being female (see Model 2) is about $12,165.50 (even after job relevant factors are accounted for in the model).
- The "Standardized Regression Coefficients" (sometimes called "beta-weights") show the predictive power of each independent variable in a uniform way *so they can be compared relevant to each other*. The values in this column are useful for two reasons: they show the strength of the correlation relationship of each independent variable with the dependent variable, and the direction of the correlation relationship (either positive or negative). Higher absolute values have a stronger impact on the dependent variable (*i.e.,* pay). For example, the "Years of Service" and "Highest Degree" variables have the highest values in Model 1 (.46 and .508 respectively), and are therefore the strongest predictors in that model.
- The "t" and the "Sig" columns contain important data. The "t" shows the *direction* of the relationship with compensation (using positive and negative values). The "Sig" column reveals the p-value (values less than .05 are

statistically significant). A basic rule is that when "t" values exceed 2.0, they become statistically significant at the .05 level (*i.e.,* higher "t" values are associated with smaller *p-values*). Notice that the p-value associated with gender is 0.005 – revealing that gender is statistically significant even after controlling for legitimate job-related factors.

- The values in the Tolerance and Variance Inflation Factor (VIF) columns are useful for investigating whether multicollinearity is an issue (see discussion on this topic below). These two values are mathematically related (VIF is inversely related to the Tolerance value). Tolerance has a range from zero to one, and the closer the value is to zero the higher the level of multicollinearity caused by that variable. VIF shows how much the standard error variance of each of the independent variables coefficients increased as a result of multicollinearity. Thus, it is a measure of the *cost* of multicollinearity in loss of precision, and is directly relevant when performing statistical tests and calculating confidence intervals (which show the *range of accuracy* for the MR model). High VIF values (a usual threshold is 10.0, which corresponds to a Tolerance value of .10) indicate that the associated variable is a cause of multicollinearity in the model.

While the Regression Coefficients Report (in Figure 9-3) places emphasis on *statistical significance* (whether the independent variables are significantly correlated with compensation – indicated when the "Sig." column is less than .05 for that variable), what about considering the *practical significance* of a pay difference? For example, an annual pay difference between groups of $5,000 that is statistically significant represents a greater concern than a pay difference of $2,000 that is also statistically significant. Even pay differences that are large, but are *not* statistically significant are still a concern to those being underpaid!

On the other hand, what about pay differences between groups that are very small (*e.g.,* $300/year where average compensation is in the $80,000/year range) that are statistically significant? Certainly these situations make it easier for employers to make corrections that remove the statistical significance findings. Certainly practical considerations like these should also be considered when interpreting MR analysis results.

Multicollinearity

If two of the variables that are being used to explain compensation are highly correlated, they are referred to as "collinear." When more than two variables are collinear, multicollinearity exists, which may limit the usability of the model. At a minimum, it is not advisable to include independent variables in the same model if they are correlated higher than .80 with each other. In this case, consider dropping one of them from the analysis.

Many more advanced statistical techniques exist for assessing multi-collinearity. SPSS provides two sets of tools that can be used for evaluating this potential limitation. The first set of tools is the Tolerance and Variance Inflation Factor (VIF) noted above. Independent variables that have Tolerance values less than .10 or corresponding Variance Inflation Factor (VIF) values higher than 10.0 indicate multicollinearity. Another set of tools is provided by the Collinearity Diagnostics report shown in Figure 9-4.

Collinearity Diagnostics

Model	Dimension	Eigenvalue	Condition Index	(Constant)	Age	PerfCode	YrsOfService	YrsInGrade	Highest Degree	Gender
							Variance Proportions			
1	1	5.560	1.000	.00	.00	.00	.00	.01	.00	
	2	.216	5.077	.00	.00	.02	.04	.61	.01	
	3	.131	6.523	.00	.00	.00	.83	.25	.02	
	4	.050	10.574	.00	.45	.20	.01	.06	.04	
	5	.037	12.237	.00	.02	.37	.08	.05	.65	
	6	.007	27.671	1.00	.52	.40	.03	.02	.27	
2	1	6.324	1.000	.00	.00	.00	.00	.00	.00	.00
	2	.243	5.100	.00	.00	.02	.00	.01	.00	.73
	3	.213	5.455	.00	.00	.01	.04	.65	.01	.10
	4	.130	6.981	.00	.00	.00	.79	.22	.02	.01
	5	.049	11.377	.00	.45	.15	.01	.04	.08	.02
	6	.034	13.589	.00	.00	.46	.11	.05	.57	.09
	7	.007	30.226	.99	.54	.36	.06	.02	.32	.05

a. Dependent Variable: BaseSalary

Figure 9-4 SPSS Collinearity Diagnostics Report

The Condition Index in the third column is the key in this report. The Condition Index measures the "dependency" of the independent variables, and values in this column will increase as additional related variables are added to the MR model (it is *cumulative*). Various guidelines are available for interpreting the results in this report. For example, SPSS provides conservative guidelines that Condition Index values over 15 indicate *possible* problems with collinearity and higher than 30 suggests a *serious* problem with collinearity.

Evaluating the Condition Index values can be done in conjunction with an evaluation of the "Variance Proportions" data also in this report, which are shown for each of the independent variables. For example, some experts advise that multicollinearity exists if (first) the Condition Index exceeds a threshold of 30 and (second) two or more Variance Proportions in those rows exceed .50.[7] Others advise using the same process, but with a .90 threshold (again for at least two independent variables) for the Variance Proportions in those rows where the Condition Index exceeds 15 or 30 (with 30 being the typical criteria of choice).[8]

If the goal of the MR analysis is simply to *predict* pay using a collection of independent variables that are statistically or practically relevant to compensation, then multicollinearity may only be a minor limitation (*i.e.*, the predictions may still be accurate). However, if the goal of the MR analyses is to understand exactly *how* the various independent variables impact compensation, multicollinearity can be a significant issue. This is because the individual *p-values* for the independent variables can be misleading and the "confidence intervals" (which shows the *range of accuracy*) may be very wide.

What can be done about multicollinearity? Perhaps the best solution is to find out why it is occurring and remove the variables that are creating the problem. This is especially true if the variables creating the problem are either redundant to other variables or not practically relevant to predicting pay. Another way to address multicollinearity is to combine the co-linear variables. This can be done by first standardizing[9] each variable then simply adding them together to create a new variable. Multicollinearity can also be reduced by "centering" the variables, which can be done by computing the mean of each independent variable and replacing each value with the difference between it and the mean.

The key to the interpretation

While reviewing the Coefficients Report in Figure 9-3, the particular area of interest is whether the gender or minority status variable is statistically significant in Model 2. If it is not, it means that gender (or minority status) did not appear to be related to differences in compensation after the effects of the other variables are accounted for and therefore there is no statistical evidence of possible pay discrimination. It is important to note that the two-model process that has been used in this example has been provided for clarity purposes only. Assessing whether the R^2 Change in Model 2 is statistically significant is effectively the same as simply placing all independent variables in the same "model" or block and then assessing whether the gender/minority status variable is statistically significant. This is exactly the process followed for the MR analysis using Excel described later. In other words, the p-value of the R^2 Change between the two MR models (where gender/minority status is the only variable in the second model) will be exactly the same as the p-value of the gender/minority status variable that is simply included in the first model with the other variables.

Interaction terms: When two variables create a third

Standard MR models that include only the "main effects" (or the natural variables like those discussed above) are forced to assume that these variables impact all the employees in the group in the *same way*. From a purely statistical perspective, this means that the employees grouped together should exhibit similar relationships to these pay-related variables for the model to work properly. However, when significant interactions are occurring between the variables, it is incorrect to interpret the MR model that includes only the natural variables. For this reason, it is useful for the researcher to determine whether *interactions* exist between the variables being used in the MR analysis. In this way, the researcher can determine the extent to which the *effect of one predictor variable depends upon levels of another predictor variable.*

The interaction between two independent variables is obtained by multiplying the two variables to create a new variable (called an "interaction term"). For example, multiplying the gender variable (coded 0 for male; 1 for females) by the "time in job" variable will create a Gender/Tenure interaction variable. By using interactions in the MR analyses, the combined dynamic of being a female and one's level of job tenure would be allowed to statistically interact with one another in their influence on the dependent variable (pay).

Interactions are typically included in the MR model by first entering each of the two variables that were used to make the interaction (*e.g.*, Gender and Tenure), and then including the interaction term in the second block of the model. By using this process, the statistical significance of the interaction effect (shown by the significance of the R^2 Change) can be attributed to the interaction of the two independent variables, *beyond what they contributed to the regression model independently.*

Step 5B1 - Conducting Multiple Regression (MR) Using Microsoft Excel

There are two ways to use Excel to perform statistical analyses. One way is to program formulas from scratch into the spreadsheet. This process, however, can be complex and is certainly time consuming. Thankfully, there is an alternative that is easy to use, relatively straightforward, and which presents the relevant statistical results in a way that is easy to understand. Before this can be done, however, the Excel "Analysis ToolPak" needs to be installed (this tool is included on the Microsoft Excel installation CD but it needs to be intentionally installed when Excel is first loaded onto a computer or added later using the instructions below).

Installing the Analysis ToolPak

The following is a step-by-step process for installing the Analysis ToolPak:

1. Have the original Microsoft Office installation CD available in case the installation process requests the CD during the process (do not place it in the drive at this time. Do so only if requested to do so).
2. Start Microsoft Excel and click on the "Tools" menu located at the top of the screen.
3. Click on the "Add-Ins" option that is located inside the "Tools" menu.
4. After clicking on the "Add-Ins" menu option, a window will open. Make sure that the check box located next to "Analysis ToolPak" has a checkmark. If there is already a checkmark in this box, it means that the Analysis ToolPak is already installed.
5. Click "OK." Excel will now begin installing the Analysis ToolPak (if it was not already installed).
6. At this point, the installation process may request inserting the Microsoft Office installation CD. If this occurs, follow the instructions, and after this process is complete, the Analysis ToolPak will be ready for use. Now, when accessing the "Tools" menu in Excel, a new menu option called "Data Analysis" will be available.

Conducting step-by-step MR analyses using Excel

This section provides a step-by-step guide to using Microsoft Excel to perform a basic MR analysis. Readers are encouraged to follow along and actually run the analysis while reading.

1. Create an Excel worksheet that contains the variables relevant for the MR analysis. Place the dependent variable (pay) in Column A. Place the independent variables (*e.g.,* age, time with company, time in job, years of education, starting salary, performance appraisal score) starting in column B and continuing across columns (with one variable per column). **It is important to make sure that all independent variables are next to each other without any separations** (columns cannot be skipped when selecting variables to include in the MR analysis – see Figure 9-5).

	A	B	C	D	E	F	G	H	I
1	BaseSalary	Age	PerfCode	YrsOfService	YrsInGrade	HighestDegree	Gender	Degree Type	SSEG
2	$79,971.72	30.00	2.00	8.2	4	3	0	0	SSEG 17
3	$85,236.07	35.00	2.00	5.3	1	4	0	0	SSEG 17
4	$95,017.50	39.00	2.00	6.1	6	4	0	0	SSEG 17
5	$95,153.21	53.00	2.00	5.6	2	4	0	0	SSEG 17
6	$100,000.00	46.00	1.00	4.6	4	4	1	1	SSEG 17

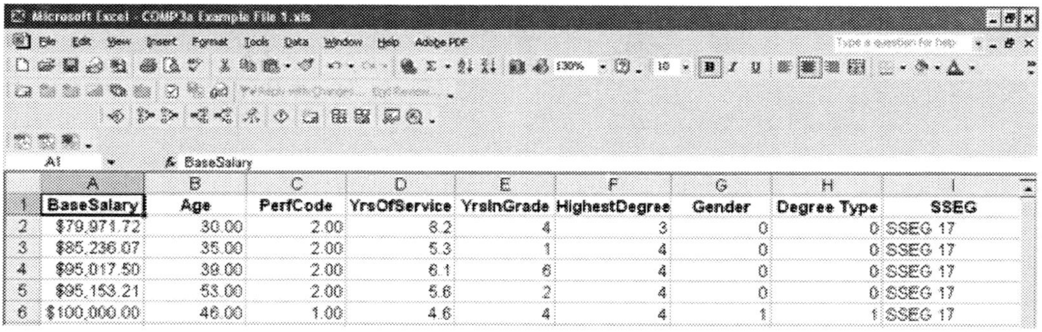

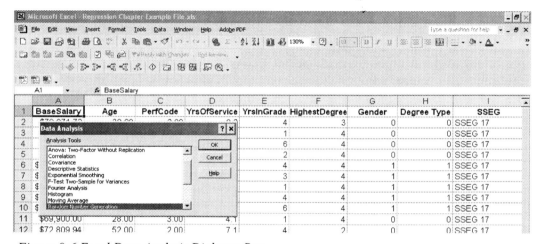

Figure 9-5 Setting Up an Excel File for Use in Multiple Regression

2. Click on the "Tools" menu, then on the "Data Analysis" menu option. The Data Analysis window shown in Figure 9-6 will appear.

	A	B	C	D	E	F	G	H	I
1	BaseSalary	Age	PerfCode	YrsOfService	YrsInGrade	HighestDegree	Gender	Degree Type	SSEG
2					4	3	0	0	SSEG 17
3					1	4	0	0	SSEG 17
4					6	4	0	0	SSEG 17
5					2	4	0	0	SSEG 17
6					4	4	1	1	SSEG 17
7					3	4	1	1	SSEG 17
8					1	4	1	1	SSEG 17
9					4	4	1	1	SSEG 17
10					6	4	1	1	SSEG 17
11	$69,900.00	28.00	3.00	4.1	1	4	0	0	SSEG 17
12	$72,809.94	52.00	2.00	7.1	4	2	0	0	SSEG 17

Figure 9-6 Excel Data Analysis Dialogue Box

3. Using the scroll bar, scroll down to access the "Regression" option and select it. The window shown in Figure 9-7 will appear. Pay particular attention to the following parts of this window. First, there is a text box titled "Input Y Range" which is where the compensation variable will be identified (which in this case is *BaseSalary*). Next, there is a text box titled "Input X Range" where the independent variables will be identified (*i.e.,* the variables that will be used to model, or explain, why employees receive the compensation they do). At the far right side of each of these text boxes is a button that, when selected, allows the computer's mouse to select the data to include.

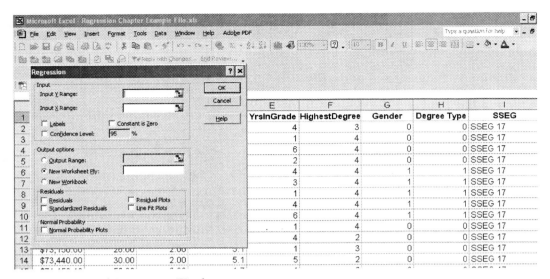

Figure 9-7 Excel Regression Window

4. Click on the button located at the right end of the "Input Y Range" text box. The computer screen will look something like what is shown in Figure 9-8.

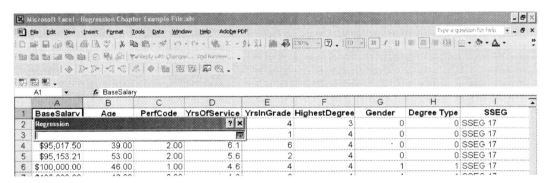

Figure 9-8 Excel Input Y Range Window

5. Place the mouse pointer over the *BaseSalary* column label that is located in cell A1. Holding down the right mouse button, highlight the *BaseSalary* title and all of the data included in column A underneath *BaseSalary*. After highlighting the data in column A and releasing the mouse button, click on the button that is located at the right edge of the Regression dialogue box. The computer screen will look something like that shown in Figure 9-9.

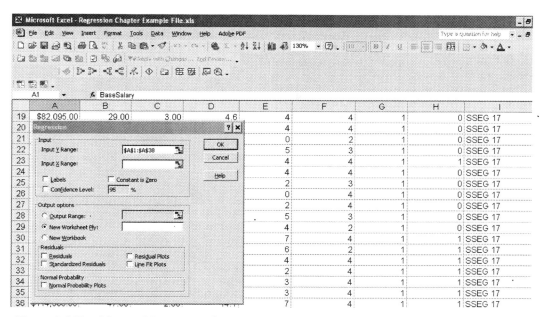

Figure 9-9 Excel Input X Range Window

6. Click on the button located at the right end of the "Input X Range" text box.

7. Place the mouse pointer over the Age column label that is located the cell B1. Holding the right mouse button down, highlight the Age title, drag the mouse to the right until column G and then all of the data included in columns B through G underneath the column labels. Note that Column G identifies the employee's gender and so this analysis will seek to determine whether reliable differences in compensation exist for males and females. For conducting an MR analysis comparing whites and minorities, the variable in column G would need to indicate the employee's white/minority status (0 = white; 1 = minority). In general, do not include both gender and minority status variables in the same analysis because the results will be difficult to interpret. After highlighting the data in columns B through G and releasing the mouse button, click on the button that is located at the right edge of the query box (similar to the step completed while selecting data for pay using the *BaseSalary* variable).

8. Note that in this example file each column has a descriptive label in row 1. Because these labels are included (which is always a good idea because it will make the results of the analysis much easier to understand), a check mark must be placed in the "Label" checkbox located just below "Input X Range." This tells Excel to ignore the first row and only use that information to label specific output information. Click "OK" and Excel will compute the requested regression analysis. The computer screen will look something like that shown in Figure 9-10.

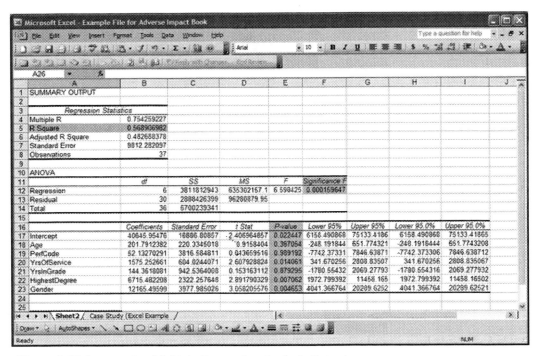

Figure 9-10 Interpreting Multiple Regression Analysis Output

Step 5B2 - Interpret Initial Results

After calculating the appropriate statistical analyses, Excel automatically opens a new worksheet and pastes the information presented in Figure 9-10. To draw the reader's attention to the important components of this analysis, various areas have been shaded (Excel does not automatically provide this shading). However, these shaded areas will be referred to in the following step-by-step guide to interpreting these results. The following steps and guidelines can be followed for analyzing the analysis results:

1. Under "Regression Statistics," view the shaded row titled "R-Square." Notice that the number presented is 0.568906982 (rounded to 0.57). Earlier in this Chapter, it was pointed out that when a correlation is squared, it indicates the percent of variation in compensation that is accounted for or *explained* by the variable (or variables) with which it is being correlated. The R-Square simply shows the percentage of variation across employees in their compensation that is explained by the *combination* of all the variables included in the model. In this case, the R-Square of .57 shows that a total of 57% of an employee's compensation appears to be explained by a combination of a) age, b) performance appraisal score, c) years of service, d) years in grade, e) highest degree earned, and f) gender.

2. In the section titled ANOVA (which stands for Analysis of Variance), notice that a cell titled "Significance F" is shaded. This is a very important part of the report. Remember that MR is designed to be used to study data where the relationship between variables is "linear." This ANOVA table is a statistical

test that measures whether the relationships between the independent variables and compensation is linear and therefore appropriate for use in MR analyses.[10] Specifically, if the number listed under Significance F is less than .05, it indicates that the relationships are characterized by a linear relationship. If the number is .05 or greater, it means that something about the data makes it inappropriate for use with MR. There are strategies for dealing with these kinds of data problems called "non-linear transformations" but they are beyond the scope of this book. Simply be aware that if the Significance F is .05 or greater, the results of the analysis will be questionable and may not be reliable. In this case, the number shown under Significance F is 0.000159647 – which is definitely less than 0.05! In this case, it is safe to assume that the relationship between compensation and the set of independent variables is linear and significant.

3. Evaluate the *p-values* for each of the independent variables. This information is highlighted to make it easier to evaluate. Notice that each independent variable is identified in a row and a variety of numbers is listed to the right of the independent variable. Each of these numbers provides important information. However, to simply answer the question of whether there is a statistically significant difference in compensation for males and females exist (after taking into account legitimate job-related factors that could explain these differences), the only number that needs to be reviewed is the p-value associated with gender. Note that the p-value associated with gender is 0.004653 (which can be rounded to 0.005). If the p-value shown is less than 0.05 (which is true in this case), it reveals that *even after controlling for legitimate job-related factors* there were statistically significant differences in the compensation of males and females. There are at least two possible explanations for this: (1) It is very possible that legitimate job-related factors that could explain the differences in compensation were not included in the analysis. Available data should be more carefully reviewed to determine if there are other variables that should be included in the MR analysis, and (2) the decision process used to establish the compensation of males and females was based on something other than legitimate job-related factors.

Step 6 - Conduct a Cohort Analysis

The last step in the compensation analysis is to conduct a Cohort Analysis for the employee groups (*e.g.,* SSEGs) where statistically significant differences exist for gender or minority status. This process can be completed by examining the highest paid males/whites and the lowest paid females/minorities (based on whether the statistically significant finding is based on gender or minority status in the at-issue SSEG) to determine if there are other factors that seem to explain why these differences exist. These can be *soft factors* or *qualitative factors* that may not be statistical in nature, or can be variables that are statistical in nature but for some reason were not captured in the MR analysis. For example, it is common practice for many employers to base starting salary on an applicant's previous salary and/or experience, but it is a rare employer that has this information included in their HRIS and readily available for inclusion in regression analyses.

In summary, while MR is a powerful tool for evaluating differences in compensation, it can only take the researcher so far. If, after careful consideration of relevant factors and analysis groupings, gender/minority status continues to be significant predictors of pay, nothing can replace the importance of a thorough review of personnel files, applicant vitae/resume, and interview notes. And for those significant differences that remain unexplainable by such factors, corrective actions should be made.

When it comes to making overall conclusions about a particular employer's pay practices and whether they have been "fair" or "discriminatory," careful attention should be given to the *trend* of the findings. For example, it is not uncommon in practice to identify a similar number of SSEGs with significant pay disparities for men and women alike (*e.g.,* five significant findings against men and five against women for the same employer, where a total of only 10 significant pay disparities were found).

Evaluating the Legal Defensibility of Regression Models
By Daniel A. Biddle, Ph.D.

The Equal Pay Act of 1963 and Title VII of the Civil Rights Act of 1964 provide the legal foundation for pay equity studies. While Title VII generally prohibits pay discrimination, the Equal Pay Act is specifically tailored around "equal pay for substantially equal work," with claims typically arising when men and women perform "substantially equal work" for unequal pay. Specifically, the Equal Pay Act holds that:

> No employer having employees subject to any provisions of this section shall discriminate, within any establishment in which such employees are employed, between employees on the basis of sex by paying wages to employees in such establishment at a rate less than the rate at which he pays wages to employees of the opposite sex in such establishment for equal work on jobs the performance of which requires equal skill, effort, and responsibility, and which are performed under similar working conditions.[11]

Title VII of the Civil Rights Act of 1964 prohibits employers from discriminating on the basis of race, color, religion, national origin or sex[12] and also states that employers cannot discriminate "against any individual with respect to his compensation … because of such individual's sex."[13] The U.S. Supreme Court has interpreted this section of Title VII as a prohibition "not only against overt discrimination, but also practices that are *fair in form, but discriminatory in operation.*"[14]

Following this statute, plaintiffs that bring a Title VII suit need to establish "the existence of a discriminatory hiring pattern and practice,"[15] and proving such a claim requires the plaintiffs to show a practice or pattern, as opposed to an "isolated or accidental, or sporadic discriminatory acts."[16] Specifically, the plaintiff in a Title VII case must prove that the plaintiff was a member of a protected class, the plaintiff was meeting the employer's legitimate expectations, the plaintiff suffered an adverse employment action, and the employer treated a similarly situated employee of the opposite sex more favorably.[17]

Therein lays the fundamental strength of multiple regression when used to analyze pay equity. Because regression is capable of *controlling* for job-related factors that may differ at *both* the individual and group levels, it is the ideal strategy for analyzing whether "the employer treated a similarly situated employee of the opposite sex more favorably." For this reason, and because the use of multiple regression has been widely-adopted as the tool-of-choice accepted by the courts for pay equity analyses, the U.S. Department of Labor's enforcement arm, the Office of Federal Contract Compliance Programs (OFCCP), has endorsed multiple regression as the ideal methodology for conducting compensation analyses.[18]

The standard process for using multiple regression to analyze pay includes grouping the employees into Similarly Situated Employee Groups ("SSEGs"), loading the model with the major job-related factors thought to predict (explain) pay, and then dropping the race/gender variable into the equation to assess whether it adds significantly to the model (*i.e.,* beyond the job-related factors, which theoretically should explain most of the variance without race or gender). If a significant disparity is observed, cohort analyses can be conducted to determine why the significant imbalance may exist, and then remedial pay changes can be applied if differences remain. Such remedial pay changes range from "just enough to get out of significance" to "complete parity" to "parity with back-pay" based upon the strength of the evidence and the circumstances of the study (*i.e.,* whether proactive, in response to an audit, or litigation).

While employers have been conducting such practices for years (and perhaps even more frequently with the formal endorsement of the OFCCP through the publication of the 2006 standards), some employers have been concerned with the potential of "reverse discrimination" or Equal Protection-based lawsuits that may arise after making pay adjustments to a given group. Faced with liability from potential class action suits or audits from "classical" pay disparity issues on one side and Equal Protection cases on the other, some employers view themselves in a "pickle." Indeed, some employers that act in good faith to conduct (and later act upon) proactive pay equity studies may find themselves open to an Equal Protection suit from the group that received no pay changes.

When the courts evaluate such circumstances, some have extracted three criteria from the U.S. Supreme Court case, Johnson. v. Transportation Agency[19]: (1) evaluating whether a "manifest imbalance" exists (which typically includes statistical significance as a minimum threshold); (2) evaluating whether the rights of individuals who were not part of the remedial pay were "unnecessarily trammeled"; and (3) evaluating whether the remedial pay adjustments were along the lines necessary to "attain a balance."[20] The Johnson decision also dictates that the burden shifts to the employer to provide a nondiscriminatory rationale for its decision after the plaintiff demonstrates that sex was taken into account in an employer's employment decision. The employer can establish such a rationale by pointing to an existing affirmative action plan.

One of the key cases that has applied the Johnson framework to compensation discrimination is Rudebusch v. Hughes.[21] As a background, in Rudebusch, the employer (a University) made pay changes to women and minorities who were below their predicted pay levels (based on a flawed regression – see discussion below), and the employer made such decisions without sufficient evidence that the differences in pay were not *statistically significant at the group level*. Forty white males filed an equal protection suit and lost at the federal district level. They appealed the case to the Ninth Circuit, where the Court affirmed in part and remanded in part. When the remanded parts of the case were tried by the District Court, the Court found that the regression model that was initially used to justify making pay changes (to only minorities and women) was fatally flawed, and thus deemed the pay changes as unjustified. As a result, the employer had to pay $2 million in back pay to the 40 white males.

When applying the Johnson framework to an Equal Protection pay case, the Ninth Circuit in Rudebusch pointed out that previous Appellate Courts (both the Fourth and Eighth Circuits) have adopted the Johnson approach in their analysis of pay equity claims. While agreeing that the Johnson case provided the proper framework for a pay equity case, they noted that there were "some significant conceptual differences between affirmative action in the promotional context and remedial measures used to cure pay inequity"[22] because the <u>Johnson</u> case involved voluntary affirmative action efforts for promotional decisions – which is quite different than pay equity.

With respect to the second <u>Johnson</u> prong (evaluating whether the rights of those who were not part of the pay plan were "unnecessarily trammeled"), the Ninth Circuit noted that promotional decisions that were the focal issue in <u>Johnson</u> involve a competition for a *finite position* where the benefits of promotion will have *lasting employment consequences*, and that operating exclusively to alleviate racial or gender-based disparities may in fact trammel upon the excluded employee's legitimate expectation to *compete equally* for the position. Thus, the Ninth Circuit pointed out that in <u>Johnson</u>, the remedial plan should make "minimal intrusion on the legitimate expectations of other employees." Drawing a clear distinction between the lawfulness of voluntary affirmative action in the promotional context compared to pay equity situations, the Ninth Circuit stated:

> But none of these concerns are presented in this case. Here, there would have been no opportunity or funds available for any pay adjustments but for the University's decision to address the manifest imbalance between the salaries of white male professors and their female and minority counterparts in the first instance. In other words, the University's decision to scrounge its budget for unused funds and make adjustments to women and minorities' salaries was driven solely by the perceived need to make such adjustments.

Further clarifying the differences between the voluntary affirmative action promotional decisions and a pay equity case, the Court stated, "Allowing Rudebusch and the white male plaintiffs to claim that their exclusion from consideration 'absolutely barred their advancement' would permit them to recharacterize [the employer's] situation as an 'opportunity for advancement' when, in fact, such an opportunity never existed in the first instance."

The Seventh Circuit <u>Ende v. Board of Regents</u>[23] case gave a similar ruling by endorsing a similar adjustment scheme for purposes of an Equal Pay Act claim brought by male faculty, stating: "it determines the incremental adjustment to females' salaries necessary to remedy the effects of past sex discrimination and eliminate sex as a determiner of salary. The formula merely [brings] the women to a salary level they would have reached in ordinary course if they had been men and not subjected to sex discrimination. It makes no sense to apply the formula to men in this context."

Regarding the third prong of the <u>Johnson</u> framework applied in the <u>Rudebusch</u> case (*i.e.,* whether the adjustments were along the lines necessary to "attain a balance"), the Circuit Court remanded this issue back to the Federal District Court for ruling. This is exactly where the case moves into the *hall of fame of lessons learned* for both academics and practitioners alike. Upon remand, the Court found that both the defense and plaintiff multiple regression studies revealed that the differences in pay were *not statistically significant,* and as such, they ultimately failed both the first <u>Johnson</u> prong (manifest imbalance) as well as the third prong (attaining a balance).[24]

The evidence for this finding was compelling. For example, the defendant's regression revealed that the difference attributable to ethnicity was only $87 and was not statistically significant. The difference between men and women was also not statistically significant.[25] The plaintiff expert's regression analysis found that the differences between men and women "would not even remotely be statistically significant" and both "gender and minority status do not come close to being statistically significant."[26] The District Court further clarified that "if 'manifest imbalance' requires a 'statistically significant disparity,' then there is no 'manifest imbalance' in this case."[27]

In addition to not demonstrating that a manifest imbalance existed between groups (through a showing of statistical significance), the plaintiff expert analysis and the court noted several internal flaws with the original regression analysis that was used as a basis for making pay changes. These included:

- Ethnicity was used as a linear variable (rather than a dummy-coded variable). This mistake alone would make most regression analyses impossible to interpret, because treating race as a linear variable gives higher credit to various race groups (e.g., whites = 1, Hispanics = 2, Asians = 3, etc.).[28]
- The regression model omitted "critical factors influencing salary levels, such as doctoral status, performance, and individual differences."[29] While building a "perfect" regression model is not a requirement, the Court in this case noted that these factors were important but were omitted from the model.
- Pay increases were given to women and minorities based upon how far each individual was from their predicted pay (using the Standard Error of Estimate, or SEE) *without the gender or race variable first being statistically significant.*
- The amount of pay increases that were given to women and minorities far exceeded the amount necessary to attain a balance. For example, the average pay increase given to women was *three times* the amount of the average difference between men and women ($2,400 versus $751).
- The regression model "forced" a market value variable into the model to use linear spacing, which distorted the effect of the other variables and led to an apparent significant gender effect.[30]

There are two major lessons that can be learned from the Rudebusch case. First, before making pay adjustments to a group, be sure the regression model clearly shows that the gender or race variable is statistically significant after controlling for job-related factors. Second, make sure that the regression model is sound, accurate, and reliable. The following guidelines are offered to help employers address these key requirements, as well as the core requirements from other related pay discrimination cases:

1. Do not make pay adjustments unless multiple regression analyses are used (opposed to other techniques) to control for realistic differences in job-related factors that may exist between groups. In most situations, using multiple regression is the only clearly acceptable way to model compensation decisions, and has decades of support in the federal courts and recent endorsement from both federal enforcement agencies that investigate and enforce pay equity cases.[31]

2. Do not make pay adjustments unless the gender or race variable is *statistically significant* after controlling for job-related factors.

3. Be sure that the pay equity analysis was designed to identify significant pay disparities that may exist for *any* group (whites and men included). In addition, determine (preferably in advance) how pay disparities will be addressed if discovered to insure that the criteria and rules will be *uniformly applied* across all gender and race/ethnic groups.

4. Do not make pay adjustments unless *the regression model itself is statistically significant*. This can be accomplished by evaluating the ANOVA associated with the model.

5. Ensure that the *strength* of the regression model is adequate for making reliable predictions. The strength of the regression model can be evaluated by referencing the Adjusted R^2 value, with Adjusted R^2 values that are statistically significant passing a minimum threshold.[32] In addition, the degree of multicollinearity among the variables should be evaluated (high multicollinearity tends to inflate standard errors associated with predictions, which can make predictions less reliable).

6. In most situations, do not make pay adjustments until after performing a *"cohort"* analysis, whereby additional variables (*i.e.,* those not included within the regression analysis) are investigated. This is because some situations may reveal that some job-related factors (both qualitative factors and quantitative factors that were not included in the regression model) may explain (and justify) pay differences between individuals that may *collectively* account for the significant differences that were observed at the *group level*.

7. Be sure that the *fundamental factors* relevant to compensation have been included in the regression analysis or evaluated in the cohort analysis. This has been one of the key factors reviewed when regression studies are contested in litigation settings. In Bazemore v. Friday,[33] the U.S. Supreme Court addressed this issue by evaluating the validity of statistical evidence that is necessary to support an inference of discrimination, but fails to consider *all possible variables*. In Bazemore, the Court reversed the lower court's refusal to accept plaintiff's regression analysis as proof of pay discrimination, noting that "discrimination need not be proved with scientific certainty." The Court rejected the lower court's conclusion that "an appropriate regression analysis should include *all measurable variables thought to have an effect*" (478 U.S. at 399, 400) [emphasis added]. Thus, in Bazemore, the Court ruled that statistical evidence may prove discrimination provided that it accounts for the *major* measurable factors causing the disparity. Rather than requiring the "perfect regression model," the courts

typically require the opposing party to prove that the omitted variables would have *substantially changed the outcome of the study*, and they typically do not allow an inference of discrimination (based on statistical evidence) to be rebutted by simply pointing out unaccounted variables that might have affected the analysis.[34]

8. Be sure that the compensation adjustments made to the disadvantaged group are no more than necessary to attain a balance. As noted in Rudebusch:

> In addition to existence of a manifest imbalance, the pay equity plan must not unnecessarily trammel the rights of others, and it must be designed to do no more than 'attain a balance' (citing Johnson v. Transportation Agency, 480 U. S. at 637-39, 1987). It is logical that, since pay equity plans are, at least theoretically, implemented to eliminate a pre-existing manifest imbalance, Title VII requires that they must not be designed to go beyond correcting the imbalance, or unnecessarily trammel the rights of others.[35]

When dealing with the important issue of "attaining balance" and "not trammeling the rights" of other groups not part of the pay adjustments, the Ninth Circuit noted in Rudebusch that, "while pay equity plans resemble affirmative action, they are not concerned (as affirmative action usually is) with providing an ultimate advantage, such as providing preferences in hiring and promotion plans. Though sometimes labeled as 'affirmative action,' a pay equity plan such as that implemented by [the defendants] seeks to eliminate *existing* salary disparities for *particular individuals* due to race and sex [emphasis added]."[36] The Federal District Court also clarified this matter by stating: "In other words, where salary is already skewed due to discrimination (as prohibited by Title VII), on account of race and sex equalization results in the *elimination* of the preferences – it does not create a preference."

9. Thoroughly discuss with legal counsel and executive staff how adjustments to compensation will be made (e.g., incrementally, lump-sum, as part of a yearly compensation/performance review, etc.).

In addition to addressing the important lessons that emerge from the Rudebusch case, employers will further safeguard their pay equity analyses (and resulting remedial pay changes) from the principles laid down in the U.S. Supreme Court case, Ricci v. DeStefano[37] by following guidelines 1-9 above. In Ricci, the Supreme Court held that, in order for employers to avoid a reverse-discrimination lawsuit in a hiring case, the employer must have a "strong basis in evidence" to believe that it will be exposed to a discrimination suit if it follows an employment practice.

While the U.S. Supreme Court may need to clarify the extent to which Ricci applies to pay discrimination cases, it is clear that at least three Circuit-level courts have regularly applied the previous Johnson Supreme Court case to evaluating whether a "manifest imbalance" exists, whether the rights of individuals who were not part of the remedial pay were "unnecessarily trammeled," and whether the remedial pay adjustments were along the lines necessary to "attain a balance." These Circuit cases have also made a point out of clarifying that voluntary affirmative action actions (such as considering race in promotions) falls under a different *type* and *level* of scrutiny than making remedial pay changes based on a robust multiple regression model.

Notes

[1] OFCCP released two proposals on systemic compensation discrimination that were published in the Federal Register on November 16, 2004 (69 FR 67246-67255).

[2] There are multiple types of compensation metrics that can be used in MR analyses, such as "Total Compensation," "Base Annual Salary," "Pay per Hour," and bonuses, just to name a few. Only one type of compensation metric should be used for each analysis, unless it makes logical sense to combine several together. For example, it might make logical sense to combine "Base Annual Salary" with commissions when computing overall compensation for sales personnel. However, this should only be done *if the factors used to pay employees based on commission were also factored into the MR analyses as independent variables*. However, all analyzed employees should have equivalent metrics (*i.e.,* if one person in the job class has their base annual salary and commissions combined for analysis purposes, all people in that same job class should have their base annual salary and commissions combined).

[3] Because employee age is often a solid predictor of pay, but is sometimes compressed due to the diminishing relationship between age and compensation that typically occurs at various age levels, sometimes using transformations on the age variable is necessary (*e.g.,* squaring).

[4] Statistically speaking, power has to do with Type I and Type II errors. Type I errors occur when a researcher concludes "there is a statistically significant difference" when there really is not. In the realm of compensation analyses, this can be costly because an employer has essentially wrongfully concluded that their employer has potentially discriminatory pay practices. Type II errors occur when the researcher concludes "a statistically significant difference does not exist," but it *actually does*. This leads employers to miss a real difference in pay practices that could have possibly been identified if the study had higher levels of statistical power.

[5] Green, S. B. (1991). How many subjects does it take to do a regression analysis? *Multivariate Behavioral Research, 26,* 499-510.

[6] Harris, R. J. (1985). *A primer of multivariate statistics* (2nd ed.). New York: Academic Press.

[7] Tabachnick, B. G., & Fidell, L.S. (2001). Using multivariate statistics (4th ed.). Needham Heights, MA: Allyn & Bacon.

[8] Hair, J. F., Anderson, R. E., Tatham, R. L., & Black, W. (1998). *Multivariate data analysis* (5th ed.). New Jersey: Prentice Hall.

[9] Standardizing variables can be done by converting them into Z-scores so they can be compared relevant to each other. This function can be readily completed using SPSS or other statistical programs.

[10] The ANOVA table simply shows whether the R^2 for the model is statistically significant. If it is non-significant, then a nonlinear relationship is *one* of the many possible reasons for the non-significance. It could be restricted range in the variance of the independent variables, low statistical power, the fact that no relationship really exists at all, or a host of other possible reasons. Analysis of residual plots is needed to identify nonlinearity.

[11] Equal Pay Act of 1963, 29 U.S.C. § 206(d)(1).

[12] Title VII of the Civil Rights Act of 1964 (42 U.S.C. § 2000e-2(a)(1)(2)).

[13] Title VII of the Civil Rights Act of 1964 (42 U.S.C. § 2000e-2(a)(1)).

[14] Griggs v. Duke Power Co., 401 U.S. 424, 431 (1971).

[15] Franks v. Bowman Transportation Co., Inc., 424 U.S. 747 (1976).

[16] Melani v. Board of Higher Education, 561 F.Supp. 769 (S.D.N.Y. 1983).

[17] Cullen v. Indiana University Board of Trustees, 2003 WL 21741693, F.3d, 7th Cir. 2003).

[18] Office of Federal Contract Compliance Programs; Interpreting Nondiscrimination Requirements of Executive Order 11246 With Respect to Systemic Compensation Discrimination. 69 Fed. Reg. No. 220, November 16, 2004. p. 35140.

[19] Johnson v. Transportation Agency, 480 U.S. 616 (1987).

[20] See Rudebusch v. Hughes, 313 F.3d 506 (9th Cir. 2002).

[21] Rudebusch v. Hughes, No. 95-CV-1313-PCT-RCB, No. CV-1077-PCT-RCB (D. Ariz.). Judgment entered June 28, 2004. Rudebusch v. Hughes, 313 F.3d 506 (9th Cir. 2002).

[22] Rudebusch v. Hughes, 313 F.3d 506 (9th Cir. 2002) (at 25).

[23] Ende v. Board of Regents, 757 F. 2d 176, 181 (7th Cir. 1985).

[24] While the Ninth Circuit's 2002 decision ultimately did not try the manifest imbalance issue (but rather assumed the issued had already been addressed by the previous Federal District case), the June 30, 2006 decision (after remand) ultimately ruled on the "attaining a balance" prong based upon the faulty premise of how the "manifest balance" was substantiated.

[25] Plaintiffs/Appellants Reply Brief, Exhibit 46, p. 2-3, T. 130). Rudebusch v. Hughes, 313 F.3d 506 (9th Cir. 2002). See also Rudebusch v. Hughes, No. 95-CV-1313-PCT-RCB, No. CV-1077-PCT-RCB (D. Ariz.). Judgment entered June 28, 2004.

[26] Plaintiffs/Appellants Reply Brief (Appendix A to Opening Brief, p. 8; 2 T. 84.). Rudebusch. v. Hughes, 313 F.3d 506 (9th Cir. 2002).

[27] Plaintiffs/Appellants Reply Brief (Citing Excerpt of Record, 147, pp. 25-26). Rudebusch v. Hughes, 313 F.3d 506 (9th Cir. 2002).

[28] Plaintiffs' Response to Defendants' Motion for Summary Judgment and Plaintiffs' Cross Motion for Summary Judgment (p. 10). Rudebusch v. Hughes, No. 95-CV-1313-PCT-RCB, No. CV-1077-PCT-RCB (D. Ariz. 2007).

[29] Rudebusch v. Hughes, No. 95-CV-1313-PCT-RCB, No. CV-1077-PCT-RCB (D. Ariz.). Judgment entered June 28, 2004 (p. 11).

[30] Plaintiffs' Response to Defendants' Motion for Summary Judgment and Plaintiffs' Cross Motion for Summary Judgment (p. 10). Rudebusch v. Hughes, No. 95-CV-1313-PCT-RCB, No. CV-1077-PCT-RCB (D. Ariz. 2007).

[31] U.S. Department of Labor (DOL), Employment Standards Administration, Office of Federal Contract Compliance Programs (June 16, 2006). Voluntary Guidelines for Self-Evaluation of Compensation Practices for Compliance With Nondiscrimination Requirements of Executive Order 11246 With Respect to Systemic Compensation Discrimination; *Federal Register*, Vol. 71, No. 116. See also EEOC Compliance Manual, Section 10-III A.3.c. (http://www.eeoc.gov/policy/docs/compensation.html#3).

[32] For example, if the R^2 of a given regression is 0.28 and the corresponding p-value is statistically significant ($p < .05$), one would also desire the Adjusted R^2 (e.g., 0.24) to be statistically significant ($< .05$).

[33] Bazemore v. Friday, 478 U. S. 385 (1986).

[34] See for example, Contractors Association v. Philadelphia, 6 F.3d 990, 1007 (3d Cir. 1993); EEOC v. General Tel. Co., 885 F.2d 575, 582 (9th Cir.), cert. denied, 498 U.S. 950 (1989); Sobel v. Yeshiva Univ., 839 F.2d 18, 34 (2d Cir. 1988), cert. denied, 490 U.S. 1105 (1989); Catlett v. Missouri Highway and Transp. Comm'n, 828 F.2d 1260 (8th Cir. 1987), cert. denied, 485 U.S. 1021 (1988); Palmer v. Shultz, 815 F.2d 84, 101 (D.C. Cir. 1987).

[35] Rudebusch v. Hughes, No. 95-CV-1313-PCT-RCB, No. CV-1077-PCT-RCB (D. Ariz.). Judgment entered June 28, 2004 (p. 16).

[36] Rudebusch v. Hughes, 313 F.3d 506 (9th Cir. 2002) (at 520).

[37] Ricci et al., v. DeStefano et al., U.S.SC, No. 07-1428 (June 29, 2009).

Chapter 10 - Internet Applicant Regulations and EEO Compliance

By Patrick M. Nooren, Ph.D.

Introduction

At the time that the Uniform Guidelines were first published in 1978, there was no way for people to instantly apply for open positions across the world, submit their resumes to "banks" of databases to be evaluated by hundreds or thousands of employers, or sift through and apply to open positions from the comfort of their homes. Remember, in 1978, personal computers were not much more than elaborate calculators and word processors. That all changed as the popularity of the Internet exploded in the early 1990s.

Websites such as Monster.com sprang to life and changed the way people applied for jobs. No longer were paper-and-pencil resumes the norm – they were now the exception. Once employers saw the utility of the Internet as a recruitment tool they began to develop their own websites to allow people to view open positions, read job descriptions, and apply for specific jobs "online" - and it did not stop there. Recruitment via the Internet evolved once again when LinkedIn and FaceBook were launched in 2003 and 2004 (respectively). Both sites allowed users to post their personal profiles (including education, work experience, and current job) online, thus allowing corporate recruiters and headhunters to "target" specific individuals who appeared to be qualified based on their posted information. Suddenly situations arose where people, who may have been otherwise happily employed, were being *solicited* to apply for open positions. The paradigm had shifted once again.

Unfortunately, rapid growth is often accompanied by growing pains. As employers began to see the utility of the Internet and social media as a means for soliciting and collecting information on prospective applicants, it became apparent that enforcement agencies were also going to have to change to reflect the need for enforcement of equal employment opportunity within this new paradigm. The requirement that employers analyze their hiring processes for discrimination did not change, but it did become much more complicated as a result of these technological advancements.

Per the 1978 Uniform Guidelines, "[t]he precise definition of the term 'applicant' depends upon the user's recruitment and selection procedures. The concept of an applicant is that of a person who has *indicated an interest* in being considered for hiring, promotion, or other employment opportunities [emphasis added]." In other words, under the Uniform Guidelines definition, *everyone* who indicated an *interest* in a position was considered an applicant and subject to analysis. In a world where applicants can use software to "spam" resumes to thousands of employers instantly or apply to hundreds of jobs at once using a "shopping-cart" model, how can employers properly analyze their hiring processes for discriminatory impact? Further, how does this definition apply within the context of social media recruitment where people are solicited to apply for a job based on the information within their personal profile? It is because of these and other similar issues that the OFCCP issued the Obligation to

Solicit Race and Gender Data for Enforcement Purposes: Final Rule (hereafter referred to as the "Internet Applicant Regulations") and associated recordkeeping rules.[1]

Because of the rapid changes in how the Internet and social media are used in the recruitment and selection process, it should be no surprise that enforcement around many of these issues is "less than clear." This Chapter will seek to provide guidance to employers who use the Internet, online job/applicant databases, and social media[2] as part of their recruitment processes.

Internet Applicant Regulations

Issued on October 7, 2005, the Internet Applicant Regulations and recordkeeping rules became effective 120 days later on February 6, 2006. The primary purpose of the rule was to clarify three important issues: 1) define "Internet applicants," 2) outline recordkeeping requirements relative to hiring done through the Internet or related electronic data technologies, and 3) describe the information employers must solicit and submit to the OFCCP to evaluate impact within their selection processes.

The Internet Applicant Regulations require that employers analyze all expressions of interest meeting the following four criteria[3]:

1. The individual submits an expression of interest in employment through the Internet or related electronic data technologies;
2. The employer considers the individual for employment in a particular position;
3. The individual's expression of interest indicates the individual possesses the basic qualifications (BQs) for the position; and,
4. The individual at no point in the employer's selection process prior to receiving an offer of employment from the employer, removes himself or herself from further consideration or otherwise indicates that he or she is no longer interested in the position.

Criteria 1: Submits An Expression Of Interest Through The Internet Or Related Electronic Data Technologies[4]

Despite its advantages, the Internet and related technologies are still relatively new, not yet adopted by all employers and/or applicants, and not evenly distributed among all race/ethnic and socioeconomic groups. In fact, according to a study by the U.S. Department of Commerce (2000)[5]:

- People with a college degree are eight times more likely to have a PC at home and 16 times more likely to have Internet access at home than those with an elementary school education.
- A high-income household in an urban area is 20 times more likely to have Internet access than a rural, low-income household.
- A child in a low-income white family is three times more likely to have Internet access than a child in a comparable black family, and four times more likely than a child in a comparable Hispanic family.

- A high-income household of Asian descent is 34 times more likely to have Internet access than a low-income household of blacks.
- A child in a two-parent white household is twice as likely to have Internet access as a child in a single-parent household. If the child in a two-parent household is black, he or she is four times more likely to have Internet access than his single-parent counterpart.
- Disabled people are nearly three times less likely to have home access to the Internet than people without disabilities.

For these reasons, there will continue to be a need for traditional paper applications/resumes for the foreseeable future. As a result, the Internet Applicant Regulations distinguish between "traditional applicants" and "Internet applicants," stating that if an employer considers expressions of interest from the Internet or related data technologies *and* more traditional paper submissions, then the Internet definition will apply. However, if the employer does not allow individuals to apply electronically, then the traditional OFCCP recordkeeping rules apply[6]: "The precise definition of the term 'applicant' depends on the user's recruitment and selection procedures. The concept of an applicant is that of a person who has indicated an interest in being considered for hiring, promotion, or other employment opportunities. This interest might be expressed by completing an application form, or might be expressed orally, depending on the employer's practice."

Realizing that technologies would continue to advance and quickly make obsolete any current definition, the OFCCP avoided a precise definition of "Internet or related electronic data technologies." However, the preamble to the Uniform Guidelines Questions and Answers Supplement does provide six examples of technologies that would meet the standard and that are currently in use today[7]:

1. Electronic mail/email: To include emails either sent or received.
2. Resume databases: These are databases of personal profiles/resumes that can be searched by employers for individuals with certain BQs (*e.g.,* Monster.com).
3. Job banks: The opposite of resume databases, these are databases of available job openings that applicants can search based upon certain criteria. Typically, job banks are created by third-party providers such as America's Job Bank or they can be maintained by companies through their own websites.
4. Electronic scanning technology: This technology scans hard-copy resumes and/or applications into a database to later be searched using relevant criteria.
5. Applicant tracking systems/Applicant service providers: Most applicant tracking systems allow individuals to apply online and then track the individual's progress, identifying where they are in the overall process, their scores in any tests/interviews, and where/why they fall out of the hiring process (if applicable). Some systems even compile applicants from both internal and external databases for combined searches.
6. Applicant screeners: Typically third-party vendors that focus on providing employers with applicants that meet certain skillset requirements.

Criteria 2: Considers The Individual For Employment In A Particular Position[8]

Identifying applicants who are considered for a particular position seems like a simple task. Unfortunately, more often than not, the exact opposite is true. According to the Internet Applicant Regulations, a person does not become an applicant until that person is "considered," and an individual is not considered until "the employer assesses the substantive information provided with the expression of interest with respect to any qualifications involved with a particular position."

So how do employers successfully navigate the complexities of documenting those they consider while concurrently meeting the legitimate business needs of a diverse and qualified, yet manageable, applicant pool? Fortunately, the Internet Applicant Regulations provide for a number of ways to address these concerns. If employers receive a high volume of applications, the Internet Applicant Regulations permit the use of standardized protocols by which employers can refrain from considering applications that are not submitted in accordance with established procedures. Requiring applicants to apply for specific positions, in a specific manner, within a specific timeframe are just some of the strategies employers can use to refine and restrict applicant pools. Not accepting unsolicited resumes or requiring that all resumes be submitted to a centralized location can also be helpful.

When pools of applicants become excessive, the Internet Applicant Regulations also permit the use of "data management techniques" to further refine the pool of those who are considered. These techniques include, but are not limited to, random sampling (*e.g.,* selecting every 10th record) and absolute numerical limits (*e.g.,* selecting the first 50 applicants resulting from a database search, etc.). When using data management techniques, it is important that they are objective and do not consider an applicant's qualifications. It is also important that, after using data management techniques, the resulting pool of applicants be similar in composition to the original pool of those submitting expressions of interest.

Social Media

An interesting dynamic occurs between the first two prongs for those employers who use social media recruitment. Typically (and historically), employees express interest in a specific position prior to being considered by the employer. Conversely, with social media recruitment, an individual is considered by the employer *prior* to being solicited to apply. As a result, some who are considered may never be asked to apply. This change in the typical approach creates some interesting difficulties when it comes to data collection/retention requirements and adverse impact analyses. The first prong of the Internet Applicant Regulations requires that, to be an applicant (and thus be included in an adverse impact analysis), one must submit an expression of interest through the Internet or related electronic data technology. It could be argued that individuals whose personal profiles are considered, but who are never solicited by the company to apply, have not "expressed an interest" and, therefore, should not be included in adverse impact analyses. However, data collection and retention requirements begin with the second prong (*i.e.,* once an individual is considered). As a result, it could also be argued that all individuals whose personal profiles are considered for a particular position should be maintained in the applicant database by the employer.[9]

Criteria 3: The Individual Meets The Basic Qualifications (BQs)[10]

For the past several decades, employers have argued that, for practical reasons, it was necessary to consider for employment only those individuals possessing the requisite BQs. Unfortunately, during that same timeframe, enforcement agencies have been required to adhere to the definition of applicant set forth in the Uniform Guidelines which was silent on the topic of qualifications. Fortunately for employers, the ability to consider an individual's BQs is a cornerstone of the Internet Applicant Regulations.

According to the Internet Applicant Regulations, acceptable BQs must be *established in advance*, prior to considering any expressions of interest (regardless of whether they are advertised to potential applicants): "The final rule provides that if the contractor does not advertise for the position, the contractor may use 'an alternative device to find individuals for consideration (for example, through an external resume database),' and establish the qualification criteria by making and maintaining a record of such qualifications for the position prior to considering any expression of interest for that position. Contractors must retain records of these established qualifications in accordance with section 60 - 1.12(a)" (p. 58953). In addition, acceptable BQs must meet *all* of the following three conditions. BQs must be:

1. Noncomparative (*i.e.,* used as hurdles);
2. Objective and not depend on subjective judgment; and,
3. Relevant to the performance of the particular position and enable the employer to accomplish business-related goals.

How can employers develop BQs that will survive scrutiny from government enforcement agencies (*e.g.,* OFCCP)? What about challenges that are brought by private plaintiff groups? Employers that are challenged because of their BQs will generally not have a difficult time defending the first two criteria above (unless, of course, they were clearly violated). This is because the first two requirements are very clear-cut and uncomplicated. Employers can address these first two requirements by insuring that BQs operate as "hurdles" (*i.e.,* are either met or not met) and are sufficiently objective that a third-party, with the contactor's technical knowledge, would be able to evaluate whether the job seeker possesses the BQs.

It is the third criteria that will carry the day, or not, when an employer's BQs are challenged. The reason for this is straightforward. This is because the "relevant to performance" criterion has *two levels*. The first level is exactly as it is written. This level applies to an employer's recordkeeping requirements. The second level, however, is where employers should be most concerned. This "second level" exists whenever the employer's BQs *create adverse impact*. Once this happens, the full weight of federal anti-discrimination laws (Title VII of the 1991 Civil Rights Act) immediately applies, which is a much higher standard. Rather than the first level (showing that the BQ is simply "relevant" to job performance), now an employer will be required to prove – using the Uniform Guidelines and other relevant standards – that the BQ is "job related for the position in question and consistent with business necessity."

This has been true of BQs that have adverse impact since the <u>Griggs v. Duke Power Company</u> (1971) case, where the BQ of having a high school diploma had adverse impact against blacks and was not justified on the basis of job-relatedness. When framed in 1978, the Uniform Guidelines adopted much of the Griggs standard for establishing the "job relatedness" threshold that selection procedures (including BQ screens) need to meet if they have adverse impact. And, this "job relatedness" standard has been essentially coined "validity" ever since.

So how can employers meet the *level two* standard (showing "job relatedness" or "validity" for their BQs when they have adverse impact)? Below are some guidelines for doing just this. First, however, the reader is referred to Chapter Five for a complete discussion on validating training, education, and experience requirements. This Chapter provides guidelines for setting up *rated and scored* BQ requirements that are limited to training, education, and experience types of BQs. The reason for this is because BQ screening systems that are scored allow applicants to demonstrate their qualifications for the job by any *combination* of education or experience (even including volunteer experience). Thus, it is essentially a *scored selection procedure*, rather than "prescreening" BQs where applicants self-report whether they possess a pre-defined level of a certain BQ. Chapter Five does not review steps for establishing BQs that are self-reported or self-rated by an applicant; such discussion is provided only here.

Steps for validating BQs that are self-reported by applicants

There are various methods that can be used to validate BQs. At the heart of all *acceptable* methods is a "linkage" or some type of clear connection that traces the BQ back to essential requirements of the job, which are usually found in a job analysis that outlines the knowledges, skills, abilities, and personal characteristics (KSAPCs) of the target position (see Chapter Two for a full discussion on conducting job analyses). Section 14C6 of the Uniform Guidelines also provides clear guidance on the type of evidence required for proving validity of BQs that are based on training or experience.

The five-step process outlined below, when conducted in order and completely, should survive a full "job relatedness" review if employers need to justify BQs that have adverse impact. However, these steps are not provided to simply justify a BQ that has adverse impact. This is because a BQ that is valid is one that is *truly anchored in the actual requirements of the job*. Making sure that the actual requirements of the job are embedded in the BQ is the net goal of any thorough BQ validation process. With this said, below are the five steps suggested for validating BQs:

1. Develop a job analysis for the target position. A job analysis process results in a document that is more in-depth than most "job description" or "job specification" documents. A Uniform Guidelines-style job analysis will include an analysis of job duties, KSAPCs, physical requirements, and other requirements (*e.g.,* licenses). Job analyses should always include input from qualified Job Experts, and it is typically recommended to include at least seven Job Experts in the process (more is helpful with positions that have more than 50 incumbents). The final job analysis should represent all KSAPCs with at least 70% agreement from Job Experts (*e.g.,* "70% of Job Experts agree that KSAPC #4 is at least critically important").

2. Isolate critical KSAPCs from the job analysis that are necessary on the *first day* on the job (*i.e.*, before any training is provided). See the "Selection Plan" section in Chapter Two for further details on setting apart KSAPCs that can be included in a selection process.

3. Develop *multiple levels* (4-9) of each BQ requirement (to be reviewed and rated by Job Experts). This can be accomplished by working with 1-2 Job Experts, trainers, or supervisors to draft a set of BQ requirements for a similar area (*i.e.*, education/experience, weight handling requirements, licenses, etc.) that *range in qualification* from the lowest to highest level that might possibly be required for entering the position. For example, consider the following four BQ levels for an HR Consultant position (the BQ in this example pertains to training, education, and experience – the same process can be used for other BQs, such as weight handling requirements).

- Level 1: Must possess BA/BS in statistics, business, psychology, or HR.
- Level 2: Must possess BA/BS in statistics, business, psychology, or HR and two years (FT/equiv.) experience in HR, personnel, or EEO field applying statistical and data analysis methods/concepts; or, Master's degree in same fields with no experience.
- Level 3: Must possess BA/BS in statistics, business, psychology, or HR and four years (FT/equiv.) experience in HR, personnel, or EEO field applying statistical and data analysis methods/concepts; or, Master's degree in same fields with two years' experience; or, Doctorate degree in same fields with no experience.
- Level 4: Must possess BA/BS in statistics, business, psychology, or HR and six years (FT/equiv.) experience in HR, personnel, or EEO field applying statistical and data analysis methods/concepts; or, Master's degree in same fields with two years' experience; or, Doctorate degree in same fields with no experience.

4. Convene a panel of 7-10 Job Experts to review and rate each draft BQ level on several factors, including:
   a. Is the BQ based on a *clear resemblance* between the specific behaviors, products, and KSAPCs required on the job?
   b. Is the BQ based on *objective criteria* related to actual job requirements? Job Experts should be instructed to answer "Yes" if a third-party with their employer's technical knowledge would be able to correctly evaluate whether the applicant possesses the qualification (without more information about their employer's judgment).
   c. Is the BQ the *minimum* level/amount needed on the *first day* of the job (before training)?
   d. Will the BQ be *easily understood* by applicants?
   e. Is the BQ designed to differentiate whether an applicant is *minimally qualified for the job* (rather than being used to differentiate one applicant from another)?

See Figure 10-1 for a sample survey that includes these questions.

BQ Level	Description	What KSAs are linked to the BQ?	Is the BQ based on a **clear resemblance** between the specific behaviors, products, and KSAs required on the job?		Is the BQ based on **objective criteria related to actual job requirements?** Answer "Yes" if a third-party with your employer's technical knowledge would be able to evaluate whether the applicant possesses the qualification (without more information about your employer's judgment).		Is the BQ the **MINIMUM level/amount needed on the FIRST DAY** of the job (before training)?		Will the BQ be **easily understood** by applicants?		Is the BQ designed to **differentiate whether an applicant is minimally qualified for the job** (rather than being used to differentiate one applicant from another?)	
		List #s from Job Analysis	Yes	No	Yes	No	Yes	No	Yes	No	Yes	No

Basic Qualification (BQ) Development Survey

Target Position: _____ Job Expert's Name: _____ Date: _____

Note: If the suggested BQs in this survey do not meet the requirements, please feel free to suggest new and/or revised BQs to management. Also, notify management if there are different BQs that a person could possess prior to the first day on the job that would be equally acceptable but would exclude fewer job applicants than the BQs offered here.

Figure 10-1 Basic Qualification (BQ) Development Survey

5. Evaluate the survey results and set the BQ at a level that represents at least 70% Job Expert consensus on that level *or lower*. For example, assume 10 Job Experts rated the four BQ levels in the example above (with level 4 being the "BA plus six years" requirement), and their ratings supported the following levels: 4, 4, 3, 3, 3, 2, 2, 1, 1, and 1. Because seven Job Experts supported setting the BQ level *at least* at level 2 (a "BA plus two years or a Master's degree with no experience"), the final BQ would be set at this level (assuming all other ratings on the suggested questions above came out with acceptable levels of agreement).

Why not just develop definitive and final BQ statements and have them "blessed" by Job Experts? Developing BQs can be done this way, but only for some jobs where the requirements are very clear and highly specific. One must consider: Would Job Experts have come up with something totally different had they not be "spoon fed" the single BQ they were asked to endorse? This is one reason why presenting multiple levels is useful.

Yet another process to use for validating BQs might be to have Job Experts "fill in the blank" with the education and experience requirements they believe are most appropriate – such as: "Applicants must possess ___ degree in ___ fields and have ___ years' experience in ___ areas." The limitation of this technique, however, is that the responses of Job Experts cannot be compared to each other because such ratings are *compound and inter-related* – one Job Expert's rating regarding a unique combination of education and experience cannot be compared to another who might have placed more value on one area than on another.

It is important to note that BQs can be used in sequence to further refine applicant pools to manageable levels, so long as the search criteria are established in advance. For example, according to the Internet Applicant Recordkeeping Rule, Frequently Asked Questions[11]:

> An employer initially searches an external job database with 50,000 job seekers for 3 basic qualifications for a bi-lingual emergency room nursing supervisor job (a 4-year nursing degree, state certification as an RN, and fluency in English and Spanish). The initial screen for the first three basic qualifications narrows the pool to 10,000. The employer then adds a fourth, pre-established basic qualification, 3 years of emergency room nursing experience, and narrows the pool to 1,000. Finally, the employer adds a fifth, pre-established, basic qualification, 2 years of supervisory experience which results in a pool of 75 job seekers. Under the Internet Applicant rule, only the 75 job seekers meeting all five BQ would be Internet Applicants, assuming the other three prongs of the "Internet Applicant" definition were met.

A strategy often utilized by enforcement agencies or plaintiff groups is to look for exceptions to supposedly objective, standardized protocols as a way of attacking the components of a selection process. Circumventing BQs to hire the nephew of the Executive Vice President can cause a chain reaction ultimately resulting in the downfall of the BQ screening process, and subsequently the entire selection process. In short, ensuring BQs are noncomparative, objective, and relevant to the performance of the particular position is only one piece of the equation. Applying BQs in a uniform and consistent manner can be equally important.

Lastly, since employers are only required to solicit demographic information from applicants, and people only become applicants once they meet *all four* prongs of the Internet applicant definition, the OFCCP realizes that it is possible for employers to evade scrutiny of their BQs by not soliciting demographic information from those deemed unqualified. Realizing this, the OFCCP has reserved the right to evaluate the impact of BQs by comparing the demographic composition of those meeting the BQs to external labor force statistics and/or census data. According to the Internet Applicant Recordkeeping Rule, Frequently Asked Questions[9]:

> The Internet Applicant rule emphasizes that OFCCP will compare the proportion of women and minorities in the contractor's Internet Applicant pool with labor force statistics or other data on the percentage of women and minorities in the relevant labor force in order to evaluate the impact of BQ. If there is a significant difference between these figures, OFCCP will investigate further as to whether the contractor's recruitment and hiring practices conform with E.O. 11246 standards.

Criteria 4: The Individual Does Not Remove Themself from Consideration[12]

How often do recruitment personnel attempt to contact applicants only to find that they have already found another position and are no longer interested? Or similarly, applicants who are allowed to proceed through the entire selection process turn out to have salary requirements that are too high for the position or are unwilling to relocate? Because of these and many similar issues, the Internet Applicant Regulations provide for the removal of applicants (from adverse impact analyses, not from record retention) if the employer concludes that an individual has removed themself from consideration, or has otherwise indicated that they are no longer interested in the position. According to the Internet Applicant Regulations, an applicant can either actively or passively remove themselves from consideration. An example of active removal would be an expressed statement of disinterest. Examples of passive removal from consideration may include (but are not limited to):

- Declining an employer's invitation to interview;
- Declining a job offer;
- Repeatedly failing to respond to an employer's telephone and/or email inquiries asking about their interest in the job;
- No-show for an interview;
- No-show for a drug test.

An employer may also presume a "lack of interest" based upon a review of the applicant's original expression of interest: incongruent salary expectations, falsification of information on the application, differences in shift requirements, or type and location of work can all be considered provided that the requirements were consistently and uniformly applied to all applicants.

Recordkeeping Requirements

The Internet Applicant Regulations are very clear that employers must maintain records of any/all expressions of interest made through the Internet or related electronic data technologies for all individuals it *considered* for a particular position, even if those individuals do not ultimately meet all four criteria of an Internet applicant.[13] For internal resume databases, the employer must maintain:

- A record for each resume added to the database;
- A record of the date each resume was added to the database;
- Corresponding to each search: 1) A record of the position for which each search for the database was made, 2) the substantive search criteria, and 3) the date of the search; and,
- Records identifying job seekers contacted regarding their interest in a particular position.

For external databases, the employer must maintain:

- A record of the position for which each search of the database was made;

- Corresponding to each search: 1) the substantive search criteria used, 2) the date of the search, 3) the resumes of any job seekers who met the BQ for the particular position who are considered by the employer;
- Records identifying job seekers contacted regarding their interest in a particular position; and,
- (Arguably) Records for all social media profiles that are considered.

It is important to note that the recordkeeping requirements do not only relate to hiring, but also to assignments, promotion, demotion, transfer, layoff or termination, rates of pay or other terms of compensation, selection for training or apprenticeship, and other requests for reasonable accommodations, the results of any physical examination, job advertisements and postings, applications, resumes, BQs, and any and all expressions of interest through the Internet or related electronic data technologies. These records must be maintained for a period of not less than two years from the date of making the record or personnel action involved, whichever occurs later (regardless of whether the individual qualifies as an Internet Applicant).[14]

Soliciting Gender and Race/Ethnic Information
Soliciting gender and race/ethnic information from applicants is not a new requirement. In fact, there are several provisions already in the regulations requiring employers to solicit this information. The Internet Applicant Regulations state that employers are required to solicit this information from only those who are applicants, or Internet Applicants (whichever definition is applicable to the particular position).[15] It is apparent that employers can solicit this information at any time using the same traditional methods they have always used (*e.g.,* tear-off sheets, postcards, etc.) as well as other methods such as web-based input and automated bulk emails. The commentary to the Internet Applicant Regulations as well as an OFCCP directive on employer data tracking responsibilities (dated April 21, 2004) reiterates that self-identification is the preferable and most reliable method for collecting this information. However, since self-identification is always voluntary, if an individual declines to identify, a visual assessment may be made. With that said, the OFCCP directive on employer data tracking responsibilities continues to state:

> When contractors are unable to elicit or ascertain specific information regarding an applicant's gender, race or ethnicity, contractors should not guess or assume. Rather, if, after making reasonable efforts to identify applicant gender, race and ethnicity information, the contractor is unable to obtain such information, the contractor must record race or gender as "unknown" in its applicant flow log. A contractor is not required to "guess" as to the gender, race or ethnicity of an applicant. Adverse impact determinations should be based on the pool of applicants where gender, race or ethnicity is known.

In short, conflicting guidance currently exists. A visual assessment may be made, but employers should not guess or assume. It is this author's opinion that employers should never guess, even when a visual assessment can be made, and should only conduct adverse impact analyses with known demographic information provided by the applicant.

When the OFCCP evaluates whether an employer has maintained information on impact and conducted adverse impact analyses per 41 C.F.R. § 60-3 with respect to Internet hiring, the OFCCP will require only those records relating to the impact of selection procedures on Internet Applicants. However, if employment tests are administered by employers as part of the selection process, data on the impact of those tests will also be required, regardless of whether those tests were administered to Internet Applicants.[16] As a result, it is important for employers to understand that the sequence in which they administer selection tests greatly impacts whether it is necessary to solicit demographic information from applicants. For example, if an employment test is administered online prior to an assessment of BQs, then employers are required to solicit demographic information from *all* who take the test. However, if only those who possess the requisite BQs take the test, then employers are only required to solicit demographic information from those who met the BQs and took the test.

Recommendations

The following are procedural and system recommendations to help employers address the Internet Applicant Regulations. Procedural recommendations refer to "best practices" employers can implement to bolster the defensibility of their policies and procedures in light of the Internet Applicant Regulations. System recommendations refer to features and functionality that internal applicant tracking systems should include to address the Internet Applicant Regulations. The recommendations can also be used to evaluate external databases for compliance. Employers who follow these recommendations will realize increased defensibility and reduced exposure related to their hiring practices.

Procedural recommendations

1. Allow for the collection of applications and responses via electronic means to all job openings (this way the Internet Applicant Regulations will apply).
2. Create an "Active Consideration Period" for applications for all positions (*i.e.,* "We will consider an application active for XX days after receipt, after which time you will need to re-apply if you wish to be considered for employment").
3. Establish policies regarding unsolicited resumes. Ensure they are uniformly and consistently applied across the employer.
4. Review job postings for BQs. Ensure they are:
    a. Non-comparative;
    b. Objective;
    c. Relevant to the performance of the particular position and enable the employer to accomplish business-related goals.
5. If BQs have adverse impact, validate them using the steps outlined in this Chapter or other similar process that provides a clear connection between the BQ and job requirements that are needed "day one" on the job.
6. Pre-define approved search criteria and data management techniques in advance of accepting applications.

7. Ensure search criteria are specific to the particular job and not "generic."
8. Ensure all recruiting/staffing personnel have been trained on the proper use of queries, search criteria, and data management techniques.
9. With legal assistance, establish standardized social media recruitment protocols and ensure all recruiting/staffing personnel have been trained on the proper use of social media recruitment.
10. Collect gender and race/ethnic data *after* the individual meets basic qualification.
11. Do not administer employment tests until *after* BQs have been assessed. Otherwise, employers will be required to solicit demographic information from all applicants who took the test, even those who are later deemed to have *not* been basically qualified for the position.

System recommendations

1. The applicant tracking system, or associated applicant tracking protocol, should include a search "log" linked to each individual job opening (*i.e.,* requisition), including:
    a. the position for which the search was made;
    b. substantive search criteria;
    c. search date(s); and,
    d. the ability to store and/or replicate results of the search for later verification.
2. In addition, applicant tracking systems must:
    a. retain each resume added and the date each was added;
    b. retain records of applicants contacted regarding their interest in a position;
    c. be able to identify if/when applicants voluntarily withdraw from the selection process and why;
    d. be able to document where exactly the applicant is within the process and whether they passed/failed each step in the process;
    e. retain all records for two years from the date of action (*e.g.,* hire, requisition closing, etc.);
    f. not include for consideration or analysis purposes those records that are beyond active consideration period (described above);
    g. retain all expressions of interest submitted via electronic data technologies that are considered *even if* the individual does not meet all criteria to become an Internet applicant.

Notes

[1] Section 41 Code of Federal Regulations (C.F.R.) § 60-1

[2] This Chapter will focus on the use of social media as it relates to adverse impact analyses and the definition of Internet applicant. It will not cover topics such as the *legality* of social media use in the recruitment process.

[3] 41 C.F.R. § 60-1.3(1)

[4] 41 C.F.R. § 60-1.3(2)

[5] U.S. Department of Commerce: "Falling Through the Net?" The Economist (24 June, 2000), p. 24. Although these differences may have reduced somewhat over the past several years, it is likely that they are still apparent to varying degrees.

[6] Uniform Guidelines, Questions and Answers 15.

[7] 69 Fed. Reg. March 4, 2004 at 10155 (in proposed draft form)

[8] 41 C.F.R. § 60-1.3(3)

[9] Of course, this is debatable, and opens up a litany of other issues beyond the scope of this Chapter, such as how would this be enforced, and how would recruiters identify an individual's gender and race/ethnicity when it is not listed on an individual's profile? While visual identification of an applicant's gender and/or race is allowed, it is not recommended by this author.

[10] 41 C.F.R. § 60-1.3(4)

[11] Located on the Internet at: http://www.dol.gov/esa/regs/compliance/ofccp/faqs/iappfaqs.htm

[12] 41 C.F.R. § 60-1.3(5)

[13] 41 C.F.R. § 60-1.12

[14] 41 C.F.R. § 60-1.12(a)

[15] 41 C.F.R. 60-1.12(c)(ii)

[16] 41 C.F.R. 60-1.12(c)

Chapter 11 - Using Croson Studies to Develop Defensible Diversity Initiatives

By Daniel A. Biddle, Ph.D. & Richard E. Biddle, M.B.A.

Introduction

On June 29, 2009, the U.S. Supreme Court handed down the first Title VII ruling that answers the difficult question: "Under what circumstances can an employer subject to Title VII implement otherwise prohibited disparate-treatment discrimination to avoid disparate impact liability?" When answering this question, the U.S. Supreme Court adopted a "strong-basis-in-evidence standard" as a matter of statutory construction for courts to use as a means of resolving conflicts between Title VII's disparate-treatment and disparate-impact provisions - "allowing violations of one in the name of compliance with the other only in certain, narrow circumstances" (Ricci, p. 23).

Twenty years prior to the Ricci case, the U.S. Supreme Court codified the "strong-basis-in-evidence standard" in Richmond v. Croson[1] – a concept that first originated three years earlier in Wygant v. Jackson Board of Education[2] by Justice Powell. Both of these cases laid down legal concepts that were relevant to the Ricci context in ways that will be fully explored in this Chapter – defining how the *strong-basis-in-evidence standard* applies to various personnel actions and diversity initiatives.

Case Background

The context of the Ricci v. DeStefano[3] case involved the City of New Haven's (Connecticut) firefighter promotional practices. The foundation for the City's selection procedure is an agreement with its firefighters' union that only a written test and an oral interview will be used as the selection devices, weighted 60% and 40% respectively. Although the weighting came about as a result of negotiations with the union, it was apparently not based on job analysis research. Candidates were required to be placed on the eligibility list in rank order of their scores, even though the measurement properties of the tests used could not distinguish between candidates in such a finite manner. The City's charter requires promoting only from the highest scoring three candidates, called the "rule of three," even though there could be other candidates just as qualified but a few decimal points away in score. The examinations were administered in November and December 2003. The results of the exams are shown in Table 11-1.

# in Group (Passing Rate %)				
Exam/Status	Total	White	Black	Hispanic
Lieutenant Exam (taking)	77	43	19	15
Lieutenant Exam (passing)	34	25 (58%)	6 (32%)	3 (20%)
Captain Exam (taking)	41	25	8	8
Captain (passing)	22	16 (64%)	3 (38%)	3 (38%)

Table 11-1 Ricci Exam Results

Under the "rule of three," the top 10 candidates were eligible for an immediate promotion to the eight open Lieutenant positions. All 10 were white. Subsequent vacancies would have allowed at least 3 black candidates to be considered for promotion to Lieutenant. Seven Captain positions were vacant at the time of the examination. Under the "rule of three," 9 candidates were eligible for an immediate promotion to Captain (7 whites and 2 Hispanics).

After giving the tests and learning that there was substantial adverse impact on minority candidates (80% Rule violations[4] and various levels of statistical significance based on each exam and how the groups could be combined), the City discarded the test results. Their decision was based on the adverse impact finding as well as on limited information that the tests might not have survived a "possible" disparate impact challenge.

The City faced two choices, both involving possible lawsuits: (1) if the City kept the test results, there could be a lawsuit from minorities who would likely not have been appointed had the lists been adopted; or (2) if the City discarded the test results, there could be a lawsuit from whites who would have likely been appointed had the lists been adopted. A potential suit from whites would be a disparate treatment suit; the suit from minorities would be a disparate impact suit. The City elected to discard the exam results and face the possible disparate treatment type of lawsuit from whites.

The U.S. Supreme Court ruled that the City's action was impermissible in this case: "Fear of litigation alone cannot justify the City's reliance on race to the detriment of individuals who passed the examinations and qualified for promotions. Discarding the test results was impermissible under Title VII." The Court further noted that a *strong basis in evidence* would be necessary for such drastic action to be allowed: "If, after it certifies the test results, the City faces a disparate-impact suit, then in light of today's holding the City can avoid disparate-impact liability based on the strong basis in evidence that, had it not certified the results, it would have been subject to disparate-treatment liability" (Ricci, pp. 33-34). The City did not provide the strong basis in evidence – only unsupported arguments were presented by the City.

Evaluating the Relevance of Ricci in both Public and Private Sectors

Because Ricci involved a promotional exam given to city firefighters (government employees), many might question the relevance of the case to private sector employers. However, both types of employers are subject to Title VII. Further, Ricci was decided on statutory grounds, not constitutional grounds. "We hold only that, under Title VII, before an employer can engage in intentional discrimination for the asserted purpose of avoiding or remedying an unintentional disparate impact, the employer must have a strong basis in evidence to believe it will be subject to disparate-impact liability if it fails to take the race-conscious, discriminatory action" (Ricci, p. 25).

Because state and local governments are *public sector employers*, their hiring, promotional, and contracting practices are covered by Title VII and are subject to the *strict scrutiny* theory of constitutional law. The Court used principles from constitutional cases for guidance: "Our cases discussing constitutional principles can provide helpful guidance in this statutory context" (Ricci, p. 23).

The cornerstone case that pertains to the strict scrutiny and strong-basis-in-evidence standards in the public sector is Richmond v. Croson.[5] In Croson, the Supreme Court codified the strong-basis-in-evidence standard that originated three years earlier in Wygant v. Jackson Board of Education.[6] Both of these cases involved the strong-basis-in-evidence standard in ways that were relevant to the framework used in Ricci.

The Croson case involved a city program that set aside 30% of city construction funds for black-owned firms that was challenged under the Equal Protection Clause of the Fourteenth Amendment. This set-aside quota was judged as a "highly suspect tool" by the Supreme Court. The Court asserted that such affirmative action steps must be subject to "strict scrutiny" and is unconstitutional unless racial discrimination can be proven to be "widespread throughout a particular industry." The Court stated that "the purpose of strict scrutiny is to 'smoke out' illegitimate uses of race by assuring that the legislative body is pursuing a goal important enough to warrant use of a highly suspect tool. The [strict scrutiny] test also ensures that the [race-conscious] means chosen 'fit' this compelling goal so closely that there is little or no possibility that the motive for the classification was illegitimate racial prejudice or stereotype."

Both public and private cases that have followed in the wake of the Croson decision have proscribed that affirmative action programs that use race-conscious remedies can pass the "strict scrutiny" test only if they are "narrowly tailored" towards eradicating the effects of past discrimination and preventing current/future discrimination. "Narrowly tailoring" the remedies means that they must take into account factors such as the necessity of the program and the plausibility of alternative remedies, the scope and duration of the remedy, the relationship of the numerical goals to minorities within the relevant labor market, and the likely effect on other gender or race/ethnic groups that are not part of the program.

Because private employers are not covered by the Fourteenth Amendment,[7] they may be held to a lesser standard than the strict scrutiny standard. Nevertheless, the ruling in Ricci states that at least part of the Court's intention was to "provide guidance to employers and courts for situations when these two prohibitions [disparate-impact liability and disparate-treatment discrimination] could be in conflict absent a rule to reconcile them. In providing this guidance our decision must be consistent with the important purpose of Title VII – that the workplace be an environment free of discrimination, where race is not a barrier to opportunity" (Ricci p. 20). This admonition appears to speak to both public and private employers alike.

Clearly, the Court used concepts from prior constitutional cases and applied them in Ricci: "This suit does not call on us to consider whether the statutory constraints under Title VII must be parallel in all respects to those under the Constitution. That does not mean the constitutional authorities are irrelevant, however" (Ricci, pp. 22-23). The basic concept put forth by the Court in Ricci applies to private and public employers – before an employer can implement intentional discrimination on a protected group (race, color, religion, sex, national origin) for the purpose of avoiding a potential disparate impact liability, the employer must have a "strong basis in evidence" that it will be subject to disparate impact liability if it fails to take the discriminatory action. The "strong basis in evidence" is the common thread for both public and private employers, and, since it is now a statutory standard, must be applied in Title VII cases involving both public and private employers.

The Strong-Basis-in-Evidence Standard

In the <u>Ricci</u> case, the Supreme Court stated: "We hold only that under Title VII, before an employer can engage in intentional discrimination for the asserted purpose of avoiding or remedying an unintentional disparate impact, the employer must have a strong basis in evidence to believe it will be subject to disparate-impact liability if it fails to take the race-conscious, discriminatory action" (<u>Ricci</u>, p. 26). The Court's analysis begins with the premise that the City's actions would violate the disparate-treatment provisions of Title VII unless there was *some valid defense,* and reasons: "All the evidence demonstrates that the City chose not to certify the examination results because of the statistical disparity based on race – *i.e.,* how minority candidates had performed when compared to white candidates . . . Without some other justification, this express, race-based decision making violates Title VII's command that employers cannot take adverse employment actions because of an individual's race" (<u>Ricci</u>, p. 19).

The Court clarified that the primary question being asked in the case was not whether the City's conduct was discriminatory but whether it had a lawful justification for its race-based action: "We consider, therefore, whether the purpose to avoid disparate-impact liability excuses what otherwise would be prohibited disparate-treatment discrimination…Our task is to provide guidance to employers and courts for situations when these two prohibitions could be in conflict absent a rule to reconcile them" (<u>Ricci</u>, p. 20). The Court continues and clarifies that, "Fear of litigation alone cannot justify an employer's reliance on race to the detriment of individuals who passed the examinations and qualified for promotions" (<u>Ricci</u>, p. 33) and concludes, "Even if respondents were motivated as a subjective matter by a desire to avoid committing disparate-impact discrimination, the record makes clear there is no support for the conclusion that respondents had an objective, strong basis in evidence to find the tests inadequate, with some consequent disparate-impact liability in violation of Title VII" (<u>Ricci</u>, p. 26).

Regarding making changes to the tests *after they had been given* – up to and including discarding the results altogether – the Court ruled that a strong basis in evidence had to be somehow demonstrated on the record. This was not done by the City. Had the City conducted a *Croson Study*[8] (defined in detail later in this Chapter) for the at-issue jobs *prior to the development of the selection processes*, they may have been justified in implementing less extreme race-conscious remedies to identify substantially equally qualified candidates for the lists with less adverse impact, such as competency-based cutoff scores, weights less likely to adversely impact minorities that subject-matter experts would indicate produce substantially equally qualified candidates, banding based upon the reliability of the tests to group substantially equally qualified candidates together, etc.

In the public sector, rules are often set up by a "merit system," negotiation with a union, tradition, or some other reason that can influence the type of selection procedures to be administered and their use. Here are some examples:

- a written test might be specified as required (rather than considering other options such as an assessment center);
- a 70% cutoff score might be required (rather than a competency-based cutoff score);
- certain weights on tests might be required (rather than using job analysis data or having subject-matter experts establish the weights based upon their opinions of relevance to the at-issue jobs, perhaps combined with a competency-based cutoff);
- the rule of three might be required (rather than identifying those substantially equally qualified candidates based upon the measurements of the tests);
- a rank-ordered list might be required (rather than grouping candidates who are substantially equally qualified together); or,
- a rigid banding based upon the same score might be required (rather than grouping substantially equally qualified candidates together).

Different practices, procedures, and tests measure different competencies – each with varying levels of psychometric precision – and they should be developed and used with respect to how they relate to the actual job requirements (more so than just tradition). The constraints outlined above are typically established so everyone knows the ground rules going into the selection process and are not necessarily based on competency and finding the most qualified applicant. If a public entity has any of these constraints, the <u>Ricci</u> case presents a blueprint of what is needed to establish a strong basis in evidence before making race-conscious remedies.

A competency-based system can often reduce unnecessary adverse impact against groups protected by Title VII compared to a selection system with rigid constraints. Tests, such as assessment centers, often create less adverse impact than traditional paper-and-pencil tests and can provide very qualified candidates.[9] Assessment centers can measure important or critical parts of jobs not measurable with paper-and-pencil tests; however, the cost is usually higher, except when the number of candidates is small. Use of competency-based cutoff scores often provides more qualified candidates with less adverse impact than an arbitrary, fixed cutoff score, such as 70%. Using job analysis data or having subject-matter experts determine weights to be used by different parts of the selection process often gives much more flexibility to a public entity for obtaining very qualified candidates with less adverse impact than fixed weights not based on job analysis data or subject-matter expert opinions. Using a banding process to group substantially equally qualified candidates based upon the reliability of the tests (how consistently the test measures what it is supposed to measure) used in the selection process can provide many more competent candidates with less adverse impact than a fixed "rule of three."

Any changes made after test administration *for the sole purpose of lowering adverse impact*, such as altering cutoff scores, alternate use of qualified weights, etc. may invite challenges. This is due to Title VII's prohibition against making race-based adjustment of test results. This is especially the case if they are outside of the "substantially equally valid" or "substantially equally qualified" doctrines or are not justified on the "strong-basis-of-evidence" standard – see the section below regarding applying the Ricci standard to common testing situations. Ricci holds that these changes should be made, based upon a strong basis in evidence, *prior* to the administration of the selection process (hence the need for a Croson Study prior to the implementation of a selection procedure):

> Title VII does not prohibit an employer from considering, before administering a test or practice, how to design that test or practice in order to provide a fair opportunity for all individuals, regardless of their race. And when, during the test-design stage, an employer invites comments to ensure the test is fair, that process can provide a common ground for open discussions toward that end. We hold only that, under Title VII, before an employer can engage in intentional discrimination for the asserted purpose of avoiding or remedying an unintentional disparate impact, the employer must have a strong basis in evidence to believe it will be subject to disparate-impact liability if it fails to take the race-conscious, discriminatory action (Ricci, pp. 25-26).

The strong-basis-in-evidence standard does not have to be evidence that is provable in court:

> Applying the strong-basis-in-evidence standard to Title VII gives effect to both the disparate-treatment and disparate-impact provisions, allowing violations of one in the name of compliance with the other only in certain, narrow circumstances. The standard leaves ample room for employers' voluntary compliance efforts, which are essential to the statutory scheme and to Congress's efforts to eradicate workplace discrimination… And the strong-basis-in-evidence standard appropriately constrains employers' discretion in making race-based decisions: It limits that discretion to cases in which there is a strong basis in evidence of disparate-impact liability, but it is not so restrictive that it allows employers to act only when there is a provable, actual violation (Ricci, pp. 23-24).

Background on Croson Studies: Justification for Taking Remedial Action

The Supreme Court's ruling in Richmond v. Croson and the related Wygant v. Jackson Board of Education case established the basic principle that a governmental employer must provide a strong basis in evidence for its determination that remedial action is necessary before it takes the action. To support an affirmative action program that requires remedial action for minorities under *strict scrutiny*, a "strong basis in evidence" of past discrimination by the specific entity must exist to support the conclusion that remedial action is necessary.[10]

A generalized assertion that there has been past discrimination in an entire industry will not be enough to justify a race-conscious program under strict scrutiny.[11] Applying this rule, however, has produced conflicting results based on various state regulations surrounding affirmative action.[12] Croson did not provide guidance as to what amount and type of factual showing would provide a strong basis in evidence that discrimination existed in a particular industry.[13]

The most probative type of evidence in government contracting cases is statistical data showing "gross statistical disparities between the proportion of minorities hired . . .and the proportion of minorities willing and able to do the work."[14] In government contracting cases, this is often shown through the use of a disparity index, which is a comparison between the share of contracts awarded to minority contractors and the percentage of qualified minority-owned firms in the local population that do such work.[15] In addition, while the combination of "convincing anecdotal and statistical evidence is potent,"[16] anecdotal evidence, by itself, will rarely suffice to justify a race-conscious remedy evaluated under strict scrutiny.[17] Specific analyses of underutilization for the at-issue jobs, past adverse impact for the practices, procedures, and tests used for the at-issue jobs, analysis of the job- relatedness of prior selection procedures used for the at-issue jobs, and evaluation of alternate employment practices is needed. These items make up a Croson Study, but are not necessarily facts ready to be proved in court. The strong-basis-in-evidence standard is not so restrictive, according to the Supreme Court, as to require employers to act only when there is a provable, actual violation (Ricci, p. 24).

In the Ricci case, the Supreme Court stated that the City of New Haven's race-based rejection of the test results based only on adverse impact against minorities cannot satisfy the strong-basis-in-evidence standard (Ricci, pp. 26-34). The racial adverse impact in this case was acknowledged by the city attorney and the head of Human Resources. There was no dispute that the City was faced with a prima facie case of disparate-impact liability, but this information alone was not enough to cancel the eligibility lists. The problem for the City is that such a prima facie case – essentially, a threshold showing of a significant statistical disparity of test scores and nothing more – falls short of being a strong basis in evidence that the City would have been liable under Title VII had it certified the test results. The Court ruled that the City could be liable for disparate impact discrimination *only if the exams at issue were not job related and consistent with business necessity, or if there existed an equally valid, less discriminatory alternative that served the City's needs but that the City refused to adopt.* And, based on the record the parties developed through discovery, there was ". . . no substantial basis in evidence that the test was deficient in either respect" (Ricci, pp. 26-28).

The City made claims that the exams were *not* job related and consistent with business necessity, but failed to produce any validation study supporting their claim. A validation study would have looked at the entire selection process and could have shown the parts that were valid and parts that were not, if there were any. Of particular interest is the fact that the city attorney asked the test developers to not provide the validation study already contemplated in the contract the test developer had with the City (Ricci, p. 6). Several people asked the City's Civil Service Board to have a validation study conducted so that it could be determined if the test process was job related and consistent with business necessity. As a result of not having a validation study on the record, the only evidence before the Court demonstrated that *detailed steps* were taken to develop and administer the tests and there were *painstaking analyses* of the questions asked to assure their relevance to the Captain and Lieutenant positions. The testimony also shows that complaints that certain examination questions were contradictory or did not specifically apply to firefighting practices in the City were fully addressed, even while the City turned a blind eye to evidence supporting the exams' validity (Ricci, pp. 28-29).

A Croson Study would have identified that a validation study was needed; a validation study would have provided the strong basis in evidence the City needed. The validation study would have provided the City with information showing the lack of validation support for the adverse impact created by the minimum qualifications, the adverse impact created by the 70% arbitrary cutoff score, the adverse impact created by the weights negotiated with the union rather than set by job analysis or by subject-matter experts, the adverse impact created by the use of a rank-ordered list that presented candidates in a way not supported by the psychometric properties of the written test and oral interview, and the adverse impact created by the certification process of the rule of three, which exceeded the psychometric properties of the tests used to create the artificial groupings of three. The City, therefore, did not provide a strong basis in evidence that the exams were not job related in order to support its decision to toss out the test results.

Likewise, the City also made a vain attempt at showing that alternative selection procedures were available with less adverse impact. The same strong-basis-in-evidence requirement was needed to support each of the City's proposed alternate employment practices. Instead, the City asked for an opinion from a testing expert who was not involved in the selection process, and who did not review the selection procedures at issue before providing advice to the City. The City asserted that the use of an assessment center to evaluate candidates' behavior in typical job tasks would have had less adverse impact than written exams, but this assertion was contradicted by other statements in the record from firefighter Ricci indicating that the City could not have used assessment centers for the exams at issue, because it would have taken too long to develop. A Croson Study would have identified that a testing expert was needed to provide alternate employment practice options and an expert would have been available to rebut firefighter Ricci's assertions regarding how long an assessment center takes to develop.

It was inevitable that the City's arguments would fail without a strong basis in evidence. The City referred to testimony that a different composite-score calculation would have allowed the City to consider black candidates for then open positions, but it produced no evidence to show that the weighting they used was indeed arbitrary, or that different weighting would be a substantially equally valid way to determine whether candidates were qualified for promotions. A Croson Study would have identified that alternate weights required subject-matter experts. These subject-matter experts would have provided the strong basis in evidence needed to provide an option for the City to consider with substantially equally qualified candidates with less adverse impact.

The City additionally argued that it could have adopted a different interpretation of its charter provision limiting promotions to the highest scoring applicants, and that the interpretation would have produced less discriminatory results; but the Supreme Court said the City's approach would have violated Title VII's prohibition of race-based adjustment of test results. "Here, banding was not a valid alternative for this reason: Had the City *reviewed the exam results and then* adopted banding to make the minority test scores appear higher, it would have violated Title VII's prohibition of adjusting test results on the basis of race" (Ricci, p. 31). A Croson Study would have identified banding as an option before the selection process to avoid the problem of race-based adjustments of scores after the fact. The City failed to provide a strong basis in evidence that any viable alternate employment practice was available (Ricci, pp. 29-33). A Croson Study would have provided the strong basis in evidence the City needed.

Essential Components of a Croson Study

The Supreme Court, in Croson and Wygant, ruled that certain actions taken by governmental entities to remedy past racial discrimination – actions that are themselves based on race – are constitutional only when there is a "strong basis in evidence" that the actions taken for remedial purposes are necessary. A Croson Study is a way to gather the "strong basis in evidence" needed. In Ricci, the Court stated: ". . . the standard appropriately constrains employers' discretion in making race-based decisions: It limits that discretion to cases in which there is a strong basis in evidence of disparate-impact liability, but it is not so restrictive that it allows employers to act only when there is a provable, actual violation" (Ricci, p. 24). A Croson Study is a practical and prudent vehicle for employers to use to minimize the likelihood of losing a Title VII case, or perhaps even being challenged.

A Croson Study is specific to the job classification or rank for which a promotional list is being considered. The Croson Study process includes an evaluation of the utilization of minorities and women as well as the adverse impact and job-relatedness of past practices, procedures, and tests used to select candidates during prior selection processes. The job-relatedness evaluation includes the assistance of subject-matter experts, as well as outside experts who can provide information for alternative selection procedures. It is not enough to simply review prior statistics of practices, procedures, and tests (*i.e.,* utilization analyses and adverse impact analyses). The job-relatedness of the practices, procedures, and tests used must also be addressed and some additional job-relatedness work might be necessary. The statistical and job-relatedness information is needed to establish a strong basis in evidence required to make temporary remedial or race-conscious or gender-conscious changes.

Problems identified from a Croson Study do not have to reach the level required of proof in court. However, problems found from a Croson Study *can be* used as a blueprint for some change and as a basis for limited actions to substantially reduce the likelihood of losing a Title VII suit, or in the best case, avoiding the suit altogether. As the Court stated: "Applying the strong-basis-in-evidence standard to Title VII gives effect to both the disparate-treatment and disparate-impact provisions, allowing violations of one in the name of compliance with the other only in certain, narrow circumstances. The standard leaves ample room for employers' voluntary compliance efforts, which are essential to the statutory scheme and to Congress's efforts to eradicate workplace discrimination" (Ricci, p. 23). Table 11-2 summarizes how various levels of justification for using race-conscious remedies for current/future selection processes can be amassed through a Croson Study.

Level of Justification Gathered for Using Race-Conscious Remedies for Future/Current Selection Process			
Element	Description	Low Range	High Range
Recruiting	Applicant outreach, job fairs, job postings, etc.	Good faith outreach towards all subgroups within relevant labor market (both local and regional).	Narrow outreach only to majority-rich sources. No good faith outreach.
Selection process	Tests used in hiring/ promotional process.	Reasonably balanced and job-related/validated tests.	Use of high adverse impact tests with no/low validity evidence.
Test use	Pass/fail cutoffs, banding, ranking, or weighting/combining.	Tests are used in a way that matches how skills are required for the position.	Ranking on high adverse impact tests with limited justification.
Utilization analysis	Comparison between current workforce composition and qualified labor pool.	No statistically significant imbalances.	Gross imbalances that are statistically and practically significant.
Adverse impact	Historical adverse impact analyses on tests.	Low/no adverse impact or adverse impact on job-related/ validated tests.	Long history of unjustified adverse impact on non-validated tests.
Alternate employment practices	Tests that are substantially valid but have less adverse impact.	Good faith efforts made to investigate and evaluate alternatives.	Alternatives not investigated or considered.

Note: "Tests" in the table represent practices, procedures, or tests (either formal or informal) as defined by the Uniform Guidelines.

Table 11-2 Elements of a Comprehensive Croson Study

For example, an employer could conduct a Croson Study that would include an evaluation of how test scores were *used* (e.g., ranked, banded, weighted, etc.) in a certain selection process for a given position. The purpose of the evaluation would be to determine whether tests scores should be used in a different way for future selection processes, or whether previously-administered tests that are pending certification (as in Ricci) should be used in the same way they were previously, or used differently based on the results of the Croson Study.

If the Croson Study determined that the tests were used and weighted in a way that matches how skills are required for the position (e.g., based on a job analysis or opinions from qualified subject-matter experts) and ranking was only used when justified, no strong basis in evidence would be gathered for using the test results in ways that could minimize adverse impact. However, if the tests were *not* used and weighted in a way that matches how skills are required for the position and ranking was conducted on high adverse impact tests with only limited justification (e.g., low reliability, bunched scores, not differentiating skills, etc.), then a strong basis in evidence would be gathered for using the test results in ways that could minimize adverse impact. Obviously, a stronger basis in evidence would be required for using the test results differently than originally presented to applicants (*i.e.,* in a post-exam situation with pending score results) than would be required for changing how the test scores would be used for a forthcoming selection process.

What Constitutes a Defensible Croson Study?

How defensible is a Croson Study? Ultimately, that depends on the extent to which the race-conscious remedies based on the Croson Study are *exclusive* versus *inclusive*. Race-conscious interventions that have the effect of being exclusive towards certain groups at the expense of being inclusive to others will be more highly scrutinized. After the landmark Adarand Constructors, Inc. v. Peña[18] case, a case where the U.S. Supreme Court held that all racial classifications, imposed by whatever federal, state, or local government actor, must be analyzed by a reviewing court under the "strict scrutiny" standard, the U.S. Department of Justice authored a memorandum to general counsels[19] regarding the implications of the case relevant to the "narrowly tailored," and "strict scrutiny" requirements surrounding race-conscious remedies (such as those that might be justified based on a Croson Study). This memorandum included several evaluation criteria regarding the use of race-conscious remedies which are summarized below:

1. Before using race-conscious remedies, consider whether *race-neutral* alternatives could be used instead.. This consideration should be obvious, but is nonetheless often overlooked by many well-meaning employers. Both public- and private-sector employers should consider race-neutral measures before resorting to race-conscious action.

2. What is the *scope* of the program (*i.e.,* in what *manner* is race used)? Is the race-conscious remedy a hard, fixed number (e.g., a quota)? Is race used as a "plus factor," or is it included in a static formula? Is it a soft or hard standard, variable or fixed? Quota systems typically require judicial instatement and enforcement, whereas "plus factors" can sometimes be used with less scrutiny. For example, Justice O'Connor's opinion for the Court in Croson criticized the scope of Richmond's original 30% minority subcontracting requirement as a "rigid numerical quota." In the Supreme Court case Gratz v. Bollinger,[20] the court reviewed the University of Michigan's affirmative action policies that used a strict "race = +20 points" program and ruled that race can be *one of many factors* considered by colleges when selecting their students, but cannot be used in such a strict formulaic manner.

3. What statistical evidence exists that substantiates possible discrimination? Evaluating this factor can include two types of statistical evidence: Utilization analyses and classical adverse impact evidence. Utilization analyses can be used to evaluate the group's current representation in the workforce (e.g., their numbers in the at-issue position) to their availability in the relevant labor market (using either the qualified applicant flow data or census EEO data). The two-tail exact binomial test can be used to evaluate whether the group is underutilized, with a statistically significant finding constituting a threshold

test[21] of possible discrimination. Classical disparate impact evidence (where the success rates of two groups are compared using the two-tail Fisher Exact Test)[22] exists if the practices, procedures, and tests administered in the past have exhibited adverse impact and have not been validated.

4. The duration of the program. Race-conscious remedies should only be instated for a sufficient time period needed to remedy the ill effects of previous discrimination.

5. The extent to which the race-conscious remedy has an exclusionary effect on whites or men. The most ideal race-conscious remedy is one that does not unnecessarily trammel the rights of any willing competitor to the process.

Many of these criteria have also been evaluated and upheld when private employers have used race-conscious remedies as part of their Affirmative Action Plans (AAPs) required under Executive Order 11246 (which requires private employers that have contracts with the federal government exceeding $50,000 and having at least 50 employees to maintain AAPs). For example, in <u>Sharkey v. Dixie Electric Membership</u>,[23] the employer's use of race-conscious remedies was challenged in a "reverse discrimination" action. Sharkey, who was white, alleged that Dixie electric engaged in discriminatory hiring practices in violation of Title VII when it failed to hire him for a vacant position even though he was qualified and instead hired an African-American applicant (in part because the at-issue job was identified in Dixie's AAP as statistically significantly underutilized). Race was only to be used as a "plus factor" if the applicant was otherwise qualified for the position. The Fifth Circuit supported Dixie's action, ruling that the action was substantially justified by means of a *valid AAP*.

In reviewing the validity of the AAP, the Court noted that the plan (1) was created on an annual basis, (2) properly identified *specific positions that were underutilized*, (3) made accurate comparisons to the relevant labor pool, (4) did not unnecessarily trammel the rights of non-African Americans, and (5) did not present an absolute bar to employment of other groups.

Similar rulings have been made by other Appellate Courts. For example, in <u>Doe v. Kamehameha School/Bernice Pauahi Bishop Estate</u>,[24] the Ninth Circuit ruled that private employers' AAPs: (1) must respond to a manifest imbalance in the work force, (2) must not unnecessarily trammel the rights of members of the non-preferred class or "create an absolute bar to their advancement," and (3) must do no more than is necessary to attain a balance.

Following the guidelines offered by these two cases can help safeguard both public sector employers and federal contractors who integrate goals into their hiring and promotional processes.

Evaluating Specific Practices in a Croson Study

Evaluating weights in a Croson Study. Examining the weights used in prior selection processes to create a ranked list is one practice a Croson Study would evaluate. For example, a public safety department may have used a 60% weight assigned to the written test based upon a collective bargaining agreement. The Croson Study may uncover that while the 60% weight had been negotiated, it had no job-relatedness or validation support. The Croson Study might find that the 60% weight actually caused more adverse impact than lower weights suggested by subject-matter experts, and that the lower weights would have provided substantially equally qualified candidates, especially if a job-related competency-based cutoff was used first on the written test before weighting was applied.

As implied above, one step that could be involved in a Croson Study is to gather data from 7-10 subject-matter experts for a mid-sized department regarding weights. These subject-matter experts would be provided information on what each test (written and oral) measures and would be asked for independent opinions regarding the weights for each test that best represent the proper qualification mix necessary for the job. This effort could lead to, for example, a conclusion that the written test weight should have a weight of 30%, be used with a minimum competency cutoff score, and would provide substantially equally qualified candidates.

In the Ricci case, however, the City demonstrated that weights of 30% / 70% would substantially reduce adverse impact but provided no evidence that the scores were substantially equally valid: "Nor does the record contain any evidence that the 30% / 70% weighting would be an equally valid way to determine whether candidates possess the proper mix of job knowledge and situational skills to earn promotions. . . On this record, there is no basis to conclude that a 30% / 70% weighting was an equally valid alternative the City could have adopted" (Ricci, p. 30). Further, they ruled that changing the weights for the sole purpose of reducing adverse impact could likely violate the race-norming prohibition of the 1991 Civil Rights Act: "Changing the weighting formula, moreover, *could well have violated* Title VII's prohibition of altering test scores on the basis of race. See §2000e-2(l)" [emphasis added] (Ricci, p. 30).

Clearly, a strong basis in evidence is needed to show that the different weighting options, perhaps with a job-related cutoff, would produce substantially equally qualified candidates. In the Ricci opinion, the Supreme Court explains its concerns *before and after* testing:

> Nor do we question an employer's affirmative efforts to ensure that all groups have a fair opportunity to apply for promotions and to participate in the process by which promotions will be made. But once that process has been established and employers have made clear their selection criteria, they may not then invalidate the test results, thus upsetting an employee's legitimate expectation not to be judged on the basis of race. Doing so, absent a strong basis in evidence of an impermissible disparate impact, amounts to the sort of racial preference that Congress has disclaimed, §2000e-2(j), and is antithetical to the notion of a workplace where individuals are guaranteed equal opportunity regardless of race.

> Title VII does not prohibit an employer from considering, *before* administering a test or practice, how to design that test or practice in

order to provide a fair opportunity for all individuals, regardless of their race [emphasis added] (Ricci, p. 25).

Another option from a Croson Study could be to use subject-matter expert opinions and data from prior exams (either given by that department, similar departments, or reported in the testing literature) with the currently proposed exam to develop weights that are likely to minimize adverse impact, then set these weights in advance of administering the tests. Using a competency-based cutoff on the written test could sometimes allow the test to be used as a pass-fail device, rather than a ranking device. Using a job-related competency-based cutoff score on the written test could be used to ensure candidates had a minimum competency, then the rest of the selection process could be used to rank or band candidates, using factors that differentiate more between marginally successful and higher levels of job performance (ideally, ranking should be based on qualification factors that differentiate job performance, rather than factors that are only needed at a minimum level for successful job performance – see further discussion later).

A Croson Study also evaluates the practice of how the math was done on developing the weights prior to creating the ranked list. Written test scores and oral interview scores may be normally distributed but they often come from different distributions. If the employer multiplied the raw score from the written test by 60%, and the raw score from the oral interview score by 40%, and then added these two scores together, it is very possible the *effective weight* for the written test could be very different than the *intended weight* (e.g., 70% rather than the 60% advertised to the candidates, needlessly increasing adverse impact). When the scores are combined and given certain intended weights, consider each person's score expressed as the deviation of their score from the mean score in each distribution in units of standard deviation. This process is referred to as standard scoring – a practice that has been used in testing since at least 1921.[25] If each candidate's score is *not* transformed into a score in relation to the standard deviation of that distribution, the relative performance of the candidate compared to others on this test will not be known.

Raw scores on written tests and oral interview tests are usually quite different. A written test may have a mean of 55 with a standard deviation of 15 (*i.e.,* 68% of the scores fall between 40-70; 95% of the scores fall between 25-85; and 99% of the scores fall between 10-100). An oral interview may have a mean of 84 and a standard deviation of 5 (*i.e.,* 68% of the scores fall between 79-89; 95% of the scores fall between 74-94; and 99% of the scores fall between 69-99). Sometimes, oral interviewers will give a candidate a score of 69 as a "failure," not using the whole distribution of failing scores.

A quick look at the mean raw score for the written and the mean raw score for the oral may detect a difference. If the standard deviations for the written and oral are different, almost certainly the *effective weights* are not going to be the same as the *intended weights*. Standard scoring is the process used to ensure the intended weights become the effective weights. With standard scoring, the candidate's raw score is subtracted from the mean score then divided by the standard deviation of the test. This conversion puts the candidate's score in perspective with the distribution of scores. After each candidate's score is converted to a standard score, the weights can be multiplied by the converted standard score to ensure the intended weight becomes the effective weight. This process was not completed by the City of New Haven, which resulted in the creation of a final list being issued where 43 of the 77 Lieutenants (56%) were out of their appropriate mathematical ranking (some as many as four positions out of their correct rank order) and 15 of the 41 Captains (37%) also being out of correct rank order.[26]

Relative Weight Analysis[27] can be used to evaluate the effective weights if raw scores have been used. Re-analyzing the raw score data in the _Ricci_ case reveals that the actual effective weights of the Lieutenants' oral and written tests were 37.2% and 62.8%, respectively; and 38.2% for and 61.8% for the Captains' oral and written tests, respectively. While only a 2-3% difference from the intended weights, small differences are, of course, meaningful to those being tested.

Use of 70% cutoff score in a Croson Study. Another practice evaluated in a Croson Study is the cutoff score used in prior examinations for the rank. If a 70% cutoff score was used, the basis for its use may be a civil service rule, charter provision, or a provision negotiated with a union. If this cutoff is found to have had adverse impact on past exams for the rank and no job-relatedness data is available to support it, then the public employer may wish to use these facts to establish a strong basis in evidence and implement a cutoff score based upon job-related competency.[28] In footnote 16 of Justice Ginsburg's dissenting opinion, she states:

> It appears that the line between a passing and failing score did not accurately differentiate between qualified and unqualified candidates. A number of fire-officer promotional exams have been invalidated on these basis. See, _e.g._, Guardians Assn., 630 F. 2d, at 105 ("When a cutoff score unrelated to job performance produces disparate racial results, Title VII is violated.") (_Ricci_, p. 32).

If a Croson Study finds that the 70% cutoff score has created unnecessary adverse impact in the past and is not supported by any job-relatedness or validation data, then a strong basis in evidence is available to the public employer to make a change. The fact that a city charter, merit system, or even state law specifies the use of a 70% rule is not enough to justify it. The Supreme Court warns against this: "A state court's prohibition of banding, as a matter of municipal law under the charter, may not eliminate banding as a valid alternative under Title VII. See 42 U.S.C. §2000e-7" (_Ricci_, p. 31). Not using a competency-based minimum score can needlessly increase adverse impact. In other situations, using a competency-based cutoff may actually increase adverse impact, although in such situations the adverse impact would be justified because the cutoff score represents the competency level necessary for success.

If an employer desires to determine a job-related, competency-based cutoff score, the steps are quite straightforward. One such process (known as the modified Angoff technique) can be completed by convening a panel of 7-10 qualified subject-matter experts to rate every item on the test with respect to the percentage of minimally-acceptable candidates who would likely answer the question correctly.

These ratings are then averaged in a "critical score" that is reduced by deducting 1, 2, or 3 Conditional Standard Errors of Measurement (CSEMs) after the test is administered and the reliability becomes known.

The classical Standard Error of Measurement (SEM) is calculated using the standard deviation and reliability of the test, shown as: $SEM = \sigma_x (1 - r_{xx})^{1/2}$ where σ_x is the standard deviation of all test scores and r_{xx} is the reliability of the entire test. It represents the variance in a score resulting from factors other than the ability being measured by the test. The concept is based on the premise that the underlying ability being measured by the test cannot be measured exactly without a perfectly reliable test. Factors cause the candidates taking the test to score higher or lower than their true score due to factors such as chance error, differential testing conditions, imperfect test measurement, and other factors unrelated to the applicant's true ability. The SEM provides an estimate of the average test score error for all candidates regardless of their ability level. The SEM assumes that errors are the same at every score throughout the distribution of candidate scores and represents a weighted average of errors associated with each score.

Because the SEM varies across the range of candidate proficiencies, and individual candidate score levels on any specific test could have different degrees of measurement error, the SEM as well as individual score level estimates, commonly referred to as *Conditional* Standard Errors of Measurement (CSEM), are typically reported.[29] The CSEM gives the estimate of reliability (error estimate) at each score point. The SEM is considered a test-level statistic and the CSEM is considered a score-level statistic. Both can be used to compute a confidence band around an observed score to determine a score range in which the *true score* (*i.e.,* a score absent measurement error) probably lies. Unlike the SEM, the CSEM takes into account the variation in measurement accuracy across the score scale into consideration. That is why the CSEM can offer a more precise error band around any one individual score.

With the Supreme Court's warning about section 2000e-2(1) of Title VII, which specifies, "It shall be an unlawful employment practice for a respondent, in connection with the selection or referral of applicants or candidates for employment or promotion, to adjust the scores of, . . . or otherwise alter the results of, employment related tests on the basis of race, color, religion, sex, or national origin," it might be prudent to pre-determine whether to use 1, 2, or 3 CSEMs to adjust the critical score. To properly determine the CSEMs, the test must first be administered, but then the pre-determined number of CSEMs can be deducted to arrive at the final cutoff for the test (there are, however, some methods for determining the CSEM prior to administration – see later discussion).

While pre-determining the number of CSEMs to use for the final adjustment may lower risk, determining the number to use *after* the test has been given is a risk if the decision is based solely upon race. Lowering a validated cutoff score by 1, 2, or 3 CSEMs to reduce adverse impact (as well as factoring in other relevant factors) is merely accounting for the lack of reliability of the test (using 1, 2, or 3 CSEMs as confidence intervals for including true scores); it does not *alter the results* or *use different cutoff scores* for different groups, but merely *uses the existing results in a different way*. It is unclear how a conservative Supreme Court would view using race as one factor. Therefore, while it would be safer to make the decision prior to test administration, there are some advantages as well as risks associated with waiting until after test administration to decide on the number of CSEMs to use.

There are several case examples where reducing cutoff scores within substantially equally qualified ranges to reduce adverse impact has been supported. Perhaps the first example is given in the Supreme Court case, U.S. v. South Carolina.[30] In the South Carolina case, the Court permitted the consideration of five statistical and human factors when choosing whether to deduct 1, 2, or 3 SEMs:

1. The size of the SEM. Large SEMs indicate low test reliability and/or high levels of variance in the applicant pool;
2. The possibility of sampling error in the study (this relates to the number of subject-matter experts who served on the cutoff development panel). Panels with only a few subject-matter experts raise concern based on this factor, especially if there are a large number of incumbents in the workforce);
3. The consistency of the results (internal comparisons of the panel results). Panels that included biased subject-matter experts raise concern here (only if they were not removed based on inter-rated reliability and/or being extreme outliers);
4. The supply and demand for incumbents in the target position (pertaining to the demand for workers needed in the work force); and
5. The racial composition of the workforce/levels of adverse impact on each of the cutoff options should be considered.

Deducting SEMs (or preferably, CSEMs) in this fashion preemptively addresses concerns or attacks that plaintiff groups may bring by arguing that lower cutoff scores are within the range of the "substantially equally valid" requirement of the Uniform Guidelines (Section 3B) and the third burden ("alternate employment practices") discussed in the 1991 Civil Rights Act. Without deducting CSEMs from validated cutoff scores, employers could find themselves wide open to *alternate employment practice* disparate impact discrimination arguments brought by enforcement agencies or plaintiff groups. Further, if the critical score has statistically significant adverse impact and 1 CSEM below does not, the employer is faced with a situation where two cutoff options that are substantially equally valid result in very different liability outcomes (one is enforceable under Title VII, the other is not).

A more recent example occurred in Isabel v. City of Memphis (2005),[31] where the City of Memphis used a written test for the sergeant promotional process. The City had negotiated a 70% cutoff for the test which had disparate impact against blacks, and the Court ruled that the cutoff score was invalid, stating: "To validate a cutoff score, the inference must be drawn that the cutoff score measures minimal qualifications…" The district court found that the cutoff score was "nothing more than an arbitrary decision and did not measure minimal qualifications." Given this context, the Court supported lowering the (arbitrary) 70% cutoff score by 4% to reduce adverse impact.

Use of score lists in rank order in a Croson Study. Another area investigated in a Croson Study is how the prior lists have been used. If the lists have been used in strict rank order, then an investigation is made using a distribution type of adverse impact analysis[32] to see if the rank order process itself adversely impacted any groups protected by Title VII. If so, then the investigation proceeds to the job-relatedness support to see the reasons for using the list in rank order. It is not enough to provide job-relatedness data using content validity to support a rank-ordered list with adverse impact. The employer must provide evidence that the test measures those *aspects of performance which differentiate among levels of job performance*. The Uniform Guidelines (1978, Section 14C9) state:

> Where a selection procedure supported solely or primarily by content validity is used to rank job candidates, the selection procedure should measure those aspects of performance which *differentiate among levels of job performance*. [emphasis added]

This requirement has been affirmed in numerous court cases. For example, in <u>Vulcan Pioneers v. NJ Department of Civil Service</u>,[33] the Court ruled that the tests were not appropriate for ranking because "subject-matter experts were not even asked whether the knowledges, skills, and abilities were appropriate for ranking; rather, they were asked to indicate whether the knowledges, skills, and abilities ought to be 'qualifying'. . . several knowledges, skills, and abilities, such as knot-tying or first aid, appear to be abilities common to all experienced firefighters, and as to which only an insignificant range of performance ought to have been possible." The Court also noted that the reliability of the examinations was poor and that the test placed a premium on test-taking ability rather than the relevant knowledges, skills, and abilities required for the job.

An additional requirement surrounding ranking that is sometimes applied in litigation has to do with the extent to which the scores are adequately dispersed around the range of interest. For example, in <u>Guardians v. Civil Service Commission of New York</u>,[34] the Court ruled that the scores were "too bunched" to be used in rank order. The Court remarked:

> Rank-ordering satisfies a felt need for objectivity, but it does not necessarily select better job performers. In some circumstances the virtues of objectivity may justify the inherent artificiality of the substantively deficient distinctions being made. But when test scores have a disparate racial impact, an employer violates Title VII if he uses them in ways that lack significant relationship to job performance.

The Court ruled that rank ordering was only permissible when a demonstration could be made of "such substantial test validity that it is reasonable to expect one- or two-point differences in scores to reflect differences in job performance." Even though the Court approved the validity of the test itself, it viewed the evidence required to use the test as a separate and distinct issue: "Our prior conclusion that the test itself may have had enough validity to be used does not, therefore, lead to approval of using its results for rank-ordered selections."

In Ricci, the differentiating evidence required to demonstrate the job-relatedness of the rank-ordered lists was not addressed by the Supreme Court majority.[35] The plaintiffs did not attack this process because the top scorers on the lists *were* the plaintiffs. Not surprisingly, the City did not criticize their own rank-ordered process, though the validation report would have, had the City asked for it.

When lists are used in a strict, rank-ordered way, they can needlessly increase adverse impact. The reliability of tests and consistency of measurement used in personnel selection is not perfect. Anyone who has taken a typing test knows that they may score 45 words a minute the first time, and then, five minutes later, re-take the test and score 43 words a minute or even 48 words a minute. In other words, achieving the identical score is highly unlikely. However, if this process is repeated with many candidates, it is possible to find the reliability of the test. There are other ways to find reliability, but reporting the reliability of tests is a requirement of the Uniform Guidelines, whenever it is feasible.[36]

Test scoring programs typically produce different types of reliability calculations. The reliability can be used to establish the reasonable range with which candidates are likely to obtain their true score. This range reflects the error of measurement for the test and can be used to group scores so that substantially equally qualified candidates are banded together based upon the test(s) used. See the next section for a discussion of the common mechanics used for the banding process.

A Croson Study could evaluate the distribution of scores of prior exams to see if the rank-order process contributed to adverse impact. If so, the Croson Study would evaluate the justification for the use of the test in a rank-ordered way to see if there is differentiating job-relatedness support that adequately addresses the Uniform Guidelines requirements. Also, the Croson Study would evaluate whether the reliability of the tests has been addressed in how the rank-ordered list had been used. If there are problems in this area, the Croson Study can be used to establish the strong basis in evidence needed to make changes to help the employer reduce unnecessary adverse impact and more properly use these selection tools, relying on the reliability of the test to group scores of substantially equally qualified candidates.

It is important that the decision to band is set up *prior* to the next test administration. Changes in the scoring process *after* test administration may place the public entity at a major risk. The Supreme Court has stated that banding would not be an option after the fact (if it was used solely to reduce adverse impact), but should rather be decided in advance as a practice the employer will adopt. "Had the City reviewed the exam results and then adopted banding to make the minority test scores appear higher, it would have violated Title VII's prohibition of adjusting test results on the basis of race. §2000e-2(l)" (Ricci, p. 31). If adverse impact is shown with the rank-ordered process after test administration, adequately addressing the differentiating validity requirements is the only hope of success in court.

Rule of three in a Croson Study. Another practice that could be evaluated in a Croson Study is the practice of how top candidates are certified to an appointing authority for final appointment. The appointment certification procedure called the "rule of three" used by a public employer may adversely impact groups protected by Title VII. Any practice, procedure, or test that causes adverse impact on a group protected by Title VII in a hiring or promotion process is subject to a disparate-impact discrimination challenge. If an adverse impact analysis of the rank-ordered distribution of scores indicates adverse impact throughout the appointing potential part of the list, the chances are very good that the rule of three will have adverse impact (as it is used to select three people at a time from the rank-ordered lists). If the Croson Study finds that the practice of the rule of three has adversely impacted a group or groups protected by Title VII, then the job-relatedness of the rule of three needs to be demonstrated. This will be hard to do when the psychometrics of a written test and oral interview will *almost never* be reliable enough to justify strict rank order in groups of just three candidates.

For example, in the Ricci case, using the known standard deviations of each test – typical reliability estimates of .90 for the written test (internal consistency) and .60 for the interview (inter-rater reliability) – and the actual correlations between these two tests ($r = .35$ and $r = .40$ for the Lieutenant and Captain process, respectively), the composite reliability of the two combined measures can be estimated ($r = .84$ and $r = .85$ for the Lieutenant and Captain process, respectively). This value can be used with the standard deviation of scores on each list to compute a Standard Error of Difference (SED) that can be used to band applicants that are deemed *substantially equally qualified*. Multiplying the SED in this example by 1.96 provides a 95% confidence interval that applicants who are within a 9.12 point spread (for the Lieutenant list) and 9.06 point spread (for the Captain list) possess scores that are statistically indistinguishable. In other words, score differences within the broader extremes of this range can be considered the product of measurement error with these tests, rather than reliably different ability levels between the candidates.

With these ranges of substantially equally qualified candidates, there might be as few as two substantially equally qualified candidates for the appointing authority to consider or as many as nine or more. It is unlikely that there will always be three. The reliability of the test is used to establish the measurement range of the test. The number of substantially equally qualified candidates will vary throughout the range of scores. But that's what a job-related selection procedure should be doing – basing the grouping of candidates *according to how their competency levels may reliably differ*.

Remember that the Supreme Court has stated that banding would not be an option after the fact if the sole reason for doing so is race-based. The decision to band needs to be made before test administration begins. "Had the City reviewed the exam results and then adopted banding to make the minority test scores appear higher, it would have violated Title VII's prohibition of adjusting test results on the basis of race. §2000e-2(l)" (Ricci, p. 31). If a public entity performs a Croson Study, evaluates the rule of three as a part of that study, and finds adverse impact in the past, it is likely to happen again. Changing to a banding process *after test administration* will probably be too late, according to the Supreme Court, if the reason is race-based. Therefore, stating *before* test administration, that banding will be used based upon the reliability of the tests involved in making the list, rather than the rule of three, is making adjustments on the basis of the test reliability, not race, and is a more prudent decision than waiting for a case to be filed after testing is done. Banding should be done based upon the measurement properties of the tests involved and not based upon an artificial number of three candidates at a time. The Croson Study can help act as the change agent to avoid disparate-impact discrimination liability because, once adverse impact is shown on a current list with the rule of three, it is probably too late (see discussion on this specific topic later).

An inherent conflict exists between a Civil Service requirement that the selection process be job related and a requirement to use a rule of three. In the 1971 Griggs v. Duke Power[37] case, it was learned from the Supreme Court that the rule of three is a practice covered under Title VII: "Under the Act, practices, procedures, or tests neutral on their face, and even neutral in terms of intent, cannot be maintained if they operate to 'freeze' the status quo of prior discriminatory employment practices." The defendant City charter established a merit system. The merit system requires the use of job-related exams:

> When the City of New Haven undertook to fill vacant Lieutenant and Captain positions in its fire department (Department), the promotion and hiring process was governed by the city charter, in addition to federal and state law. The charter establishes a merit system. That system requires the City to fill vacancies in the classified civil service ranks with the most qualified individuals, as determined by *job-related examinations* [emphasis added] (Ricci, p. 3).

The Griggs case, quoted above, tells us that "examinations" must be interpreted as "practices, procedures, or tests." The City's merit system states the requirement to use the rule of three:

> After each examination, the New Haven Civil Service Board (CSB) certifies a ranked list of applicants who passed the test. Under the charter's "rule of three," the relevant hiring authority must fill each vacancy by choosing one candidate from the top three scorers on the list (Ricci, p. 3).

Perhaps the conflict between being required to use job-related practices and also being required to use the rule of three has been anticipated when the Supreme Court in Ricci issued a clear warning to the public sector that relying upon a state court's prohibition of banding may not be enough: "A state court's prohibition of banding, as a matter of municipal law under the charter, may not eliminate banding as a valid alternative under Title VII. See 42 U. S. C. §2000e-7" (Ricci, p. 31). Title VII states in part:

> Nothing in this subchapter shall be deemed to exempt or relieve any person from any liability, duty, penalty, or punishment provided by any present or future law of any State or political subdivision of a State, other than any such law which purports to require or permit the doing of any act which would be an unlawful employment practice under this subchapter. (42 U.S.C. §2000e-7).

A Croson Study can gather the data regarding adverse impact of the rule of three and crystallize the issue for public sector management to address before being required to by a court. With a Croson Study completed, more options are available to the public employer.

Has Ricci Created an Internal Conflict in the 1991 Civil Rights Act?

Two sections of Title VII may now have a conflict. Section 2000e-2(l)[38] is the section dealing with the "Prohibition of discriminatory use of test scores." Section 2000e-2(k)(1)(A)(ii)[39] deals with the "Burden of proof in disparate impact cases," specifically the "alternate employment practice" provision. Reading these two sections in light of the Uniform Guidelines' interpretation of the alternate employment practices application (see section 60.3B)[40] confirms potential conflicts, causing practitioners to wonder how they can be reconciled.

Upon closer examination, there is a way to minimize the conflict created by five conservative Supreme Court Justices who added substantial constraints to the interpretation published by the Equal Employment Opportunity Commission, the Department of Justice, the Civil Service Commission and the Department of Labor in section 3B of the Uniform Guidelines on Employee Selection Procedures (1978).

In Ricci, the Supreme Court states regarding section 2000e-2(l): "If an employer cannot re-score a test based on the candidates' race, §2000e-2(*l*), then it follows *a fortiori* that it may not take the greater step of discarding the test altogether to achieve a more desirable racial distribution of promotion-eligible candidates – absent a strong basis in evidence that the test was deficient and that discarding the results is necessary to avoid violating the disparate impact provision" (Ricci, p. 24).

When addressing the proposed alternate employment practice of changing the weights from 60% on the written test and 40% on the oral interview to 30% / 70%, the Ricci majority stated: "Nor does the record contain any evidence that the 30% / 70% weighting would be an equally valid way to determine whether candidates possess the proper mix of job knowledge and situational skills to earn promotions. Changing the weighting formula, moreover, *could* well have violated Title VII's prohibition of altering test scores on the basis of race. See §2000e-2(*l*). *On this record*, there is no basis to conclude that a 30% / 70% weighting was an equally valid alternative the City could have adopted" [emphasis added] (Ricci, p. 30).

In the Ricci decision, the Supreme Court addressed section 2000e-2(l) again dealing with the alternative employment practice of banding: "Here, banding was not a valid alternative for this reason: Had the City reviewed the exam results *and then* adopted banding to make the minority test scores appear higher, it would have violated Title VII's prohibition of adjusting test results on the basis of race. §2000e-2(*l*)…" [emphasis added] (Ricci, p. 31).

The alternative employment practice provisions of Title VII in the Civil Rights Act of 1991, gives a specific day for an important reason. It states in section 2000e-2(k)(1)(A)(ii): "the complaining party makes the demonstration described in subparagraph (C) with respect to an alternative employment practice and the respondent refuses to adopt such alternative employment practice." The (C) section states: "The demonstration referred to by subparagraph (A)(ii) shall be in accordance with the law as it existed on *June 4, 1989*, with respect to the concept of 'alternative employment practice'" [emphasis added]. On June 5, 1989, <u>Wards Cove v. Atonio</u>[41] was decided in a way by the Supreme Court that was objectionable to a majority of Congress. The objectionable part of the <u>Wards Cove</u> decision states:

> Finally, if on remand the case reaches this point, and respondents cannot persuade the trier of fact on the question of petitioners' business necessity defense, respondents may still be able to prevail. To do so, respondents will have to persuade the fact finder that "other tests or selection devices, without a similarly undesirable racial effect, would also serve the employer's legitimate [hiring] interest[s]"; by so demonstrating, respondents would prove that "[petitioners were] using [their] tests merely as a 'pretext' for discrimination." Albemarle Paper Co., supra, at 425; see also Watson, 487 U.S., at 998 (O'Connor, J.); id., at 1005-1006 (Blackmun, J., concurring in part and concurring in judgment). If respondents, having established a prima facie case, come forward with alternatives to petitioners' hiring practices that [490 U.S. 642, 661] reduce the racially disparate impact of practices currently being used, and petitioners refuse to adopt these alternatives, such a refusal would belie a claim by petitioners that their incumbent practices are being employed for nondiscriminatory reasons.
>
> *Of course, any alternative practices which respondents offer up in this respect must be equally effective as petitioners' chosen hiring procedures in achieving petitioners' legitimate employment goals.* Moreover, "[f]actors such as the cost or other burdens of proposed alternative selection devices are relevant in determining whether they would be equally as effective as the challenged practice in serving the employer's legitimate business goals." Watson, supra, at 998 (O'Connor, J.). "Courts are generally less competent than employers to restructure business practices," <u>Furnco Construction Corp. v. Waters</u>, 438 U.S. 567, 578 (1978); *consequently, the judiciary should proceed with care before mandating that an employer must adopt a plaintiff's alternative selection or hiring practice in response to a Title VII suit.* [emphasis added]

The specific words regarding alternate employment practices from <u>Albemarle</u> (prior to June 4, 1989) were: "...the respondents have not until today been specifically apprised of their opportunity to present evidence that even validated tests might be a 'pretext' for discrimination in light of alternative selection procedures available to the Company."[42] The <u>Watson</u> decision (prior to June 4, 1989) stated the following regarding alternate employment practices: "Factors such as the cost or other burdens of proposed alternative selection devices are relevant in determining whether they would be equally as effective as the challenged practice in serving the employer's legitimate business goals. The same factors would also be relevant in determining whether the challenged practice has operated as the functional equivalent of a pretext for discriminatory treatment."[43]

While Congress obviously wanted to put fewer constraints on how alternate employment practices had been interpreted by a conservative Supreme Court, the 1991 Civil Rights Act could only do so much by reversing any impact the Wards Cove case could have. The Supreme Court's narrowing to employment goals from business goals was erased. The warning that "the judiciary should proceed with care before mandating that an employer must adopt a plaintiff's alternative selection or hiring practice in response to a Title VII suit" was clearly reversed by the 1991 Civil Rights Act.

Applying the Ricci Standard to Common Testing Situations

What are the implications for employers of the Supreme Court's analysis of the test-related evidence that was available in the record? This was a unique case with unusual circumstances that are not typically encountered in EEO settings (*i.e.,* tossing out a list solely on the basis that it had adverse impact against minorities and, as a result, having whites sue on the basis of disparate treatment). The classical Title VII burdens established under the U.S.SC's unanimous ruling in Griggs and codified by the 1991 Civil Rights Act remain intact. In the aftermath of Ricci, some recent lower-court cases clarified this point. For example, in the post-Ricci case, U.S. v. City of New York,[44] the court clarified that the Ricci case does not change the law as it relates to the burden-shifting requirements outlined in Title VII. While the major tenets of Title VII remain, Ricci does provide specific guidance to employers regarding making race-based decisions after an employment test has been given – *i.e.*, let the results stand unless they can prove (using the strong-basis-in-evidence standard) that the test was likely not valid or that other substantially equally valid (lower adverse impact) options were available but were overlooked.

Considering (1) the Ricci admonishment regarding changes after a selection process has been administered absent a "strong basis in evidence" that not acting will cause a disparate impact situation, (2) the "Prohibition of discriminatory use of test scores" in Title VII's section 2000e-2(l), and (3) the alternate employment practices in Title VII's 2000e-2(k)(1)(A)(ii) (and related doctrine codified in the Guidelines, Sections 3B, 5G, 14B[5] and [6], and 14C[8] and [9] with respect to "alternate use with less adverse impact"), the following examples have been prepared to illustrate how employers can address real employment situations. Each example will be discussed in the context of the employers in situations with and without a *strong basis in evidence* (*i.e.,* evidence that the test(s) used were not sufficiently valid) as well as *before or after* the test administration.

Changing weights. For purposes of this discussion, the process of changing weights means changing from union-negotiated or arbitrary weights to a set of job-related weights based on job analysis data or ratings from a panel of subject-matter experts. Because developing test weights based upon job research results in weights that accurately reflect job requirements, such a process is actually likely to produce a *more qualified* applicant list than union-negotiated or arbitrary weights, and may produce more or less adverse impact.

Changing weights before test administration with or without a strong basis in evidence. This practice is acceptable, even if adverse impact was a motivating factor behind starting the process to research and identify the actual job-related weights (based on both the "alternate employment practice" requirement of the 1991 Civil Rights Act and the related "substantially equally valid" doctrine of the Guidelines). For example, an employer, in an attempt to both maximize the validity of the process and reduce undesirable adverse impact, may conduct research and determine that assessment centers are an effective means of reducing adverse impact while measuring competencies that are typically untapped by written tests, and decide to include an assessment center as part of the overall weighted testing process. Another example would be an employer that uses both a written test and an assessment center (weighted arbitrarily 50% / 50%) and decides to conduct a study to re-weigh the tests according to their *relative importance* to the job. Yet another example would be using the written test with a validated cutoff score as a pass/fail device only (especially if it only measures abilities needed at a baseline level, rather than differentiating abilities), and then weighting the assessment center 100% (especially if it measured differentiating abilities).

      Changing weights <u>after</u> test administration <u>without</u> a strong basis in evidence. This practice would not be defensible post-<u>Ricci</u>.

      Changing weights <u>after</u> test administration <u>with</u> a strong basis in evidence. The Supreme Court ruled in <u>Ricci</u> that "changing the weighting formula, moreover, *could well have violated* Title VII's prohibition of altering test scores on the basis of race. See §2000e-2(l)" [emphasis added] (<u>Ricci</u>, p. 30). Their key caveat to this statement was, "*On this record*, there is no basis to conclude that a 30% / 70% weighting was an equally valid alternative the City could have adopted" [emphasis added] (<u>Ricci</u>, p. 30). If, however, the City presented a set of weights (based on job analysis data or qualified subject-matter expert opinions) that were in fact substantially equally valid – or perhaps even *more valid* – than the original set used by the City, but reduced adverse impact, they might have been accepted. For example, if the City used job analysis data or subject-matter expert opinions to determine that a 50% / 50% weighting scheme was substantially equally valid (or even more valid) than the 60% / 40% weights that were used, and the job related set reduced adverse impact, such a weighting scheme could have been adopted. However, merely suggesting alternative weights *without also demonstrating* that they were substantially equally valid to sufficiently address the "alternate employment practice" requirement of the 1991 Civil Rights Act and the related "substantially equally valid" doctrine of the Guidelines would obviously not be acceptable, as they were rejected in the <u>Ricci</u> case.

      Lowering cutoffs. Because cutoffs split the entire applicant group into two groups – passing and failing – they should be set in a way that maximizes the differentiation between the qualified versus unqualified applicants. The most effective cutoff scores have the highest levels of Decision Consistency Reliability – a type of reliability that evaluates how consistently the test classifies "qualified" and "non-qualified," or those who pass the test versus those who fail.[45] Cutoffs that are set too high will eliminate too many applicants who are actually qualified. Cutoffs that are set too low have the opposite effect – they will select in too many unqualified applicants. Cutoffs that are accurately set using a job-related process like the Angoff method are likely to have higher levels of Decision Consistency Reliability than arbitrary cutoffs.

Even if a cutoff is set using a job-related method like the Angoff technique, the test used to measure applicant qualification levels along the continuum of scores will have a certain degree of score consistency (reliability) with respect to measuring the same. As discussed earlier, accounting for this lack of perfect measurement can be done by reducing the critical score by 1-3 CSEMs. Also discussed below is the possibility of lowering cutoffs without respect to the consideration of such measurement error.

Lowering cutoffs before test administration without a strong basis in evidence. Although this example implies lowering cutoffs in a way that is *not* based on the psychometric properties of the test (e.g., without considering the reliability or CSEM), it is likely defensible because it was done before the administration of the test. However, lowering cutoffs without respect to the psychometric properties of the test (or the ability continuum inherent within the score distribution) may possibly result in setting a standard that is below the qualification levels needed for the job. It is recommended to use the psychometric properties of the test and a job-related cutoff procedure.

Lowering cutoffs before test administration with a strong basis in evidence. If an employer determines a job-related cutoff before the test is given and desires to account for the measurement error of the test, they can defensibly lower the cutoff using CSEMs and determine the exact number (either 1, 2, or 3) beforehand. Most CSEM methods require post-administration statistics for computation. However, the Lord-Keats method[46] can be used for estimating CSEMs before a test has been administered, although it is more advisable to simply state up front whether 1, 2, or 3 CSEMs will be deducted and then use the most accurate CSEM computations after test administration.

Lowering cutoffs after test administration with a strong basis in evidence. If an employer administers a test that is used with an arbitrary cutoff, and they subsequently determine that neither the test nor the cutoff score are sufficiently valid (establishing a strong basis in evidence), lowering the cutoff score to reduce or eliminate adverse impact may be permissible. In fact, the Court ruled in Ricci that having a strong basis in evidence may even justify a *more severe* action – retracting the test results altogether. Lowering the cutoff score with consideration of the psychometric properties of the test would be helpful to support this situation, as would knowing the test score level associated with the minimum levels needed for the job (e.g., a cutoff score set using the modified Angoff technique).

Lowering cutoffs after test administration without a strong basis in evidence. Provided that the employer lowers the cutoff based upon the psychometric limitations of the test, lowering the cutoff by 1-3 CSEMs may be permissible based on both the "alternate employment practice" requirement of the 1991 Civil Rights Act and the related "substantially equally valid" doctrine of the Guidelines. It should be noted here that the race-norming prohibition of the 1991 Civil Rights Act (§2000e-2[l]) expressly states that *using different cutoff scores* for different groups is prohibited; however, this should be differentiated from lowering a cutoff score, which is applied to *all* test takers in the distribution, within a range that is within the substantially equally valid confines. If the employer arbitrarily lowers the cutoff for race reasons only without a strong basis in evidence, this practice would not be supported post-Ricci.

Banding. As discussed above, test score banding is widely practiced in the testing field and has been endorsed far more times than denied in litigation settings.[47] However, if banding is adopted after a test has been administered for the sole purpose of reducing adverse impact, the foundations laid down in <u>Ricci</u> apply as follows.

  Banding <u>before</u> test administration <u>with or without</u> a strong basis in evidence. Before a test is administered, employers can pre-determine to use banding, even though the span of the bands can only be determined after the test(s) have been administered (because the psychometric properties of the tests cannot be known until afterwards).

  Banding <u>after</u> test administration <u>without</u> a strong basis in evidence. This practice is not permissible after <u>Ricci</u>.

  Banding <u>after</u> test administration <u>with</u> a strong basis in evidence. Provided that this process is based upon the psychometric properties of the test(s) involved, banding using 1-3 Standard Errors of Difference[48] may be permissible based on both the "alternate employment practice" requirement of the 1991 Civil Rights Act and the related "substantially equally valid" doctrine of the Guidelines. Table 11-3 provides a summary of these recommendations.

Strong-Basis-in-Evidence Requirement (i.e., evidence of non-validity and/or no alternate employment practice)				
Practice	**No Risk**	**Some Risk**	**Moderate Risk**	**High Risk**
Changing weights.	Before administration.	After administration based on correct math (e.g., using standard scores v. raw scores to weight tests).[1]	After administration based on updated/ corrected job analysis data or SME panel opinions.[2]	After administration changing weights without job research just to reduce adverse impact.[3]
Lowering cutoffs.	Deciding to lower a job-related cutoff using 1-3 CSEMs before or after administration.[4]	Deciding to lower an arbitrary cutoff before testing (not related to using 1-3 CSEMs).	Lowering an arbitrary cutoff score after administration just to reduce adverse impact.	
Banding.	Deciding to band before test administration.	Banding based on arbitrary or weak statistical methods.	Widening pre-determined bands or deciding to band after administration just to reduce adverse impact.[5]	
Taking part or whole test actions or changes after identifying adverse impact.	Considering future alternate employment practices with lower adverse impact, making changes, or validating for subsequent administrations.	Removing test items based on qualified Differential Item Functioning (DIF) analyses.[6]		Retracting or not certifying test results.

Notes: (1) Changing from raw scores to standard scores will typically have an effect of changing the effective weights. (2) Using accurate and reliable job analysis data and/or input from a panel of qualified SMEs (such a change could result in higher or lower adverse impact). (3) Note that the Court in <u>Ricci</u> ruled that changing the weights for the *sole purpose* of reducing adverse impact *could* likely violate the race-norming prohibition of the 1991 Civil Rights Act (<u>Ricci</u>, p. 30). Given the "could" caveat offered by the court, it is safe to say that weights that were not "substantially equally valid" would mostly likely constitute a violation; whereas weights within a substantially equally valid range "may" cause a violation. (4) This process is supported and based upon the psychometric characteristics of the test. (5) In the Ricci decision, the Supreme Court addressed section 2000e-2(*l*), again dealing with the alternative employment practice of banding: "Here, banding was not a valid alternative for this reason: Had the City reviewed the exam results *and then* adopted banding to make the minority test scores appear higher, it would have violated Title VII's prohibition of adjusting test results on the basis of race. §2000e-2(*l*)..." (Ricci, p. 31). (6) Removing test items based on DIF studies should be governed by the psychometric/validity properties of the item.

Table 11-3 Strong-Basis-in-Evidence Requirement Applied to Testing Scenarios

Applying Ricci to Other Title VII Situations (Outside of Testing)

Within a few short weeks after the Supreme Court's ruling in Ricci, the HR legal field began exploring its possible reach to situations outside of the typical disparate impact/disparate treatment framework. Some stretched the Ricci precedent to mean that meeting the strong-basis-in-evidence rule prevented employers from taking *any* actions based on their adverse impact findings – sending messages to the EEO compliance community that proactive adverse impact analyses were either moot (at best) or impermissible (at worst). Others offered cautionary guidance, implying that HR practitioners should tread lightly when it comes to applying disparate impact theory to transactions such as layoffs or proactive compensation analyses.[49] Some courts have even felt the need to clarify the fact that Ricci does not change the standard Title VII disparate impact theory applied in testing cases.[50]

When evaluating the span of Ricci, it is important to recognize the context under which the case was tried. In Ricci, the strong-basis-in-evidence standard was laid down within a set of extreme circumstance – candidates who had competed in a public-sector promotional process (where the competitive ground rules were laid down *a priori*) were faced with losing their promotional opportunities *after* being previously-deemed qualified. In addition, it was within the public sector; it dealt with promotional processes that were judged by the Court as acceptable (albeit based on a very limited evidence record); and it weighed the permissibility of redacting promotional eligibility based on publically announced criteria. Given these circumstances, it is safe to say that the facts in Ricci set the case far to one side of the continuum of HR practices that might be subjected to Title VII scrutiny. Table 11-3 has provided how different testing practices may fall along this same continuum.

The extent to which the Ricci precedence may apply to other (non-testing) situations will now be explored. Because adverse impact pertaining to layoff (Reduction in Force, or RIF) decisions and compensation analyses are two of the most common situations where disparate impact theory is applied outside of testing, the discussion will be limited to just these two practices.

Applying Ricci to Reduction in Force (RIF) decisions. The primary practical implication from Ricci is that if employers are using practices, procedures, and/or tests that are fair and valid, they are on safe ground when using them – *even when they have adverse impact, unless an alternate employment practice that is substantially equally valid with less adverse impact has been presented to the employer and the employer rejected it*. The Ricci ruling squarely stated that employers should let the results of an employment-related test stand *unless* they have a strong basis in evidence for disregarding the results from the test (based on the factors discussed above). In addition, any steps taken to reduce adverse impact (that are outside the bounds permitted within Title VII's "substantially equally valid" doctrine) should be made prior to the test being administered, unless there is a strong basis in evidence that race-conscious remedies are necessary (as would be defined through a Croson Study process).

When employers undergo a RIF process, they should be sure that the criteria used for making RIF decisions are based upon a bona fide seniority system and/or are job-related and uniformly applied. If the RIF process results in adverse impact based on race or gender and a bona fide seniority system is not being used, the same burdens that are relevant to a disparate impact hiring case will apply – *i.e.*, the employer will need to justify their RIF criteria based on the 1991 Civil Rights Act validation standard anchored to the <u>Griggs</u> case ("job related for the position in question and consistent with business necessity"), which is essentially "making a demonstration of validity." Under this same framework, a plaintiff in such a RIF case could prevail under the "alternate employment practice" theory (*i.e.,* by successfully arguing RIF practices or criteria that were "substantially equally valid," but had less adverse impact and the employer refused to use the alternate employment practice presented to it).

If the RIF process is not based on a bona fide seniority system and has adverse impact based on age (which is common in RIF cases), the Supreme Court has ruled in <u>Smith v. City of Jackson</u>[51] that there are important textual differences between the Age Discrimination in Employment Act (ADEA) and Title VII. The ADEA permits any "otherwise not prohibited" action "where the differentiation is based on *reasonable factors other than age*." The result is that the ADEA's requirement for justifying adverse impact based on age is much less than the <u>Griggs</u> requirement. An employer does not need to "demonstrate validity" but rather only needs to show that *reasonable factors other than age* accounted for the adverse impact.

So, under <u>Ricci</u>, can an employer calculate adverse impact before making RIF decisions and base individual RIF decisions on whether such decisions put them on the adverse impact radar? If their RIF process is defensible (with either a bona fide seniority system or job-related validity and uniformly applied), the adverse impact is justified and the employer is safe if challenged under either a race/gender or an age-related claim of adverse impact. However, if their RIF process has adverse impact and is not based on a bona fide seniority system or uses un-validated criteria, they leave themselves vulnerable to a Title VII lawsuit.

There are a few differences that specifically apply when comparing RIFs to the redacted promotional process that occurred in <u>Ricci</u>. <u>Ricci</u> dealt with a promotional process where all of the candidates knew the promotional process and criteria *in advance* and then competed within this pre-defined framework to earn their slots on a promotion slate. By competing in such a process, the employees developed certain "legitimate expectations" that were upset by the redacting of the eligibility list: "Examinations like those administered by the City create legitimate expectations on the part of those who took the tests. As is the case with any promotion exam, some of the firefighters here invested substantial time, money, and personal commitment in preparing for the tests" (<u>Ricci</u>, p. 24). Only with a strong basis in evidence could the employer consider tossing the lists generated by the selection process, if adverse impact existed. By contrast, RIF decisions are competitive per se, but are typically based on pre-existing factors that are both individually (e.g., seniority, performance reviews, etc.) and employer based (e.g., needs within a specific department, desire to keep certain core functions, etc.). By keeping initial RIF decisions confidential, an employer is able to proactively analyze its *proposed* decisions for adverse impact prior to making its final decisions known. The intent of this initial analysis is to (perhaps) allow the employer to adjust its RIF decisions based upon the results of the analyses and the existence of adverse impact. Absent a strong basis in evidence, this adjustment of RIF decisions would likely not withstand legal scrutiny, but because the initial RIF decisions are confidential, it would be much harder for a potential plaintiff to realize what is happening. The best advice for employers making RIF decisions is to ensure that the RIF decisions are job-related and consistent with business necessity, and to live with their initial decisions.

Applying <u>Ricci</u> to compensation analyses. Since the passage of the 1963 Equal Pay Act and the 1964 Civil Rights Act, the courts and federal government have been involved in making sure the compensation practices of employers are free of pay discrimination. While all subgroups are protected under these Acts, women and/or minorities are typically the plaintiffs in such actions. The U.S. Equal Employment Opportunity Commission (EEOC) and the U.S. Department of Labor's enforcement arm, the Office of Federal Contract Compliance Programs (OFCCP) have proactively regulated and enforced policies for analyzing the compensation practices of thousands of U.S. corporations – employers that are federal contractors.

While active in their enforcement efforts, the government's tools for identifying systematic compensation discrimination for the first two decades following the Equal Pay Act and Civil Rights Act have been limited. For example, from the 1990s to 2004 (when the draft version of the now final compensation standards were released), the typical "red flag" analyses used for identifying possible compensation discrimination consisted simply of making average salary comparisons between men and women and whites and minorities by job grouping variables such as job title or job group.[52] In the courtrooms, more sophisticated multiple regression procedures had been used but with mixed response, being called incomprehensible and deemed questionable in some courtrooms while being accepted and considered necessary in others.[53] The vast majority of high-level litigation, however, adopted this use of multiple regression for analyzing compensation data for possible discrimination.

On November 16, 2004, however, all this changed when the OFCCP released a new set of draft guidelines that solidified the role of multiple regression analysis in evaluating compensation discrimination. These draft guidelines went through a public review process and were released in final form on June 16, 2006, as a set of two documents. The first set, titled "Interpreting Nondiscrimination Requirements of Executive Order 11246 with Respect to Systemic Compensation Discrimination,"[54] essentially constitutes OFCCP's formal guidelines they follow when analyzing compensation data received from federal contractors. The second set is titled, "Voluntary Guidelines for Self-Evaluation of Compensation Practices for Compliance With Nondiscrimination Requirements of Executive Order 11246 With Respect to Systemic Compensation Discrimination,"[55] and is provided as a set of useful guidelines that federal contractors may want to proactively follow to ensure that their compensation analyses will be done using procedures and techniques that will address the Interpretive Standards.

The Voluntary Guidelines provide both a strong recommendation that federal contractors use multiple regression techniques to proactively identify pay disparities between groups, as well as proactively provide "make whole relief" when pay discrimination is identified. In fact, under federal affirmative action regulations, employers that are federal contractors are required to conduct pay analyses *annually* to ensure that minorities and women are being fairly treated.[56] This is a similar function to what Croson Studies are designed to do – identify problems and prepare a path for correction. In addition, when contractors are scheduled for an on-site review for their compensation practices, Item 11 of the Scheduling Letter requests that the employer provide "annualized compensation data (wages, salaries, commissions, and bonuses) by either salary range, grade, or level showing total number of employees by race and gender and total compensation by race and gender."[57] When supplied by the contractor, this information is analyzed by the OFCCP for possible statistical indicators of pay discrimination. To encourage contractors to use the multiple regression and related techniques described in the Voluntary Guidelines, the OFCCP offers a program called "compliance coordination" which, in effect, states that the OFCCP will forego independent review of a contractor's raw compensation data and will simply review the contractor's compliance with the Guidelines themselves.

While nearly four decades of enforcement in the courts and the federal enforcement guidelines lay a substantial foundation for conducting proactive pay analyses, what are the outer boundaries surrounding pay investigations, and does Ricci weigh into where these lines are drawn? It should first be stated that while minorities and women are most often the targeted group for inquiry in a pay review, the 1963 Equal Pay Act and the 1964 Civil Rights Act also protect whites and men and, to the extent that pay studies reveal significant pay discrepancies against these groups, they should be (and have been) enforced.

But what about situations – like in Ricci – where efforts to comply with civil rights laws based on a possible violation against one group apparently creates a situation where discrimination can occur against another? Such situations are not limited to just promotional testing circumstances – they have also occurred in pay analysis cases. For example, in Rudebusch v. Hughes[58] a federal judge ruled that Northern Arizona University violated the civil rights of 40 white male faculty members by giving salary raises exclusively to female and minority professors.

In this case, the University implemented a "pay equity" plan that gave one-time pay increases that averaged $3,000 for minorities and $2,400 for women. Whites, however, received no increases. Such changes were made based on a (limited) regression model that was used to make $207,613 of pay increases to *just female and minority male faculty members* whose salaries fell below the predicted salary of a similarly situated white male faculty member. While this practice – *i.e.*, making pay adjustments based upon significant disparities – is in fact a common one (in fact, mandatory for compliance in some cases), the problem with this employer is that no non-minority men were granted salary increases – *even those with salaries below their predicted levels*. In addition, the court noted three major inadequacies with the pay study used to justify making changes to minority and female pay levels.

The first inadequacy was that the study indicated that the *highest single pay disparity* was only 2.0 standard deviations from the predicted salary. This is not to be confused with an entire group's pay triggering the 2.0 standard deviation test required for showing statistical significance. The highest single pay disparity in <u>Rudebusch</u> being "2.0 standard deviations from the predicted salary" pertains to the distance of a single individual away from their predicted salary level – not an entire group factor (e.g., gender) being statistically significant at the 2.0 standard deviation level.

The next inadequacy was the fact that, "although over half the minority faculty made less than the predicted salary, a very large percentage of white male faculty also made less than the predicted amount."[59] The court deemed this as some degree of evidence that other factors besides discrimination may be to blame in explaining the imbalances.

The third limitation pointed out by the Court had to do with the regression study itself. The Court deemed the regression model "inadequate" because it did not include critical performance factors that were fundamental to predicting pay for the at-issue position (teachers):

> As a final point, we have concerns about the way in which Hughes calculated and made the adjustments in this case. Particularly when, as was the case here, adjustments depend upon a regression analysis that does not account for performance factors such as academic credentials, performance, merit, teaching, research, or service – factors that are the major criteria for faculty compensation on campuses across the country – the failure to make some sort of more individualized determination of what sort of adjustments are warranted in any given case will not satisfy strict scrutiny. (<u>Rudebusch</u>, para. 33).

Given this legal background that is specific to investigating pay disparities, coupled with the more general guidance given in <u>Ricci</u> regarding the strong-basis-in-evidence standard, the following advice is given regarding conducting proactive pay investigations:

- Never make pay adjustments without statistically significant evidence (e.g., comparing means only, etc.) that accounts for realistic qualification differences that may exist between groups. Using multiple regression is the only acceptable way to complete this process, and has enjoyed decades of the support and recent endorsement from federal enforcement agencies.
- Never make pay adjustments until after performing a "cohort" analysis whereby additional variables (*i.e.,* those not included within the regression analysis) are investigated.
- Conduct multiple regression studies under attorney-client privilege.
- Make sure that pay investigations look for possible pay disparities that may exist for *any group* (whites and men included), and when pay adjustments are made, be sure that the criteria and rules are *uniformly applied* across all gender and race/ethnic groups.
- When pay adjustments are made based on a multiple regression model, ensure that the model itself is statistically significant, the strength of the regression

model is sufficiently adequate for making predictions, and the fundamental factors that are relevant to pay are included.[60]

All employers – especially federal contractors – are encouraged to invest in expert statistical and legal expertise to insure their compensation evaluations and pay adjustment methodology is sound. Table 11-4 summarizes the post-<u>Ricci</u> recommendations for RIFs and compensation analysis.

Strong-Basis-in-Evidence Requirement				
Practice	**No Risk**	**Some Risk**	**Moderate Risk**	**High Risk**
Layoffs (RIFs)	Evaluating adverse impact of possible RIF decisions.	Changing validated RIF criteria to lower adverse impact after learning about adverse impact.	Changing moderately-validated RIF criteria to lower adverse impact after learning about adverse impact.	Making RIF decisions based entirely on adverse impact results.
Compensation analyses	Making pay changes to *any* statistically significantly impacted group based on a *strong* regression model.	Making pay changes to *any* statistically significantly impacted group based on a *moderate* regression model.	Making pay changes to *any* statistically significantly impact group based on a *weak* regression model.	Making pay changes to only minorities or women based on weak regression models (or non-regression methods).

Table 11-4 Strong-Basis-in-Evidence Requirement Applied to Non-Testing Scenarios

Conclusions

The <u>Ricci</u> case sends a clear message to employers that they need to perform a Croson Study to establish a *strong basis in evidence* for concluding that a race-conscious remedial action, such as throwing out the results of a list, or a test, is necessary in order to avoid adversely impacting a group protected by Title VII of the Civil Rights Act and which they not feel are not job related enough to withstand a court challenge. Conducting a Croson Study under attorney-client privilege to determine if race-conscious remedies may be appropriate on a limited basis for a limited time in some situations is a prudent step for any employer to take that would like to justify race-conscious remedies that are part of their diversity initiatives. A Croson Study can provide a strong basis in evidence to provide more flexibility regarding the type of test, the weights to be used, the cutoff, and alternate selection procedures, which can be developed and administered to substantially reduce unnecessary adverse impact while selecting qualified candidates.

And finally, employers that evaluate alternate employment practices under a Croson Study should make sure to compile evidence, not just rhetoric, to support the position that the alternate employment practice (such as banding, a different set of weights, a different cutoff score, another test such as the use of an assessment center) will provide substantially equally qualified candidates with less adverse impact.

Note

[1] Richmond v. Croson, 488 U.S. 469, (1989).

[2] Wygant v. Jackson Board of Education, 476 U.S. 267 (1986).

[3] Ricci et al., v. DeStefano et al., U.S.SC, No. 07-1428 (June 29, 2009).

[4] An 80% violation occurs when the selection rate of the focal group is less than 80% of the reference group's selection rate. The 80% test is only sometimes used as a practical evaluation of possible adverse impact (statistical significance tests are the most definitive standard – see Biddle, 2006).

[5] Richmond v. Croson, 488 U.S. 469, (1989).

[6] Wygant v. Jackson Board of Education, 476 U.S. 267 (1986).

[7] U.S. Constitution, Amendment 14: "All persons born or naturalized in the United States, and subject to the jurisdiction thereof, are citizens of the United States and of the State wherein they reside. No State shall make or enforce any law which shall abridge the privileges or immunities of citizens of the United States; nor shall any State deprive any person of life, liberty, or property, without due process of law; nor deny to any person within its jurisdiction the equal protection of the laws." The Equal Protection Clause limits only the powers of government bodies, and not the private parties on whom it provides equal protection.

[8] "Croson Studies" come from a 1989 Supreme Court decision that decided local governments could not establish preferences based upon race and gender unless there is proof of prior discrimination. Race is a suspect classification that is subject to strict judicial scrutiny. Richmond v. Croson, 488 U.S. 469, (1989). A "Croson Study" is used to justify minority business participation and that is narrowly tailored to remedy past discrimination.

[9] Dean, M. A., Bobko, P., & Roth, P. L. (2008). Ethnic and gender subgroup differences in assessment center ratings: A meta-analysis. *Journal of Applied Psychology, 93*, 685-691.

[10] City of Richmond v. Croson, 488 U.S. 469, 500 (1989).

[11] Id. at 498.

[12] Donze, P, L. (2000). Supreme court's denial of certiorari in Dallas fire fighters leaves unsettled the standard for compelling remedial interests. *Case Western Reserve Law Review, 50*, 759-796.

[13] Alphran, D.M. (2003). Proving discrimination after Croson and Adarand: If it walks like a duck, *U.S.F. Law Review, 37*, Rev. 887, 892-93.

[14] Engineering Contractors Assn. v. Metropolitan Dade County, 122 F.3d 895, 907 (11th Cir. 1997), cert. denied, 118 S. Ct. 1186 (1998) (quoting Ensley Branch, NAACP v. Seibels, 31 F.3d 1548, 1565 [11th Cir. 1994]); see also Contractors Assn. v. City of Phila., 6 F.3d 990, 1004 (3d Cir. 1993).

[15] Contractors Assn., 6 F.3d at 1005.

[16] Id. at 1003 (quoting Coral Constr. Co. v. King County, 941 F.2d 910, 919, 9th Cir. (1991).

[17] Contractors Assn., 6 F.3d at 1003; Coral Constr., 941 F.2d at 919; Engineering Contractors, 122 F.3d at 925; Concrete Works, Inc. v. City & County of Denver, 36 F.3d 1513, 1521 (10th Cir. 1994); Croson, 488 U.S. at 509.

[18] Adarand Constructors, Inc. v. Peña (63 U.S.L.W. 4523, U.S. June 12, 1995).

[19] U.S. Department of Justice (June 28, 1995). Legal guidance on the implications of the Supreme Court's decision in Adarand Constructors, Inc. v. Peña: Memorandum to general counsels (author).

[20] Gratz v. Bollinger, 539 U.S. 244 (2003).

[21] See, for example, pp. 22-24 in Biddle, D. (2006). *Adverse impact and test validation: A practitioner's guide to valid and defensible employment testing*, Second Edition. Burlington, VT: Gower Publishing Company; Biddle, R.E., (November 1995). Disparate impact reference

trilogy. *Labor Law Journal*; Biddle, R.E., (April 1996). The role of two statistical approaches in EEO cases. *Labor Law Journal.*

[22] The Lancaster mid-P correction should be used when computing the Fisher Exact Test. See http://www.disparateimpact.com for a web-based tool that can be used for calculating these adverse impact statistics.

[23] Sharkey v. Dixie Electric Membership Corporation, No. 06-31199, 5th Cir., (Jan. 23, 2008).

[24] Doe v. Kamehameha School/Bernice Pauahi Bishop Estate, 470 F. 3d 827, 840 (9th Cir., 2006).

[25] http://www.merriam-webster.com/dictionary/standard+score. See also: Francis, R. W. (Fall, 2006). Common errors in calculating final grades, *Thought & Action.*

[26] The means and standard deviations of the oral interview and written were 63.43 / 12.35 and 71.44 / 10.79 respectively for the Lieutenant process and 69.45 / 11.72 and 72.05 / 10.43 respectively for the Captain process.

[27] Johnson, J.W. & Lebreton, J.M. (2004). History and use of relative importance indices in organizational research. *Organizational Research Methods, 7* (3), 238-257.

[28] Biddle, R.E. (Spring, 1993). How to set cutoff scores for knowledge tests used in promotion, training, certification, and licensing. *Public Personnel Management.*

[29] A computer program for calculating the conditional SEM is available from the first author. Standard 2.14 of the APA Standards requires that conditional standard errors of measurement are used and reported if constancy of measurement error cannot be assumed (which is normally the case) and states, "Where cut scores are specified for selection or classification, the standard errors of measurement should be reported in the vicinity of each cut score" (American Educational Research Association, the American Psychological Association, and the National Council on Measurement in Education (1999), *Standards for Educational and Psychological Testing.* Washington DC: American Educational Research Association.

[30] U.S. v. South Carolina, 445 F. Supp. 1094 (D.S.C. 1977), aff'd U.S. Supreme Court (434 U.S., 1026, 1978).

[31] Isabel v. City of Memphis, 404 F. 3d 404, 6th Cir. (2005).

[32] For example, the Mann-Whitney U test can be used for evaluating whether the effect of ranking caused adverse impact against a group (see, for example, Bridgeport Guardians v. City of Bridgeport, 933 F.2d 1140, 1991; Bryan v. Koch, 492 F. Supp. 212, 220 (S.D.N.Y.), aff'd, 627 F.2d 612 (2d Cir.1980); and Fritz v. Baker, No. 87 Civ. 5662 (S.D.N.Y. Jan. 17, 1990) (1990 WL 3921), aff'd without opinion, 914 F.2d 239 (2d Cir. 1990). See an illustrated approach in Biddle, R.E. (Spring, 1993). How to set cutoff scores for knowledge tests used in promotion, training, certification, and licensing. *Public Personnel Management.*

[33] Vulcan Pioneers v. NJ Department of Civil Service, 625 F. Supp. 527, 539, NJ (1985).

[34] Guardians v. CSC of New York, 630 F.2d 79, 2nd Cir. (1980).

[35] In footnote 16 of Justice Ginsburg's dissenting opinion she states: "…Notably, the exams were never shown to be suitably precise to allow strict rank ordering of candidates. A difference of one or two points on a multiple-choice exam should not be decisive of an applicant's promotion chances if that difference bears little relationship to the applicant's qualifications for the job."

[36] The reliability of selection procedures justified on the basis of content validity should be a matter of concern to the user. Whenever it is feasible, appropriate statistical estimates should be made of the reliability of the selection procedure. (See 41 CFR Part 60-3.14[C][5])

[37] Griggs v. Duke Power, 401 U.S. 424, (1971).

[38] Title VII Section 2000e-2(l) Prohibition of discriminatory use of test scores: It shall be an unlawful employment practice for a respondent, in connection with the selection or referral of applicants or candidates for employment or promotion, to adjust the scores of, use different

cutoff scores for, or otherwise alter the results of, employment related tests on the basis of race, color, religion, sex, or national origin.

[39] Title VII Section 2000e-(k)(1)(A)(ii)(k) Burden of proof in disparate impact cases. (1) (A) An unlawful employment practice based on disparate impact is established under this subchapter only if – (i) a complaining party demonstrates that a respondent uses a particular employment practice that causes a disparate impact on the basis of race, color, religion, sex, or national origin and the respondent fails to demonstrate that the challenged practice is job related for the position in question and consistent with business necessity; or (ii) the complaining party makes the demonstration described in subparagraph (C) with respect to an alternative employment practice and the respondent refuses to adopt such alternative employment practice. (B) (i) With respect to demonstrating that a particular employment practice causes a disparate impact as described in subparagraph (A)(i), the complaining party shall demonstrate that each particular challenged employment practice causes a disparate impact, except that if the complaining party can demonstrate to the court that the elements of a respondent's decision making process are not capable of separation for analysis, the decision making process may be analyzed as one employment practice. (ii) If the respondent demonstrates that a specific employment practice does not cause the disparate impact, the respondent shall not be required to demonstrate that such practice is required by business necessity. (C) The demonstration referred to by subparagraph (A)(ii) shall be in accordance with the law as it existed on June 4, 1989, with respect to the concept of "alternative employment practice."

[40] Uniform Guidelines section 60.3B: Consideration of suitable alternative selection procedures. Where two or more selection procedures are available which serve the user's legitimate interest in efficient and trustworthy workmanship, and which are substantially equally valid for a given purpose, the user should use the procedure which has been demonstrated to have the lesser adverse impact. Accordingly, whenever a validity study is called for by these guidelines, the user should include, as a part of the validity study, an investigation of suitable alternative selection procedures and suitable alternative methods of using the selection procedure which have as little adverse impact as possible, to determine the appropriateness of using or validating them in accord with these guidelines. If a user has made a reasonable effort to become aware of such alternative procedures and validity has been demonstrated in accord with these guidelines, the use of the test or other selection procedure may continue until such time as it should reasonably be reviewed for currency. Whenever the user is shown an alternative selection procedure with evidence of less adverse impact and substantial evidence of validity for the same job in similar circumstances, the user should investigate it to determine the appropriateness of using or validating it in accord with these guidelines. This subsection is not intended to preclude the combination of procedures into a significantly more valid procedure, if the use of such a combination has been shown to be in compliance with the guidelines.

[41] Wards Cove Packing Co. v. Atonio, 490 U.S. 642 (1989)

[42] Albemarle, supra, at 425.

[43] Watson v. Fort Worth Bank & Trust, 487 U.S. 977 (1988).

[44] U.S. v. City of New York, 07-cv-2067, NGG, RLM (2009).

[45] See Biddle, 2006.

[46] Most CSEM methods require post-administration statistics for computation. However, the Lord-Keats method can be used for estimating CSEMs before a test has been administered (see Lord, F. M. [1984]. Standard errors of measurement at different ability levels. *Journal of Educational Measurement, 21*, 239-243).

[47] See, for example, Aguinis, H. (2004). *Test-score banding in human resource selection: legal, technical, and societal issues.* Praeger Publishers.

[48] See Biddle, D. (2008). Overview of C-SEM Methods. In Hurtz, G. M. (Chair), Integrating conditional standard errors of measurement into personnel selection practices. Symposium presented at the Annual Conference of the Society for Industrial and Organizational Psychology. San Francisco, CA, April 2008. See also, Biddle, D. Kuang, D. C.Y., & Higgins, J. (2007, March). Test use: ranking, banding, cutoffs, and weighting. Paper presented at the Personnel Testing Council of Northern California, Sacramento.

[49] See, for example: Cave, B. (2009, July 15). Ricci v. DeStefano Supreme Court finds that city discriminated against white employees. Labor and Employment Bulletin. Retrieved from http://www.bryancave.com/files/Publication/b1149e33-b667-436b-9cc4-d0d6f8ecbd27/Presentation/PublicationAttachment/352c8bfc-5f1f-4e53-8dd1-d1cb9e97cb56/LaborAlert7-15-09.pdf.
Hammell, J.W. & Curtin, Z. M. (2009, July 10). Ricci v. DeStefano: Supreme Court holds employer liable for trying to avoid claims of adverse-impact discrimination. Dorsey & Whitney LLP.
Retrieved from http://www.dorsey.com/ricci_analysis/

[50] U.S. v. City of New York (07-cv-2067, NGG, RLM), the court clarified that the Ricci case does not change the law as it relates to the burden-shifting requirements outlined in Title VII.

[51] Smith v. City of Jackson (03-1160, 544 U.S. 228, 2005, 351 F.3d 183, affirmed).

[52] Truesdell, W. H. (2003). *Secrets of affirmative action compliance* (6th ed.). The Management Advantage, Inc. (Author). p. 311. p. 311.

[53] Pedhazur, E. J. (1997). *Multiple regression in behavioral research: Explanation and prediction* (3rd ed). Wadsworth.

[54] OFCCP – U.S. Department of Labor (DOL), Employment Standards Administration, Office of Federal Contract Compliance Programs (November 16, 2004). *Interpreting Nondiscrimination Requirements of Executive Order 11246 With Respect to Systemic Compensation Discrimination* (Notice). Federal Register, Vol. 69, No. 220.

[55] OFCCP – U.S. Department of Labor (DOL), Employment Standards Administration, Office of Federal Contract Compliance Programs (June 16, 2006). *Interpreting Nondiscrimination Requirements of Executive Order 11246 With Respect to Systemic Compensation Discrimination* (Notice). Federal Register, Vol. 71, No. 116.

[56] 41 CFR 60.2.17(b)(3).

[57] Interpretive Standards, p. 35125.

[58] Rudebusch v. Hughes (313 F.3d 506 (9th Cir. 2002).

[59] Teske, J. (Fall 2003). The significance of statistical significance: Ninth Circuit clarifies usefulness of statistical evidence when implementing pay equity adjustments in Rudebusch v. Hughes. *Loyola of Los Angeles Law Review*. Rev. 153.

[60] Checking to see whether the model itself is significant can be accomplished by evaluating the ANOVA associated with the model; the strength of the regression model can be evaluated using the Adjusted R2 value; the predictive efficiency of the model can also be weighed by evaluating the Adjusted R2 as well as the degree of multicollinearity among the variables (which tends to inflate standard errors associated with predictions), as well as making sure that the most relevant (fundamental) pay factors are included in the model.

Appendix A - Choosing the Correct Tool for Adverse Impact Analyses

By Daniel A. Biddle, Ph.D. & Scott B. Morris, Ph.D.

> *This chapter describes the importance of using adjustments to the classic Fisher Exact Test when conducting adverse impact analysis. Please note that the procedures for calculating adverse impact that are advocated in this chapter can be accessed at no cost at http://www.disparateimpact.com.*

Overview

Since the Uniform Guidelines (1978) defined adverse impact as a *substantially different success rate* between two groups, 2 X 2 contingency tables have been used to evaluate whether the success rates between two groups on a selection procedure are statistically significant. While various statistical methods have been use to analyze 2 X 2 tables, the Fisher Exact Test (FET) has been widely adopted, especially when sample sizes are small. In more recent years, however, the statistical field at large has expressed concern regarding the default use of the FET when the strict *conditional assumptions* are not met and has proposed several alternative tests that meet a wider variety of 2 X 2 conditions. In addition, using modern data simulation techniques, the statistical field at large has confirmed that the FET is extremely conservative (*i.e.,* has a low Type I error rate) when compared to other available tests. This section reviews the use of the Lancaster (1961) mid-P as a reasonable solution for the challenges posed by the FET, and reviews the Type I and Type II error rates of this test compared to other alternatives.

Introduction

Since even before the 1978 publication of the Uniform Guidelines, adverse impact analyses have been conducted by employers to evaluate passing rate differences between subgroups on various practices, procedures, and tests. Methods for conducting such analyses have typically included impact ratio tests that comparatively evaluate the success rates between two groups (*e.g.,* the 80% Rule), statistical significance tests, and practical significance tests (Zedeck, 2009). While these methods have remained consistent, the actual tools (*i.e.,* statistical procedures) have evolved, with some exceptions.

This section discusses one such exception. While the medical and statistical fields have recently gravitated towards more powerful statistical techniques for analyzing 2 X 2 tables, and have grown to recognize serious limitations as well as constraints with the conventional Fisher Exact Test (FET) for analyzing 2 X 2 tables, the HR and personnel psychology fields have not been so quick to adapt. Specifically, the FET has been contested in the statistical literature since 1945 (Mehrotra, et. al., 2003) and most practitioners in the statistical field now reserve its use for situations where its *strict conditional assumptions* can be met and its conservative nature taken under consideration when evaluating its results (Upton, 1992; Lydersen, Fagerland, & Laake et. al., 2009).

The limitations with the FET (its conditional assumptions and conservative nature) that have already been revealed in the literature will be discussed, and a widely-accepted correction to the FET that produces more balanced results will be proposed. In addition, the results of our data simulation studies that reveal how the FET limitations specifically apply to adverse impact analyses will be provided. Our research confirms that one of the predominantly endorsed corrections to the FET, namely the Lancaster (1961) mid-P (LMP) adjustment, maintains the exactness of the FET in the sense that it is based on an exact discrete distribution rather than a normal approximation, but circumvents the major constraints and criticisms that apply to the FET. The theory surrounding the LMP adjustment will be discussed and the calculation process explained. Finally, the results of a Monte Carlo simulation where the FET, LMP, and commonly-applied Z-test (or equivalently, the Chi-Square test) are used in various common HR settings (where adverse impact tests are applied) will be discussed. Resources are also provided for computing a variety of 2 X 2 statistical analyses and recommendations are provided.

Statistical Significance Testing and Adverse Impact

A common statistical significance test for evaluating adverse impact is the Chi-square test, or equivalently, the Z-test for the difference between two proportions. The Chi-square test was originally developed by Karl Pearson in 1900 for analyzing 2 X 2 tables (two groups with two possible outcomes, such as pass or fail) to determine whether the *observed* frequencies in the table cells depart from the *expected* values at a level that exceeds what could be expected by chance alone (Plackett, 1984). Various corrections to the Chi-square test have been developed through the years, with the Yates and Cochran corrections being the most common. The Z-test for the difference between proportions, which is equivalent to Pearson's Chi-square test, has also been used with endorsement from federal enforcement agencies (OFCCP, 1993). Both the Chi-square test and the Z-test are based on large-sample theory and may not be appropriate in small samples. Specifically, when any of the expected cell frequencies are less than 5 (some even set this threshold at 10 – see Stokes, Davis, & Koch, 2001) the ability of the test to achieve the nominal Type I error rate is questionable. For this reason, the FET has typically been advised when the sample size falls below 30, or the expected numbers in any cell fall below 5 (a rule originally advanced by Fisher in 1925 but still often cited today).

Analyzing the statistical significance of a 2 X 2 table can be applied to virtually any type of employment transaction where the success rates of two groups can be compared – *e.g.*, the outcome of layoffs, demotions, hires, promotions, or other similar personnel transactions where there are only two possible outcomes (*e.g.*, promoted v. not promoted; hired v. not hired, etc.). While most techniques are designed for analyzing only a single 2 X 2 table, methods have also been developed for analyzing multiple 2 X 2 tables (with the Mantel-Haenszel technique being the most common – see Biddle, 2006).

As with any statistical significance test, researchers can choose between one-tail and two-tail alternatives as well as choose the statistical significance level of the test (*e.g., .05*). Hazelwood School District v. United States (1977) was the first U.S. Supreme Court case to pave the way for using the two-tail "2 or 3 standard deviation" rule when interpreting adverse impact findings, and nearly every EEO case since has used 2 standard deviation minimum threshold (equating to the .05 significance level) as the minimum threshold for showing adverse impact, coupled with a two-tail alternative. In the adverse impact context, a one-tail statistical test investigates the possibility of discrimination occurring in *just one direction* (*e.g.,* against women when making a men versus women comparison). A two-tail test takes the neutral assumption that discrimination *could have occurred in either direction* (*e.g.,* against men or against women) and hence spends its statistical power investigating discrimination in both directions.

Sampling Models for 2 X 2 Contingency Tables

Statistical significance tests involve a comparison of the observed result to what might have occurred due to chance. As such, each test requires an operational definition of chance results. In the context of 2 X 2 tables, three distinct models have been developed based on differing operational definitions. The choice among these models has been a matter of debate among statisticians for decades, and has important implications for the choice of the best statistical test (Camilli, 1990). Central to this debate are the *conditional assumptions*. The conditional assumptions pertain to whether the marginal totals of the table (either the row or column, or both) are assumed to be *fixed a priori* by the study design or whether they can be assumed to be drawn from a larger population. Collins and Morris (2008) summarize the three contexts (or "models") in which 2 X 2 tables can be evaluated, which are summarized briefly below.

   Model 1: Independence Trial (also referred to as "conditional" sampling in the 2 X 2 framework). All marginal totals are assumed to be *fixed in advance* (*i.e.,* proportion of each group and selection totals are fixed). The data are not viewed as a random sample from a larger population.

   Model 2: Comparative Trial (also referred to as a "binomial" sampling in the 2 X 2 framework). Either the row or column totals are fixed in advance. For example, the applicants are viewed as random samples from two distinct populations (*e.g.,* men and women). The proportion from each population is fixed (*i.e.,* the marginal proportion on one variable is assumed to be constant across replications). The second marginal proportion (*e.g.,* the marginal proportion of applicants who pass the selection test) is estimated from the sample data.

   Model 3: Double Dichotomy (also referred to as "multinomial" sampling in the 2 X 2 framework). In this model, neither the row nor the column marginal totals are assumed to be fixed. Applicants are viewed as a random sample from a population that is characterized by two dichotomous characteristics. No purposive sampling or assignment to groups is used, and the proportion in each group, as well as the success rate can vary across samples.

   These three models can be summarized as having "fixed," "mixed," and "free" marginal assumptions. As will be discussed in greater detail later, the current state of the statistical and medical research literature holds that the various 2 X 2 tests available fit these three models with more or less precision.

An additional issue that is sometimes raised regarding the use of 2 X 2 analyses in the EEO context is the fact that most analyses are conducted retroactively. It is not recommended, however, to view this as a deciding factor regarding which sampling methodology to apply because the selection model (*i.e.,* how the data were collected in reality) should dictate which statistical model is most appropriate, not the fact that the data are retrospective.

Balancing Type I and Type II Errors

One of the most important considerations when choosing a statistical test – especially one that will result in making a high-stakes finding such as adverse impact – is how the test balances Type I versus Type II statistical errors. In the adverse impact context, Type I errors (*i.e.,* rejecting the null hypothesis when the null hypothesis is true) occur when the test results indicate there is a statistically significant difference between the groups (*i.e.,* adverse impact) when there is no difference in the population. Defendants (employers) may be more concerned with this type of error than plaintiffs. Type II errors (*i.e.,* failing to reject the null hypothesis when the null hypothesis is false) occur when the test results indicate there is a not statistically significant difference between the groups (*i.e.,* no adverse impact) when there *actually is* a difference in the population. Plaintiffs may be more concerned with this type of error than defendants. The *error rate* associated with Type I errors refers to the rate at which the test *falsely concludes statistically significant adverse impact exists*. The error rate associated with Type II errors refers to the rate at which the test *misses adverse impact when it actually exists.*

Beyond the typical differences between employer and plaintiff concerns regarding the types of errors that may occur when conducting an adverse impact analysis, the *context* in which the analysis is made should also be considered. For example, in a typical "reactive" situation where the adverse impact analyses are being made in response to litigation or enforcement, employers might be very concerned with either error type if the at-issue test has been thoroughly validated. In this same situation, however, plaintiff groups or enforcement agencies may be concerned about wasting time and resources on cases that may be based on a false finding of adverse impact (*i.e.,* a Type I error). When employers conduct proactive analyses, the concern over making either error type is not great (because no action is required).

Because making a false conclusion of adverse impact and missing adverse impact are both "errors" that should be avoided, selecting a statistical test that adequately balances the two error types is critical. For example, if an employer uses a test with low statistical power (*i.e.,* one that has a high Type II error rate), they may "miss" adverse impact that actually exists. On the flipside, using a test with a high Type I error rate may falsely conclude adverse impact exists and raise concern when none was necessary.

Exact v. Approximation Techniques for Analyzing Adverse Impact

An additional consideration that should be weighed when choosing a statistical test for analyzing 2 X 2 tables is selecting between an *exact* versus an *approximation* test. An exact test operates by summing the probability values from the observed 2 X 2 table and the probability values from all tables that are more extreme – *i.e.,* all possible tables that have probabilities equal to or less than the first observed table. In this way, the probability values are obtained from the *hypergeometric distribution* rather than the approximate normal distribution, which is a pre-assembled probability table designed to simulate these probability values.

Either the exact or approximate test can be computed using a one-tail or two-tail test. A one-tail test is more powerful than a two-tail test when investigating adverse impact because it requires only a 5% level of significance level in *one direction* in the probability distribution, whereas the two-tail test allows 2.5% on each end of the probability distribution (*i.e.,* it assumes that the focal group's success rate could have been either more or less than the reference group's).

Using the exact method followed by the FET, the total probability value for the first tail is calculated by summing all probability values from each hypothetical 2 X 2 table that is *more extreme* (*i.e.,* fewer passing) than the original table, until there are 0 successes in the disadvantaged group. To compute the second tail exact probability, the iteration process is repeated but in the *opposite direction* (*i.e.,* increasing the success rate of the group that started with the highest success rate one at a time until either group reaches 0 unsuccessful subjects). Then the probability values from each iterated table that is *equal to or less than* the probability value of the first observed table are summed (Agresti, 1990, p. 62).

For example, the probability value of a 2 X 2 table where 22 men applied for a position and 14 were hired and 8 were not (a 64% success rate), and 9 women applied with 2 hired and 7 not hired (a 22% success rate) is .0383. The full set of possible outcomes and their probabilities are given in Table 12-1. The next iteration in this same direction (making it less favorable for women) is 15 men hired and 7 not hired, and 1 women hired and 8 not hired (with a corresponding probability of .0051). The next iteration is 16 men hired and 6 not hired, and 0 women hired and 9 not hired (with a corresponding probability of .0002). Summing these three probability values produces the total one tail probability value of .0436.

The second tail probability is calculated by iterations going the other direction (increasing the number of women hired while decreasing the number of men hired, one at a time until 0 is reached for either group, while keeping the total hired the same), and only summing probability values of iterated tables that are equal to or less than the original table. Following this method, there are only two 2 X 2 tables that qualify to include in the second tail probability: (1) all 9 women hired with 7 men hired and 15 not hired (a probability value of .0006) and (2) 8 women hired, 1 not hired, 8 men hired and 14 not hired (a probability value of .0096). The next 2 X 2 table in order (7 women hired, 2 not hired, 9 men hired and 13 not hired) has a probability value (.0596), which is not equal to or lower than the probability value of the original table (.0383), so it is not included. Adding the probabilities of the relevant tables in both tails produces a total, two-tail probability value of 0.0538 (.0436 from the first tail plus the second tail, which is .0006 + .0096 = 0.0102), which just barely misses the .05 significance level.

Number of Women Hired	Hypergeometric Probability
0	0.0002
1	0.0051
2	0.0383
3	0.139
4	0.2711
5	0.2957
6	0.1807
7	0.0596
8	0.0096
9	0.0006

Table 12-1 Probability Outcomes Assuming Fixed Marginal Frequencies

Limitations of the Fisher Exact Test for Adverse Impact Analysis

Shortly after Ronald Fisher framed his exact test (Fisher, 1925), some statisticians began challenging its use across different 2 X 2 scenarios (*e.g.,* Barnard, 1945) as well as its conservative nature (see Yates, 1984). While these early contests were theoretical in nature, more recent criticisms have been based on the results of modern data simulation analyses that provide a more in depth scan of the statistical behavior of various 2 X 2 tests (Sekhon, 2005; Collins & Morris, 2008; Crans & Shuster, 2008; Lin & Yang, 2009; Lydersen, et. al., 2009). These recent studies have revealed two major limitations of the FET: the fact that its strict conditional assumptions are *rarely met in actual practice* and the conservative nature of the FET. Each is discussed below.

The Conditional Assumptions of the FET

The first limitation deals with the *conditional assumptions* required for correctly applying the FET. The statistical field has (especially more recently), convened at a consensus that the FET can *only be accurately applied in the first model* – the Independence Trial Model (fixed margins). Because this model does not represent typical personnel selection data, "there is reason to question the appropriateness of the FET for adverse impact analysis" (Collins & Morris, 2008). The appropriateness of treating the margins as fixed has been at the heart of much of the debate that has surrounded the FET for over 50 years.

Some statisticians contend that the Independence Trial Model requires that "both of the margins in a 2 X 2 table are fixed by construction – *i.e.,* both the treatment and outcome margins are *fixed a priori*" (Sekhon, 2005; see also Romualdi, et. al., 2001; Hirji et. al., 1991; and D'Agostino, et. al., 1988). In other words, for the conditional assumptions of the Independence Trial Model ("fixed margins") to be met, the investigator needs to identify the marginal totals of both the rows and columns *prior to conducting the experiment that will produce the numbers within each.* It is common in experimental research to specify in advance the relative numbers in each treatment conditions, thereby fixing the row marginals. Alternatively, retrospective research will often select a specified number of cases within each outcome category, thereby fixing the column marginals. However, it would be unusual to specify the frequency of both the predictor and outcome before collecting any data (Gimpel, 2007). While recommended by some, this condition seems to be only rarely met in practice.

Collins and Morris (2008) argued that the data available for adverse impact analysis is rarely consistent with the fixed marginal assumptions. Research in personnel selection does not involve the kinds of purposive sampling (*e.g.,* random assignment) that make it reasonable in experimental designs to treat the group size as fixed. The number of applicants in minority and majority groups is unlikely to be consistent across samples. Collins and Morris argued that selection decisions based on a fixed cutoff score are best represented by the Double Dichotomy Model, with neither marginal fixed. Other kinds of decision rules, such as top-down selection, may reasonably be viewed as having fixed column marginals (*i.e.,* fixed number who are selected), but not fixed row marginals (*i.e.,* fixed number of minority applicants).

It is tempting to view promotion or layoff decisions as involving a fixed pool of candidates (and therefore fixed number of minority applicants), and a fixed number of persons selected. This might lead one to view the Independence Trial as the most appropriate model in this situation. However, once the set of individuals is fixed, it becomes unclear what comprises the sample space on which probabilities are defined. That is, in order to make a probability statement or compute a *p-value*, it is necessary to articulate what other results could have possibly resulted from the analysis due to chance. The sample space of significance tests is often conceptualized in terms of possible random samples from a larger population, but this approach does not apply if one treats the set of observed scores as fixed.

Some proponents of the FET (*e.g.,* Yates, 1984) argue for defining the sample space in terms of alternate assignment of persons to treatment conditions. In this approach, the set of individuals is fixed, but alternate results can be conceived of as resulting from the process of random assignment. While this may be a reasonable approach in the context of experiments, the concept of random assignment does not seem relevant to the analysis of adverse impact.

Yates (1984) articulated a completely different justification for conditioning on the marginals, based on the idea of conditional inference. The argument is that when evaluating the null hypothesis, judgments should be informed by what is known about ancillary statistics that do not directly impact the hypothesis being tested. In the context of adverse impact, the argument would be that the proportion of minorities in the sample, and the overall selection rate, provide essentially no information about degree to which selection rates differ across groups, and therefore should be treated an ancillary statistics. Conditioning on the marginals is appealing, because it separates the evaluation of adverse impact from the probability of obtaining a particular marginal distribution. After all, why should the evidence of adverse impact be treated as stronger or weaker just because there are more or fewer minorities in the sample?

By conditioning on the marginal frequencies, the test evaluates the probability of the data in relation to comparable settings (*i.e.,* those with the same number of minority applicants and the same overall selection rate).

Although the idea of conditioning on ancillary statistics has appeal to many statisticians (*e.g.,* Upton, 1992), this approach has been criticized by others. Little (1989) showed that the marginal frequencies are not fully ancillary in the 2 X 2 case, and therefore do contribute some information about the null hypothesis. More importantly, Gastwirth (1995) showed that this is particularly problematic in the context of adverse impact analysis. For statistics to be ancillary, the process determining the fixed marginal counts *must be independent of the process under study* (Gastwirth, 1995). However, employment data analyzed in adverse impact settings is often the result of a *sequence* of employment decisions, with each case being dependent on previous employer-decisions made further downstream in the process.

Take for example a promotion decision. The set of candidates considered for a promotion decision will have been previously selected using some screening procedure that may have considered some of the same factors that that are used to make the promotion decision. Therefore, the prior selection process, which determined the number of minority applicants, will not be independent of the success ratio of the promotion decision, the parameter of interest. Gastwirth (1995) advises checking this assumption before calculating conditional tests in situations where the available sample results from a previous selection process that may be *affected by the same factors involved in the process being examined* (because the success ratio of the hiring rates and promotion rates would be correlated).

An additional challenge with meeting the conditional assumptions of promotional settings is that employers may first try to fill promotional opportunities with in-house employees from a *variety* of lower positions (with each position having different potential weight and availability percentages for each group), and then turn to outside resources (where the comparison group is external availability, which is clearly binomial) if the slot cannot be filled internally. Situations like these blur the "fine line" between "fixed," "mixed," and "free" marginal assumptions.

Even in layoff (RIF) situations, where it appears that the row and column totals may be fixed in advance, sometimes the decision-making process is *continually flexible* until the final decision list has been made, thus weakening the strict conditional assumptions tied to the FET. In addition, the numbers and success/failure ratios in the process often depend on the employer's previous selection and promotional practices.

When applying the three models to typical adverse impact analyses (*e.g.,* hiring, promotion, terminations, layoffs, etc.), it becomes clear that the conditional assumptions of the FET will only rarely be met. And, when the conditions are not met, many statisticians recommend the use of an unconditional test, such as Barnard's test adopted in StatXact® or the Boschloo test widely advocated in the medical research field. Alternatively, Lancaster's mid-P (LMP), while it is based on the underlying mechanics and probability calculations of the (conditional) FET, includes an adjustment that accurately emulates the results of unconditional exact test outputs (Lin & Yang, 2009; Hirji, 2006; Agresti, 2007; Lydersen, 2009; and Hwang & Yang, 2001).

.

The debate over the use of conditional versus unconditional tests has been going on for decades, and is not likely to be resolved any time in the near future. The goal here is more modest – to evaluate the use of an alternate significance test as a decision-making aid in evaluating adverse impact. In this context, of primary concern are the error rates for the decision rule. Specifically, the concern with the likelihood of false-positives (Type I errors) and false-negatives (Type II errors) will be addressed. This leads to the second, and more important criticism of the FET - that the test is overly conservative.

The Conservative Nature of the FET

The second issue with the FET pertains to its *unnecessary conservative* nature. The statistical field at large holds that the FET is too conservative (see Reference Authorities Regarding the Limitations of the Fisher Exact Test in the Reference section of this book for a partial listing of citations that hold this position). In this context, *conservative* refers to the fact that the desired significance level, for example 0.05, cannot be attained exactly due to the discrete distribution of the data, and lesser (sometimes much less) values must be used.

Discreteness occurs because, for small sample sizes, the number of possible outcomes considered by the FET is small (Agresti, 2007). As a result, the *p-value* can take on only a limited number of possible values, and often none of the possible outcomes will have *p-values* close to but less than the nominal significance level. Therefore, the obtained probability of a Type I error will be less than the nominal alpha level, often considerably lower.

Consider the example described in Table 12-1. For these marginal frequencies, the test will be significant ($\alpha = .05$) if the number of women hired is 0, 1, 8 or 9. Less extreme results would have *p-values* greater than .05 (*i.e.,* .054 for 2 women hired and .113 for 7 women hired), and therefore would not be classified as significant. The probability of obtaining one of these results (*i.e.,* 0, 1, 8 or 9) under the null hypothesis is .015 – *i.e.,* only about 1.5% of the probability distribution space is covered by these 4 possible outcomes, which is considerably lower than the nominal significance level (.05). That is, if the test were applied repeatedly in this setting (with the same fixed marginals), the Type I error rate would be .015 rather than .05.

It is important to note that the problem is not with the *p-values*, which are accurate given the conditional assumptions, but rather results from the use of a decision rule where the *p-value* is compared to $\alpha = .05$. Upton (1992) argued that the conservativeness of the FET is due to the common practice of fixing the nominal significance level at 0.05. For example, if one were to instead set $\alpha = .055$, the results with 2 women hired would also be significant and the Type I error rate (.054) would be quite close to the nominal level. Thus, the problem of conservatism can be avoided by directly interpreting *p-values*, rather than reporting results as significant or non-significant based on a fixed alpha level. However, in Title VII situations (as well as most statistical research fields), fixed significance levels are the required standard, so the detrimental consequences of discreteness remain.

This limitation results in the FET having "less power than conditional mid-P tests and unconditional tests" while these other tests "generally have higher power yet still preserve test size" (Lydersen, et. al, 2009). For this limitation alone, several statisticians have recommended that the "traditional FET should practically never be used" (Lydersen, et. al, 2009) because the "actual significance level (or size) being much less than the nominal level" (Lin & Yang, 2009). Agresti (2007) recommends using the mid-P adjustment even in situations where the fixed marginal assumptions can be met "because the actual error rates [of the FET] is *smaller than the intended one*" (p. 48). Other categorical statistical books also recommend the mid-P as an effective way to meet the challenges offered by a discrete distribution when trying to apply a statistical test to correctly answer the .05 question (*e.g.*, Simonoff, 2003; Rothman, 1986; Hirji, 2006).

While these issues have been percolating in the statistical journals for decades, the more recent application of Monte Carlo simulations conducted on the FET now provide a more complete insight into just how conservative the FET can be, with estimates ranging between 40% below the desired .05 significance level (with small sample sizes around 25) to 15-30% under the .05 level with larger sample sizes ranging between 75 and 125 (and even up to 200) (Lydersen, et. al., 2009). Stating these *p-values* in standard deviation units, the Lydersen study reveals that the effect of these limitations inherent to the FET sets a 2.5 standard deviation threshold (in small samples 10 and smaller), rather than the desired 2.0 threshold, a 2.18 standard deviation threshold in samples around 25, and a standard deviation threshold of about 2.1 in larger samples between 75 and 200. So, when practitioners think they are using a 2.0 standard deviation threshold test to analyze adverse impact, the conservative nature of the FET has a net effect of *setting the bar much higher*.

While the FET has nearly always been regarded as conservative in the literature, several data simulation studies have researched the effectiveness of various 2 X 2 table tests with respect to Type I and Type II errors and adherence to the desired nominal statistical levels (*i.e.*, .05 alpha level). These studies provide insight into the extent of the FET's conservative nature compared to other 2 X 2 tests. Our research identified a total of nine studies which collectively reviewed 22 different 2 X 2 test methods for free, mixed, and fixed marginal settings (see Table 12-2). Seven of the 2 X 2 tests listed in Table 12-2 (P, U, UP, Z, Y, PCX, and PCX1) are all based on large sample approximation theory (several of these tests are the same or similar algebraically, but were referenced separately to maintain identity with the originating study). While some of the studies (*e.g.*, Mehrotra, Chan, & Berger, 2003) reviewed the performance of various 2 X 2 tests in unconditional settings (mixed or free margins), each study included an evaluation of the unadjusted FET by means of comparison to demonstrate the difference between these various tests in various 2 X 2 settings. The summary results of these studies are provided in Table 12-2.

Comparative Studies Evaluating Various 2x2 Tests (including the FET), 1994-2009

Study/Year	Tests Evaluated	Conclusions/Recommendations	Recommend Uncorrected FET
Berger (1994)	F, B, Bc, P, Z, Pc, U, Z, & Uc.	B and Bc tests are best in unconditional settings.	Not for most 2 X 2 situations; only if samples are pre-determined in advance of study.
Campbell (2007)	F, PCX, PCX1, F2, MP2, LMP	Use the PCX1 for free/mixed margin 2 X 2 tables where all expected numbers are at least 1; otherwise use the FET.	Only if both margins are fixed by the investigator (however, "the research design is rarely used").
Collins & Morris (2008)	F, UP, Z, Y	The P test is preferred over the F.	No, because of overly conservative Type I error rates and substantially lower power.
Crans & Shuster (2008)	F, A-FET	FET results were continually below the desired .05 level (less than 0.035 for nearly all samples < 50 and did not approach 0.05 for n > 100).	No, adjustment to nominal significance level needed (A-FET test is proposed).
Fuchs (2001)	F, A, ET, SR, UM	There is no reason to use the very conservative exact test. The SR and UMPU are not recommended. A-MET and ET tests are permissible.	No. There is no justified reason to use the uncorrected FET.
Hwang & Yang (2001)	P, BB, F, PCX, LMP	Study results justify using LMP.	No, expected p-values or LMP are preferred.
Lin & Yang (2009)	F, CIP, LMP, BB, SS	The CIP F is recommended over F. LMP and BB depend on the nominal level and imbalance of sample sizes. BB and CI adjusted BB preferred.	No, CI modified F, LMP, or BB should be used.
Lydersen, Fagerland, & Laake (2009)	PCX, B, F, LMP	Exact unconditional tests are ideal; the B unconditional test is preferred, or can be approximated by LMP (for small samples) or PCX (in large samples). Traditional F should practically never be used	No, the F not recommended because it is unnecessarily conservative with lower power than conditional LMP/unconditional tests.
Mehrotra, Chan, & Berger (2003)	F, D, BB, P, U	B test is more powerful and preferred over the F test. The modified B, P, and modified P may be used for all sample sizes. U and modified P for equal sample sizes are more powerful than F over most (but not all) points. (Comparisons are made in the context	No, the B unconditional test outperforms the F and is recommended

Notes: A-FET - Adjusted F (see Crans & Shuster (2008); A-MET Test (Adjusted-More Extreme Tables) (see Fuchs, 2001); B - Boschloo's (1970) Test; BB Berger & Boos Test (1994); Bc - CI-Modified B Test (see Berger, 1994); CIP - CI p-value (see Lin & Yang, 2009); D - Santner & Snell's Exact Unconditional Test (see Mehrotra, Chan, & Berger, 2003); ET - The Randomized Critical Region of the Equal-Tails Test (ET test) (see Fuchs, 2001); F - Fisher's Exact Test (unadjusted); F2 - Fisher Exact Test (by doubling the one-sided P value - see Campbell, 2007); LMP - mid-P Fisher Exact Test (using conventional two-tail computation - see StatXact, 2009); MP2 - mid-P Fisher Exact Test (by doubling the one-sided mid-P level - see Campbell, 2007); P - Suissa & Shuster's (1985) Z-pooled Test (see Berger, 1994); Pc - CI-Modified Z-pooled Test (see Berger, 1994); PCX - Pearson's Chi-Squared Test with one degree of freedom (see Campbell, 2007); PCX1 - Chi-Square N-1 Test (with one degree of freedom - see Campbell, 2007); SR - The Single-Randomization Test (see Fuchs, 2001); U - Suissa & Shuster's (1985) Z-unpooled Test (see Berger, 1994); Uc - CI-Modified Z-unpooled Test (see Berger, 1994); UM - UMPU Test (see Fuchs, 2001); UP - Upton's Chi-Square (see Collins & Morris, 2008); Y - Yates's Chi-Square Test (see Collins & Morris, 2008); Z - Z-Test (see Collins & Morris, 2008).

Table 12-2 Studies Evaluating 2 X 2 Tests (including the FET), 1994-2009

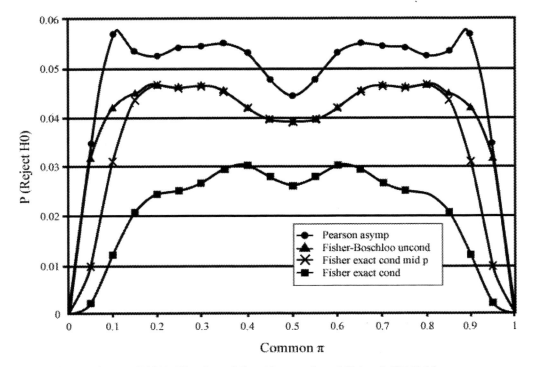

Figure 12-1 Lyderson (2009): The Actual Significance Level Using 2 X 2 Tables

Figure 11-1 shows how the four different 2 X 2 tests (the Z-Test, the Boschloo exact unconditional test, the LMP, and FET, in this order) are able to track with the desired .05 significance level. While the Z-Test trends slightly over the .05 level, the FET consistently stays between .02 and .03. The unconditional exact test and LMP share the same trend in between these two extremes.

Lydersen concluded that unconditional tests preserve the significance level and generally are more powerful than the FET for moderate to small samples. He also advocates using unconditional tests in most 2 X 2 situations (particularly because unconditional tests more appropriately fit the circumstances surrounding 2 X 2 analyses) – especially now that many commercially available software programs facilitate unconditional tests. Lydersen also supports using the FET with mid-P adjustment and notes that it gives about the same results as an unconditional test. He concludes by stating, "Unconditional tests and the mid-P approach ought to be used more than they now are. The traditional Fisher's exact test should practically never be used" (p. 1159).

The Crans and Shuster (2008) Study. The work completed by Crans and Shuster was directly targeted towards determining the extent of the conservative nature of the FET (hence the title, "How conservative is Fisher's exact test? A quantitative evaluation of the two-sample comparative binomial trial"). Their work concluded that the two-sided test results of the FET for sample sizes of 10-125 were in fact conservative, attaining actual test sizes much less than 0.05 (the test results of the FET was less than 0.035 for nearly all sample sizes below 50 and did not approach 0.05 even for sample sizes over 100). They concluded that the conservativeness of the FET, as evaluated by how close the actual test size is compared with the desired significance level of 0.05, "is indeed quite conservative, even for sample sizes greater than 100 subjects per group." One of the figures (see Figure 12-2) produced in their research shows the null power function of the FET (for sample sizes of 10, 25, 50, and 100).

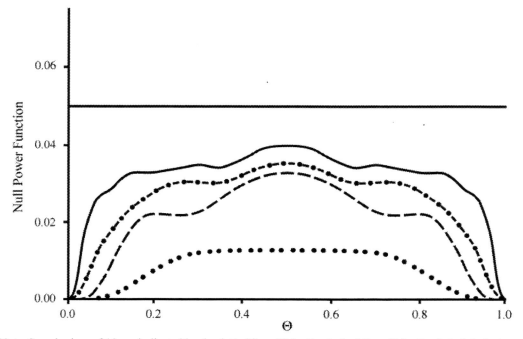

Note: Sample sizes of 10 are indicated by the dotted line, 25 by the dashed line, 50 by the dotted-dashed line, and 100 by the solid line.

Figure 12-2 Crans & Shuster (2008): The FET Null Power Function

Figure 12-2 demonstrates just how far below the desired .05 level of significance the FET can be – especially with smaller sample sizes. Figure 12-3 (also from their research) demonstrates the same phenomena in a slightly different way.

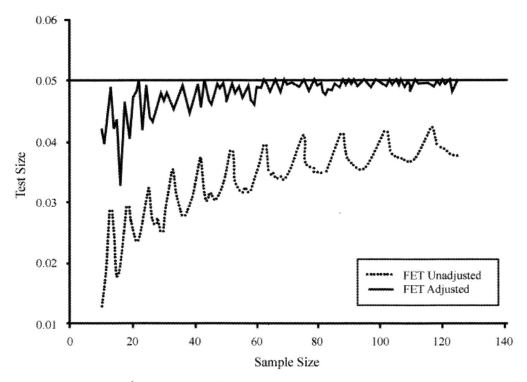

Figure 12-3 Crans & Shuster (2008): FET Test Sizes Using a 0.05 Significance Level

The dashed line represents the FET which is shown to be well below the desired .05 level of significance based on various sample size configurations. The solid line represents a corrected version of the FET that operates much like a mid-P adjustment.

The Crans and Shuster study identified that the actual size of the FET ranged from 0.013 to 0.043 for sample sizes of 10-125 per group. The smallest values were observed with samples sizes smaller than 25, where the actual size of FET was always less than 0.03 (40% below the desired nominal level). For larger sample sizes (100-125), the FET test size ranged from 0.036 to 0.042. Their conclusion was that the unadjusted FET remained conservative even when the sample sizes reach 125 per group and should not be used unless appropriately adjusted.

The Collins and Morris (2008) Study. Collins and Morris noted that much of the debate surrounding the appropriateness of the FET has been framed in the context of experimental research that differs in important ways from the types of data available for adverse impact analysis. They explored the performance of alternate significance tests in the context of typical employment practices. For employment decisions based on a test with a fixed cutoff score, the data are best represented by the Double Dichotomy Model. A simulation was conducted using this model with small sample sizes (20 to 100). Consistent with the preceding research, the FET demonstrated conservative Type I error rates and power considerably lower than the Z-test for the difference in proportions. Although the Z-test produced Type I error rates in excess of .05 under some conditions, the magnitude of the inflation was typically small, except in the smallest sample size condition where larger errors were found. Considering the balance of both Type I and Type II errors, slight inflation of Type I error rates seems acceptable if it is accompanied by substantial gains in power.

For other types of employment decisions (*e.g.,* top-down selection, banding), Collins and Morris (2008) argued that none of the three statistical models accurately represent the nature of the data. They reported results from simulations that directly modeled these kinds of decisions, finding a similar pattern of results.

These three studies provide a thorough review of the FET's conservative nature when it comes to reviewing adverse impact analyses using the .05 level of significance. Similar research findings (and comparisons between the FET and other techniques) have also been conducted by others with very similar findings (Lin & Yang, 2009; Sekhon, 2005).

Admissibility of the FET in Title VII Litigation

The U.S. Supreme Court case, <u>Daubert v. Merrell Dow Pharmaceuticals</u> (1993), established the current standard for admitting expert testimony in federal courts. In Daubert, seven members of the Court agreed that expert evidence offered in federal litigation needs make use of "scientific methodology" to formulate and test hypotheses to prove or falsify the hypothesis. One requirement they court instated with this standard is that the investigative tools need to have a known or potential error rate and need to be "reliably applied to the facts at hand." For decades now, the courts have established that the .05 threshold has been set in stone as the standard for identifying and deliberating adverse impact. Choosing a test that can accurately set this .05 standard – not claim the standard yet deliver something higher (such as the FET) – is key in choosing an effective legal strategy.

The Court also ruled that the theory or technique used must be *falsifiable, refutable, and testable, as well as subjected to peer review and publication.* An additional evaluation criteria is the "degree to which the theory and technique is *generally accepted* by a relevant scientific community [emphasis added]." The concern about the FET with respect to this criteria is that, while it has enjoyed a long stent in the EEO enforcement community, it has recently been subjected to serious waves of challenge (*e.g.,* Agresti, 2007; Agresti & Gottard, 2007; Collins & Morris, 2008; Crans & Shuster, 2008; Lin & Yang, 2009; Lydersen, et. al., 2009) and, in many communities, left aside for other more powerful techniques (*e.g.,* Berger, 1994, 1996; Boschloo, 1970; Collins & Morris, 2008; Crans & Shuster, 2008; Lin & Yang, 2009). Because of these recent developments, practitioners are advised to update their adverse impact techniques to incorporate the techniques advocated here.

The uncorrected FET has been used (by default) for years in Title VII litigation; so has the Z-test (or Chi-Square) in both corrected and uncorrected forms. However, the FET does not appear to have been specifically challenged (compared to alternatives) under the more recent criticisms that have been leveled in more recent years. This is likely because, for such challenge to occur, the rare situation would need to emerge where a litigated adverse impact case is significant using one test and not significant using the other, and each test subjected through the legal choosing process (where the battle of experts ensues and the judge decides on the appropriateness of one test over the other given the situation at hand). Given the background described above, the FET would not likely survive a Daubert challenge. However, if a situation emerged where the opposing experts in an EEO case agreed upon the 2 X 2 sampling circumstances on the case, one of the 2 X 2 models could be mutually adapted. Even if the situation was as close to a conditional circumstance as possible, deciding whether to correct for discreteness might still be an issue of contention (see Agresti, 2007, p. 49).

With over 20 articles published in statistical research journals (see Table 12-2) and the majority of categorical statistical texts over the last 10 years giving only *conditional use* permission to the FET (a circumstance rarely met in adverse impact settings), thoroughly documenting the FET's conservative nature, and recommending or endorsing other techniques like the Z-test, LMP, or unconditional exact methods (such as the Barnard or Boschloo tests), employers would be much safer in litigation settings using the same.

Beyond the legal implications and challenges that may come from analysis systems that use the FET, HR professionals as "liability analysts" are likely to want to use more balanced methods that better fit all three 2 X 2 situations and do not produce such conservative results. The mid-P provides one alternative that fits all three 2 X 2 analysis conditions; the Barnard (1945) and Boschloo test (Boschloo, 1970; Berger, 1994) can provide highly accurate and balanced tests for the "mixed" and "free" 2 X 2 situations.

Lancaster's mid-P (LMP) as the Solution

For the reasons discussed above, it is recommended that employers/practitioners use the Lancaster mid-P correction to the FET, which effectively corrects the FET to more accurately reflect the probability values of the adverse impact case analyzed in *any* of the three 2 X 2 models. While unconditional exact tests (like the Barnard or Boschloo tests) can be correctly used for mixed and free marginal situations, they were not tailored for "truly" fixed marginal situations.

The mid-P, however, can be used for all three 2 X 2 situations. This is because in the clearly conditional "fixed" model, the LMP provides a correction for discreteness that adjusts the FET to a less conservative alpha level (Agresti, 2007). In mixed and free marginal settings, the functional mechanics of the LMP result in computed values for various settings that accurately emulate the results of unconditional exact tests.

For example, the Lin and Yang (2009) study (set in the context of a free marginal model) revealed correlations between the LMP and the Boschloo unconditional exact test sizes exceeding $r = .99$. The two tests also produced very similar alpha levels in simulation cases where the nominal alpha level was set to .05 (with nine sample size configurations between 10-10 and 40-160 for focal and reference groups), with average alpha levels of .0508 (1.6% over the .05 level) and .0468 (6.3% under the .05 level) for the LMP and Boschloo unconditional exact tests. By comparison, the FET produced an average alpha level of .0337 in these same scenarios (33% below the desired .05 level). When comparing the performance of the three tests across multiple scenarios with specified nominal alpha levels of .01, .05, and .10, the LMP showed the closest adherence to the desired alpha level, with an average alpha of 99.53% of the specified alpha level across the various scenarios. By comparison, the FET, Boschloo, and Z-test were 64.43%, 91.03%, and 123.05% of the specified alpha levels under these same conditions.

The versatile nature of the LMP is a key characteristic for practitioners and employers. One can only imagine the difficulties of having to go through a decision tree to choose which of the three models is most appropriate for each and every adverse impact analysis, then only having to defend exactly which margin was fixed, mixed, or free in litigation or enforcement settings. In addition, practitioners would be faced with choosing between the various 22 tests that are available for analyzing 2 X 2 tables, with strengths and limitations in each. Then one needs to choose whether any corrections will be made for discreteness. Our research and data simulation (below) has shown that the LMP is highly balanced (between Type I and Type II errors) and has been well supported in the literature for analyzing 2 X 2 tables in a variety of adverse impact situations.

Computational Mechanics of the LMP

Perhaps one of the reasons that the LMP received such early adoption was its ease of computation. The LMP is simply computed by subtracting ½ of the probability value of the first (observed) 2 X 2 table and then summing the *p-values* from the remaining tables that are equal to or smaller than the first.

Using the adverse impact example above (where 22 men applied for a position and 14 were hired and 8 were not and 9 women applied with 2 hired and 7 were not), the probability value of the first (observed) table is .0383 (and one-half of this value is 0.01915). Adding the *p-values* from the remaining tables (following the same procedure described in the example above – *i.e.,* only summing probability values of iterated tables that are equal to or less than the original table, before reducing it by one half) results in a significant two-tail LMP value of 0.035 (compared with the non-significant FET probability value of 0.0538).

Note that LMP probability values can also be computed from the outputs produced by many existing software programs that follow the conventional cumulative probability procedure described in our example. This can be accomplished by starting with the conventional two-tailed FET probability, and then subtracting from this the probability value of the observed 2 X 2 table. Functions for computing the hypergeometric probability for the observed table are available from many statistical programs. In Excel, the hypergeometric probability can be computed using the function HYPGEOMDIST (h_{min}, n_{min}, h_{tot}, N), where h_{min} is the number hired from the minority group, n_{min} is the number of minority applicants, h_{tot} is the total number hired from both groups, and N is the total sample size, Using the above example, this would be HYPGEOMDIST (2,9,16,31) = .0383. The mid-P has also been included in several commercially-available software programs as well as several of the unconditional tests (Berger, 2010; StatXact, 2009). Free on-line calculators are also available that provide the LMP and Z-test (Abramson, 2004; Biddle Consulting Group, 2011).

While the simple act of subtracting ½ of the first observed probability value may seem overly-simplistic, the theory behind the mid-P has been proven by its originator (Lancaster, 1961) and further tested and justified by others (see Hwang & Yang, 2001; Hirji, 2006). Because the *p-values* of tables with smaller sample sizes are larger, and decrease (rather quickly) with larger sample sizes, the LMP functions as a self-diminishing correction – providing larger corrections for discreteness in smaller samples, and no practical correction in larger samples.

There are several reasons that the mid-P is proposed here as a "best choice" option. Some of these have been pointed out by Hirji (2006, pp. 218-219). In the Section titled, Why the mid-P?, Hirji provides the basis for endorsing the mid-P as the preferred exact method (for either conditional or unconditional situations). Some of these reasons are: (1) Statisticians who hold very divergent views on statistical inference have either recommended or given justification for the mid-P method, (2) the power of the mid-P tests is generally close to the shape of the ideal power function, (3) in a wide variety of designs and models, the mid-P rectifies the extreme conservativeness of the traditional exact conditional method without compromising the Type I error in a serious manner, and (4) empirical studies show that the performance of the mid-P method resembles that of the exact unconditional methods and the conditional randomized methods. Hirji concludes by stating: "The mid-P method is thus widely-accepted, conceptually sound, practical, and among the better of the tools of data analysis. Especially for sparse and not that large a sample size discrete data, we thereby echo the words of Cohen and Yang (1994) that it is among the 'sensible tools for the applied statistician'." Additional resources and supporters of the LMP method are provided in the Reference section of this book under References Supporting the Use of Lancaster's mid-P Adjustment to the FET.

Simulation

Research on the performance of alternate significance tests for 2 X 2 tables has shown that the results depend, in part, on the model used to generate the data. The existing research on alternate tests has generally adopted one or more of these models. The relevance of these studies, of course, depends on the fidelity with which the simulated data represents the nature of data found in a particular domain. Because the data available for adverse impact analysis may not follow any of the existing statistical (Collins & Morris, 2008), it is unclear to what extent the existing literature will generalize to adverse impact analysis.

To avoid this limitation, the current study attempted to model more directly the processes that generate data for adverse impact analyses. Specifically, data were initially generated to represent applicant test scores, and then a selection rule was applied to determine pass/fail decisions. Two types of selection rules were simulated: top-down selection and fixed cutoff score. All data simulation data sets were produced using "free" marginal assumptions.

Simulation of Top-Down Selection

In many selection decisions, the number of hires is based on the number of positions available. Candidates are ranked based on the results of a test or composite score from a test battery and then individuals are selected top-down until all positions are filled. In this approach, the cutoff for passing the test is not established before-hand. The effective cut-score is determined by last candidate selected. As such, the effective cutoff is not fixed across repeated administrations, and whether an individual passes or fails the test depends in part on the scores of other candidates in the applicant pool.

These characteristics make top-down selection distinct from any of the existing statistical models for 2 X 2 tables (Collins & Morris, 2008).

Method. Top-down selection decisions were simulated using a Fortran 90 program created for this research. Data were generated to represent test scores from two normally distributed populations (minority and majority) with variance of 1.0 and a specified mean difference. Two levels of the group difference (0.0 and 1.0) were simulated to represent situations with different degrees of adverse impact. The mean difference of 0.0 reflects a situation with no adverse impact.

Each sample had a fixed total sample size specified by the condition. Sample sizes of 20, 50 and 100 were examined to represent a range of sizes typical of selection settings. Because the alternate statistical tests tend to converge for large samples, it was decided to focus on relatively small sample sizes.

For each sample, the number of minority applicants was determined from a binomial distribution based on the total sample size and proportion of minorities for the condition. The proportion of minorities in the population was set at .1, .3. and .5 to represent settings with low, moderate and high minority representation. The remainder of the sample represented the majority group.

Scores were then generated for minority and majority applicants from a standard normal distribution. Scores for the minority group were adjusted by subtracting the group mean difference for the condition. Scores from both groups were then sorted, and the top scores were selected to fill a fixed number of positions. The number of slots was fixed across samples, and was determined by multiplying the total sample size by the total selection rate specified for the condition.

Selection rates of .1, .3, .5, and .7 were simulated to represent a wide range of selection settings. In practice, selection rates vary considerably depending on labor market conditions and the purpose of the test. For example, tests used for initial screening often have relatively large selection rates, because the goal is to screen out individuals who do not possess minimum qualifications. In contrast, tests used for final hiring decisions will often be much more selective.

Using this decision rule, the number of applicants from each group who passed and failed the selection decision was determined, and used to calculate each of the adverse impact significance tests (Z-test, FET, and LMP). Following the common practice when evaluating adverse impact, a two-tailed significance level of .05 was used. Significant results in either direction were included in the calculation of Type I error rates, but power calculations only counted significant results in which the minority selection rate was lower than the majority selection rate.

The simulation generated 10,000 samples under each condition of the mean difference (3), sample size (3), proportion of minorities (3), and selection rate (4), comprising 108 conditions. Empirical rejection rates were computed using only samples that provided usable data, that is, samples with at least one applicant from each group. Rejection rates for the conditions with no mean difference reflect Type I error rates, while rejection rates for the conditions with a mean difference represent estimates of statistical power.

Results. Type I error rates are summarized in Table 12-3. Consistent with past research, the simulation found that the FET was considerably more conservative than the other methods. On average, the Type I error rate for the FET (.022) was considerably lower than the nominal alpha level of .05, and was about half the size of the Type I error rate for the Z-test (.048). The LMP test was generally similar to but slightly more conservative than the Z-test, with an average Type I error rate of .040. These values translate to Type I error thresholds of 2.28, 1.98, and 2.06 standard deviations for the FET, Z-test, and LMP test respectively.

Type I Error (Rejection) Rates of Alternate Significance Tests for a Top-Down Selection System					
Selection Rate	Proportion Minority	N	Z-Test	FET	LMP
0.1	0.1	20	0.107	0.008	0.043
0.1	0.1	50	0.05	0.021	0.037
0.1	0.1	100	0.051	0.026	0.046
0.1	0.3	20	0.05	0.005	0.027
0.1	0.3	50	0.04	0.021	0.042
0.1	0.3	100	0.051	0.025	0.053
0.1	0.5	20	0.022	0.001	0.007
0.1	0.5	50	0.052	0.013	0.057
0.1	0.5	100	0.051	0.042	0.043
0.3	0.1	20	0.038	0.006	0.038
0.3	0.1	50	0.045	0.017	0.043
0.3	0.1	100	0.049	0.021	0.049
0.3	0.3	20	0.037	0.021	0.037
0.3	0.3	50	0.054	0.036	0.051
0.3	0.3	100	0.051	0.036	0.051
0.3	0.5	20	0.038	0.031	0.038
0.3	0.5	50	0.052	0.027	0.062
0.3	0.5	100	0.055	0.042	0.054
0.5	0.1	20	0.011	0.002	0.002
0.5	0.1	50	0.048	0.01	0.018
0.5	0.1	100	0.055	0.02	0.037
0.5	0.3	20	0.038	0.012	0.021
0.5	0.3	50	0.05	0.021	0.03
0.5	0.3	100	0.049	0.03	0.037
0.5	0.5	20	0.046	0.015	0.022
0.5	0.5	50	0.066	0.033	0.033
0.5	0.5	100	0.057	0.035	0.035
0.7	0.1	20	0.035	0.004	0.035
0.7	0.1	50	0.049	0.017	0.045
0.7	0.1	100	0.045	0.018	0.045
0.7	0.3	20	0.041	0.021	0.041
0.7	0.3	50	0.049	0.035	0.047
0.7	0.3	100	0.046	0.035	0.047
0.7	0.5	20	0.04	0.032	0.04
0.7	0.5	50	0.049	0.028	0.063
0.7	0.5	100	0.054	0.042	0.051

Note: Nominal a =.05. FET = Fisher Exact Test. LMP = Lancaster mid-P adjusted Fisher Exact Test.

Table 12-3 Type I Error Rates of 2 X 2 Tests (Top-Down Selection)

All tests tended to be conservative in extremely small samples (n = 20) and to show larger coverage probabilities as sample size increased (see Figure 12- 4). The Z-test produced Type I error rates below .04 only at the smallest sample size (n = 20). For larger sample sizes, the average coverage probabilities for the Z-test were close to the nominal alpha level. The LMP test was often conservative at the smallest sample size, with Type I error rates as low as .01, but less so at sample sizes of 50 or 100. Type I error rates also increased with sample size for the FET, but even under the largest sample size (n = 100), Type I error rates were still quite conservative (as low as .02).

Although the average Type I error rate for the Z-test was very close to the nominal level, there were many instances where the error rate exceeded .05. In most cases the inflation was minor, generally less than .055. However, when the sample size, proportion of minorities and selection rate were all small, substantial inflation was observed (.107). It is worth noting that the smallest expected cell frequency for this condition was 0.2, considerably less than the minimum of 5 generally recommended for this test.

The LMP test also showed inflated Type I error rates under some conditions, but generally lower in magnitude than the Z-test. The worst case was a Type I error rate of slightly over .06, which occurred for a sample size of 50 with 50% minority applicants and either a 30% or 70% selection rate.

Overall, the Z-test exceeded the .05 level in 13 of the 36 (36%) simulation configurations (with an average Type I error rate of .058 in the cases that exceeded the .05 level), the LMP exceeded the .05 level in 8 of the 36 (22%) simulation configurations (with an average Type I error rate of .055 in the cases that exceeded the .05 level), and the FET never exceeded the .05 level, but averaged 0.022, or about 55.1% below the target .05 level.

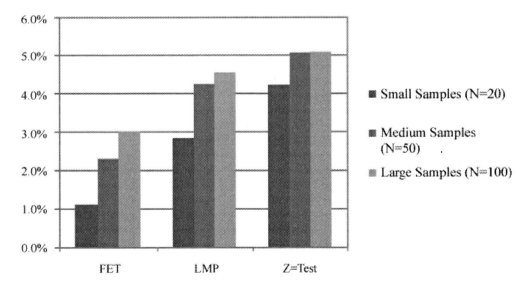

Figure 12-4 Average Type I Error Rates of 2 X 2 Tests (Top-Down Selection)

Conservative Type I error rates are a concern because a more conservative test will tend to have lower statistical power. Table 12-4 summarizes the power of the alternate tests to detect adverse impact when there was a large test score difference ($d = 1.0$) between groups. The relationship between the standardized mean difference and the adverse impact ratio depends on the selection rate, with lower selection rates producing greater adverse impact. Adverse impact ratios corresponding to each of the simulated selection rates are summarized in Table 12-4.

Power of Alternate Significance Tests for a Top-Down Selection System when a Large Group Difference Exists on the Test (d = 1.0)						
Selection Rate	Proportion Minority	IR	N	Z-Test	FET	LMP
0.1	0.1	0.12	20	0	0	0
0.1	0.1	0.12	50	0	0	0
0.1	0.1	0.12	100	0	0	0
0.1	0.3	0.13	20	0.001	0	0
0.1	0.3	0.13	50	0.029	0	0.051
0.1	0.3	0.13	100	0.475	0.229	0.501
0.1	0.5	0.15	20	0.065	0.002	0.023
0.1	0.5	0.15	50	0.433	0.172	0.459
0.1	0.5	0.15	100	0.751	0.718	0.722
0.3	0.1	0.22	20	0.001	0	0.001
0.3	0.1	0.22	50	0.058	0.025	0.025
0.3	0.1	0.22	100	0.327	0.168	0.327
0.3	0.3	0.26	20	0.14	0.069	0.14
0.3	0.3	0.26	50	0.564	0.452	0.525
0.3	0.3	0.26	100	0.882	0.834	0.885
0.3	0.5	0.3	20	0.289	0.256	0.289
0.3	0.5	0.3	50	0.73	0.636	0.761
0.3	0.5	0.3	100	0.962	0.951	0.96
0.5	0.1	0.34	20	0.048	0.009	0.009
0.5	0.1	0.34	50	0.32	0.12	0.188
0.5	0.1	0.34	100	0.6	0.428	0.526
0.5	0.3	0.39	20	0.274	0.142	0.196
0.5	0.3	0.39	50	0.698	0.567	0.624
0.5	0.3	0.39	100	0.943	0.915	0.925
0.5	0.5	0.45	20	0.352	0.191	0.24
0.5	0.5	0.45	50	0.815	0.722	0.723
0.5	0.5	0.45	100	0.979	0.965	0.965
0.7	0.1	0.48	20	0.247	0.074	0.247
0.7	0.1	0.48	50	0.471	0.312	0.471
0.7	0.1	0.48	100	0.69	0.57	0.69
0.7	0.3	0.55	20	0.322	0.266	0.322
0.7	0.3	0.55	50	0.703	0.673	0.705
0.7	0.3	0.55	100	0.94	0.928	0.938
0.7	0.5	0.62	20	0.292	0.264	0.292
0.7	0.5	0.62	50	0.732	0.635	0.764
0.7	0.5	0.62	100	0.963	0.95	0.96

Note: IR = population adverse impact ratio. FET = Fisher Exact Test. LMP = Lancaster mid-P adjusted Fisher Exact Test.

Table 12-4 Power of 2 X 2 Tests (Top-Down Selection, d = 1.0)

Power generally improved for all methods with increases in sample size, the selection rate and the proportion of minority applicants. Of particular importance is the smallest expected frequency. Under most conditions, power was similar for the Z-test and the LMP test, both of which had steeper power curves than the FET. This is illustrated in Figure 12-6 with the power curves when the overall selection rate was 30%. When the selection rate was 50%, the power curve for the LMP test fell between that of the Z-test and the FET (see Figure 12-7).

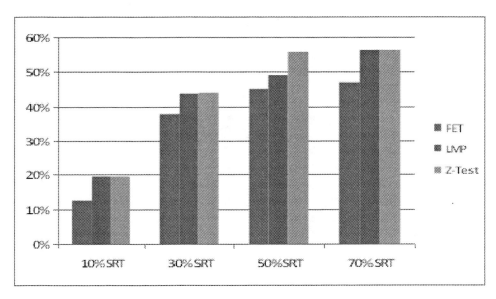

Figure 12-5 Power of 2 X 2 Tests (Fixed Cutoff Selection, d = 1.0)

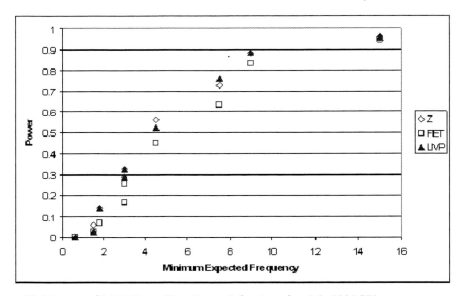

Figure 12-6 Power of 2 X 2 Tests (Top-Down Selection, d = 1.0, 30% SR)

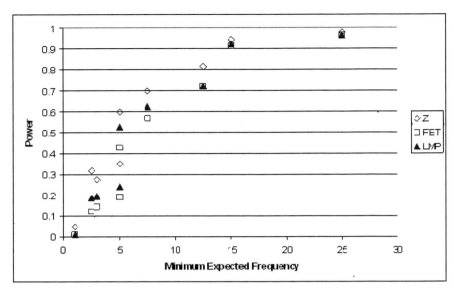

Figure 12-7 Power of 2 X 2 Tests (Top-Down Selection, d = 1.0, 50% SR)

The average power across all scenarios in Table 12-4 was 44.7%, 36.8%, and 42.9% for the Z-Test, FET, and LMP respectively. In lower adverse impact settings (impact ratios of 10% or 30%), the average power was 31.7%, 25.1%, and 31.5%, and in high adverse impact settings (impact ratios exceeding of 50%), the average power was 57.7%, 48.5%, and 54.4% for the Z-Test, FET, and LMP. The most notable power differences between the tests were observed in the cases with higher impact ratios, where the average power of the Z-test and the LMP exceeded the FET by 19% and 9% respectively (for the cases with a 50% impact ratio), and by 15% (Z-test) and 15% (LMP) for the 70% impact ratio.

In summary, in the top-down selection situation, the advantage of using the FET (if the conditional assumptions can be met) is that it provides a 100% strict adherence to the .05 nominal level (*i.e.,* it will never exceed the .05 level of significance). This benefit, however, does not come without a substantial cost – namely an average alpha level about 55% lower than the desired .05 level (overall), coupled with 22% less power than the Z-test and 17% less power than LMP (average across all cases studied), and 19% and 12% less power in high-adverse impact settings (>30% impact ratios) for these two tests, respectively.

Simulation of a Fixed Cutoff

Standardized tests are often evaluated using a cutoff score representing a desired proficiency level. All persons above this cutoff score pass the test, and decisions among this group are made using other criteria. Cutoff scores are typically established before administering the test, based on test norms or standard-setting procedures that link the cutoff to job requirements. In such cases, the cutoff score will be fixed across replications, and the number of candidates passing the test will vary due to sampling error.

Method. Data representing fixed cutoff decisions were simulated using the same procedure as the top-down simulation, with the exception of the decision rule.

For each condition, a selection rate was specified for the majority population, and this was used to set the cutoff score. Specifically, the cutoff score was defined as a Z-score such that the proportion of a standard normal distribution falling above the cut score was equal to the selection rate for the majority population.

Results. The results for the fixed cutoff scenario were quite similar to those for top-down selection. Type I error rates were generally quite close to the nominal alpha level for the Z-test, were slightly conservative for the LMP test, and were quite conservative for the FET (see Table 12-5). Under the most extreme condition examined (10% selection rate, 10% minority, n = 20), the Z-test had an inflated Type I error rate of .09; however, the rejection rates were mostly less than 0.055. Type I error rates for the LMP rarely exceeded .05, and never exceeded 0.052. When the sample size was small, the LMP tended to be conservative, with an average Type I error rate of .031, noticeably smaller than the average of 0.047 for the Z-test, but substantially better than the average of 0.014 for the FET.

Type I Error Rates of Alternate Significance Tests for a Fixed Cutoff Selection System					
Selection Rate	Proportion Minority	N	Z-Test	FET	LMP
0.1	0.1	20	0.09	0.012	0.04
0.1	0.1	50	0.058	0.021	0.037
0.1	0.1	100	0.044	0.022	0.04
0.1	0.3	20	0.042	0.009	0.023
0.1	0.3	50	0.04	0.022	0.042
0.1	0.3	100	0.049	0.03	0.048
0.1	0.5	20	0.025	0.007	0.015
0.1	0.5	50	0.044	0.02	0.039
0.1	0.5	100	0.05	0.033	0.048
0.3	0.1	20	0.047	0.009	0.026
0.3	0.1	50	0.035˙	0.017	0.037
0.3	0.1	100	0.049	0.031	0.05
0.3	0.3	20	0.042	0.016	0.036
0.3	0.3	50	0.053	0.036	0.049
0.3	0.3	100	0.053	0.039	0.05
0.3	0.5	20	0.048	0.02	0.037
0.3	0.5	50	0.053	0.032	0.046
0.3	0.5	100	0.054	0.04	0.052
0.5	0.1	20	0.027	0.007	0.016
0.5	0.1	50	0.04	0.02	0.036
0.5	0.1	100	0.055	0.035	0.051
0.5	0.3	20	0.051	0.022	0.043
0.5	0.3	50	0.05	0.031	0.045
0.5	0.3	100	0.052	0.037	0.05
0.5	0.5	20	0.051	0.019	0.042
0.5	0.5	50	0.055	0.038	0.043
0.5	0.5	100	0.054	0.043	0.043
0.7	0.1	20	0.043	0.008	0.024
0.7	0.1	50	0.04	0.021	0.043
0.7	0.1	100	0.045	0.028	0.044
0.7	0.3	20	0.042	0.016	0.034
0.7	0.3	50	0.051	0.033	0.046
0.7	0.3	100	0.047	0.035	0.046
0.7	0.5	20	0.051	0.024	0.041
0.7	0.5	50	0.054	0.034	0.049
0.7	0.5	100	0.052	0.038	0.05

Note: Nominal α =.05. FET = Fisher Exact Test. LMP = Lancaster mid-P adjusted Fisher Exact Test.

Table 12-5 Type I Error Rates of 2 X 2 Tests (Fixed Cutoff Selection)

Overall, the Z-test exceeded the .05 level in 16 of the 36 (44%) simulation configurations (with an average overage of about 11% in the cases that exceeded the .05 level), the LMP exceeded the .05 level in 2 of the 36 (6%) simulation configurations (with an average overage of about 3% in the cases that exceeded the .05 level), and the FET never exceeded the .05 level, but averaged .0251, about 49.7% below the target .05 level. Similar to the top-down selection results, the average Type I error rate for the FET was substantially below the .05 level (.0251) compared to the Z-test (.048) and the LMP (.041). These values translate to Type I error thresholds of 2.24, 1.98, and 2.05 standard deviations for the FET, Z-test, and LMP test respectively.

The Z-test and the LMP test produced similar levels of power under most conditions (see Table 12-6). In the few cases where the two methods showed non-trivial differences, the Z-test had greater power, yielding power as much as 0.068 higher than the LMP test. The largest differences occurred mostly when the selection rate was either 30% or 70% and the sample size was small (n = 20). Both the Z-test and the LMP test had substantially greater power than the FET under most conditions.

Power of Alternate Significance Tests for a Fixed Cutoff Selection System when a Large Group Difference Exists on the Test (d = 1.0)						
Selection Rate	Proportion Minority	IR	N	Z-Test	FET	LMP
0.1	0.1	0.12	20	0	0	0
0.1	0.1	0.12	50	0	0	0
0.1	0.1	0.12	100	0.001	0	0.001
0.1	0.3	0.13	20	0.003	0.001	0.002
0.1	0.3	0.13	50	0.026	0.011	0.032
0.1	0.3	0.13	100	0.224	0.118	0.215
0.1	0.5	0.15	20	0.054	0.015	0.032
0.1	0.5	0.15	50	0.179	0.086	0.173
0.1	0.5	0.15	100	0.51	0.378	0.494
0.3	0.1	0.22	20	0.005	0.001	0.003
0.3	0.1	0.22	50	0.045	0.025	0.042
0.3	0.1	0.22	100	0.29	0.162	0.3
0.3	0.3	0.26	20	0.098	0.038	0.082
0.3	0.3	0.26	50	0.435	0.356	0.389
0.3	0.3	0.26	100	0.805	0.746	0.807
0.3	0.5	0.3	20	0.245	0.127	0.186
0.3	0.5	0.3	50	0.606	0.507	0.581
0.3	0.5	0.3	100	0.901	0.866	0.893
0.5	0.1	0.34	20	0.066	0.023	0.044
0.5	0.1	0.34	50	0.262	0.16	0.25
0.5	0.1	0.34	100	0.565	0.474	0.55
0.5	0.3	0.39	20	0.266	0.15	0.239
0.5	0.3	0.39	50	0.648	0.56	0.638
0.5	0.3	0.39	100	0.928	0.909	0.923
0.5	0.5	0.45	20	0.364	0.238	0.326
0.5	0.5	0.45	50	0.751	0.684	0.727
0.5	0.5	0.45	100	0.965	0.955	0.963
0.7	0.1	0.48	20	0.223	0.084	0.155
0.7	0.1	0.48	50	0.418	0.324	0.413
0.7	0.1	0.48	100	0.672	0.611	0.673
0.7	0.3	0.55	20	0.351	0.242	0.318
0.7	0.3	0.55	50	0.72	0.653	0.702
0.7	0.3	0.55	100	0.951	0.936	0.947
0.7	0.5	0.62	20	0.41	0.27	0.365
0.7	0.5	0.62	50	0.799	0.745	0.76
0.7	0.5	0.62	100	0.977	0.97	0.971

Note: IR = population adverse impact ratio. FET = Fisher Exact Test. LMP = Lancaster mid-P adjusted Fisher Exact Test.

Table 12-6 Power of 2 X 2 Tests (Fixed Cutoff Selection, d = 1.0)

The average power across all scenarios (see Table 12-6) was 41%, 34.5%, and 39.4% for the Z-Test, FET, and LMP respectively. In lower adverse impact settings (impact ratios of 10% and 30%), the average power was 24.6%, 19.1%, and 23.5%, and in high adverse impact settings (impact ratios of 50% and 70%), the average power was 57.4%, 49.9%, and 55.4% for the Z-Test, FET, and LMP. As with the top-down simulations, higher power differences were observed between the tests in cases with higher impact ratios, where the average power of the Z-test and the LMP exceeded the FET by 16% and 12% respectively (for the cases with a 50% impact ratio), and by 14% (Z-test) and 10% (LMP) for the 70% impact ratio.

In the fixed cutoff situation, the tradeoff for having the strict assurance of maintaining the .05 alpha level (offered by the FET) is the net effect of setting the alpha level about 50% lower than the desired .05 level (overall across studies). The other tradeoff is the substantial reduction in power, where the FET falls 19% and 15% below the Z-test and LMP respectively (average of all cases studied), and 15% and 11% less power in high-adverse impact settings (*i.e.,* cases with >30% impact ratios).

Conclusion

The choice among procedures for testing statistical significance in 2 X 2 tables has been an issue of continuing research and debate for decades. Our review of the literature identified no less than 22 tests to choose among, each with its own particular assumptions, strengths and weaknesses (Upton, 1982). The availability of alternative significance test suggests that employers who find themselves as defendants in Title VII settings will be called on to defend not only the results of their adverse impact analysis, but also how those statistics were calculated.

Although the FET has long been the statistic of choice for small sample adverse impact analysis, the statistics literature has raised serious concerns about its strict assumptions and conservative results (Lydersen, et. al, 2009). The literature has also highlighted the need for using tests with higher power without excessive Type I error rates (Overall & Hornick, 1982).

Our study has shown that the LMP and Z-test evade the scrutiny that is levied against the FET (*i.e.,* being overly conservative and tied to strict conditional assumptions). In addition, this benefit is coupled with alternative tests producing higher levels of power, while still adhering closely to the desired .05 significance level. Specifically, the FET produced effective average alpha levels that were 55.1% below the .05 alpha level (in top-down settings) and 49.7% below (in fixed cutoff settings). The LMP and Z-test produced values that were closer to the target .05 level, with average alpha levels of .04 and .048 (in top-down settings) and .041 and .048 (in fixed cutoff settings). Our study (as well as those reported herein) demonstrates that these trends are more pronounced in small sample sizes (n < 50) and continue until sample sizes exceed 200. Our study also revealed that the target .05 alpha level was only rarely exceeded in the case of the LMP. Further, although the Z-test sometimes showed Type I error rates above the .05 alpha level, the excess error was typically small, rarely exceeding .055.

When sample size is small, it is of particular importance to evaluate the potential that statistical results could have occurred due to chance. Statistical significance tests play a key role identifying whether the observed degree of adverse impact is larger than would be expected due to random sampling error. Unfortunately, in the small sample conditions where sampling error is of greatest concern, significance tests generally have low power to detect real group differences. While the problem of low power is to some degree unavoidable, this situation highlights the importance considering power when choosing among alternate statistical tests. This is especially true in settings where higher impact ratios exist (50% - 70%), where our study exhibited the most notable power differences between the tests (15% - 19% for the Z-test and 9% - 15% for the LMP).

A theoretical critique of the assumptions of the FET, along with Monte Carlo simulation results (from this study and others reported herein) raise serious concerns about the use of the FET for adverse impact analysis. With widespread evidence in the literature that the FET tends to be conservative (producing Type I error rates substantially below the nominal alpha level) and this conservative tendency resulting in lower power than other available tests, practitioners may find themselves in less defensible positions in Title VII enforcement settings when using the FET compared to other alternatives.

Practitioners who work on both sides of Title VII litigation and federal enforcement settings should desire balanced tests for analyzing adverse impact. Tests with low power will miss adverse impact that exists – adverse impact that could possibly be identified later by enforcement agencies or plaintiff experts running different tests on the same samples under study. This could lead to false assurance of the part of employers using more conservative tests like the FET. In addition, practitioners who use the FET outside of conditions they can argue are truly "fixed by design" may find themselves having to defend their positions against a substantial amount of literature that restricts use of the FET to these limited circumstances.

The two (more powerful) alternatives proposed in this study provide reasonable replacements for the FET. Power was generally similar for the two methods, although the Z-test showed greater power under some conditions. In contrast, the LMP mid-P test provided better control of Type I errors than the Z-tests. Based on these results, it is recommended to use the Z-test for larger samples, and the LMP test when sample size is small.

In the (very rare) circumstance where the LMP and Z-test produce different *p-values* on cases that are on the cusp of the .05 alpha level (with one test below and the other above), a more definitive results could be obtained by consulting one of the unconditional exact tests (*e.g.,* the Barnard test adopted in StatXact® or the Boschloo test – see Berger, 2010). However, the cases where the Z-test, LMP, or these unconditional exact tests will substantially differ are few and far between, and will be discovered even less frequently on the .05 cusp. When such instances occur, evaluating the practical significance of the finding (by evaluating which tests are triggered and the number of subjects that would need to change places to remove the findings of each) will be increasingly important, and this point is suggested as a topic for future research.

Appendix B - The Conditional Standard Error of Measurement (CSEM)

By Daniel A. Biddle, Ph.D., Leonard S. Feldt, Ph.D., & Daniel C. Kuang, Ph.D.

Overview

The implications of using CSEMs are *wide* and *substantial* for the HR practitioner. Classical SEMs are widely used by HR practitioners in two ways – both of which have substantial impact on countless applicants that are ranked on various score lists: score *banding* and *adjusting cutoff scores*. The process for using CSEMs to set score bands is discussed in this section.

Test score banding is commonly practiced by HR professionals as a way of preserving utility (over simply using cutoffs) while minimizing adverse impact (over top-down ranking). Banding procedures typically use the Standard Error of Difference (SED), which is calculated by multiplying the classical Standard Error of Measurement (SEM) by the square root of 2, along with a confidence interval multiplier (*e.g.,* 95% using a 1.96 multiplier) to categorize groups of "substantially equally qualified" applicants. While this classic technique was used for years, it has now been well established that the *conditional* nature of the SEMs (meaning that the width of the SEM changes throughout the score distribution), demands using CSEMs (rather than SEMs) when creating bands to accurately capture the dynamic nature of reliability through the score distribution. Most CSEM techniques typically produce *smaller* values than classical SEM calculations in the upper range of the score distribution, which translates to smaller groups of applicants being categorized because of the added precision of the conditional measurement precision (the classical SEM simply averages measurement error across the entire score range).

Background

The traditional Standard Error of Measurement (SEM)[1] should no longer be used in practice unless the researcher is confident that measurement error is consistent throughout the score range – a circumstance that is rare indeed.[2] Rather, the *conditional* SEM should be used because it accurately reflects the *variation of measurement precision* throughout the range of scores.

The fact that measurement precision (*i.e.,* represented in SEM units) varies throughout the score range was allegedly first discovered by William G. Mollenkopf, a professor at Princeton University, while studying under the prestigious Harold Gulliksen (author of The Theory of Mental Tests in 1950).[3] Mollenkopf's studies resulted in a 1949 publication in Psychometrika titled, "Variation of the standard error of measurement of scores" and was subsequently followed by dozens of articles that explored the same phenomena.

Leading up to the last decade, the most significant milestone for the CSEM research thread occurred with the publication of the 1999 *Standards for Educational and Psychological Testing*, where – for the first time in measurement history – the *conditional* SEM was codified into APA standards (Standard 2.2 and 2.14). The conditional SEM has been regularly used in the educational measurement community since its inception, however, the concept only began showing up in I-O psychology publications in more recent years (*e.g.,* Bobko & Roth, 2004; Biddle, 2005, Biddle, Kuang, & Higgins, 2007).

More than a dozen various CSEM techniques have accumulated since the first mention of the concept over 60 years ago. Some techniques are original; others are "improved" techniques that include minor adjustments to the original author's work. Some techniques are based on "strong true score models," which are tied to strong statistical and theoretical (*i.e.,* parametric) assumptions. Binomial error models and IRT models for computing CSEMs generally fall into this category. Other CSEM models are categorized as "weak true score models" and encompass the "difference" methods that were used by the original CSEM authors. Such methods are referred to as the "difference" methods because they compute the CSEM based on the variance between two split halves of the same test. These methods are referred to as the "weak" methods because they are not fundamentally tied to theoretical or parametric distributional assumptions.

While the techniques for computing CSEMs are widely varied, they are fortunately rather close in their outputs. For example, Qualls-Payne (1992) showed that the average C- SEM produced by the difference method (across 13 different score levels) produced CSEM values that were very close to five other methods (including binomial and IRT methods). Further, a study conducted by Feldt, Steffen, & Gupta (1985) shows that, while the difference methods are less complicated than some other methods (*i.e.,* those based on ANOVA, IRT, or binomial methods), it is "integrally related" and generally produces very similar results.

IRT-based CSEM methods typically require a large sample size for calibrating accurate parameter estimates (*e.g.,* Tsutakawa & Johnson, 1990, recommend a minimum sample size of approximately 500 for accurate parameter estimates) and the use of sophisticated software (*e.g.,* BILOG). Further, they can only be used for tests that meet certain psychometric assumptions (*e.g.,* uni-dimensionality). The binomial error methods are generally less computationally intensive, and require only KR-21 reliability, the mean and standard deviation of test scores, and the number of items on the test. As "strong" methods, both of these techniques are tied to distributional assumptions.

The "difference" methods reviewed here focus on the Mollenkopf-Feldt (M-F) method, which uses polynomial regression to "smooth" the CSEM values that are calculated using the variance between scores on two split test halves. Specifically, the M-F CSEM method can be executed by following the steps outlined in the section below.

After computing CSEMs, score bands can be created by centering confidence intervals around classically computed Estimated True Scores, using the formula: *ETS* $= ((X-M)* r_{xx} + M$ (where X is the examinee's obtained score, M is the average test score of all examinees, and r_{xx} is the reliability of the test) and the desired Confidence Interval (*e.g.,* 1.96 for 95% confidence when considering 2 CSEMs). This personnel score banding approach is based on the original M-F method and was modified for the personnel score banding (as originally defined in Biddle *et al.*, 2007).

As a "weak" model, it is not tied to the strong statistical assumptions inherent to other models (*e.g.*, IRT or the binomial methods). It has the added value of being tolerant of various item types (*e.g.*, binary or polytomous items) and having sample size requirements similar to those of most multiple regression situations. One of the additional advantages of the M-F method is that it is based on the actual item responses and characteristics of *each data set* (binomial models can even be computed without item-level data because they are based on the binomial probability distribution). The method allows data from *each test administration* to form varying CSEM values at each score interval. Some research conducted by the author has shown that the M-F method is highly correlated (r = .88) to the CSEM models based on binomial methods.

Steps for Banding Using the M-F Procedure

The steps for computing the M-F CSEM are relatively straightforward. They do, however, require using statistical software to compute regression analysis and several steps that must be made in succession to develop accurate bands. Fortunately, there are software programs available for completing these steps (Biddle Consulting Group, 2011). The systematic process for computing M-F CSEMs and subsequent score bands is described below.

Step 1. Divide the test into two halves that are approximately equal in difficulty and variance, and have the *same number of items*. Because the M-F method is a "difference" CSEM method, it is important that the test halves are balanced by having the same number of items contributing variance to the equation. If the test has an odd number of items, one of the items can be removed from the test (for CSEM computing purposes only). It is also important that all of the items on the test have the same point values, as the M-F method cannot be used on a test that includes mixed binary and polytomous (multi-point) items. Fortunately, the method *can* be used for tests with polytomous items, however, all items on the test need to be the same type (*i.e.*, either binary or polytomous).

In addition, to have the same number and type of items, the two test halves should be psychometrically similar. While a number of sophisticated techniques are available for assembling and evaluating the comparability between tests (referred to as tau equivalency – see Haertel, 2006), it is recommended that at least some minimal uniform procedure be developed and followed. In many cases, simply dividing the test using an even/odd split (with the same number of items on each half) will be sufficient. However, if such a split results in two test halves that have substantially different means or standard deviations, using a more intensive splitting method is recommended.

Because the M-F CSEM approach already takes the mean difference between test halves into account (by subtracting them out of the equation), the SD of each test should receive attention. With this in mind, the following steps are suggested to insure the test halves are parallel:

1. Calculate the mean difficulty level for each item (*i.e.,* the average passing rate for each item), shown as *p*.
2. Sort the items by mean difficulty level (*p*).
3. Split the test items (using odd/even) into two forms with the same number of items (if the test has an odd number of items, remove one). The two forms should have fairly equivalent means, which is one component of establishing parallel forms.
4. Compute the standard deviation for each test half.
5. Use a pre-specified criteria/threshold for the difference between both forms. If the difference exceeds a criteria/threshold, then swap items from hardest to easiest until they are within the threshold.[4]

     Step 2. Calculate an "adjusted difference score" for each applicant by subtracting their score on test half 1 from their score on test half 2 and the mean from test half 1 from the mean from test half 2, noted as: $Y = ((X_1 - X_2) - (\overline{X}_1 - \overline{X}_2))^2$ where X_1 and X_2 are the two test halves and $\overline{X}_1$ and $\overline{X}_2$ are the means for each test half. This process results in calculating an "adjusted difference score" for each applicant that will be used as a dependent variable, Y in the subsequent regression equation.

     For example, for a test with two halves that have means of 26.28 and 26.45 respectively and a first examinee who scored 60 on the test, 28 on half 1 and 32 on test half 2, the formula would be displayed as: $Y = ((28-32)-(26.28-26.4))^2$ which computes to a value of 14.67. This calculation is repeated for each examinee in the data set to create Y values that will be used as the dependent variable in the multiple regression analysis, described next.

     Step 3. Conduct a multiple regression analysis using the dependent variable Y from the step above and the total test score (X^1), total test score squared (X^2), and total test score cubed (X^3) as the independent variables. Set the constant in the regression to 0 because this is the theoretical floor of CSEM values.

     Step 4. Use the resulting three beta coefficients to compute CSEM values for each score in the distribution using the formula:

$$\sqrt{((\beta_1 * X^1) + (\beta_2 * X^2) + (\beta_3 * X^3))}$$

For example, to calculate the CSEM for the raw score of 70, the three predictors 80 (X_1), 640 (X_2), and 512000 (X_3) are multiplied with their three corresponding beta coefficients β_1 (1.5597) β_2 (-0.01914) and β_3 (0.000006) as demonstrated here

$$\sqrt{((70*1.5597) + (490*-0.01914) + (343000*0.000006))}$$

This results in a CSEM of 2.667 for the score of 70.

By way of technical thoroughness, a clarification should be made at this point. The dependent variable, Y, must be defined as the square of the difference score – *not the square root of it*. Thus,

$$Y = \left((X_1 - X_2) - (\overline{X}_1 - \overline{X}_2)\right)^2 .$$

This squared quantity for an examinee is *not* equal to Y^2. In effect, the regression analysis must be carried out as a process of developing smoother estimates of the *conditional error variance*. Only *after* the curve is fitted to the data for smoothing the variances are the square roots of the predicted *Y* values taken to obtain the CSEM for various score values. At first blush, this may seem identical to defining the squared deviation as Y^2. It is not. The square root of the average of a set of values is not equal to the average of the square roots of the values. This can be illustrated as follows:

$$\sqrt{((25+144)/2)} = 9.19 \text{ vs. } (5 + 12)/2 = 8.50.$$

When the values are closer together, the difference is not so great. Consider these values:

$$\sqrt{((9+16)/2)} = 3.53 \text{ vs. } (3 + 4)/2 = 3.50.$$

The CSEM must be taken as the square root of the mean of the predicted *Y*, as defined above. The process cannot be abbreviated by defining *Y* as the positive square root of the squared deviation and then smoothing these predicted *Y* values.

Step 5. Multiply each CSEM by the desired Confidence Interval (*e.g.,* 1.96 for 95% confidence intervals). This creates the width of the bands to be used in Step 7.

Step 6. Calculate Estimated True Scores (ETS) for each score in the distribution, using the formula: $ETS = ((X\text{-}M)^* \, r_{xx} + M)$ where X is the score, *M* is the average test score of all examinees, and r_{xx} is the reliability of the test. This will result in fraction scores for each observed score, which is fine because these are estimations of true scores.

Step 7. Create score bands by centering confidence intervals around the ETS values so that the lower boundary and upper boundary of the bands do not overlap. See Table 13-1 for an example.

Score Bands Using the M-F CSEM Method						
Observed Score	ETS	M-F CSEM	95% Lower Conf. Int.	95% Upper Conf. Int.	CSEM Band	Classic Band
80	77.68	0	77.68	77.68	1	1
79	76.77	0.77	75.26	78.28	1	1
78	75.85	1.17	73.57	78.14	1	1
77	74.94	1.46	72.08	77.8	1	1
76	74.02	1.69	70.7	77.35	1	1
75	73.11	1.9	69.39	76.83	1	1
74	72.19	2.08	68.11	76.28	1	1
73	71.28	2.25	66.87	75.68	1	1
72	70.36	2.4	65.66	75.06	2	1
71	69.45	2.54	64.48	74.42	·2	1
70	68.53	2.67	63.31	73.76	2	1
69	67.62	2.79	62.15	73.08	2	2
68	66.7	2.9	61.02	72.39	2	2
67	65.79	3.01	59.89	71.69	2	2
66	64.87	3.11	58.78	70.97	2	2
65	63.96	3.2	57.68	70.24	2	2
64	63.04	3.29	56.59	69.5	2	2
63	62.13	3.38	55.5	68.75	2	2
62	61.21	3.46	54.43	68	2	2
61	60.3	3.54	53.36	67.23	2	2
60	59.38	3.61	52.31	66.46	2	2
59	58.47	3.68	51.26	65.68	2	2
58	57.55	3.74	50.21	64.89	3	3

Table 13-1 Score Bands Using the M-F CSEM Method

Table 12-1 demonstrates that creating bands is a *bi-directional process*. Because CSEMs vary in size (typically being smaller towards the upper end of the distribution and largest near the mean) and the ETS adjustment centers the CSEM bands slightly below each observed score at the higher range, the upper and lower confidence intervals of each CSEM need to be simultaneously evaluated to determine where they touch. For example, Bands 1 and 2 divide at the score of 72 because the upper confidence interval limit at the CSEM at 72 [2.40 *1.96 = 4.70 plus 70.36 (the ETS at the observed score of 72)] is 75.06, which touches the lower confidence interval of the highest possible score with a non-zero CSEM (79).

Classic bands are also displayed in Table 13-1 for comparative purposes. Using the conventional SED formula (SEM * $\sqrt{2}$) based on the reliability of the test (0.9151) and SD (12.76) the SED 10.31 can be calculated and centered on observed scores. This process produces wider bands in general, particularly in the upper part of the distribution, when compared to M-F CSEM banding. In this data set, the classic band procedure starts the second band 4 points lower than the M-F CSEM method.

Given a sufficiently large sample size (starting generally at 100+ subjects), the process described above should produce stable CSEMs and related score bands. However, in situations where fewer than 100 subjects are involved, and particularly in situations with less than 50 subjects, the classical SEM should be used instead of the CSEM if the CSEM produces higher overall values. This is because the regression-based estimates will tend to overestimate CSEMs when smaller samples are involved. In addition, sometimes negative CSEM values will occasionally occur with small data sets are analyzed. These values should be set to the theoretical minimum value of 0.

Notes

[1] $SEM = \sigma_x (1 - r_{xx})^{1/2}$ where σ_x is the standard deviation and r_{xx} is the reliability of the test.

[2] The SEM is only constant in symmetrical, mesokurtic score distributions [see Mollenkopf, 1949).

[3] Ten years prior to this "discovery" made by Mollenkopf, Rulon (1939) showed that the SEM is equal to the standard deviation of the differences between the two half-test scores (which could be calculated at any score interval and thus resulting in the SEM at various levels). However, Rulon's emphasis was not placed on the conditional nature of SEMs; the same was only a focus of the later work first conducted by Mollenkopf.

[4] The BCG (TVAP®) has these steps automated. Such a complicated process is not necessary; however, some steps should be taken to ensure the forms are approximately similar.

References

1991 Civil Rights Act (42 U.S.C. §2000e-2[k][1][A]).

Abraham, S. (1996). Effects of leader's communication style and participative goal setting on performance and attitudes. *Human Performance, 9* (1), 51.

Albemarle Paper v. Moody, 422 U.S. at 431, 95 S.Ct. 2362 (1975).

Alexander, E.R., Helms, M.M. & Wilkins, R.D. (1989). The relationship between supervisory communication and subordinate performance and satisfaction among professionals. *Public Personnel Management, 18*, 415-429.

Allen, T.D. & Rush, M.C. (1998). The effects of organizational citizenship behavior on performance judgments: a field study and a laboratory experiment. *Journal of Applied Psychology, 83*, 247-260.

Angoff, W.H. (1971). 'Scales, Norms, and Equivalent Scores', In Thorndike RL, *Educational Measurement*, pp. 508-600. Washington, DC: American Council on Education.

Agresti, A. (1990). *Categorical Data Analysis*. New York: John Wiley & Sons.

American Educational Research Association, the American Psychological Association, and the National Council on Measurement in Education (1999). *Standards for Educational and Psychological Testing*. Washington DC: American Educational Research Association.

Anastasi, A. & Urbina, S. (1997). *Psychological Testing* (7th ed.). Upper Saddle River, New Jersey: Prentice Hall (pp. 199-200).

Anderson v. Premier Industrial Corp. (62 F.3d 1417, 1995 WL 469429, 6th Cir., 1995) (unpublished opinion).

Anrig, G. (January, 1987). 'Golden Rule: Second thoughts', *APA Monitor*.

Arnold v. Postmaster General (Civil Action Nos. 85-2571, 86-2291, U.S. Dist. Ct. for the District of Columbia, 667 F. Supp. 6, 1987).

Association Against Discrimination in Employment, Inc. v. City of Bridgeport (479 F. Supp. 101, 112-13 D. Conn., 1979).

Barrick, M. R. & Mount, M.K. (1993). Autonomy as a moderator of the relationships between the Big Five personality dimensions and job performance. *Journal of Applied Psychology, 78* (1), 111-118.

Barrick, M., & Mount, M. (1991). The Big 5 personality dimensions and job performance: A meta-analysis. *Personnel Psychology, 44,* 1-26.

Berger, M.A. (2000). The Supreme Court's trilogy on the admissibility of expert testimony. In D. Rubenfeld (Ed.), *Reference manual on scientific evidence* (2nd ed., pp. 10-38). Federal Judicial Center.

Bernard v. Gulf Oil Corp., 890 F.2d 735, 5th Cir. (1989).

Biddle, D.A. (2005). *Adverse impact and test validation: A practitioner's guide to valid and defensible employment testing* (1st ed.). Ashgate Publishing Company: Burlington, VT.

Biddle, D.A. (2006). *Adverse impact and test validation: A practitioner's guide to valid and defensible employment testing* (2nd ed.). Ashgate Publishing Company: Burlington, VT.

Biddle, D., Kuang, D. C.Y., & Higgins, J. (2007, March). *Test use: ranking, banding, cutoffs, and weighting.* Paper presented at the Personnel Testing Council of Northern California, Sacramento.

Biddle Consulting Group, Inc. (2011). Test Validation & Analysis Program (TVAP, Version 7) [Computer Software]. Folsom, CA: Author.

Bloom, B.S. (Ed.) (1956). *Taxonomy of Educational Objectives: The Classification of Educational Goals: Handbook I, Cognitive Domain.* New York, Toronto: Longmans, Green.

Bobko, P., Roth, P.L. (December, 2004). Personnel selection with top-score-referenced banding: On the inappropriateness of current procedures. *International Journal of Selection and Assessment, 12* (4), 291-298.

Boston Chapter, NAACP Inc. v. Beecher (504 F.2d 1017, 1021, 1st Cir. 1974).

Bouman v. Block (940 F.2d 1211, C.A.9, Cal., 1991).

Bradley v. Pizzaco of Nebraska, Inc. (926 F.2d 714, C.A.8, Neb., 1991).

Breslow, N.E. & Day, N.E. (1980). *Statistical Methods in Cancer Research,* Vol. I. 'The Analysis of Case-Control Studies', WHO/IARC Scientific Publication, No. 32.

Brown v. Chicago, WL 354922, N.D. III (1998).

Brown v. Delta Air Lines, Inc. (522 F.Supp. 1218, 1229, n. 14, S.D., Texas, 1980).

Brown, S.P. & Leigh T.W. (1996). A new look at psychological climate and its relationship to job involvement, effort, and performance. *Journal of Applied Psychology, 81*, 358-368.

Brunet v. City of Columbus (1 F.3d 390, C.A.6, Ohio, 1993).

Brunet v. City of Columbus, 1 F.3d 390, U.S. Ct. App. Sixth Cir. (1993).

Camilla, G. (1990). The test of homogeneity for 2 X 2 contingency tables: A review of and some personal opinions on the controversy. *Psychological Bulleting, 108,* 135-145.

Cascio, W. (1998). *Applied Psychology in Human Resource Management,* Upper Saddle River, NJ: Prentice-Hall, Inc.

Castaneda v. Partida (430 U.S. 482, 496, 1977).

Chang v. University of Rhode Island (606 F.Supp. 1161, D.R.I., 1985).

Chow, G. C. (1960). Tests of equality between sets of coefficients in two linear regressions. *Econometrica, 28,* 591-605.

Chao, G., O'Leary-Kelly, A., Wolf, S., Klein, H., Gardner, P. (1994). Organizational socialization: its content and consequences. *Journal of Applied Psychology, 79* (5), 730-743.

Cicero v. Borg Warner Automotive (75 F.Supp.2d 695, November, 1999)

Clady v. County of Los Angeles (770 F.2d 1421, 1428, 9th Cir., 1985).

Cleary, T. A. (1968). Test bias: Prediction of grades of negro and white students in integrated colleges. *Journal of Educational Measurement, 5,* 115-124.

Cohen, J., & Cohen, P. (1975). *Applied multiple regression/correlation analysis for the behavioral sciences.* Hillsdale, NJ: Lawrence Erlbaum.

Contreras v. City of Los Angeles (656 F.2d 1267, 9th Cir., 1981).

Cooper v. University of Texas at Dallas (482 F. Supp. 187, N.D. Tex., 1979).

Cormier v. PPG Industries, 519 F.Supp. 211, W.D. La. 1981, aff'd 702 F.2d 567 5th Cir. (1983).

Covington v. District of Columbia (Nos. 94-7014, 94-7015, 94-7022, 94-7107, U.S. Ct of Appeals, 313 U.S. App. D.C. 16; 57 F.3d 1101, 1995).

Csicseri v. Bowsher (862 F.Supp. 547, D.D.C., 1994).

Dees v. Orr, Secretary of the Air Force (No. Civil S-82-471 LKK, U.S. Dist. Ct., Eastern District of California, 1983).

Delgado-O'Neil v. City of Minneapolis, No. 08-4924 (U.S. District Court, D. Minnesota, August 4, 2010).

DeGroot, M. H., Fienberg, S. E., Kadane, J. B. (1985). *Statistics and the Law*, New York, NY: John Wiley & Sons.

Dennis L. Harrison v. Drew Lewis (Civil Action No. 79-1816, U.S. Dist. Ct. for the District of Columbia, 559 F. Supp. 943, 1983).

Dickerson v. U. S. Steel Corp. 472 F. Supp. 1304, E.D. Pa. (1978).

Donnel v. General Motors Corp (576 F2d 1292, 8th Cir., 1978).

Dothard v. Rawlinson (433 U.S. 321, 1977).

Dye, D. A., Reck, M., & McDaniel, M. A. (1993, July). The validity of job knowledge measures. *International Journal of Selection and Assessment, 1* (3), 153-157.

EEOC v. Federal Reserve Bank of Richmond (698 F.2d 633, C.A.N.C., 1983).

EEOC v. United Virginia Bank (615 F.2d 147, 4th Cir., 1980).

Ellinger, A. D., Ellinger, A.E., Keller, S.B. (2003). Supervisory coaching behavior, employee satisfaction, and warehouse employee performance: A dyadic perspective in the distribution industry. *Human Resource Development Quarterly, 14* (4), 435-458.

Feldt, L. S., Steffen, M., & Gupta, N. C. (1985, December). 'A comparison of five methods for estimating the standard error of measurement at specific score levels', *Applied Psychological Measurement, 9* (4), 351-361.

Franks v. Bowman Transportation Company (495 F. 2d 398, 419, 8 FEP, 66, 81, 5th Cir., 1974; and 12 FEP 549, 1976).

Gastwirth, J.L. & Greenhouse, S.W. (1987). 'Estimating a common relative risk: Application in equal employment', *Journal of the American Statistical Association, 82,* 38-45.

Gatewood, R. D. & Feild, H.S. (1994). *Human Resource Selection,* Orlando, FL: The Dryden Press.

Gault v. Zellerbach (172 F.3d 48, 1998 WL 898831 at 2, 6th Cir.,1998) (unpublished opinion).

Gerstner, C.R., Day, D.V. (1997). Meta-Analytic review of leader-member exchange theory: Correlates and construct issues. *Journal of Applied Psychology, 82,* 827-844.

Golden Rule Life Insurance Company v. Mathias (86 Ill.App.3d 323, 41 Ill. Dec. 888, 408 N.E.2d 310, 1980)

Griggs v. Duke Power Co. (91 S. Ct. 849, 1971).

Guardians Association of the New York City Police Dept. v. Civil Service Commission (630 F.2d 79, 88, 2d Cir., 1980; cert. denied, 452 U.S. 940, 101 S.Ct. 3083, 69 L.Ed.2d 954, 1981).

Guion, R. M. (1998). *Assessment, Measurement, and Prediction for Personnel Decisions,* Mahwah, NJ: Lawrence Erlbaum Associates.

Gutman, A. (2005). Adverse impact: judicial, regulatory, and statutory authority. In F. J. Landy (Ed.), *Employment discrimination litigation: Behavioral, quantitative, and legal perspectives* (pp. 20-46). San Francisco: Jossey Bass.

Haertel, E. H. (2006). Reliability. In R. L. Brennan (Ed.). *Educational measurement* (4th ed., p. 83). Westport, CT: Praeger Publishers.

Hazelwood School District v. United States (433 U.S. 299, 1977).

Heck, R.H. (1995). Organizational and professional socialization: Its impact on the performance of new administrators. *Urban Review, 27,* 31-49.

Hedges, L. V. & Olkin, I. (1985). *Statistical methods for meta-analysis.* Academic Press.

Hermelin, E. & Robertson, I. (2001). A critique and standardization of meta-analytic validity coefficient in personnel selection. *Journal of Occupational and Organizational Psychology,* 74, 253-277.

Hirji, K.F. (2006). *Exact analysis of discrete data.* New York, NY: Taylor and Francis.

Hogan v. Pierce, Secretary, Housing and Urban Development (No. 79-2124, U.S. Dist. Ct District of Columbia, 1983).

Hoops v. Elk Run Coal Co., Inc. (95 F.Supp.2d 612, S.D.W.Va., 2000).

Hunter, J.E. (1983). A causal analysis of cognitive ability, job knowledge, job performance and supervisory ratings. In F. Landy and S. Zedeck and J. Cleveland (Eds.), *Performance measurement theory* (pp. 257-266). Hillsdale, NJ: Erlbaum.

EEOC v. Atlas Paper, (868 F.2d. 487, 6th Cir., cert. denied, 58 U.S. L.W. 3213, 1989).

Hunter, J., & Hunter, R. (1984). Validity and utility of alternative predictors of job performance. *Psychological Bulletin, 96*, 72-98.

Hunter, J. E., & Schmidt, F. L. (2004). *Methods of meta-analysis: Correcting error and bias in research findings* (2nd ed.). Newbury Park, CA: Sage.

Jenkins, D.G., Mitra, A., Gupta, N., & Shaw, J.D. (1998). Are financial incentives related to performance? A meta-analytic review of empirical research. *Journal of Applied Psychology, 83,* 777-787.

Johnson, B. T, Mullen, B., & Salas, E. (1995). Comparison of three major meta-analytic approaches. *Journal of Applied Psychology, 80*, 94-106.

Johnson v. Garrett, III as Secretary of the Navy (Case No. 73-702-Civ-J-12, U.S. Dist. Ct. for the Middle District of Florida, 1991).

Joint Standards – American Educational Research Association, the American Psychological Association, and the National Council on Measurement in Education (1999). *Standards for Educational and Psychological Testing.* Washington DC: American Educational Research Association.

Judge, T. A. & Ferris, G. R (1993). Social context of performance evaluation decisions. *Academy of Management Journal, 36*, 80-105.

Judge, T. A. Thoresen, C.J., Bono, J. E., Patton, G.K. (2001). The job satisfaction-job performance relationship: A qualitative and quantitative review. *Psychological Bulletin, 127* (3), 376-407.

Kacmar, K.M., Witt, L.A., Zivnuska, S. & Gully, S.M. (2003). The interactive effect of leader-member exchange and communication frequency on performance ratings. *Journal of Applied Psychology, 88*, 764-772.

Kolen, M. J., Hanson, B. A. &, Brennan, R. L. (1992). 'Conditional standard errors of measurement for scale scores', *Journal of Educational Measurement, 29* (4), 285-307.

Landy, F. J. & Farr, J. L. (1983). The measurement of work performance: Method, theory, and applications. San Diego, CA: Academic Press.

Landy, F. J. (2003). Validity generalization: then and now. In K. R. Murphy (Ed.), *Validity generalization: a critical review* (pp. 155-195). Mahwah, NJ: Erlbaum.

Lanning v. Southeastern Pennsylvania Transportation Authority, 181 F.3d 478, 80 FEPC., BNA, 221, 76 EPD P 46,160 3rd Cir.(Pa.) June 29, 1999 (NO. 98-1644, 98-1755).

Lautenschlager, G. J., & Mendoza, J. L. (1986). A step-down hierarchical multiple regression analysis for examining hypotheses about test bias in prediction. *Applied Psychological Measurement, 10,* 133-139.

Lord, F. M. (1984). 'Standard errors of measurement at different ability levels', *Journal of Educational Measurement, 21* (3), 239-243.

Louv, W.C. & Littell, R.C. (1986). 'Combining one-sided binomial tests', *Journal of the American Statistical Association, 81,* 550-554.

Manko v. U.S. (No. 79-1011-CV-W-9, U.S. Dist. Ct. for the Western District of Missouri, 636 F. Supp. 1419, 1986).

Martin v. United States Playing Card Co. (172 F.3d 48, 1998 WL 869970, 6th Cir., 1998) (unpublished opinion).

McKay v. U.S. (Civil Action No. 75-M-1162, U.S. Dist. Ct. for the District of Colorado, 1985).

Meglino, B. M., Ravlin, E. C. Adkins, C. L. (1989). A field test of the value congruence process and its relationship to individual outcomes. *Journal of Applied Psychology, 74* (3), 424-432.

Mehrotra, D. & Railkar, R. (2000). 'Minimum risk weights for comparing treatments in stratified binomial trials', *Statistics in Medicine, 19,* 811-825.

Mollenkopf, W. G. (1949). Variation of the standard error of measurement of scores. *Psychometrika, (14)* 3, 189-229.

Moore v. Summers (113 F.Supp.2d 5, D.D.C., 2000).

Morgeson, F. P., Delaney-Klinger, K., Hemingway, M. A. (March, 2005). The importance of job autonomy, cognitive ability, and job-related skill for predicting role breadth and job performance. *Journal of Applied Psychology, 90* (2), 399-406.

Mosteller, F., Rouke, R.E.K., & Thomas, G.B. (1970). *Probability with Statistical Applications* (2nd ed.). Menlo Park, CA: Addison-Wesley.

Mozee v. American Commercial Marine Service Co. (940 F.2d 1036, C.A.7, Ind., 1991).

Murphy, K. R., & Shiarella, A. H. (1997). Implications of the multidimensional nature of job performance for the validity of selection tests: Multivariate frameworks for studying test validity. *Personnel Psychology, 50,* 823-854.

Murphy, K. R. (2003). The logic of validity generalization. In K. R. Murphy (Ed.) *Validity generalization: a critical review.* Mahwah, NJ: Erlbaum.

NAACP Ensley Branch v. Seibels, 13 E.P.D. 11,504 at pp. 6793, 6803, 6806, N.D.Ala. (1977). aff'd in relevant part, rev'd in other part, 616 F.2d 812,818 and note 15 (5th Cir.), cert. den., 449 U.S. 1061 (1980).

Neisser, U., Boodoo, G., Bouthard, T.J., Boykin, A.W., Brody, N., Ceei, S.J., Halpern, D.F., Loehlin, J.C., Perloft, R., Sternberg, R.J., & Urbina, S. (1996). 'Intelligence: Knowns and Unknowns', *American Psychologist, 51,* 77-101.

Nunnally, J. C., & Bernstein, I. H. (1994). *Psychometric Theory* (3rd ed.). New York: McGraw-Hill.

OFCCP (Office of Federal Contract Compliance Programs) (1993). *Federal Contract Compliance Manual.* Washington, D.C.: Department of Labor, Employment Standards Administration, Office of Federal Contract Compliance Programs (SUDOC# L 36.8: C 76/1993).

Osborne v. Brandeis Machinery & Supply Corp. (1994 WL 486628, 6th Cir., June 15, 1994) (unpublished opinion).

Ottaviani v. State University of New York at New Paltz (679 F.Supp. 288, D.N.Y., 1988).

Overall, J.E., & Hornick, C.W. (1982). An evaluation of power and sample-size requirements for the continuity-corrected Fisher exact test. *Perceptual and Motor Skills, 54,* 83-86.

Paige v. California Highway Patrol (No. CV 94-0083 CBM [Ctx], U.S. District Court, Central District of California, Order Entered August 12, 1999).

Palmer v. Shultz (815 F.2d 84, C.A.D.C., 1987)

Peng, C.J. & Subkoviak, M. (1980). 'A note on Huynh's normal approximation procedure for estimating criterion-referenced reliability', *Journal of Educational Measurement, 17* (4), 359-368.

Peters, L. H., O'Connor, E. J., & Rudolph, C. J. (1980). The behavioral and affective consequences of performance-relevant situational variables. *Organizational Behavior and Human Performance, 25,* 79-96.

Pincus, D. (March, 1986). Communication, satisfaction, job satisfaction, and job performance. *Human Communication Research, 12* (3), 395.

Podsakoff, P. MacKenzie, S., Bommer, W. (1996). Meta-analysis of the relationships between Kerr and Jermier's substitutes for leadership and employee job attitudes, role perceptions, and performance. *Journal of Applied Psychology, 81* (4), 380-399.

Police Officers for Equal Rights v. City of Columbus (644 F.Supp. 393, S.D.Ohio, 1985).

Pritchard, R., Jones, S., Roth, P, Stuebing, K, & Ekeberg, S. (1988). Effects of group feedback, goal setting, and incentives on organizational productivity. *Journal of Applied Psychology, 73* (2), 337-358.

Psychological Services, Inc. (PSI), (2006). Professional Employment Test (PET) validation research summary.

Qualls-Payne, A. L. (1992). 'A comparison of score level estimates of the standard error of measurement', *Journal of Educational Measurement, 29* (3), 213-225.

Rhoades, L. & Eisenberger, R. (2002). Perceived organizational support: A review of the literature. *Journal of Applied Psychology, 87*, 698-714.

Ricci v. DeStefano (U.S.SC, No. 07-1428, 2009).

Rulon, P. J. (1939). A simplified procedure for determining the reliability of a test by split-halves. *Harvard Educational Review, 9*, 99-103.

Sackett, P. R., Schmitt, N., Ellingson, J. E., and Kabin, M. B. (2001). 'High stakes testing in employment, credentialing, and higher education: Prospects in a post-affirmative action world', *American Psychologist, 56*, 302-318.

Sackett, P. R., Schmitt, N., Tenopyr, M. L., Kehoe, J., & Zedeck, S. (1985). Commentary on forty questions about validity generalization and meta-analysis. *Personnel Psychology, 38*, 697-798.

Sagie, A. (1994). Participative decision making and performance: A moderator analysis. *The Journal of Applied Behavioral Science, 30* (2), 227.

Schleicher, D. J., Watt, J. D. Greguras, G.J. (2004). Reexamining the job satisfaction-performance relationship: The complexity of attitudes. *Journal of Applied Psychology, 89* (1), 165-177.

Schmidt, Hunter, & Urry (1975). *Statistical power in criterion-related validation studies.* U.S. Civil Service Commission: Washington, DC.

Schmidt, F. L., & Hunter, J. E. (1977). Development of a general solution to the problem of validity generalization. *Journal of Applied Psychology, 62*, 529-540.

Schmidt, F. L., & Hunter, J. E. (1998). The validity and utility of selection methods in personnel psychology: practical and theoretical implications of 85 years of research findings. *Psychological Bulletin, 124* (2), 262-274.

Schmitt, N., Clause, C., & Pulakos, E. (1996). Subgroup differences associated with different measures of some common job relevant constructs. In C. Cooper & I. Robertson (Eds)., *International review of industrial organizational psychology*, 115-140. New York: Wiley.

Serlin, R. C., & Levin, J. R. (1980). Identifying regions of significance in aptitude-by-treatment interaction research. *American Educational Research Journal, 17*, 389-399.

Shadish, W.R., Cook, T.D., & Campbell, D.T. (2002). *Experimental and quasi-experimental designs for generalized causal inference*. Boston: Houghton-Mifflin.

Shutt v. Sandoz Crop Protection Corp. (934 F.2d 186, 188, 9th Cir., 1991).

Sinclair, M.D. & Pan, Q. (2009). Using the Peters-Belson method in equal employment opportunity personnel evaluations. *Law, Probability and Risk 8*, 95−117.

SIOP – Society for Industrial and Organizational Psychology, Inc. (1987, 2003). *Principles for the Validation and Use of Personnel Selection Procedures* (3rd & 4th ed.). College Park, MD: Author.

Smither, J.W., Reilly, R.R., Millsap, R.E., Pearlman, K., & Stoffey, R. W. (1993). Applicant reactions to selection procedures. *Personnel Psychology, 46*, 49-76.

Stauffer, J. M. & Buckley, M. R. (May 2005). The existence and nature of racial bias in supervisory ratings. *Journal of Applied Psychology, 90* (3), 586-591.

Steel, R.P., Shane, G.S. & Kennedy, K.A. (1990). Effects of social-system factors on absenteeism, turnover, and job performance. *Journal of Business and Psychology, 4*, 423-430.

Stokes, M. E., Davis, C. S., & Koch, G. G. (2001). *Categorical data analysis using the SAS system* (2nd ed.). Cary, NY: SAS Institute.

Strong v. Blue Cross of California, No. BC382405 (Los Angeles Superior Court, 2010).

Subkoviak, M. (1988). 'A practitioner's guide to computation and interpretation of reliability indices for mastery tests', *Journal of Educational Measurement, 25* (1), 47-55.

Tarone R.E. (1988). 'Homogeneity score tests with nuisance parameters', *Communications in Statistics,* Series A; *17,* 1549-1556.

Thorndike, R. L. (1951). 'Reliability', In E. F. Lindquist (Ed.). *Educational Measurement* (pp. 560-620). Washington DC: American Council on Education.

Tinker v. Sears, Roebuck & Co. (127 F.3d 519, 524, 6th Cir.,1997).

Trout v. Hidalgo (Civ. A. Nos. 73-55, 76-315, 76-1206, 78-1098, U.S. Dist. Ct. of Columbia, 517 F. Supp. 873, 1981).

Tsutakawa, R. K. & Johnson, J. C. (1990). The effect of uncertainty of item parameter estimation on ability estimates. *Psychometrika, 55,* 371-390.

Tubre, T. & Collins, J. (2000). Jackson and Schuler (1985) revisited: A meta-analysis of the relationships between role ambiguity, role conflict, and job performance. *Journal of Management, 26* (1), 155-169.

Uniform Guidelines – Equal Employment Opportunity Commission, Civil Service Commission, Department of Labor, and Department of Justice, *Adoption of Four Agencies of Uniform Guidelines on Employee Selection Procedures,* 43 Federal Register, 38,290-38,315 (August 25, 1978), referred to in the text as *Uniform Guidelines*; Equal Employment Opportunity Commission, Office of Personnel Management, Department of Treasury, *Adoption of Questions and Answers to Clarify and Provide a Common Interpretation of the Uniform Guidelines on Employee Selection Procedures,* 44 Federal Register 11,996-12,009 (1979).

U.S. Department of Labor: Employment and training administration (2000), *Testing and Assessment: An Employer's Guide to Good Practices.* Washington DC:

Department of Labor Employment and Training Administration.

U.S. v. City of Garland, WL 741295, N.D.Tex. (2004).

U.S. v. South Carolina (434 U.S. 1026, 1978).

Vuyanich v. Republic National Bank (N.D. Texas 1980, 505 F. Supp. 224).

Wards Cove v. Atonio (109 S.Ct. 2115, 1989).

Watson v. Fort Worth Bank & Trust (487 U.S. 1977, 1988).

Weiner, J. (1997). POST public safety dispatcher psychological assessment resource report. Sacramento, CA: POST Media Distribution Center.

Williams v. Owens-Illinois, Inc. (665 F2d 918, 9th Cir, Cert denied, 459 U.S. 971, 1982).

Waisome v. Port Authority (948 F.2d 1370, 1376, 2d Cir.,1991).

Zamlen v. City of Cleveland (686 F.Supp. 631, N.D. Ohio, 1988).

Zedeck, S. (2009). Adverse Impact: History and evolution. In J. L. Outtz (Ed.), *Adverse impact: Implications for organizational staffing and high stakes staffing* (pp. 3-27), New York, NY: Taylor & Francis.

Reference Authorities Regarding the Limitations of the Fisher Exact Test

Andres, M.A. & Tejedor, H. (1995). Is Fisher's exact test very conservative? *Computational Statistics & Data Analysis, 19* (5), 579-591.

Andres, M.A. (1991). A review of classic non-asymptotic methods for comparing two proportions by means of independent samples. *Communications in Statistic – Simulation and Computation, 20* (2&3), 551-583.

Agresti, A. (2007). *An introduction to categorical data analysis* (2nd ed.). Wiley.

Agresti, A. & Gottard, A. (August, 2007). Nonconservative exact small-sample inference for discrete data. *Computational Statistics & Data Analysis Archive, 51* (12), 6447-6458.

Barnard, G.A. (1945). A new test for 2 X 2 tables. *Nature, 156,* 177, 783-784.

Berger, R. L. (1994). Power comparison of exact unconditional tests for comparing two binomial proportions. *Institute of Statistics Mimeo Series,* No. 2266.

Berger, R. L. (1996). More powerful tests from confidence interval p-values. *The American Statistician, 50,* 314-318.

Boschloo, R. D. (1970). Raised conditional level of significance for the 2 X 2-table when testing the equality of two probabilities, *Statistica Neerlandica, 24,* 1-35.

Camilli, G. & Hopkins, K. D. (1978). Applicability of Chi-square to 2 X 2 contingency tables with small expected frequencies. *Psychological Bulletin, 85,* 163-167.

Camilli, G. & Hopkins, K. D. (1979). Testing for association in 2 X 2 contingency tables with very small sample sizes. *Psychological Bulletin, 86,* 1011-1014.

Campbell, I. (2007). Chi-squared and Fisher-Irwin tests of two-by-two tables with small sample recommendations. *Statistics in Medicine, 26,* 3661.3675.

Collins, M. W. & Morris, S. B. (2008). Testing for adverse impact when sample size is small. *Journal of Applied Psychology, 93,* 463-471.

Crans, G. G. & Shuster, J. J. (2008). How conservative is Fisher's exact test? A quantitative evaluation of the two-sample comparative binomial trial. *Statistics in Medicine, 27* (8), 3598-3611.

D'Agostino, R.B., Chase, W., Belanger, A. (1988). Appropriates of some common procedures for testing the equality of two independent binomial populations. *The American Statistician, 42*(3), 198-202.

Fisher, R.A. (1925). *Statistical methods for research workers.* Edinburgh, Scotland: Oliver & Boyd.

Fuchs, C. (June, 2001). UMPU and alternative tests for association in 2 X 2 tables. *Biometrics, 57*, 535-538

Gastwirth, J.L. & Greenhouse, S.W. (1995). Biostatistical concepts and methods in the legal setting. *Statistics in Medicine, 14*, 1641-1653.

Gimpel, H. (2007). Preferences in Negotiations: The Attachment Effect (Lecture Notes in Economics and Mathematical Systems): Author.

Hirji, K.F. (2006). *Exact analysis of discrete data.* New York, NY: Taylor & Francis.

Hirji, K. F., Tan, S. & Elashoff, R.M. (1991). A quasi-exact test for comparing two binomial proportions. *Statistics in Medicine, 10*, 1137-1153.

Hwang, G. & Yang, M.C. (2001). An optimality theory for mid-P values in 2 X 2 contingency tables. *Statistica Sinica, 11*, 807-826.

Lancaster, H.O. (1961). Significance tests in discrete distributions. *Journal of the American Statistical Association, 56*, 223.234.

Lidell, D. (1976). Practical tests of 2 X 2 contingency tables. *The Statistician*, 25, 295-304.

Lin, C.Y & Yang, M.C. (2009). Improved p-value tests for comparing two independent binomial proportions. *Communications in Statistics - Simulation and Computation, 38* (1), 78-91.

Little, R.J.A. (1989). Testing the equality of two independent binomial proportions. *American Statistician*, 43, 283-288.

Lydersen, S. Fagerland, M.W. & Laake, P. (2009). Recommended tests for association in 2 X 2 tables. *Statistics in Medicine, 28*, 1159-1175.

McDonald L. L., Davis B. M. & Milliken G.A. (1977). A non-randomized unconditional test for comparing two proportions in a 2 X 2 contingency table. *Technometrics, 19*, 145-150.

Mehrotra, D.V., Chan, I.S.F. & Berger, R.L. (2003). A cautionary note on exact unconditional inference for a difference between two independent binomial proportions. *Biometrics, 59*, 441-450.

Morris, S. B. (2001). Sample size required for adverse impact analysis. *Applied HRM Research, 6*, 13-32.

Overall, J. E., Rhoades, H. M., & Starbuck, R.R. (1987). Small-sample tests for homogeneity of response probabilities in 2 X 2 contingency tables. *Psychological Bulletin, 102* (2), 307-314.

Overall, J. E. (Summer, 1980). Continuity correction for Fisher's exact probability test. *Journal of Educational Statistics, 5* (2), 177-190.

Overall, J. E. & Hornick, C. W. (1982). An evaluation of power and sample-size requirements for the continuity-corrected Fisher exact test. *Perceptual and Motor Skills, 54*, 83-86.

Overall, J. E., Rhoades, H. M. & Starbuck, R. R. (1987). Small-sample tests for homogeneity of response probabilities in 2 X 2 contingency tables. *Psychological Bulletin, 102*, 307-314.

Overall, J. E. & Starbuck, R. R. (1983). F-test alternatives to Fisher's exact test and to the chi-square test of homogeneity in 2 X 2 tables. *Journal of Educational Statistics, 8*, 59-73.

Pett, M.A. (1997). *Nonparametric statistics for health care research: statistics for small samples and unusual distributions.* Sage Publications.

Romualdi, C., Bortoluzzi, S., Danieli, G.A. (2001). Detecting differentially expressed genes in multiple tag sampling experiments: comparative evaluation of statistical tests. *Human Molecular Genetics, 10* (19), 2133-2141.

Routledge, R. D. (1992). Resolving the conflict over Fisher's exact test. *Canadian Journal of Statistics, 20*, 201-209.

Sekhon, J.S. (2005). *Making inference from 2 X 2 tables: the inadequacy of the Fisher exact test for observational data and a Bayesian alternative.* Survey Research Center, University of California, Berkeley.

Simonoff, J. S. (2003). *Analyzing categorical data.* Springer-Verlag: New York, NY.

Suissa, S. & Shuster, J. J. (1985). Exact unconditional sample sizes for the 2 by 2 binomial trial. *Journal of the Royal Statistical Society, Series A, General 148*, 317-327.

Yates, F. (1984). Tests of significance for 2 X 2 contingency tables. *J.R. Statist. Soc. A,* Vol. 147, 426-463.

References Supporting the Use of Lancaster's mid-P Adjustment to the FET

Journal References

Abramson, J.H. (2004, December). WINPEPI (PEPI-for-Windows): Computer programs for epidemiologists. Retrieved from http://www.epi-perspectives.com/content/1/1/6.

Barnard, G.A. (1989). On alleged gains in power from lower p-values. *Statistics in Medicine, 8,* 1469-1477.

Cohen, G.R. & Yang, S.Y. (1994). Mid-P confidence intervals for the Poisson expectation. *Statistics in Medicine, 13,* 2189-2203.

Franck, W.E. (1986). P-values for discrete test statistics. *Biometrical Journal, 28* (4), 403-406.

Hirji, K. F. (1991). A comparison of exact, mid-P, and score tests for matched case-control studies. *Biometrics, 47*: 487-496.

Hirji, K.F. (2006). *Exact analysis of discrete data.* New York, NY: Taylor and Francis.

Hirji, K., Tan, S. J. & Elasho, R.M. (1991). A quasi-exact test for comparing two binomial proportions, *Statistics in Medicine, 10,* 1137-1153.

Hirji, K., Tang, M. L., Vollset, S.E. & Elasho, R.M. (1994). Efficient power computation for exact and mid-P tests for the common odds ratio in several 2 X 2 tables, *Statistics in Medicine, 13,* 1539-1549.

Lancaster, H.O. (1961). Significance tests in discrete distributions. *Journal of the American Statistical Association, 56,* 223.234.

Miettinen, O.S., & Nurminen, M. (1985). Comparative analysis of two rates. *Statistics in Medicine, 4,* 213-226.

Plackett, R. L. (1984). Discussion of Yates' 'Tests of significance for 2 X 2 contingency tables.' *Journal of Royal Statistical Society,* Series A, 147, 426-463.

Seneta, E., Berry, G. & Macaskill, P. (September, 1999). Adjustment to Lancaster's mid-P. *Journal Methodology and Computing in Applied Probability, 1* (2), 229-240.

Stone, M. (1969). The role of significance testing: some data with a message. *Biometrika, 56*, 485493.

Upton, G.J.G. (1982). A comparison of alternative tests for the 2 X 2 comparative trial. *Journal of the Royal Statistical Society, Series A (Statistics in Society), 145*(3), 86-105.

Upton G.J.G. (1992). Fisher's exact test. *Journal of the Royal Statistical Society, Series A,* 155: 395-402.

Williams, D. A. (1988). Tests for differences between several small proportions. *Applied Statistics, 37*, 421-434.

Statistical Textbooks

Agresti, A. (2007). *An introduction to categorical data analysis* (2nd ed.). Wiley.

Anscombe, F. J. (1981). *Computing in statistical science through APL.* Springer-Verlag, New York.

Hirji, K. F. (2006). *Exact analysis of discrete data.* CRC Press, Taylor & Francis Group. Boca Raton, FL.

Pratt J. W. & Gibbons J. D. (1981). *Concepts of nonparametric theory.* Springer-Verlag, New York.

Rothman K, J. (1986). *Modern epidemiology.* Little, Brown: Boston, MA.

Simonoff, J.S. (2003). *Analyzing categorical data.* Springer-Verlag: New York, NY.

Index